Hilary Putnam

MANCHESTER
UNIVERSITY PRESS

For Barry Wilkins

Hilary Putnam

Realism, reason and the uses of uncertainty

CHRISTOPHER NORRIS

Manchester University Press

Manchester and New York

distributed exclusively in the USA by Palgrave

Published by Manchester University Press
Oxford Road, Manchester M13 9NR, UK
and Room 400, 175 Fifth Avenue, New York, NY 10010, USA
www.manchesteruniversitypress.co.uk

Distributed exclusively in the USA by
Palgrave, 175 Fifth Avenue, New York, NY 10010, USA

Distributed exclusively in Canada by
UBC Press, University of British Columbia, 2029 West Mall,
Vancouver, BC, Canada V6T 1Z2

British Library Cataloguing-in-Publication Data
A catalogue record for this book is available from the British Library

Library of Congress Cataloging-in-Publication Data applied for

ISBN 0 7190 6195 4 *hardback*
      0 7190 6196 2 *paperback*

First published 2002

10 09 08 07 06 05 04 03 02   10 9 8 7 6 5 4 3 2 1

Typeset in Adobe Garamond
by Northern Phototypesetting Co. Ltd, Bolton
Printed in Great Britain
by Biddles Ltd, Guildford and King's Lynn

Contents

ACKNOWLEDGEMENTS   *page* vii

INTRODUCTION   1

1   Realism, scepticism and naturalism: stages on the Putnam road   8

2   Realism, reference and truth: the problem with quantum mechanics   40

3   Squaring with Wittgenstein: versions of 'realism' in Putnam's later philosophy   71

4   Can realism be naturalised? Putnam on sense, commonsense and the senses   104

5   How many positrons make five? science, scepticism and the 'ready-made world'   135

6   The 'many faces' of realism: reference, meaning and theory-change   167

7   Is logic revisable? Putnam, Quine and 'contextual apriority'   192

8   The Platonist fix: why 'nothing works' (according to Putnam) in philosophy of mathematics   218

9   Putnam, Peano and the *malin génie*: could we possibly be wrong about elementary number-theory?   246

AFTERWORD   273

INDEX OF NAMES   274

Acknowledgements

The impetus for writing this book came chiefly from discussions with colleagues and friends in the Philosophy Section at Cardiff. That it still provides such a civilised, congenial and intellectually stimulating workplace despite the whole range of destructive pressures brought to bear by government and 'quality'-control agencies – not to mention the Research Assessment Exercise – is in large part due to their collective resilience and loyalty in the face of bureaucracy run wild. I am especially grateful to Gideon Calder and Jessica Osborn for reading an early draft of the typescript and suggesting how the argument could be tightened or clarified at various points; to Duncan McFarland, Alex Miller and Alessandra Tanesini for keeping me respectably up-to-date with the literature on Wittgenstein, anti-realism, rule-following and related topics; to Andrew Belsey for helping to track down some elusive passages in Putnam; and to Barry Wilkins for running the Philosophy Section and remaining stoically good-humoured through so many day-to-day crises. Robin Attfield, Pat Clark, Michael Durrant, Andrew Edgar, Peter Sedgwick, Christine Southwell and Alison Venables have all – in different ways – been great sources of restored motivation and encouragement.

Christa Knellwolf left Cardiff for Canberra and blue skies when this project was still at quite an early stage but made some extremely useful suggestions in the period of vaguely formed thoughts leading up to it. My sub-title 'the uses of uncertainty' was amnesically lifted – I now realise – from a fine critical study of Flaubert by Jonathan Culler which I read many years ago and which obviously left a lasting impression. Needless to say my intellectual debts extend far beyond the restrictions imposed by limited space and powers of memory. Still I should like to thank the various people – at home and abroad – who have invited me to offer guest lectures or seminars based on portions of the work-in-progress and have thus provided a welcome opportunity for seeing how the arguments fared under pressure of friendly but persistent questioning. 'You know who you are', it is tempting to add, so don't all rush to take the credit or blame.

There is often the danger, with projects like this, of developing a single-track devotion to the topic that cuts one off from all the interesting things that are going on just down the corridor or just across the road. It is therefore a pleasure to acknowledge the mindbroadening companionship of several colleagues 'outside' philosophy who have kept me from becoming too obsessive over the past few years. Ken Gloag (of the Music Department at Cardiff) has done a fine job since taking over as coordinator of the jointly taught MA scheme in Music, Culture and Politics. Along with Rob Stradling – who nursed the scheme into existence some six years ago – he deserves every credit for having opened up some immensely rewarding opportunities for interdisciplinary teaching and research. I should also like to thank the postgraduate students in Philosophy with whom I have worked over the past few years – among them Jason Barker, Viv Beedle, Paul Gorton, Paul Hampson, Carol Jones, Keith McDonald, Alastair Nicholson, Marianna Papastephanou, Laurence Peddle, Daniele Procida and Basil Smith – for offering any number of helpful ideas in the course of seminar discussion and for making Cardiff a genuine research community in a sense of that phrase totally unknown to the present-day arbiters of academic 'quality' and 'excellence'. If this seems a somewhat discordant note on which to end then let me raise the tone by wishing Hilary Putnam many more years of creatively self-critical thought about the various topics that he, more than anyone, has kept philosophically alive.

Christopher Norris
Cardiff

Note

Some parts of this book have appeared previously as journal articles or contributions to various edited volumes. I should like to thanks the publishers and editors concerned for their permission to reprint this material, mostly in revised form. The Introduction was skilfully edited by Julian Baggini and published at around half-length in *The Philosophers' Magazine*. Chapter 1 first appeared in *Critical Interfaces: contributions in philosophy, literature and culture in honour of Herbert Grabes*, edited by Gordon Collier, Klaus Schwank and Franz Wieselhuber (Trier: Wissenschaftlicher Verlag, 2001); Chapter 2 in *International Studies in the Philosophy of Science*, edited by James Robert Brown; Chapter 3 in *Southern Humanities Review*, edited by my old friend Dan Latimer and colleagues at Auburn University; Chapter 4 in *Principia: an international journal of epistemology* (special thanks to Cezar Mortari); Chapter 5 in *Pretexts: studies in writing and culture* (with best wishes to John Higgins and other members of the editorial board); Chapter 6 in *adef: revista de filosofia*, translated into Spanish by Olimpia Lombardi and Maria Angélica Fierro; and Chapter 9 in the *Journal for General Philosophy of Science*, published by Kluwer.

Introduction

During the past four decades Hilary Putnam has become widely recognised as a leading contributor to various developments within the Anglo-American tradition of analytic and, arguably, 'post-analytic' philosophy. No thinker has done more to broaden the horizons of philosophical debate in an academic culture that has otherwise tended toward increasing (some would say damaging) specialisation. His interests have ranged over many fields, among them the philosophy of science, logic and mathematics, epistemology, cognitive psychology, linguistics, philosophical semantics, ethics, the social sciences and historiography. He has also – since the early 1980s – made a point of keeping up with philosophical developments in the 'other', i.e., continental or mainland-European tradition and thus helped to remind his more orthodox colleagues that there is intellectual life beyond the hallowed precincts of Cambridge, Oxford, Harvard (his long-time home university), Princeton or Yale.

All the same Putnam has refused the kinds of easy escape-route offered by those various disenchanted types – postmodernists, neo-pragmatists and 'strong' textualists – who advise that we should simply abandon that old-style analytic approach. Indeed there is a deep and impressive continuity about Putnam's work despite his uncommon willingness to constantly re-think previous positions in response to constructive criticism. What sets his work decidedly apart from fashionable forms of 'post-analytic' thought is Putnam's steady conviction that philosophy has to do with genuine – not merely artificial or hypercultivated – problems which need to be looked at from various angles but which cannot be made to disappear simply by applying some form of Wittgensteinian therapy or by 'redescribing' them in some shiny new vocabulary. While rejecting the idea of a fixed agenda of basic (philosophically 'central') topics for debate, Putnam has nevertheless shown a keen awareness of the way that such problems tend to resurface with unexpected force just when they have apparently been laid to rest. Nowhere is this more apparent than in his constant return to the issue of realism and the various modes of anti-realist thought that have become such a prominent feature of the intellectual landscape over the past three decades. It is also evident in Putnam's refusal to let go of problems – like Nelson Goodman's 'new puzzle' of induction or the quandaries resulting from Quine's doctrine of wholesale ontological relativity – which other thinkers have tended to approach with fixed preconceptions for or against. What chiefly distinguishes Putnam's thought is his willingness to see the point of contrary arguments even while rejecting the relativist notion that in the end these divergences of view come down to just so many different language-games or optional styles of talk.

'We philosophers', he wrote with disarming candour in 1977, 'are frequently torn ... between opposing considerations, but we very infrequently show it *in print*. What we do is let ourselves be torn in private until we "plonk" for one alternative or other; then the published paper only shows what we plonked for, and not the being torn'. It is a great virtue in Putnam's work that he has resisted this desire to cover his tracks or adopt the more standard professionalised appearance of having thought things through to a definite conclusion before going public. All the same he has never given up the belief – most explicit in his earlier writings – that philosophy *ought* to be in the business of seeking out better (more adequate) solutions to a range of well-defined problems, despite the strong likelihood that any such advance will soon run up against a whole new range of criticisms and counter-arguments. Of course there is no great merit in the willingness to constantly change one's mind if the changes come about through lack of conviction or a failure to grasp some crucial point. However, Putnam manifestly knows a great deal not only about philosophy but also about mathematics, physics, the history of science, and a good many other specialist fields where his contributions have often served as a stimulus to fresh enquiry. Indeed, he is one of the very few philosophers whose work is regularly cited by physicists and mathematicians who otherwise tend to take a dim view of philosophical incursions into their own expert domain.

This is why Putnam's re-thinkings and self-professed doubts carry more weight than the confident assertions of other philosophers who have shown nothing like that degree of willingness to weigh the strength of contrary arguments. Thus – for instance – he has engaged over and again with the debate about scientific realism, with problems in the interpretation of quantum mechanics, with issues concerning the (supposed) *a priori* status of mathematical truths, and – most doggedly of all – with the question whether logic might be 'revisable' under pressure from various kinds of empirical counter-evidence thrown up by the physical sciences. In each case Putnam has often seen fit to revise his views, with the pattern mostly working out as a shift from 'strong' (objectivist or causal) realism to a middle-ground standpoint which seeks to retain the intuitive appeal of that position while conceding the force – within limits – of certain anti-realist or framework-relativist arguments. Thus his work has been central to this prominent debate in recent philosophy of logic, language and science even though he cannot easily be claimed for either side in a quarrel that has tended to create sharply polarised ideas of what counts as a useful or relevant contribution.

My own view of Putnam's philosophical development – briefly stated – is that his early essays were on the right track in defending a causal-realist theory of reference and knowledge-acquisition and that his subsequent retreat from that position gave rise to more problems and unresolved dilemmas than convincing or adequate solutions. That is to say, it seems to me that Putnam has been over-impressed by the strength of sceptical arguments from Wittgenstein, Quine,

Dummett, Goodman and others for the ultimate (in-principle) revisability of even our most basic standards of rational and evidential warrant. But I am also aware – uncomfortably so – that these changes-of-mind on Putnam's part are the upshot of long and intensely self-critical reflection on the problems faced by any realist philosophy that has to appeal beyond the best-current evidence to a realm of objective truths. One reason for writing about him was that I felt my own convictions to be challenged more powerfully by Putnam's having once espoused them and then found them problematic than by any arguments put forward by thinkers of a more fixed anti-realist persuasion.

This is also why I have focused on one particular set of issues in Putnam's work and not attempted anything like a comprehensive or fully representative study. Chief among them is the issue – posed most sharply by Michael Dummett – as to whether we can ever be justified in asserting the existence of verification-transcendent truths, that is to say, objective truths that may lie beyond reach of our present-best (or even our utmost attainable) knowledge. Such would be the case, for instance, with the unverifiable statements (1) that there exists a duplicate solar system in some epistemically inaccessible region of the expanding universe, *or* (2) that the indefinite decimal expansion of *pi* contains a certain sequence of numbers – say a hundred successive sevens – that has not yet been discovered and which might lie beyond reach of even the most powerful computer-assisted search programme. According to the realist such statements must be *either* true *or* false – i.e., possess an objective truth-value – quite aside from any local or contingent limits on the scope of our perceptual acquaintance, epistemic capacities, computational powers, evidential warrant, mathematical proof-procedures, and so forth. In other words they must be taken as conforming to the principle of bivalence which allows for no third (or indeterminate) value such as 'neither-true-nor-false'. This latter class of statements can then be safely confined to future conditionals – such as Aristotle's famous example of the sea-battle that may or may not take place tomorrow – whose truth-value is as yet undecided from a temporally indexed standpoint. To the anti-realist, conversely, it is self-evident that bivalence fails in cases like (1) and (2) above in so far as we possess no means of acquiring or manifesting the kind of knowledge that would properly vouch for our having grasped their operative truth-conditions. Thus, in Dummett's words, any 'gaps in our knowledge' must also be viewed as 'gaps in reality' since it cannot make sense – on this verificationist view – to postulate the objective truth (or falsehood) of statements belonging to the so-called 'disputed class'. Moreover, he takes this argument to hold not only for mathematics and the physical sciences but also for any number of undecidable statements concerning the historical past, such as 'Julius Caesar sneezed twice while crossing the Rubicon' or 'Margaret Thatcher's left ear twitched imperceptibly as she ordered the sinking of the *General Belgrano*'. To which the realist will standardly respond that the truth-value of such statements is in no way dependent on our happening to know – or our possessing the means to find out – whether or not they express some historically factual state of affairs. Where the anti-realist goes wrong, the realist will claim, is in confusing ontological with epistemological issues, or questions concerning what is (or was) objectively the case with questions concerning the scope and limits of humanly attainable knowledge.

This is one of those issues that Putnam has returned to on many occasions, always with a view to understanding what motivates the anti-realist position while also pointing out its deeply problematical and counter-intuitive character. The same applies to Putnam's long series of engagements with various forms of sceptical or relativist thinking in epistemology and philosophy of science. Here again, there is a clearly marked pattern of retreat from the strong causal-realist approach that typifies his early writing on issues of reference, meaning and truth to the theories of 'internal' or framework-relative (quasi-)realism put forward in his later books and essays. What has chiefly prompted that retreat is Putnam's almost hypersensitive awareness of the range of counter-arguments that are standardly brought against any proponent of so-called 'metaphysical' realism. I therefore devote a large part of this book to examining the nature of those various objections – especially from the Wittgensteinian quarter – and charting the course of Putnam's attempts to formulate some alternative (scaled-down) version of the realist claim that would meet them half-way and thus avoid what he sees as their more extreme and disabling consequences. This has been a major theme in his writings since the mid-1970s and also provides a useful point of entry to wider debates that have shaped Putnam's sense of the most important issues in the wake of old-style logical empiricism.

Hence my decision to start by discussing his 1994 series of Dewey lectures – 'Sense, Nonsense, and the Senses: an inquiry into the powers of the human mind' – where Putnam offers a survey of his own philosophical development to date and also puts the case for a different approach ('commonsense' or 'natural' realism) that would leave no room for scepticism to get a hold. It seems to me that this strategy ultimately fails – as likewise with his earlier 'internal-realist' or pragmatist versions of the case – in so far as it yields some crucial argumentative ground at just the point where relativists and anti-realists can press their objections home to most telling effect. What emerges is the impossibility of assuaging sceptical doubt once it is agreed that the game must be played on rules that the sceptic has always laid down in advance. Thus there is simply no hope of coming up with an answer that would make such doubts appear somehow beside the point if one has already withdrawn so far from a realist position as to allow that the existence, nature and properties of objects in the (so-called) 'external world' are *in some sense* ineluctably framework-relative or 'internal' to our various language-games, descriptive schemes, methods of verification, etc. For the way is then open to other, more extreme varieties of relativist, constructivist, or 'strong'-descriptivist approach that would count 'reality' a world well lost for the sake of multiplying world-versions and throwing off such irksome realist constraints.

One can see the impact of such thinking most clearly in Putnam's responses to Nelson Goodman, marked as they are by his refusal to accept Goodman's arguments at full strength but also by his readiness – in my view his over-readiness –

to treat them as posing a strong challenge to any form of 'metaphysical' realism. It is likewise evident in Putnam's various discussions of Wittgenstein and his effort – most recently in the Dewey lectures – to argue the case for Wittgensteinian realism as something more than 'realism' relative to this or that language-game, communal practice, or acculturated form-of-life. Above all it shows up in Putnam's strenuous but frankly inconclusive (even baffled) attempts to resolve the long-standing conceptual problems with quantum mechanics, or at any rate to devise an interpretation that would accommodate the full range of quantum observational and predictive data. Of course there is no denying that quantum mechanics is problematic on *any* current construal, including David Bohm's 'hidden-variables' theory which conserves the idea of objective and continuous (i.e., measurement-independent) values of particle position and momentum but which does so at the price of having to admit faster-than-light non-local interaction between widely separated particles. All the same this may seem an acceptable cost if, as Bohm argues, such effects of remote quantum 'entanglement' cannot be used to transmit information and therefore need not be thought to throw any massive paradox into our post-Einsteinian conceptions of space-time reality. At least one may question whether Putnam's broad acceptance of the orthodox theory as setting the agenda for debate and his consequent rather quick dismissal of the Bohmian alternative doesn't lead him to over-estimate the problems that quantum mechanics *inevitably* poses for any 'classical' realist ontology. (See especially my discussion in Chapters 2 and 5.) Also it gives reason to doubt whether Putnam is justified in recommending the adoption of a deviant (i.e., non-bivalent or three-valued) logic as a means of resolving such anomalies as quantum superposition or wave/particle dualism. For this would seem very much a strategy of last resort, given the existence of Bohm's alternative (logic-preserving) construal and also the problems that arise in assessing *any* theory for logical consistency and truth if there is always the option of switching logics so as to accommodate recalcitrant empirical data.

This proposal goes along with Putnam's wider argument for the in-principle revisability of a good many truths whose *a priori* status has been or might yet conceivably be subject to challenge. They include (most crucially for Putnam) the accomplished shift from Euclidean to non-Euclidean geometry, and again – at a long stretch of counter-factual imagining – the possibility that we might come across some contradiction in the axioms of Peano arithmetic. I shall have a good deal to say about this aspect of his work and the problems that result when Putnam extends the range of 'revisable' items from matters of empirical warrant, *via* truth-claims grounded in certain supposed *a priori* intuitions, to those axioms of logic and arithmetic which possess a quite different (strictly non-negotiable) order of necessary truth. Indeed, this is another area where Putnam's early work in philosophical semantics – involving as it did a constant appeal to such modal-logical distinctions – can be seen to have offered a stronger basis for deciding which items might be revisable under pressure from conflicting evidence and which hold good beyond peradventure since they obtain in all conceivable (or logically possible) worlds. Then again, there is the class of *a posteriori* necessary truths – such as 'water is the substance with molecular constitution H_2O' or 'gold is the metallic element with atomic number 79' – whose status has to do with their specifying just what counts (in any world physically compatible with ours) as an instance of the natural kind in question. These truths are *a posteriori* since discovered through a process of empirical investigation but are also 'metaphysically' necessary in so far as they cannot but obtain across all such worlds. It seems to me that Putnam's insights in those early essays are among his most enduring contributions to philosophical semantics, philosophy of logic, and the epistemology of science. At any rate I have taken them as a point of departure in this study and also as something of a benchmark for assessing his later, more sceptical approach to a range of kindred topics.

I would defend this selective approach on a number of grounds, quite aside from my own particular interest in the realism *versus* anti-realism debate. For one thing these issues are central to Putnam's thinking, early and late, and therefore provide the best means of getting a grip on his exceptionally wide range of philosophical concerns. For another, they constitute a guiding thread through his engagement with various philosophers – among them Wittgenstein, Quine, Dummett and Goodman – whose arguments have clearly left a mark on his later thinking despite what I take to be the strong 'backward' pull toward a realist position that would hold out against their more sceptical conclusions. Putnam is unique in having registered the impact of these arguments while none the less retaining a strong sense of their failure to account for our knowledge of the growth of scientific knowledge. Thus I have focused on his work in philosophical semantics – where this debate is taken up most directly – and on his writings in philosophy of logic, mathematics and the physical sciences where they are likewise of central concern. This has meant paying less (or no) attention to a number of Putnam's other interests, among them cognitive psychology, the social sciences, ethics, aesthetics, historiography and literary theory. It has also prevented me from offering any adequate discussion of his various engagements with philosophy in the so-called 'continental' (i.e., post-Kantian mainland-European) line of descent from Hegel to Gadamer and Derrida. More's the pity, some may feel, since Putnam is one of the few prominent analytic philosophers who have attempted to sustain such a dialogue across and despite the deep-laid forms of institutional prejudice that have often stood in its way. All the same I would hope that readers with a primary interest in any of these subject areas will recognise the extent to which Putnam's thinking about the realism issue is germane to his thinking about questions of meaning and truth across a range of other disciplines.

I have perhaps said enough to indicate that I find many problems with the shift in Putnam's philosophical stance since he started out on the long trek from his early objectivist and causal-realist position, *via* internal (or framework-relative) realism, to the 'natural', pragmatist, or 'commonsense' outlook adopted in his later work. Still, to my mind, there is no contemporary philosopher who has shown such a readiness to take full measure of opposing views while insisting that the effort to get things right is more important than any advantage to be had by claiming the current professional high ground. 'Out of the quarrel with others we make rhetoric', so Yeats famously wrote, whereas 'out of the quarrel with ourselves we make poetry'. In Putnam's case the philosophic 'quarrel' has been conducted through a process of constant dialogical exchange with himself and other thinkers which often makes it hard to draw any such distinction. Thus, despite yielding ground in response to various anti-realist arguments, Putnam has also offered some pointed criticisms – especially of Wittgenstein and Dummett – which I have chosen to emphasise here since his own usual practice is to put the best possible case for positions that he finds problematic or unpersuasive. This attitude emerges most strikingly in Putnam's various attempts to make sense of Nelson Goodman's ultra-nominalist or strong-constructivist approach, one that few philosophers have managed to engage in so open-minded yet searchingly critical a fashion. Here again he has regularly worked on the assumption that philosophical beliefs – one's own included – are best tried out against the widest range of available counter-arguments, even if those arguments appear to push scepticism well beyond the point of rational or commonsense acceptability.

Indeed it has been a guiding principle of Putnam's work to allow that any case put forward in good earnest by an intelligent thinker is likelier than not to contain some important truth, or at any rate some partial insight that merits close attention from those who incline toward a contrary view. This is also very evident in his writings about Quine, without doubt a major influence early and late, yet one whose strongly naturalistic conception of philosophy's role *vis-à-vis* the physical sciences has prompted Putnam to embark upon a long series of intensely self-critical questionings and revaluations. Seeing all around a complicated issue is often a lot more difficult than adopting a stance – on whichever side – that permits nothing to challenge or to complicate one's own fixed view of the matter. Quite simply there is more to be *learned* from reading Putnam than from reading the work of more doctrinally committed thinkers – anti-realists and relativists of various type among them – who set out to defend their own position against all comers. I trust that these qualities in Putnam's thought have left some impression on the following pages, not least when I pursue the points of disagreement outlined above.

Note

I have not provided references for works mentioned or passages cited here since they are all discussed at greater length – with full bibliographical details – in subsequent chapters of this book.

I

Realism, scepticism and naturalism: stages on the Putnam road

It is never safe to assume that the latest Putnam-in-print represents Putnam's latest thoughts on any given topic, especially when the topic is that of realism, concerning which he has undergone numerous well-known changes of mind. Nevertheless I shall take it that his Dewey Lectures – published in the *Journal of Philosophy* – give a good idea of where he currently stands on a range of issues connected with the realism debate (Putnam 1994). Let me say straight off that I admire Putnam for his readiness to make a clean breast of all this and to go public on every occasion when he finds something wrong with his own previous thinking. The Dewey Lectures are written very much from the viewpoint of one who has occupied various positions along the way and found them all wanting in some crucial respect despite having been momentarily tempted in this or that direction. This gives his writing a certain preemptive quality, as if to warn any reader on the lookout for problems or objections that he (Putnam) is sure to have thought of them already, and that they are somewhere to be found in his recent work as footnotes, parentheses or qualifying clauses. Of course there is a strong possibility that he will have something more to say on the topic and perhaps – though this seems altogether less likely – something that will mark yet another radical change of mind. Still these lectures give a welcome chance to listen in on Putnam's continuing dialogue with himself and other thinkers, among them (most prominently) James, Dewey, Wittgenstein, Austin and Dummett. Besides that, they offer an occasion for assessing the current state of play with regard to the realism issue and enquiring whether there has been any progress toward a constructive settlement.

Putnam evidently thinks that there has – at least to the extent of clearing away some unnecessary obstacles and false dilemmas – and, moreover, that the issue can best be resolved by adopting his latest recommendations. In brief, these amount to an outlook of 'natural realism' which strongly endorses the commonsense view that 'the objects of normal, "veridical" perception are usually "external" things', and therefore that 'successful perception is just a seeing, or hearing, or feeling, etc., of things "out there", and not a mere affectation of a person's subjectivity by those things' (Putnam 1994: 454). His reason for placing the scare quotes around those terms is not that Putnam doubts the possibility of veridical perception or the existence of a real (mind- or observer-independent) world whose objects, properties, causal powers, microstructural attributes, and so forth, must be thought of as deciding the truth or falsehood of any beliefs that we hold or any statements that we make concerning them. Rather, he thinks that such language tends to reinforce the grip of some bad old pseudo-dilemmas, chiefly by setting up a dualism of 'mind' and 'world' and then treating this as a problem that requires some more or less specialised philosophical solution. Worst of all, it produces the notion of an 'interface' – a two-way juncture or meeting-point – where inputs from the (so-called) 'external world' are somehow matched up with our perceptual apparatus or powers of cognitive processsing. From Descartes, via Kant's First *Critique*, to the logical empiricists this has been the chief stumbling-block of all attempts to close that problematic gap between knowledge and the objects of knowledge. Hence the various failed attempts to 'overcome' or 'resolve' this problem by empiricists, rationalists, phenomenologists, central-state materialists, cognitive psychologists and a good many others who have basically stuck to the same agenda even while striving to think their way through or beyond it. Here Putnam takes a lead from John McDowell on the impossibility of getting any clearer about these issues so long as we persist in thinking that way (McDowell 1994). 'Winning through to natural realism', he writes, 'is seeing the *needlessness* and the *unintelligibility* of a picture that imposes an interface between ourselves and the world' (Putnam 1994: 487).

Putnam is by no means the first to suggest that we should change the agenda – simply stop thinking in those old 'Cartesian-*cum*-materialist' terms – rather than continue to flog the dead horse of an epistemological tradition whose sole result has been the constant production of ever-more technically sophisticated realist positions and ever-more resourceful sceptical arguments for rejecting those positions. Indeed almost everyone who has written on this topic during the past few decades has professed to view it as in some sense a non-issue, or as the kind of hyperinduced pseudo-problem which calls for treatment in the therapeutic mode, rather than for anything like a 'constructive' philosophical solution. Among the therapies most often proposed are Wittgenstein's idea of coaxing us down from the heights of metaphysical abstraction to a sensible acceptance of shared practices or cultural life-forms as the furthest we can get toward justifying our various beliefs; Wilfrid Sellars' deconstruction of the 'myth of the given' as a false idea and source of much epistemological confusion; Quine's advice (in 'Two Dogmas of Empiricism') that we should junk the residual Kantian dualisms of recent analytic philosophy and accept a thoroughly holistic conception of meaning, evidence, and truth; Donald Davidson's subsequent trumping of Quine as regards his attachment to a third such residual dogma, namely the scheme/content dualism or the notion of manifold conceptual frameworks that variously organise empirical data; deflationist theories which treat the truth-predicate as cancelling out for all practical purposes since it adds nothing (bar an extra degree of rhetorical emphasis) to our various standing beliefs or commitments; and of course Richard Rorty's wholesale debunking of the Western post-Cartesian epistemological tradition in favour of a strong-descriptivist approach that urges us simply to 'change the subject' and devise new language-games (vocabularies, metaphors, narratives, etc.) that find no room for that boring old talk of truth, reality, and accurate representation (see Wittgenstein 1958; Sellars 1963; Quine 1961; Davidson 1984; Horwich 1990; Rorty 1979 and 1982). So Putnam has some prominent allies in his view that the realism debate should take a fresh turn and that any such advance will need to circumvent the more traditional ways of framing it, rather than producing endless refinements to an outworn epistemological paradigm. On the other hand he sees some of these proposals – Rorty's especially – as pushing too far in a 'post-philosophical' direction which claims to leave all the problems behind through an exercise of strong-willed creative 'redescription' while in fact leaving them firmly in place for want of any adequate alternative.

This is one reason – along with several others which I shall come to shortly – why Putnam is now keen to set the record straight with regard to his own previous positions on the realism issue. It may be useful at this point to flag those positions for ease and economy of future reference. By 'Putnam 1' I shall designate the philosopher who, in some influential early essays, put forward a strong causal-realist theory of meaning, reference and truth (see especially Putnam 1975[2]a, 1975[2]b, 1975[2]c). On this account we use certain words – paradigmatically proper names and natural-kind terms – in order to pick out certain individuals or entities whose range of descriptive criteria may vary widely across time or between different stages in the process of knowledge-acquisition but which none the less retain stability of reference in consequence of having once been applied to just *that* specific person or just *that* particular kind of object. A similar approach – though with more emphasis on its modal-logical implications – was developed at about the same time by Saul Kripke in his lectures that were eventually published under the title *Naming and Necessity* (Kripke 1980). Thus the name 'Aristotle' would still apply to Aristotle *ipse* – the person conceived when his father's sperm fertilised his mother's egg – even if we made a whole range of startling new discoveries about him, such as that he had not in fact tutored Alexander, been a pupil of Plato, authored the *Posterior Analytics*, and so forth. Likewise, the natural-kind term 'gold' has retained its continuity of reference despite having been subject to various shifts in its range of descriptive criteria or defining attributes, e.g., from 'yellow ductile metal soluble in *aqua regia*' to 'metallic element with atomic number 79'.

For Putnam, as for Kripke, this 'new' theory of reference was designed to get over certain problems with the then dominant Frege–Russell or 'descriptivist' approach, in particular the fact that it seemed logically to entail some downright absurd consequences, such as the standing (if remote) possibility that Aristotle might yet turn out *not* to have been Aristotle, or gold *not* to have been gold all along (Frege 1952; Russell 1905). That is to say, if reference was ultimately fixed by the going range of descriptive or identifying criteria then there seemed no way of avoiding such a clearly unacceptable outcome. The new theory managed to avoid it by flatly denying the descriptivist premise and asserting that reference was fixed in the first place by an act of ostensive designation ('This child shall be called Aristotle', 'This substance is what we call "gold"') which thereafter held firm across and despite any subsequent changes in the currency of knowledge. It also helped to explain how some such usages might have been wrong though warranted in purely descriptivist terms, as for instance when people mistook 'fool's gold' (iron pyrites) for genuine samples of the kind, or when they misidentified whales as fish on grounds of resemblance and for want of any better (more scientifically informed) understanding. Hence one possible use of a natural-kind term: 'to a refer to a thing which belongs to a natural kind which does *not* fit the "theory" associated with the natural-kind term, but which was believed to fit that theory (and, in fact, to be *the* natural kind which fit the theory) when the theory had not yet been falsified' (Putnam 1975[2]a: 143). And again, as against the Frege–Russell descriptivist approach: 'what *really* distinguishes the classes we count as natural kinds is itself a matter of (high-level and very abstract) scientific investigation and not just meaning analysis' (*ibid.*: 141).

Putnam's was also a 'strong' causal-realist approach in the sense that – more explicitly than Kripke's – it explained this fixity of reference not only through the verbal 'chain' of transmission from one usage to the next but also with respect to those essential or underlying properties (subatomic structures, molecular configurations, chromosomal features, etc.) which distinguished various candidate items. Thus there might well be deviant or non-standard cases – such as white gold, green sweet-tasting lemons, or non-striped tigers – which could still be reliably classified under their proper (natural) kind by ignoring those deceptive surface characteristics and instead taking stock of the best available scientific knowledge. Or again: by adopting more precise forms of microphysical characterisation (such as 'acid' = 'proton-donor') we can avoid the various sorts of error that typically occur when we judge by surface or phenomenal appearances. 'This is, of course, one reason', he writes, 'for the failure of phenomenalistic translation schemes' (1975[2]a: 142). Putnam 1 also developed this line of argument through his well-known series of 'Twin-Earth' thought-experiments, involving the hypothesis of a counterpart planet where for instance the term 'water' refers to a liquid substance with all the same phenomenal attributes – wetness, transparency, identical boiling-point, freezing-point, cleansing properties, precipitation as rain under certain atmospheric conditions, etc. – but with the molecular constitution XYZ instead of H_2O (Putnam 1975[2]c). In such cases a space-traveller from Earth who arrived on Twin Earth and commented (understandably) 'There is a lot of water around here!' would have misidentified the watery substance, just as would a traveller from Twin Earth who landed on Earth and made the same remark. Only as a result of more detailed scientific investigation – i.e., by applying certain methods of chemical analysis – would both parties discover their mistake and avoid any further confusion.

Then again, different members of the same species (for instance, European cats and Siamese cats) may diverge widely in appearance and behaviour despite their common species-membership. Here the standard test is that two such creatures, so long as they are of opposite sex and biologically fertile, should be able to mate and produce likewise fertile offspring. Counterfactually speaking,

[i]f Twin Earth 'cats' were never able to mate with Earth cats (and produce fertile offspring), then not only biologists but laymen would say that Twin Earth cats are another species. They might of course say that they were another species of *cat*; but if it turned out that Twin Earth cats evolved from, say, pandas rather than felines, then in the end we would say that they were not really cats at all, and Twin Earthers would similarly say that Earth cats were not really cats at all. (Putnam 1988: 35)

Putnam's point in all this, like Kripke's, was partly to pursue certain modal-logical arguments with a bearing on the status of various (e.g., contingent or transworld necessary) truths. However what I mainly want to emphasise here is the extent to which Putnam 1 was committed to a realist and causal-explanatory account of how language displayed the referential capacity to articulate the growth of scientific knowledge through a process of increasing refinement, precision and depth-ontological grasp. That is to say, his approach went further than Kripke's toward a theory of reference grounded in the basic tenets of scientific realism, among them – as in the passage from his Dewey lectures cited above – the existence of a largely mind- and language-independent 'external world' whose salient features (such as natural kinds) could none the less be objects of 'veridical perception'. What makes this possible – according to Putnam 1 – is the fact that reference is truth-tracking in the sense of being open at any given stage to further developments in scientific knowledge or better, more adequate means of distinguishing those various objects and kinds (see also McCulloch 1995). Of course not everyone has to be *au fait* with the latest scientific theories in order to refer successfully in most cases or to know what they are talking about reliably enough for most practical (everyday-communicative) purposes. Thus non-experts can carry on referring to 'gold' without being able to specify its atomic number, just as people can talk about 'water' despite knowing nothing of its molecular constitution, or pick out instances of the animal kind 'tiger' while possessing not the least grasp of genetics or molecular biology. That is, they can rely on the 'linguistic division of labour' which ensures that there are experts around with the right sort of knowledge, specialists who can always be consulted if need should arise and who serve to monitor the currency of informed (scientifically up-to-date) usage (Putnam 1975[2]c: 227–9). All the same – and crucially for Putnam's argument – these experts are entitled to have the last word in disputed or borderline cases, since theirs is precisely the sort of expertise that decides what shall count as a paradigm sample in terms of (for instance) its molecular constitution or other such microstructural attributes.

In other words the linguistic 'division of labour' stops well short of any Wittgensteinian appeal to communal usage ('language-games', 'practices' or cultural 'forms of life') as the furthest one can get toward justification for truth-claims of whatever kind. Indeed one very marked difference between 'early' and 'late' Putnam is the extent of his willingness to treat this as a persuasive line of argument. Putnam 1 clearly finds it unpersuasive to the point of manifest absurdity. Thus: 'Wittgensteinians, whose fondness for the expression "form of life" appears to be directly proportional to its degree of preposterousness in a given context, say that acquiring the customary use of such a word as "tiger" is coming to share a form of life' (1975[2]a: 149). At this point it is worth comparing a passage from the Dewey Lectures which shows how far Putnam has moved in a Wittgensteinian direction.

> Now, there is indeed a property that all instances of pure gold have in common, namely, consisting of (a mixture of isotopes of) the element with atomic number 79, but the English word 'gold' is not synonymous with 'element with atomic number 79'. Indeed, the ordinary meaning of the word 'gold' cannot be expressed as a property or a conjunction of properties at all. As Ludwig Wittgenstein pointed out, there are many words we can use perfectly well – one example, which has become famous, was the word 'game' – although there is no one property common to all the things to which the word correctly applies. (Putnam 1994: 449)

Clearly there is large shift of emphasis here from his earlier focus on those paradigm samples of natural-kind identity which were taken as providing a reference-class for other, less precise or scientifically accountable usages. At any rate Putnam was then very anxious to disown any idea that the 'linguistic division of labour' amounts to no more than a minor variation on this standard Wittgensteinian theme. Rather, it gives non-experts the credit for knowing pretty much – or in most cases – what their terms refer to but only on condition that their usage comes out in agreement with the opinion of those who can claim to possess a more precise knowledge of the various items concerned. Also, such usage is 'sensitive to future discovery' in the sense that anyone who referred (say) to 'atoms' during the period between the ancient Greek atomists and Dalton, or anyone who talked about 'gold' before its atomic number was known, must surely be taken as picking out *that* kind of thing but as doing so in partial ignorance of *just what it was* they were picking out and with *just what degree* of genuine scientific warrant. This is a crucial load-bearing point for the realist since it explains how, for instance, different theories of the atom – from Democritus to Dalton and thence from Thomson to Rutherford, Einstein and Bohr – can be taken as denoting a shared referent despite their radically divergent conceptions of atomic (or subatomic) structure. (See also Putnam 1978: 22–5.)

Thus Putnam 1 has a strong counter-argument to that strain of linguistic-communitarian thinking, largely inspired by Wittgenstein, which would have it that nothing can fix the reference or decide the truth-value of our various terms, descriptions, theories, ontological commitments, and so forth, beyond the mere fact that 'this language-game is played' in a certain cultural context. Moreover his approach is squarely opposed to descriptivist accounts in the Frege–Russell line of descent, along with ontological-relativist theories (like that of Quine) which push yet further in that direction by treating the concepts of truth and reference as 'internal' to some given framework or conceptual scheme (Quine 1961 and 1969). Above all, it offers a sturdy realist rejoinder to those, such as Rorty, who urge that we should junk the whole tradition of epistemology from Descartes down since there is just no way to make sense of the idea that language can somehow 'cut nature at the joints' by picking out natural kinds with increased precision or achieving ever more 'adequate' or 'accurate' representations of them (Rorty 1979). Rather – he thinks – we should now take a lead from the poets and other creative types who can help to get us out of that old philosophical rut by devising novel and adventurous modes of redescription. Thus physicists might always revolutionise their field – bring about some radical Kuhnian paradigm-change – by reading around in sociology, anthropology, art-history, or literary theory, while literary theorists can likewise jazz up their discourse by borrowing the odd metaphor from physics or molecular biology (Rorty 1991[1]). To reject such overtures is merely to display an attachment to quaint old realist habits of thought which persist in dividing up subject-areas or methods of enquiry as if these somehow 'corresponded' to distinctions in the nature of extra-discursive reality. But if Putnam 1 is right then Rorty is clearly way off the mark with his idea that the range of existing academic disciplines – i.e., the various physical, social and human sciences – are so many language-games or *façons de parler* which arose at a certain time for certain culture-specific reasons and which have long since passed their sell-by date. On the contrary, what accounts for the evidence of progress in subject-areas like physics or molecular biology is their having developed the right sorts of method (observational, descriptive, predictive or causal-explanatory) for picking out their various discipline-specific objects of investigation.

II

So much for Putnam 1, the strong causal-realist whose views I have summarised here at some length partly because – in my opinion – they still merit serious attention, and partly since they offer a contrastive background to his later philosophical development. Putnam 2 is the thinker who underwent a radical change of mind and who came to believe – in broad agreement with those whose arguments he had previously rejected – that the realist case was simply incoherent if it involved the appeal to an order of mind- and language-independent reality that *by very definition* exceeded our utmost powers of perceptual or conceptual grasp (Putnam 1981 and 1983). Such was of course the great problem bequeathed by Kant, namely that of explaining how we could ever profess to have veridical knowledge of an 'external world' if that world and all its contents were accessible to us only by way of our sensory inputs, perceptual modalities, spatio-temporal intuitions, *a priori* concepts, capacities of synthesising judgement, and so forth (Kant 1964). In other words it is the problem that arises when commentators strive to make sense of Kant's claim to be both a 'transcendental idealist' and an 'empirical realist', that is to say, one who in principle accepts the absolute impossibility of attaining direct (unmediated) knowledge of the world while none the less supposing that world to exist along with all the features, properties and characteristics that would figure in a fully adequate objective account, could we but achieve such a thing. At which point, of course, the sceptic will respond that this is the merest of figleaf 'realisms', a last-resort doctrine that posits the existence of a noumenal 'reality' beyond knowledge or experience, a *je ne sais quoi* utterly devoid of empirical or even (as Kant would have it) determinate conceptual content. Such is at any rate the standard form of counter-argument, repeated – with various technical refinements – by advocates of an anti-realist position in epistemology, philosophical semantics, philosophy of science, historiography, and a range of other present-day disciplines where this issue has returned very much to centre-stage. (See Dummett 1978; Luntley 1988; Tennant 1987; Vision 1988; Wright 1987.)

On his own retrospective account in the Dewey Lectures Putnam 2 never went so far as to espouse this extreme reactive position. Rather he chose to characterise himself as an 'internal realist', one for whom it still made perfectly good sense to talk about real-world objects and events, but only in so far as they figured within some particular framework of interest-relative concepts, schemas or categories (Putnam 1981 and 1987). This approach he took to be broadly Kantian though shorn of Kant's unfortunate metaphysical excesses, among them the doctrine of faculties, the appeal to *a priori* (transcendentally valid) grounds of knowledge and judgement, and of course the idea of a noumenal reality behind phenomenal appearances. That is to say, Putnam wished to have no truck with the mysterious Kantian *Ding-an-sich* which must somehow be thought of as the precondition for our every act of cognitive judgement, yet whose nature it is – by the limits laid down for human understanding in general – to exceed any possible representation through our powers of intuitive-conceptual grasp. Of course Putnam is not alone in finding this doctrine hard to swallow and in seeking some alternative, revisionist account that would jettison the notion of noumenal reality while retaining Kant's more useful and productive insights. Other thinkers in the recent analytic tradition have likewise mounted a rescue operation that stresses those Kantian insights – especially the cardinal role of judgement as a mediating term between sensuous intuitions and concepts – but which also makes a virtue of talking Kant down from the giddy metaphysical heights (Brandom 1994; McDowell 1994; Nagel 1997). Indeed this is one of the more interesting points of convergence between current analytic philosophy of mind and language and the various post-Kantian interpretive debates that have marked the mainland-continental line of descent from Fichte, Schelling and Hegel to Husserl and beyond. (See for instance Beiser 1987; Glendinning (ed.) 1999; Norris 2000.)

What chiefly distinguishes the 'back-to-Kant' movement in current analytic philosophy is an awareness that logical empiricism gave rise to various kindred problems, not least the gap between raw sense-data (or phenomenal intuitions) and the concepts, theories or explanatory laws by which we make sense of those otherwise inchoate data. The logical-empiricist programme started out in briskly confident fashion (Carnap 1967; Reichenbach 1938, 1951) but these difficulties with it soon opened the way to more sceptical modes of argument. Hence Quine's radical-empiricist talk of the constant bombardment of our nerve-endings by a barrage of incoming physical stimuli which supposedly provide our sole means of access to 'external' reality, but which are then subject to as many alternative construals as there exist different ontologies, conceptual schemes, or selective ways of picking out the range of favoured candidate items, whether centaurs, Homer's gods, numbers, mathematical sets, or brick houses on Elm Street (Quine 1961). Davidson famously rejected this framework-relativist approach by arguing that talk of 'conceptual schemes' was the third residual dogma of logical empiricism, and that by dropping it we could regain 'unmediated contact' with those various physical objects and events whose 'antics' rendered our sentences true or false (Davidson 1984: 198). Rorty pushed this argument to the limit – with presumed warrant from Davidson – by completely severing the link between a causal account of knowledge-acquisition through direct exposure to sensory stimuli and those kinds of normative justification which we standardly provide in accordance with this or that language-game, social practice, or cultural life-form (Rorty 1979 and 1991[1]). Moreover, he could claim that this was just the inevitable outcome of those problems with logical empiricism which had spawned a whole series of compromise 'solutions', all of them subject to the same sort of difficulty and none of them able to rescue the project of old-style analytic philosophy. Rather, we should see that the causal account of belief-acquisition has absolutely no norma- tive epistemological bearings, and that the normative business (i.e., that of offer- ing reasons, theories, justifications, etc.) takes place in an altogether separate realm where the only constraints are linguistic or social, and where the choice falls out between 'normal' and 'revolutionary' modes of discourse. Thus there is nothing – at least no philosophical argument – that can take us from such brute physical contingencies as the impact of photons on Galileo's eyeball to such justificatory issues as whether or not Galileo was right to hold out against the orthodox astronomical wisdom of his time (Rorty 1991[1]: 81). To suppose that there is – or that the gap might be closed by some jointly normative and causal- explanatory approach – is merely to commit the sort of category-mistake which (in Rorty's view) bedevils all forms of realist epistemology.

I have offered this thumbnail sketch of developments in the wake of logical empiricism in order to explain both the current 'rediscovery' of Kant by analytic philosophers and the particular role that Kant has come to play in Putnam's recent thinking. What has struck commentators like McDowell is the way that 'judge- ment' functions in the First *Critique* as a synthesising power whose operations are always already at work when we 'bring intuitions under concepts', that is to say, which precludes any thought of treating these latter as separate stages or aspects of the cognitive process whose relationship then becomes impossible to explain (McDowell 1994). Thus it is only with reference to the act of judgement – conceived as something basic and hence irreducible to its various constituent parts – that we can break free of those vexing dilemmas confronted by analytic philos- ophy in the wake of logical empiricism. Moreover, there is a close analogy here – or so it is suggested – with Frege's logico-semantic case for judgements as the bearers of propositional content, and propositions (rather than their separate component terms) as the ultimate units of intelligible meaning (Frege 1952). This stands in marked contrast to Quine's way of swinging right across from the notion of manifold discrete physical stimuli impacting on our nerve ends to the notion of our total state of knowledge at any given time as a 'fabric' or 'web' of interwoven beliefs where every item is open to revision should some conflict arise or some tension develop with a belief-held-true at another point in the fabric, whether near the so-called logical 'core' or the observational 'periphery' (Quine 1961). What thus drops out of Quine's thinking – and explicitly so – is that Kantian–Fregean idea of propositional judgements as the bearers of determinate truth-values, and hence as playing a pivotal role in philosophy of mind and language. For Quine they represent nothing more than a half-way or compromise stage in the progress that has led from the hopelessly reductive term-by-term empiricist conception of Locke, Berkeley and Hume to the full-fledged holistic theory of meaning and truth that treats every incoming sensory stimulus as facing the entire 'tribunal' of present-day accredited scientific knowledge. In which case clearly the way is wide open for sceptics like Rorty to draw their wonted conclusion that truth *just is* whatever we make of it of it according to the currently most favoured range of languages or descriptive attributes.

So if Kant has made something of a comeback in recent analytic philosophy it is largely on account of his theory of judgement and the scope this offers for resisting such forms of fargone sceptical, relativist or linguistic-constructivist thinking. McDowell is most explicit in this regard, devoting a large part of his recent book *Mind and World* (1994) to an exposition of the Kantian theory and to arguing that it offers the best way forward from the problems encountered with logical empiricism and thereafter with the various putative 'solutions' put forward by thinkers like Quine, Davidson, and Rorty. The case is somewhat similar with Putnam 2 whose theory of 'internal realism' relies very heavily on the Kantian claim that one can give up the idea of our somehow having access to a mind-independent (or framework-transcendent) reality without thereby giving way to the notion that reality is itself a construct or figment of our various conceptual or descriptive schemes. Nevertheless – as commentators have often noted – Putnam 2 finds it hard to maintain this position in a consistent way, tending as he does to emphasise its 'realist' credentials when confronted with sceptics like Rorty who would urge him in the opposite direction, and to stress its 'internal' (or frame-work-relativist) aspect when reflecting on problems with the kind of externalist (or causal-explanatory) realism that he himself once endorsed. (See especially Alston 1996; Williams 1996.) Chief among these problems is the standard sceptical objection, as summarised above: that realism quite literally cannot make sense if it entails our having knowledge of an 'external world' whose existence and properties are verification-transcendent and hence unknowable by very definition. Sometimes Putnam 2 takes the strongest line against arguments of this sort, namely that they confuse ontology with epistemology, or the question: 'have we reason to assert that there exists a reality independent of our current best beliefs concerning it?', and the question: 'can we know for sure in what particular respects those beliefs either match or fail to match certain portions of objective reality thus conceived?' But elsewhere Putnam seems prone to such confusion himself, most often when explaining why he has now given up his own previous position, or when responding to critics of a realist mind who reproach him on just those grounds. Then one finds him arguing – usually with reference to Kant and/or to pragmatists like James and Dewey – that the only kind of 'realism' worth defending is one that acknowledges its framework-internal and interest-relative character (Putnam 1978, 1981, 1987). Thus: '[i]nasmuch as Kant had a view which included a correspondence view of truth *within* the empirical realm (on my reading, anyway) *and* a stress on the mind-dependence of all truth, there is (I like to think) something Kantian in the view with which I end up' (1978: 5). That is, just so long as we understand – as McDowell is likewise at pains to make clear – that this is 'a demythologised Kantianism, without "things in themselves" and "transcendental egos"' (*ibid.*: 6).

Nevertheless, such passages give a hold for critics like Rorty who can point to them as clear evidence that Putnam's is a merely notional 'realism', a term that might just as well drop out of his vocabulary, since it is doing no work except to provide a rhetorical defence against those other metaphysically deluded opponents who still hanker for the old groundless certitudes (Rorty 1998). It seems to me that Rorty is right in one respect at least: that there is no viable defence of realism to be had by taking certain arguments from Kant (i.e., the appeal to an order of intersubjectively valid intuitions, concepts and categories) and then giving these arguments a pragmatist spin by discounting the entire Kantian 'metaphysics' of transcendental deduction to *a priori* grounds of knowledge. What results – as Rorty is quick to remark – is a relativism that dare not speak its name, or a framework-internal 'realism' that can be relativised to so many different conceptual, linguistic or socio-cultural frameworks that it ceases to carry the least argumentative force. Nor is it at all clear that Putnam 2 could strengthen his position by appealing more explicitly – like McDowell – to the Kantian notion of judgement as a primordial faculty in the nature of human understanding whose function it is to bridge that otherwise problematical gap between concepts and sensuous (phenomenal) intuitions. For it has long been recognised – by 'analytic' and 'continental' exegetes alike – that Kant's exposition at this point becomes notably perplexed and obscure, as when he relates the activity of judgement to that of the 'productive imagination', itself a 'blind but indispensable function of the soul', yet one concerning which we can have no knowledge, despite its being the precondition for every kind of knowledge we can possibly attain (Kant 1964: 112).

Continental epistemology after Kant is very largely a series of responses to this problem, starting out with the debate between 'subjective' and 'objective' idealism (Fichte *versus* Schelling), taken up in grand synthesising style by Hegel, and carried on by a succession of strong revisionists – Nietzsche and Heidegger among them – who claim to transvalue that entire tradition of thought by pursuing its more radical implications (Behler (ed.) 1987; Beiser 1987; Ewing (ed.) 1957; Glendinning (ed.) 1999; Heidegger 1990; Rorty 1982 and 1991[2]). It is not hard to see how these chapters in Kant's 'continental' reception-history find a parallel in the various positions adopted by analytic philosophers on either side of the realism issue. Thus a thinker like Rorty stands to that debate as Nietzsche stood to the tradition of nineteenth-century idealism, that is to say, in the role of an antinomian sceptic who has taken the latterday 'linguistic turn' and who acknowledges no limit (certainly no limit in the nature of reality or truth) to the powers of inventive redescription. At any rate there is little comfort for realists of whatever epistemological stripe in those darkly suggestive passages to be found in the 'Transcendental Aesthetic' of Kant's First *Critique*. I have argued elsewhere at greater length that the recent 'back-to-Kant' movement among analytic philosophers such as McDowell and Nagel cannot resolve these problems since it tends to take the Kantian notion of 'judgement' very much at face value (Norris 2000). Thus the notion is appealed to as successfully explaining how sensuous intuitions are 'brought under' adequate concepts, or again – by analogy – how thinkers in the wake of logical empiricism might call upon judgement as an intermediary term that reconciles the various antinomies bequeathed by that short-lived though widely influential movement of thought. Yet, as we seen, Kant's idea of judgement goes along with that of 'productive imagination', which he describes in terms so cryptic and obscure as to have engendered a whole range of conflicting or revisionist interpretations.

However my main interest here is in Putnam's response to these issues and, more specifically, his various successive changes of mind on the question of just what counts as a viable 'realist' position. The Dewey Lectures mark another such change and one that shows Putnam – the thinker I shall henceforth refer to as 'Putnam 3' – now keen to stake out a position which avoids any charge of retreating to the strong causal realism of Putnam 1 while it also rejects the kinds of anti-realist (or Rorty-style cultural relativist) argument that proved so hard for Putnam 2 to resist despite his express misgivings in that regard. This requires quite a lot of tacking back and forth between his own previous thoughts at various stages along the way and what other philosophers have had to say on topics of related concern. In particular it involves an account of just what he meant by 'internal realism', just how this differed from any kind of 'strong' anti-realist position, yet also why he – Putnam 3 – has since moved on to a 'natural-realist' approach which supposedly resolves all these problems.

III

Probably the best place to start is with a long footnote where Putnam offers some corrective advice to those who have got him wrong or perhaps (he concedes) been understandably misled by his own earlier lack of clarity on various points. 'Am I then giving up "internal realism"?', he somewhat rhetorically asks.

> Well, while in *Reason, Truth and History* I identified 'internal realism' with what I am here calling 'moderate verificationism', in *The Many Faces of Realism* I identified it with the rejection of the traditional realist assumptions of (1) a fixed

totality of all objects; (2) a fixed totality of all properties; (3) a sharp line between properties we 'discover' in the world and properties we 'project' onto the world; (4) a fixed relation of 'correspondence' in terms of which truth is supposed to be defined. I rejected those assumptions not as false assumptions, but as, ultimately, unintelligible assumptions. As will become clear in the sequel, I still regard each and every one of those assumptions as unintelligible, although I would argue for that conclusion in a different way. So whether I am still, to some extent, an 'internal realist' is, I guess, as unclear as how much I was including under that unhappy label. (Putnam 1994: 463n)

This passage raises as many further questions as it claims to resolve. In particular it leaves one puzzled as to why Putnam should conflate such a range of very different 'traditional' realist doctrines as those listed above. Thus (1) and (2) are plainly ontological claims about the mind- or knowledge-independent status of real-world objects or properties, while (3) invokes the need for a clear distinction between ontological and epistemological issues, and (4) wheels in the correspondence-theory of truth which is really – as other writers have stressed – a topic whose bearing on the realism issue is at best indirect and at worst a cause of much confusion (Devitt 1986). Still, the passage brings welcome clarification on a few points and will therefore serve as a useful basis for discussing Putnam's latest views.

In rejecting items (1) and (2) above – rejecting them, moreover, as not merely 'false' but downright 'unintelligible' – Putnam can be seen as bidding farewell to any version of the causal-realist theory of reference according to which we pick out objects (or kinds of objects) precisely through their various individuating properties, attributes, microstructural features, and so forth. Still, there is a certain ambiguity here since the 'fixed totality' that Putnam speaks of might be taken as 'fixed' either in objective (knowledge-independent) terms, in which case he is rejecting ontological realism, or as 'fixed' just to the extent that we have discovered the right sorts of reference-fixing property, in which case he is rejecting epistemological realism, and hence adopting a more moderate sceptical line. In other words it is the same ambiguity that characterised the writings of Putnam 2 and which often made it hard to decide between the 'strong' and 'weak' versions of his internal-realist case. Anyway, there seems good reason to conclude that Putnam 3 has a lot more in common with Putnam 2 than with Putnam 1, at least in so far as he professes to find something strictly 'unintelligible' in the realist position on whichever construal.

This conclusion is borne out by Putnam's avowal in the above-cited passage that what he previously called 'internal realism' is pretty much equivalent to what he now prefers to call 'moderate verificationism'. The rest of the passage makes it clear that he still subscribes to that position, even though he would now put the arguments for it 'in a different way'. If one asks what precisely the difference amounts to then it seems to involve a disinclination to be counted among the strong constructivists or the doctrinaire anti-realists but also a countervailing belief that any 'realism' worth defending will need to take account of the case put forward by advocates of both those positions. The resultant instability of Putnam's stance comes out in item (3) of the above-cited list, namely his continuing to reject the idea of 'a sharp line between properties we "discover" in the world and properties we "project" onto the world'. On the face of it this places Putnam firmly in the camp of those – such as Nelson Goodman – who would seek to do away with such distinctions since, in their view, the 'world' *just is* what we make of it through this or that favoured descriptive scheme or mode of projection (Goodman 1978; McCormick (ed.) 1996). At least it seems to bring him out on a wavelength with strong descriptivists like Rorty who want to draw the line somewhere short of Goodman's full-fledged ontological relativism but who reject any version of the realist argument which presumes to draw that line between in-the-world (objective) properties and those that answer to our currently favoured descriptive purposes or interests.

So the big question is whether Putnam 3 – the Putnam whose views are represented in the Dewey Lectures – can produce any argument that will head off the powerful objections (as he still sees them) to 'metaphysical' realism while blocking the slide to a relativist position that he now thinks all too easily confused with his earlier theory of internal realism. Or, otherwise put, it is the question whether Putnam's 'moderate verificationist' stance can put up sufficient resistance to the blandishments of Rortian strong descriptivism. In order to succeed in this aim he would have to show that one can have it both ways, on the one hand denying the existence of objective (verification-transcendent) truths, while on the other denying that truth can be 'internal' to our various descriptive schemes or thought of as discursively or socially 'constructed' in the wholesale projectivist sense. Such is at any rate the main challenge that Putnam takes on in the Dewey Lectures and one that lends them a considerable interest in the present-day context of debate.

By 'moderate verificationism' Putnam clearly means something less extreme than the kinds of hardline verificationist doctrine that characterised old-style logical positivism or its various successor movements, among them Dummett-style anti-realism and perhaps – though this is less clear – the type of constructive-empiricist argument advanced by Bas van Fraassen (Dummett 1978, 1991; van Fraassen 1980). It is typical of Putnam that he shows this willingness to see all around a difficult question and re-think his own views when confronted with a sample of where they might lead when espoused by a thinker – such as Dummett – who takes them to the 'logical' limit and beyond. Thus Putnam firmly rejects the idea that any scientific statement concerning unobservables or any truth-claim incapable of present verification must therefore be considered to possess no determinate truth-value, that is to say, no value of objective truth or falsehood quite aside from our present best empirical procedures, methods of proof, means of ascertainment, or whatever. After all, 'in Democritus's writings, as we know of them, the notion of an "atom" was a metaphysical one, but one to which *we* can give a sense, even if Democritus himself could not' (Putnam 1994: 502). In other words – and at this point Putnam 1 comes briefly though strikingly back on stage – there is a sense in which earlier ('metaphysical') uses of a term such as *atom* are truth-tracking or sensitive to future discovery in so far as they pick out entities whose existence will later be confirmed by more advanced means of theoretically supported observation. So Dummett must be wrong – in the grip of a false theory – if he is driven to deny what is so strongly borne out by the record of scientific progress to date, not to mention the more everyday experience of having our conjectures sometimes confirmed (shown to have been true all along) when the clinching piece of evidence at last comes in.

All the same, it would clearly be a mistake to conclude that Putnam 3 is here joining hands with Putnam 1 – the 'metaphysical' realist – and reaffirming his earlier position despite all the arguments mounted against it by Putnam 2. What he now puts forward is an alternative position ('natural realism') that would cut straight through these stalled philosophical debates and appeal to a range of self-evident facts about our being-in-the-world as sentient creatures with a well-tried capacity for finding things out and thereby keeping reliably in touch with our ambient physical environment. Thus – again following McDowell – the best solution to all those old epistemological dilemmas is one that requires 'an appreciation of how sensory experiences are not passive affectations of an object called a "mind" but (for the most part) experiences of aspects of the world by a living being' (Putnam 1994: 483). This amounts to a kind of 'second naiveté', an approach that wins through to natural realism not by any process of sophisticated argument but rather by seeing 'the *needlessness* and the *unintelligibility* of a picture that imposes an interface between ourselves and the world' (*ibid.*: 487). That is to say, Putnam 3 sees just as little point in the labours of the so-called 'metaphysical' realist – one who vainly thinks to meet the sceptic's challenge by asserting the existence of mind-independent objects, properties, causal dispositions, microstructural attributes, and so forth – as in the sceptic's well-worn response to that challenge which declares them to lie beyond reach of our utmost powers of verification. Rather – he urges – we should now change the topic, leave off debating these wearisome issues, and recognise that 'truth' and 'reality' pose no problem just so long as we are reliably in touch with the world through our various (normally functioning) perceptual and cognitive inputs.

Such is the route that Putnam has travelled on that 'long journey from realism back to realism' which he now offers as the chief lesson of his own philosophical development to date. This hard-won attitude is 'naive' in the sense that it avoids certain kinds of false sophistication in epistemology and philosophy of mind, that is to say, the sorts of argument that have regularly led to a stand-off between realists and sceptics, with the realists maintaining the existence of objective (mind-independent) truths, and the sceptics coming back on cue with their rejoinder that such truths are by very definition beyond our epistemic or conceptual ken. It is an attitude, Putnam claims,

> which fully appreciates the deep difficulties pointed out by the seventeenth-century philosophers, but which overcomes those difficulties instead of succumbing to them; a standpoint which sees that the difficulties do not, in the end, require us to reject the idea that in perception we are in unmediated contact

with our environment. We do not have to accept the interface conception.
(Putnam 1994: 488–9)

This passage may well put us in mind of some of Davidson's more laconic remarks concerning those various physical objects and events whose 'antics' – as registered by our sensory apparatus – must be taken to decide the truth-value of our corresponding statements and beliefs (Davidson 1984: 198). Still there is a question as to whether this 'second naiveté' can really take account of the problems thrown up during three centuries of intensive debate among empiricists, rationalists, Kantians, and the various latterday schools of thought ('analytic' and 'continental' alike) that have claimed somehow to resolve or supersede the classical problem of knowledge. Putnam's latest idea – which he describes more or less interchangeably as 'pragmatism', 'commonsense', or 'natural realism' – is that this problem can henceforth be made to disappear by rejecting the dualist 'interface conception' bequeathed to us mainly by Descartes and Locke. We can thus win through to a sensible acceptance that reality *just is* (indeed must be) the way that we commonly perceive it when our cognitive faculties are functioning aright and there is nothing to suggest that we might be the victims of perceptual distortion, sensory overload or aberrant physical conditions.

However, this raises the question yet again as to how far the problem of knowledge can be dealt with – or made to look merely 'pointless' and 'unintelligible' – by appealing to the plain self-evidence of our various cognitive dealings with the world. Putnam takes a lead from William James's sturdily pragmatist assurance that in the end there is no choice but to endorse this position, at least if we wish to avoid the sorts of futile debate that have occupied philosophers in the mainstream tradition from Locke, Berkeley, Hume and Kant on down. Thus, '[t]he traditional claim that we must conceive of our sensory experiences as *intermediaries* between us and the world has no sound arguments to support it, and, worse, makes it impossible to see how persons can be in genuine cognitive contact with a world at all' (Putnam 1994: 454). Further back-up is provided by Austin's *Sense and Sensibilia*, a book which – in Putnam's opinion – made brilliantly short work of such ideas in the context of old-style logical positivism and its phenomenalist theory of sense data as the ultimate constituents of knowledge (Austin 1962). So Putnam agrees with a good many recent thinkers – McDowell and Nagel among them – in thinking this a disastrous wrong turn, one that amounts to nothing more than a re-run of the seventeenth-century 'way of ideas' transposed into a different idiom but carrying all the same surplus metaphysical baggage. (See also Hacking 1980.) After all, '[n]o conception that retains anything like the traditional notion of sense data can provide a way out, [since] such a conception must always, in the end, leave us confronted by what looks like an insoluble problem' (Putnam 1994: 462–3). Much better opt for a 'natural-realist' attitude which resolves that problem at a stroke by simply reaffirming – as a matter of fact – that we *are* in cognitive contact with the world and that we *can* know this to be the case in virtue of our history and everyday experience as sentient creatures with a well-proven knack for discovering things about it.

Yet it is still open to the sceptic to respond: well, this 'second naiveté' sounds pretty much like naiveté pure and simple, whatever Putnam's defensive protestations to the contrary. In other words, it marks a regression to the kind of precritical 'commonsense' outlook which merely refuses to accept that there exists any genuine problem of knowledge, despite the fact that so many philosophers – not least Putnam himself – have devoted such enormous intellectual labours to addressing just that problem. Worse still: it offers no remotely adequate response to the sceptic's two main challenges, namely (1) how the realist can claim to have knowledge of an objective (mind-independent) world or of objective (verification-transcendent) truths concerning it, and (2) why we should be so complacent as to think that our 'natural' (commonsense) attitude to these matters is in any way reliable, let alone worthy of receiving such privileged treatment. After all, the chief lesson to be learned from the history of the natural sciences to date is that progress most often comes about through a decisive break with commonsense-intuitive modes of understanding, and even with the kinds of knowledge once thought of as *a priori* or self-evident to reason, e.g., Euclidean geometry or Newtonian space-time physics (Coffa 1991). So if the realist hopes to enlist science on his or her side of the argument – as for instance by appealing to the record of progress in these or other fields – then she will surely not want to rest her case on any version of the 'natural' or 'commonsense' attitude which has so often failed the scientific test.

Then again, the realist may choose to go the other route and argue – as against 'strong' verificationists like Dummett – that the natural attitude is one which involves the existence of objective, belief-independent truths about the world, quite aside from the issue as to whether we are now (or even as to whether we could ever be) in a position to attain knowledge of them. To confuse these questions – he or she will maintain – is the sceptic's or the verificationist's greatest blunder, one that comes about through their failure to distinguish ontological from epistemological issues, or their mistaken idea (to borrow a nice phrase from Nicholas Rescher) that such truth-talk commits the realist to a belief in the 'ontological finality of science as we have it' (Rescher 1987: 61). But then of course the sceptic will respond with his query as to what kind of 'knowledge' it can possibly be which somehow gives the realist warrant for claiming to 'know' that there are truths unknown (or unknowable) to us, or features of the world that transcend our furthest powers of verification. In other words they will deny that we can make any sense of the realist's vaunted distinction between ontology and epistemology, at least in so far as this is thought to have substantive implications for our thinking about issues of truth, knowledge or rational warrant.

IV

In his Dewey Lectures Putnam takes all these issues on board and attempts to steer a way through them that will neither incline too far in a sceptical or anti-realist direction nor lay itself open to sceptical challenge by adopting too strong a realist stance. This is why, as I have said, Putnam 3 has to manage such a tricky process of renegotiation with the arguments advanced by his own previous selves, the strong causal-realist who was Putnam 1 and the 'internal realist' (albeit with pronounced sceptical-relativist leanings) who was Putnam 2. It also explains – as I shall now go on to suggest – why the 'commonsense' approach that these lectures recommend is incapable of bearing the weight placed upon it by Putnam's desire to have the best of both worlds, or to strike a middle-ground position that renders him proof against attack from either the sceptical or the realist quarter. As a result, his new theory is so thickly hedged about with qualifying clauses and disclaimers that Putnam 3 often sounds very much like Putnam 2, despite his avowed aim of putting a clearly marked distance between them. The main problem is that he brings in a wide range of arguments, some of which tend to undermine others, or to generate internal conflicts and tensions which can only be resolved – if at all – by recourse to the notion of 'natural realism' as a kind of compromise settlement. What I propose to do now is examine some of these tensions and suggest that Putnam 3 would have strengthened his case by reaffirming the (so-called) 'metaphysical' realism of Putnam 1, since the middle-ground theory still leaves him open to anti-realist construals of the sort that could plausibly claim to find warrant in the writings of Putnam 2, despite all his statements to contrary effect.

Where such construals get a hold is chiefly through Putnam's self-avowed 'second naiveté', that is to say, his physicalist appeal to those sensory stimuli that impact on our nerve-ends from one moment to the next. This latter conception is one that has lived on through the various recent attempts – by thinkers such as Quine and Davidson – to exorcise the problems of old-style logical empiricism by adopting a naturalised epistemology that purports to put us 'directly' back in touch with reality *via* those same 'unmediated' physical stimuli. As we have seen, Putnam 3 has a habit of using similar language when putting the case for commonsense ('natural') realism as a means of deliverance from all our philosophical perplexities. However, it is far from clear how such arguments can possibly head off the kinds of anti-realist or sceptical rejoinder rehearsed three paragraphs above. That is, it can always be pointed out – as by Quine in 'Two Dogmas of Empiricism' – that this physicalist approach is perfectly compatible with the widest latitude of interpretation given the existence of diverse conceptual frameworks or ontological schemes (Quine 1961). Davidson of course takes issue with Quine on just this point, i.e., as regards the very idea that we could ever have rational grounds for imputing such a wholesale divergence between different languages, theories, paradigms, frameworks, schemes or whatever. But his own argument makes the same leap from a physicalist language of direct sensory 'impacts' to a holistic theory of meaning and interpretation where truth-values are distributed – as in Quine – through a process of optimum overall adjustment in keeping with the Principle of Charity (Davidson 1984). And from this point, again, it is no great distance to Rorty's idea that one can be as 'realist' as one likes about the impact of photons on Galileo's eyeball while still thinking it an open question as to whether Galileo or the church doctors got it right about the moons of Jupiter.

Putnam is understandably keen to deny any kinship between his construal of realism and those versions (like Rorty's) that reduce it to a mere label of convenience, an honorific term devoid of substantive philosophical content and intended mainly to block any challenge from the realist quarter. Nevertheless, as we have seen, he does take a similar physicalist line – one with clear echoes of Quine and Davidson – when suggesting how we can best overcome the 'myth of the interface', that is, the residual dualist conception which makes such a mystery of the mind/world relationship. Here again he follows McDowell (along with Austin) in arguing that this conception has been nothing short of 'disastrous' in every branch of metaphysics and epistemology. Thus, according to McDowell, 'the key assumption responsible for this disaster is the idea that there has to be an interface between our cognitive powers and the external world – or, to put the same point differently, the idea that our cognitive powers cannot reach all the way to the world' (Putnam 1994: 453). But the question then arises, for Putnam as for McDowell, as to whether one can make out a realist case which will jointly satisfy a number of stringent conditions. These are that it should (1) avoid any recourse to 'sense-data' or other such redundant intermediary terms; (2) put us back in 'unmediated contact with our environment' and thereby restore our 'natural cognitive relations to the world'; (3) none the less reject any version of the Sellarsian 'myth of the given', or the idea of a world that offers itself up for some privileged range of correct descriptions; (4) provide something more substantive (epistemologically speaking) than the bare-bones physicalist 'realism' proposed by Rorty; and (5) move somewhat in a Kantian direction in order to achieve these aims while renouncing Kant's entire 'metaphysical' apparatus and all the problems that go along with it. However, it is far from clear that those conditions can be met (or even rendered logically compatible) by adopting the kind of commonsense-realist attitude that Putnam here recommends. Nor can it be said that either he or McDowell have made out a fully convincing case for this scaled-down (detranscendentalised) version of Kant as a means of overcoming the 'interface' myth or of bridging the illusory gulf between mind and world.

The idea – briefly stated – is that Kant's twin faculties of 'receptivity' and 'spontaneity' might provide a more adequate (since non-dualist) way of conceiving the strictly indissoluble relation between experience and judgement, intuitions and concepts, or what is given in the 'manifold' of sensuous (phenomenal) impressions and what allows those otherwise inchoate impressions to achieve intelligible form (McDowell 1994). If so then this naturalised reading of Kant would resolve all the problems that philosophy gets into when it assumes that there exists a 'problem of knowledge' – a genuine and deep *philosophical* problem – and that any adequate solution will need to go some lengthy and complicated ways around. Still there is something decidedly odd about enlisting Kant (of all thinkers!) as the guide toward a better and simpler solution that can cut straight through these unnecessary tangles and bring us philosophical peace. For one thing, Kant's imprimatur is not to be had on terms that would relinquish that whole 'metaphysical' machinery – including the idea of a noumenal reality behind or beyond appearances – and would thus knock away the entire conceptual scaffolding of his project in the First *Critique*. For another, the notions of 'receptivity' and 'spontaneity' are developed by Kant in the context of a transcendental argument which claims to have established the conditions of possibility for knowledge and experience in general, a claim that neither Putnam nor McDowell is willing to accept. Moreover, as I have said, there is much that is notoriously obscure in that section of the 'Transcendental Aesthetic' where Kant introduces those notions and where they bear the chief weight of his purported solution to the problem of Humean scepticism. Lastly, it is ironic – to say the least – that this solution is now invoked by thinkers (such as Putnam 3) in quest of a common-sense-realist approach that preempts all the standard anti-realist arguments by adopting a naturalised or de-transcendentalised version of the Kantian claim. For if one thing is clear from the history of recent debate on this topic it is that Kant's philosophy has most often been construed as lending support to the anti-realist case through its denial that we can ever have 'unmediated' contact with a mind-independent reality or a realm of objective, verification-transcendent truths (Stroud 1984; Williams 1996).

All of which throws some sizeable problems into Putnam 3's McDowell-inspired attempt to redeem what is of service in Kant's epistemology while still hanging on to the Davidsonian idea which would have it that we are somehow directly in touch with a world of physical objects and events whose various 'antics' render our beliefs and statements true or false. As usual with Putnam it is a pretty safe bet that these problems will have struck him at some earlier stage and prompted a change of argumentative tack. In this case the shift was that which persuaded him – back in the mid-1970s – that a functionalist account of meaning and interpretation simply wouldn't do since it ran up against a number of insoluble difficulties. Among them were the Duhem–Quine thesis regarding the underdetermination of theories by evidence and also – more specifically – the Löwenheim–Skolem Theorem in philosophy of mathematics according to which 'every consistent theory has an enormous number of different possible interpretations, even nonisomorphic interpretations' (Putnam 1994: 459). This result struck Putnam as completely undermining any functionalist argument in philosophy of mind, cognitive psychology or philosophical semantics. After all, if 'the totality of truths about mathematical "objects" expressible in the language of mathematics cannot fix which objects we are referring to even up to isomorphism', then surely 'one could prove similar results about any language, including everyday language, or the language we use in empirical science' (*ibid*.: 459–60). The functionalist may then have recourse to certain stipulative constraints, as for instance by requiring 'that certain predicates must apply to certain objects whenever the "inputs" to the neural computer (say, the outputs of the "perception modules") are of a specified kind' (*ibid*.: 460). But this solution works only for a limited range of specified inputs and predicates, and therefore cannot claim to overcome the general problem, whether in the field of functionalist cognitive psychology or for philoso-phers concerned with wider issues of reference, meaning and truth. Thus 'all other predicates in the language excepting only those explicitly definable by means of the operationally constrained predicates will still have a huge multiplicity of unin-tended interpretations, including quite bizarre ones' (*ibid.*: 460).

So it was, on his retrospective account, that Putnam 2 gave up his earlier (realist) theory and adopted a standpoint of 'internal realism' according to which the reference of terms – along with the truth-value of statements containing them – was 'fixed' only relative to some given framework or conceptual scheme. If he now has certain misgivings in that regard (since it laid him open to cooption by sceptics of a deeper dye) he is none the less still convinced that objections such as those outlined in the above paragraph are enough to undermine the position of Putnam 1. Thus, 'if the sort of realism we have been familiar with since the early modern period, including the causal theory of perception, is right, then every-thing that happens within the sphere of cognition leaves the objective reference of our terms, for the most part, almost wholly underdetermined' (Putnam 1994: 460). Yet he also wants to insist that some commentators – Rorty in particular – have definitely got him wrong when they claim that 'internal realism' is just another name (or strategic euphemism) for the full-fledged constructivist outlook which denies any means of distinguishing 'reality' from our various descriptions, conceptual schemes, paradigms, linguistic representations, and so forth. Thus Putnam 3 is distinctly uneasy with the kinds of argument foisted onto Putnam 2 yet can see no philosophically acceptable way of sinking his differences with Putnam 1.

V

In the Dewey Lectures he offers a two-pronged line of response, on the one hand asserting – as against Dummett – that we can and must uphold the existence of objective (verification-transcendent) truths, while on the other seeking a middle-ground position with regard to the epistemological debate between realists and anti-realists. Verificationism of the Dummett variety he takes to be simply 'disas-trous' in so far as it entails a whole range of insupportable consequences, among them the 'loss of the world (and the past)' which results from arguing that state-ments can have no reference or truth-value except in those cases where we happen to possess documentary warrant, scientific evidence, or some adequate proof-procedure. What drops out entirely on Dummett's account – as likewise on defla-tionist theories of truth such as that first proposed by Frank Ramsey – is the basic conviction that reality is not exhausted by our present best knowledge of it nor even by the best knowledge we could hope to attain, given our various perceptual, cognitive and intellectual limits (Ramsey 1990; also Horwich 1990). Putnam is at his most commonsensically realist when rejecting this whole line of thought. For in his view, despite Dummett's sometimes more qualified or circumspect version of the case, verificationism always ends up by yielding crucial argumentative ground to an outlook of global anti-realism concerning scientific truth-claims or statements about the past. The same applies to deflationist accounts in so far as they reduce truth to a product of linguistic or logico-semantic definition. Thus '[d]eflationism is unable to acknowledge the reality of past events (as things that truly happened), even though it retains the old form of words ("It happened or it did not happen") as a *mere* form of words' (Putnam 1994: 499). And again, lest any lingering doubts remain as to Putnam 3's realist credentials: '[t]his attenuated sense in which the deflationist continues to permit us to speak of a sentence's being true or false fails to capture what is significant about true sentences (as opposed to false ones): true sentences possess a substantive property that false sentences lack – namely, the property of corresponding to reality' (*ibid.*: 499) For the deflationist, necessary truths of the kind: 'either x is true or the negation of x is true' have this character solely in virtue of their logical form, rather than because one or other of the disjuncts can be known to possess what Putnam calls 'the relevant sort of substantive rightness'. Indeed, Putnam thinks that Dummett is more clear-sighted about this, accepting as he does – though not without qualms – that such an argument has some fairly drastic implications. Above all, it goes clean against our commonsense-realist idea of past events as inherently 'fixed' by reason of their very pastness and hence as possessing an objective truth-value quite aside from any limits of our present-best knowledge concerning them or any scope they may offer for a range of latterday (perhaps strong-revisionist) readings.

Thus 'neither Dummett nor the verificationist … can accommodate the ordinary sense in which certain statements about the past are substantively true' (*ibid.*: 499). Moreover, they are unable to acknowledge the sense in which certain mathematical theorems or scientific statements may be true *even though* we currently possess no method (proof-procedure, observational technique, causal-explanatory hypothesis, etc.) that would count as establishing their truth beyond reasonable doubt. The best-known example is Goldbach's Conjecture according to which every even number is the sum of two primes. This theorem has been tested to the limit of current computational powers and has so far run up against no counter-instances. It is therefore strongly (indeed overwhelmingly) borne out by the best corroborative evidence to hand, as well as possessing a high degree of intuitive-conceptual warrant. All the same, so the anti-realist holds, it cannot possibly be tested for *every* number in that infinite series, and must hence be counted 'neither-true-nor-false', or as belonging to the so-called 'disputed class' of indeterminate statements with respect to which we are obliged to abandon the classical logic of bivalent truth-values. So likewise with well-formed substantive hypotheses in the physical sciences where as yet conclusive evidence is lacking but where the realist maintains (*contra* Dummett) that they *must* be either true or false since their objective truth-value is 'verification-transcendent', i.e., in no way subject to the vagaries or the merely contingent limitations of scientific knowledge as we have it. Deflationists about truth – Paul Horwich among them – may balk at Dummett's more extreme version of the verificationist case and reject any notion of abandoning the logical principle of bivalence, even though they agree (in Putnam's words) 'that [truth] is not a "substantive property" about which some metaphysical story needs to be told' (Putnam 1994: 497; Horwich 1990). But again, by entering this caveat, they are effectively conceding that truth *just is* whatever we are entitled to assert as such according to our present best state of knowledge or our most advanced powers of verification. In short, '[w]hat is wrong in deflationism is that it cannot properly accommodate the truism that certain claims about the world are (not merely assertable or verifiable but) *true*' (Putnam 1994: 501).

As I have said, it is arguments like these that bring out the old realist in Putnam, the thinker who goes furthest – though never all the way – toward reoccupying ground once defended with great vigour and conviction by Putnam 1. However, what prevents him from narrating all this as a full-scale *voyage de retour au pays natal* is his nagging sense that deflationists like Horwich are right when they deny that truth is the kind of '"substantive property" about which some metaphysical story needs to be told' (*ibid.*: 497). That is, Putnam wants it to be something more 'substantive' (i.e., more contentful or world-involving) than is allowed for by Dummett's anti-realist talk of warranted assertability, or by the strong deflationist's account of truth as a logical place-filler that applies across the board and then cancels out for all practical assertoric purposes. Yet he shares their view that any form of 'metaphysical' realism – any 'story' that involves certain deep further facts about the nature of reality and our knowledge of it – simply won't hold up in the face of so many recent strong counter-arguments. At one point Putnam briefly protests that theirs is a skewed way of posing the issue and (by implication) that the defender of realism need not and should not accept it. Thus:

> [i]f we structure the debate in the way in which both Dummett and the defla-
> tionists do, then we are left with a forced choice between (a) either Dummett-
> ian antirealism or deflationism about truth, or (b) a retreat to metaphysical
> realism. Both Dummett's 'global antirealism' and the deflationist advertise their
> accounts as rescuing us from metaphysical realism. But, surely, one of the sources
> of the continuing appeal of metaphysical realism in contemporary philosophy is
> a dissatisfaction with the only apparent alternatives. (Putnam 1994: 498)

Yet it may well be thought that Putnam has given in to the same kind of forced (and unnecessary) choice, namely that of rejecting as 'metaphysical' any realist theory of truth with substantive philosophical and scientific content. For such a theory would entail providing some definite account – such as that offered by Putnam 1 – of the properties, attributes, microstructural features, causal dispositions, and so forth, that determine both the nature of physical reality and the truth-content of our various statements and theories concerning it.

This pejorative use of the term 'metaphysical' of course has its origins in logical positivism and has since then resurfaced at regular intervals whenever there is a turn toward kindred forms of verificationist thinking (Carnap 1959). It is a usage that Putnam might be expected to avoid, given his objections as summarised above. Yet he allows it to dictate the very terms of his argument by debarring any appeal to the kind of 'metaphysical' realism that would locate the conditions for our truth-apt statements in the way things actually stand with the world, rather than the way they happen to figure according to our current-best evidential warrant. This is the main point on which Putnam 3 still concurs with Putnam 2, that is, with the internal-realist Putnam who was greatly (I would say overly) impressed by the strength of various arguments against his own earlier position. These included the argument from mereological sums, i.e., the problem in set-theory and quantificational logic that one can devise as many composite 'objects' as there exist different ways of grouping things together or counting them up, so that for instance – Putnam's examples – there is an object consisting of 'my left ear and your nose', or an issue as to the genuine objecthood of a table-lamp whose shade always falls off whenever it is moved (Putnam 1994: 450). Thus it can make no sense to conceive of some fixed totality of objects or some determinate way the world is (along with all its bits and pieces) that would constitute the ulti-mate nature of physical reality and permit us to distinguish genuine from merely factitious candidate items. Such is the problem with 'metaphysical' realism as Putnam now understands it. In which case, plainly, there is not much hope for any theory – such as that espoused by Putnam 1 – which upholds the existence of natural kinds and maintains that our descriptions are truth-tracking (or sensitive to future discovery) in so far as they go beyond phenomenal appearances and purport to specify the real, microstructural, or depth-ontological nature of things.

The extent to which Putnam has changed his mind on this matter comes out in his remarks about David Lewis and the idea that 'at least the basic cases of refer-ence involve what he [Lewis] has called "elite classes" or "natural classes", classes of objects not only in the actual world but in other "possible worlds" as well, which are singled out by reality itself' (Putnam 1994: 466; Lewis 1984). Now Putnam may very well take exception – as would a good many realists – to Lewis's highly 'metaphysical' version of the realist case, in particular his interpretation of modal logic as entailing the 'real' (if not 'actual') existence of all those alternative possible worlds (Lewis 1986; also 1973). However, it is clear that Putnam's objec-tion goes much further than that. Indeed, it extends to any form of realist 'meta-physics' that would entail the attribution of objective features, properties, causal dispositions, etc., as a means of distinguishing real-world entities from their various possible-world counterparts. Thus, according to Putnam, '[t]hese classes of things … are clearly just Lewis's substitute for the older "properties"' (Putnam 1994: 466). And again:

> Since knowledge claims are claims about the distribution of 'properties' over the 'objects', and logical functions (negations, disjunctions, conjunctions, and multiple generalisations) of such claims, it follows, on this picture, that there is a definite totality of all possible knowledge claims, likewise fixed once and for all independently of language users and thinkers. (*ibid.*)

In other words, what Putnam 3 now rejects as a bad case of 'metaphysical' illusion is just the kind of argument that Putnam 1 had put forward in support of a realist approach to issues of meaning, reference, and truth. For it was then a main part of his argument that such 'properties' pertained to real-world objects and decided the truth-value of our various referential statements and theories quite aside from our present state of knowledge or powers of verification.

Of course – he concedes – Lewis's claim has to do with the way things 'actually' are in our particular (physically instantiated) world, rather than fixing ultimate limits to the range of logically consistent counterfactual hypotheses. Thus there exists (on Lewis's account) a vast multiplicity of possible worlds that are just as 'real' – metaphysically speaking – but which happen not to be the world that we inhabit along with all its properties, physical constants, laws of nature, and so forth. Nevertheless Lewis takes that world to exert a very definite constraint on our veridical claims concerning it, as distinct from the various alternative claims whose truth-conditions are those laid down by modal or possible-worlds logic, or – beyond that – by the scope for differences of cultural-linguistic perspective. Thus in Putnam's words, summarising Lewis: '[t]he nature of the language users or the thinkers can determine which of the possible knowledge claims they are able to think or verbalise, but not what the possible knowledge claims are' (1994: 466). However, Putnam 3 still concurs with Putnam 2 – as against Putnam 1 – that there is just no way of assigning such limits to the totality of existent objects, properties, structures, etc., nor again (by the same token) to the totality of genuine referring expressions and veridical statements concerning them. For that would entail that those limits be fixed 'once and for all independently of language users or thinkers' (*ibid.*). And of course Putnam is now firmly convinced that there are too many obstacles in its way – such as that of mereological sums and the Löwenheim–Skolem theorem – for this to be a viable argument.

VI

My own view is that Putnam 1 was on the right track and that none of these subsequent sceptical doubts has the force attributed to them by Putnam 2 or again, in more guarded or qualified a fashion, by the thinker (Putnam 3) whose views are represented by the Dewey Lectures. Putnam 1 – lest we need reminding – was the realist in matters semantic and epistemological who subscribed to the twin propositions (a) that 'terms in a mature scientific theory typically refer', and (b) that 'laws of a mature scientific theory are typically approximately true' (1975[2]d: 290). He was also the thinker who could use phrases like 'typically refer' and 'typically approximately refer' without any suspicion of letting the issue go by default or falling back on fuzzy phraseology in the absence of a clear all-purpose criterion for what should *count* as 'reference' and 'truth' in any given context. Thus for instance:

> there is nothing in the world which *exactly* fits Bohr's description of an electron. But there are particles which *approximately* fit Bohr's description: they have the right charge, the right mass, and, most important, they are responsible for key *effects* for which Bohr thought 'electrons' were responsible; for example, electric current (in a wire) is flow of these particles. The Principle of Reasonable Doubt

dictates that we treat Bohr and other experts as referring to *these* particles when they introduced and when they now use the term 'electron'. (Putnam 1975[2]d: 275)

For of course it is just the point of scientific realism construed as early Putnam construes it that our current state of knowledge is by no means final but always open to future correction, refinement, or revision in so far as there is always the standing possibility that it may give way to some better, more adequate or depth-explanatory account.

However, it is a different matter when the revisability-principle is extended – as Putnam 2 would suggest – to logic, mathematics, arithmetic, and the formal sciences where truth-conditions or standards of valid argument are commonly presumed to hold firm against any prospect of empirical disconfirmation. His thoughts on this topic go back a long way and, as usual, have undergone a complex process of revision and qualified re-statement. (See especially Putnam 1983.) Still, his worries with respect to the strong revisability-claim have most often been outweighed by his readiness to treat it as a perfectly intelligible working hypothesis subject, like any other, to testing against whatever kinds of evidence might turn up. Hence his suggestion – after much trying-out of alternative stronger candidates – that perhaps the only genuine (revision-proof) *a priori* truth is the statement: 'not every statement is both true and false' (Putnam 1983c). Hence also his claim that we might just conceivably discover good reason to reject or revise the conceptual foundations of arithmetic and basic set-theory. For, as Putnam sees it, there is no valid argument for drawing a line at some definite point (say between 'empirical' sciences like physics or chemistry and 'formal' sciences like arithmetic and logic) which marks the limit of revisability under pressure from counter-evidence. This is why the case of Euclidean geometry has figured so importantly in Putnam's thinking about the status of *a priori* truths. What it seems to offer is a knock-down proof that such truths are indeed revisable and that any attempt to draw such a line must always acknowledge the standing possibility of its having to be re-drawn or abandoned as a result of some future discovery that would count decisively against it. Thus, according to Putnam, we are prevented from seeing this not so much by the sheer *a priori* necessity of certain mathematical truths but rather by their depth of entrenchment within our existing mathematical practices or logical procedures. In which case the way appears open to other, more extreme or less cautious versions of the argument, among them Wittgenstein's (and Kripke's) communitarian conception of 'following a rule' and – at the limit – Goodman's idea that there exist as many 'valid' projections or ways of correctly carrying on as there exist alternative conceivable views of what counts as a viable practice (Wittgenstein 1958; Kripke 1982; Goodman 1978). And from here it is no great distance to the cultural-relativist or 'strong'-sociological claim that such practices vary from one context to another with no possibility of judging between them in 'objective' or truth-evaluative terms.

It is clear enough from the various passages cited above that Putnam would firmly reject this argument and deny that the strong revisability-thesis entails any such wholesale anti-realist or cultural-relativist upshot. Also, as early Putnam well knew, it is an argument that fails to produce any remotely plausible answer to the question why modern (mathematics-based) science has managed to achieve such a striking degree of observational-predictive and causal-explanatory success. On the other hand it is not so clear just how he can draw the necessary line between that class of well-entrenched or supposedly *a priori* 'truths' that are always in principle up for revision and those other truths that must taken as holding firm whatever our present or future state of knowledge concerning them. The problem with Putnam's favourite instance – that of the passage from Euclidean to non-Euclidean geometry – is that it leaves room for equivocation as between a purely formal understanding of geometrical axioms and proofs and an 'applied' interpretation which takes them as possessing empirical or real-world descriptive content. Martin Gardner makes this point with admirable clarity in a passage from his essay 'How Not to Talk About Mathematics'. Thus:

> Euclidean geometry was formalized by Hilbert, and others, as an uninterpreted system. One interpretation is to take its symbols as representing abstract points, lines, planes and so on. Even so, one is still inside a formal system which says nothing about the world 'out there'. To get to *that* world one must apply what Carnap called correspondence rules which link such ideal concepts as points and lines to observed physical structures . . . . Insofar as geometry applies to the outside world, it loses its certainty. By the same token, it is necessarily true only when its empirical meanings are abandoned. (Gardner 1996: 291)

It seems to me that Putnam's strong revisability-claim with regard to logic and arithmetic results from his failure to remark this distinction and his consequent tendency to assume that empirical counter-instances have just as much force against the formal (logical) truths of Euclidean geometry as against its various applied interpretations. Gardner offers some striking examples of similar confusion, as for instance when it is argued that Euclid's theorem that the angles of a triangle add up to a straight angle has been 'proved false' with the advent of non-Euclidean geometry, or that General Relativity has disconfirmed the entire Euclidean structure of formal (axiomatic-deductive) reasoning. What we should rather conclude, he suggests, is that 'in a formal non-Euclidean geometry the [straight-angle] theorem is false'. Nevertheless, 'in the Euclidean system it remains true for all possible (noncontradictory) worlds because it expresses a tautology that follows from the system's axioms and rules. It says nothing at all about the structure of physical space' (Gardner 1996: 285).

Of course one may adopt a strongly empiricist view – as Putnam sometimes does – and reject this argument as merely a product of our entrenched belief that there *must* be some other than framework-relative distinction between empirical 'matters of fact' and *a priori*, analytic, or logically necessary 'truths of reason'. Such is the full-scale Quinean revisionist view that has clearly left its mark on Putnam's later thought even though he has expressed doubts with regard to the problem it poses for any viable account of knowledge, evidence, and truth (1983a, 1983b, 1983d). What it chiefly fails to explain is what the physicist Eugene Wigner called 'the unreasonable effectiveness of mathematics' in the natural sciences (Wigner 1960). That is to say, if one abandons mathematical realism – the belief that there exists a realm of objective truths concerning such entities as numbers, sets, or purely formal (i.e., physically uninterpreted) geometrical axioms – then it is impossible to explain why mathematics should have proved so enormously fruitful of discoveries in the applied scientific domain. The point is not so much that those truths hold good in whatever situation or under whatever interpretation but rather that when they come up against some empirical counter-instance this has to be explained by factors that in no way impugn their necessity (or strictly unrevisable status) within mathematics, logic, or the formal sciences.

Thus – Gardner again – it is no argument against the basic arithmetical law of addition that if you mix two quarts of water, one at temperature 40 degrees and the other at temperature 50 degrees, you will get a half-gallon whose temperature is not 90 but something more like 45 degrees (Gardner 1996: 285). Or again, one would scarcely be minded to conclude that '1 + 1 = 3' as a result of placing two rabbits together in strict confinement for a period of several months and then discovering a third (smaller) rabbit, or that '1 + 1 = 1' in consequence of two water-drops having coalesced when nobody was looking (Musgrave 1993: 188). But in that case, Gardner asks, is it any more rational to suppose Euclidean geometry to have been 'disproved' through the discovery that its principles failed to hold good for alternative (non-Euclidean) spatial frameworks or coordinate systems? Or that the rules of elementary arithmetic are open to challenge because, under Special Relativity, those rules can be shown not to apply for the addition of relative velocities? In the same way, he writes, '[t]he discovery of irrational numbers did not demolish proofs that all integers are either odd or even, nor did the discovery of quarternions invalidate the commutative law of arithmetic' (Gardner 1996: 287). Rather, these discoveries prompted an enlargement of the concept of 'number' while leaving the established ground-rules – or the axioms of Peano arithmetic – firmly in place.

It seems to me that Putnam's long history of wrestling with the revisability issue in respect to logic and mathematics is very largely the result of his failure to observe the kinds of distinction that Gardner here invokes. No doubt one can 'rationally' entertain a whole range of counterfactual possibilities, such as that of elementary Peano arithmetic turning out to contain contradictions or basic set-theory at length giving rise to paradoxes undreamt of by Russell or Frege. After all, there is the example of Euclidean geometry, which – as Putnam constantly reminds us – serves to make the point that even the most entrenched '*a priori*' truths might eventually come up against some item of recalcitrant evidence that forced us to revise or renounce them. However, there is a crucial difference between these cases and one that tends to be blurred in Putnam's later writing. That is to say, the revisability-thesis may well be convincing with regard to some instances – such as Euclidean geometry – where there exists an ambiguity as between their formal and applied (i.e., physically 'interpreted') construals. But when it comes to arithmetic Putnam can envisage having adequate grounds for rejecting the Peano axioms only with the aid of a further variation on his well-known 'brain-in-a-vat' thought experiment. In this story the crazed but cunning 'superscientist' controls all his sensory inputs and causes him to think – to believe without question – that Saul Kripke has discovered an inconsistency in Peano arithmetic which has then been checked out and accepted by the entire mathematical and logical community. 'Perhaps I do not have time to check the proof myself; but I would believe, and rationally so, I contend, that Peano arithmetic *is* inconsistent on such evidence' (Putnam 1983d: 126). From which he concludes – Putnam *ipse* at the moment of writing these words and presumably not wired up in the manner described – that 'even "Peano arithmetic is consistent" is not a fully rationally unrevisable statement' (*ibid.*: 126).

Like many such sceptical arguments – from Descartes down – this supposition cannot be excluded on grounds of intuitive self-evidence or as a matter of sheer apodictic warrant. But it does break down on that casual admission that brain-in-a-vat Putnam may not have had time to carry out a first-hand corroborative check on Kripke's devastating result. For only then – having followed the proof-procedure through – could he be 'rationally' justified in accepting it, rather than relying on the hallucinated hearsay evidence of all those expert logicians and mathematicians. (Of course this would apply just as much to Putnam or anyone else in a normal waking situation with all their sensory inputs intact and functioning as usual.) Moreover it is in the very nature of arithmetical truths – as Descartes was the first to insist – that they *could not* be 'rationally' proved false or contradictory no matter how far one might be deluded as to the supposed self-evidence of the senses or the existence of an external world. Thus Putnam's argument collapses at the point where he has to let in that tell-tale concession and excuse brain-in-a-vat from checking the proof for himself. Nor can it be saved by opportunely invoking the 'linguistic division of labour', that is to say, the early-Putnam allowance that not everyone has to possess expert knowledge about (e.g.) the molecular constitution of water or the atomic structure of gold in order to refer to those natural kinds with a fair degree of confidence and reliability (Putnam 1975[2]c: 227–9). For of course any application of this principle to the case of Peano arithmetic would presuppose that mathematical proofs were on a par with empirical discovery-procedures – that they didn't require a different order of validating warrant – and would thus beg the main point at issue.

A similar objection might well be raised to other instances of Putnam's retreat from an objectivist outlook in philosophy of logic and mathematics under pressure from various hypothetical counter-arguments. Thus the puzzle about mereological sums might better be viewed as the kind of limit-case problem that arises – somewhat like Kant's Antinomies – at the point where thinking overreaches itself in the attempt to give determinate conceptual content to speculative ideas of reason. Or again, to resume the argument from Gardner, it will seem a deep problem only in so far as one elides the distinction between numbers or sets as formal, physically 'uninterpreted' entities and numbers or sets when applied to particular (no doubt variously divisible) objects or groups of objects (Gardner

1996). After all, as Putnam himself remarks, 'the mathematician is studying something objective, even if he is not studying an unconditional "reality" of non-material things', while equally 'the physicist who states a law of nature with the aid of a mathematical formula is abstracting a real feature of a real material world, even if he has to speak of numbers, vectors, tensors, state-functions, or whatever to make the abstraction' (Putnam 1975[1]a: 60). Of course this leaves the question wide open as to just what 'realism' entails in philosophy of mathematics and whether any naturalised account like that suggested in the above passage can possibly explain what Kant regarded as the two most salient characteristics of mathematical knowledge, namely its character of absolute necessity and its singular fruitfulness in terms of new discovery (Kant 1964). Indeed it is this naturalistic approach which leads Putnam to endorse what amounts to an *anti*-realist position, or at any rate one far removed from the usual (objectivist or Platonist) construal of realism in philosophy of mathematics. Whence his belief that mathematical truths – no matter how firmly entrenched – are always in principle subject to revision under pressure of conflicting empirical evidence or even – at the limit of 'rational' conceivability – as a result of our discovering some hitherto unnoticed contradiction in the axioms of Peano arithmetic.

However, Putnam is also keenly aware of the problems this creates when it comes to explaining why mathematics should seem to possess such a powerful claim to objective or verification-transcendent truth, along with its extraordinary range and depth of application in the physical sciences. In my view Putnam let go of some of his own best arguments when he started out on the long trek from a modal-realist ontology that could accommodate these various orders of truth-claim to an 'internal-realist' position and thence to a pragmatist or naturalised 'commonsense' outlook that treated such issues as merely a product of our bewitchment by false ('metaphysical') conceptions of reality and truth. This left him – so I have argued – with fewer resources for maintaining the different validity-conditions that apply in the physical and the formal sciences, for deciding what should properly (unrevisably) count as an instance of *a priori* truth, and also for upholding that order of *a posteriori* necessity that attaches to certain empirical discoveries, such as 'water = H_2O' or 'gold is the metallic element with atomic number 79'. With the blurring of these various crucial distinctions went a tendency to push much further in a sceptical direction than Putnam has ever been willing to accept as a matter of straightforward doctrinal adherence. Hence his protracted engagement with philosophers – among them Wittgenstein, Quine, Goodman and Dummett – whose arguments have clearly had a strong impact on Putnam's thinking despite his unease with their ultimate consequences. Hence also the signs of a lingering attachment to Putnam 1-type realist principles that still shows through on occasion in the Dewey Lectures despite his regarding them officially as so many remnants of an old 'metaphysical' worldview. As I have said, it is this readiness to see every side of a complex philosophical question that gives his work such a rare sense of intellectual honesty and depth. Certainly Putnam has done more to elucidate these issues and explain their persistent grip on our thinking than any other philosopher in recent times.

References

Alston, William P. (1996). *A Realist Conception of Truth.* Ithaca, NY: Cornell University Press.

Austin, J.L. (1962). *Sense and Sensibilia.* Oxford: Clarendon Press.

Behler, E. (ed.) (1987). *The Philosophy of German Idealism.* New York: Continuum.

Beiser, Frederick C. (1987). *The Fate of Reason: German philosophy from Kant to Fichte.* Cambridge, MA: Harvard University Press.

Brandom, Robert B. (1994). *Making It Explicit: reasoning, representing, and discursive commitment.* Cambridge, MA: Harvard University Press.

Carnap, Rudolf (1959). 'The Elimination of Metaphysics Through Logical Analysis of Language'. In A.J. Ayer (ed.), *Logical Positivism.* New York: Free Press. 60–81.

—— *The Logical Structure of the World and Pseudoproblems in Philosophy,* trans. R. George. Berkeley & Los Angeles: University of California Press.

Coffa, J. Alberto (1991). *The Semantic Tradition from Kant to Carnap: to the Vienna Station.* Cambridge: Cambridge University Press.

Davidson, Donald (1984). 'On the Very Idea of a Conceptual Scheme'. In *Inquiries into Truth and Interpretation.* Oxford: Oxford University Press. 183–98.

Devitt, Michael (1986). *Realism and Truth,* 2nd edn. Oxford: Blackwell.

Dummett, Michael (1978). *Truth and Other Enigmas.* London: Duckworth.

—— (1991). *The Logical Basis of Metaphysics.* London: Duckworth.

Ewing, A.C. (ed.) (1957). *The Idealist Tradition.* Illinois: The Free Press.

Frege, Gottlob (1952). 'On Sense and Reference'. In Max Black and P.T. Geach (eds), *Translations from the Philosophical Writings of Gottlob Frege.* Oxford: Blackwell. 56–78.

Gardner, Martin (1996). *The Night Is Large: collected essays, 1938–95.* Harmondsworth: Penguin.

Glendinning, Simon (ed.) (1999). *The Edinburgh Encyclopedia of Continental Philosophy.* Edinburgh: Edinburgh University Press.

Goodman, Nelson (1978). *Ways of Worldmaking.* Indianapolis: Bobbs-Merrill.

Hacking, Ian (1980). *Why Does Language Matter to Philosophy?* Cambridge: Cambridge University Press.

Heidegger, Martin (1990). *Kant and the Problem of Metaphysics,* trans. R. Taft. Bloomington, IN: Indiana University Press.

Horwich, Paul (1990). *Truth.* Oxford: Blackwell.

Kant, Immanuel (1964). *Critique of Pure Reason,* trans. N. Kemp Smith. London: Macmillan.

Kripke, Saul (1980). *Naming and Necessity.* Oxford: Blackwell.

—— (1982) *Wittgenstein on Rules and Private Language: an elementary exposition.* Oxford: Blackwell.

Lewis, David (1973). *Counterfactuals.* Oxford: Blackwell.

—— (1984). 'Putnam's Paradox', *Australasian Journal of Philosophy,* LXII. 221–36.

—— (1986). *On the Plurality of Worlds.* Oxford: Blackwell.

Luntley, Michael (1988). *Language, Logic and Experience: the case for anti-realism.* London: Duckworth.

McCormick, P.J. (ed.) (1996). *Starmaking: Realism, Anti-realism, and Irrealism.* Cambridge, MA: MIT Press.

McCulloch, Gregory (1995). *The Mind and its World.* London: Routledge.

McDowell, John (1994). *Mind and World.* Cambridge, MA: Harvard University Press.

Musgrave, Alan (1993). *Common Sense, Science and Scepticism: a historical introduction to the theory of knowledge.* Cambridge: Cambridge University Press.

Nagel, Thomas (1997). *The Last Word.* Oxford: Oxford University Press.

Norris, Christopher (2000). *Minding the Gap: epistemology and philosophy of science in the two traditions.* Amherst, MA: University of Massachusetts Press.

Putnam, Hilary (1975[1]). *Mathematics, Matter and Method* (*Philosophical Papers,* Vol. 1). Cambridge: Cambridge University Press.

—— (1975[1]a). 'What Is Mathematical Truth?', in Putnam 1975[1]. 60–78.

—— (1975[2]). *Mind, Language and Reality* (*Philosophical Papers,* Vol. 2). Cambridge: Cambridge University Press.

—— (1975[2]a). 'Is Semantics Possible?'. In Putnam 1975[2]. 139–52.

—— (1975[2]b). 'Explanation and Reference'. In Putnam 1975[2]. 196–214.

—— (1975[2]c). 'The Meaning of Meaning'. In Putnam 1975[2]. 215–71.

—— (1975[2]d). 'Language and Reality'. In Putnam 1975[2]. 272–90.

—— (1978). *Meaning and the Moral Sciences*. London: Routledge & Kegan Paul.

—— (1981). *Reason, Truth and History*. Cambridge: Cambridge University Press.

—— (1983). *Realism and Reason*. (*Philosophical Papers*, Vol. 3). Cambridge: Cambridge University Press.

—— (1983a). 'Possibility and Necessity'. In Putnam 1983. 46–68.

—— (1983b). '"Two Dogmas" Revisited'. In Putnam 1983. 87–97.

—— (1983c). 'There Is At Least One *A Priori* Truth'. In Putnam 1983. 98–114.

—— (1983d). 'Analyticity and Apriority: beyond Wittgenstein and Quine'. In Putnam 1983. 115–38.

—— (1987). *The Many Faces of Realism*. La Salle, IL: Open Court.

—— (1988). *Representation and Reality*. Cambridge, MA: MIT Press.

—— (1994). 'Sense, Nonsense, and the Senses: an inquiry into the powers of the human mind', *Journal of Philosophy*, XCI:9. 445–517.

Quine, W.V.O. (1961). 'Two Dogmas of Empiricism'. In *From a Logical Point of View*. Cambridge, MA: Harvard University Press. 20–46.

—— (1969). *Ontological Relativity and Other Essays*. New York: Columbia University Press.

Ramsey, Frank (1990). *Philosophical Papers*, ed. D.H. Mellor. Cambridge: Cambridge University Press.

Reichenbach, Hans (1938). *Experience and Prediction*. Chicago: University of Chicago Press.

—— (1951). *The Rise of Scientific Philosophy*. Berkeley & Los Angeles: University of California Press.

Rescher, Nicholas (1987). *Scientific Realism: a critical reappraisal*. Dordrecht: D. Reidel.

Rorty, Richard (1979). *Philosophy and the Mirror of Nature*. Oxford: Blackwell.

—— (1982). *Consequences of Pragmatism*. Brighton: Harvester Press.

—— (1991[1]). *Objectivity, Relativism, and Truth*. Cambridge: Cambridge University Press.

—— (1991[2]). *Essays on Heidegger and Others*. Cambridge: Cambridge University Press.

—— (1998). *Truth and Progress*. Cambridge: Cambridge University Press.

Russell, Bertrand (1905). 'On Denoting', *Mind*, XIV. 479–93.

Sellars, Wilfrid (1963). *Science, Perception and Reality*. London: Routledge & Kegan Paul.

Stroud, Barry (1984). *The Significance of Philosophical Scepticism*. Oxford: Oxford University Press.

Tennant, Neil (1987). *Anti-Realism and Logic*. Oxford: Clarendon Press.

van Fraassen, Bas (1980). *The Scientific Image*. Oxford: Clarendon Press.

Vision, Gerald (1988). *Modern Anti-Realism and Manufactured Truth*. London: Routledge.

Wigner, Eugene (1960). 'The Unreasonable Effectiveness of Mathematics', *Communications in Pure and Applied Mathematics*, XIII. 1–14.

Williams, Michael (1996). *Unnatural Doubts: epistemological realism and the basis of scepticism*. Princeton, NJ: Princeton University Press.

Wittgenstein, Ludwig (1958). *Philosophical Investigations*, trans. G.E.M. Anscombe. Oxford: Blackwell.

Wright, Crispin (1987). *Realism, Meaning and Truth*. Oxford: Blackwell.

2

Realism, reference and truth:
the problem with quantum mechanics

I

In the previous chapter I described some of Putnam's successive changes of mind on the issue of scientific realism and its implications for epistemology, philosophical semantics and philosophy of logic. These have led him from a strong realist position backed up by a causal account of reference and natural-kind identity, *via* a middle-period theory of 'internal' realism with marked sceptical leanings, to a pragmatist or naturalistic approach which treats such issues as merely 'metaphysical' and claims to come out on commonsense ground where at last we can forget about that old Cartesian rift between mind and world. (See Putnam 1975[2], 1981, 1994.) Thus early Putnam agreed with Richard Boyd that 'terms in a mature scientific theory typically refer' and, moreover, that 'laws of a mature scientific theory are typically approximately true' (Putnam 1975[2]d: 290). His words 'typically' and 'approximately' involved no concession to the relativist case since they simply made the point that scientific knowledge is never final but should rather be thought of as 'truth-tracking' to the extent that it identifies ever more salient or depth-explanatory structures and properties of an objective, mind-independent reality.

On this account reference is initially fixed by picking out natural kinds (such as 'water', 'gold', 'lemon', 'acid' or 'tiger') and assigning them a name which is then passed on through the causal 'chain' of transmission. At first the identifying criteria may be pretty vague, as for instance '"water" = *that* kind of colourless transparent liquid which falls as rain, possesses certain useful cleansing attributes, boils and freezes at certain temperatures, enables objects of a certain density to float in it', etc., or '"gold" is *that* kind of yellow ductile metal that dissolves in weak nitric acid', or '"tigers" are *that* kind of oversized cat-like carnivorous creature with stripes' (see Putnam 1975[2]a, 1975[2]b and 1975[2]c). Later on these rough-and-ready categorisations give way to more scientifically adequate means of identification, such as the discovery that '"water" = substance with the molecular structure H_2O', or that '"gold" is the metallic element with atomic number 79', or that 'tigers' are a distinctive animal species with certain genetic-chromosomal attributes. As a result of such advances in knowledge we can henceforth adjudicate with respect to deviant or non-standard cases, like that of 'fool's gold' (iron pyrites), or water-like liquids with a different molecular structure, or non-striped tigers as distinct from superficially tiger-like animals which turn out to have a wholly different genetic constitution. However, there is still continuity of reference since the name sticks for any genuine (scientifically verified) sample of the kind and drops out for those other – as we now know – non-genuine samples.

So this theory is realist in the threefold sense that it explains (1) how terms can be taken to refer to certain real-world existent objects and properties thereof; (2) how reference is reliably conserved across sometimes quite radical changes of theory; and (3) how those changes are truth-tracking (or 'sensitive to future discovery') in so far as they mark definite stages in the progress from vague or superficial criteria to more adequate (depth-structural) means of identification. (See also McCulloch 1995.) Putnam has a whole range of other examples to make the point, e.g., that of 'lemons' which once answered to the rough description: 'yellow, sour-tasting fruits with a certain kind of peel', but which can now be picked out more precisely – and distinguished (say) from lemon-like oranges – by reference to their chromosomal structure. Or again, in so far as their acidic content is a characterising feature of lemons, we can now specify just what sorts of substance the term 'acid' properly denotes not merely by adducing such vague criteria as sour taste, corrosive properties, or tendency to turn litmus-paper red but in terms of its subatomic structure, i.e., that '"acid" = proton-donor'. On this early-Putnam theory of reference – also developed at about the same time by Saul Kripke – such truths are a matter of *a posteriori* necessity, that is to say, the kinds of truth that are discovered through a process of empirical investigation (since they cannot be known *a priori*) but which still hold good necessarily across all worlds that are physically compatible with this one (Kripke 1980; Schwartz (ed.) 1977).

At any rate Putnam was at this time a firm believer in scientific realism as the best – indeed the only – viable approach when it came to accounting for our knowledge of the growth of scientific knowledge. Also it explained much better than the rival (Frege–Russell descriptivist) theory how we can make sense of shifts in the meaning of terms such as 'gold', 'water' and 'acid', let alone more radical shifts like those that had overtaken the theoretical understanding of terms such as 'atom' and 'electron' (Frege 1952; Russell 1905). On this latter account, 'to say that something belongs to a natural kind is just to ascribe to it a conjunction of properties' (Putnam 1975[2]a: 140). But then there is the problem – much exploited by Kuhnian and other relativistically inclined philosophers of science – that any change of theory or descriptive criteria must be taken to bring about a wholesale shift in the range of objects and conjunct properties referred to. In which case there is no sense in talking about the progress of scientific knowledge since different theories will each involve a different ontological scheme – with its own stock of putative realia – and will hence rule out the possibility of making meaningful comparisons between them in point of rationality, truth or descriptive-explanatory power (Kuhn 1970; also Quine 1961). On the causal theory, conversely, such talk makes perfectly good sense since it has to do with objects and properties – prototypically natural kinds – that have been referred to under various (more or less adequate) descriptions at various stages of scientific advance but which have none the less retained sufficient continuity of reference for those descriptions to be taken as referring to the same sorts of thing. In short, '[i]t is not *analytic* that natural kinds are classes which play certain kinds of roles in theories; what *really* distinguishes the classes we count as natural kinds is itself a matter of (high level and very abstract) scientific investigation and not meaning analysis' (Putnam 1975[2]a: 141).

I shall not repeat the story from Chapter 1 of how middle-period Putnam abandoned this approach and adopted an 'internal-realist' position according to which any realism worth defending would need to admit the scheme-relative or framework-internal character of all truth-claims or reality-ascriptions (Putnam 1981). Sufficient to say that it seems to have resulted from the impact on his think- ing of various sceptical arguments, among them Quine's (1961) doctrine of onto- logical relativity, Wittgenstein's (1958) appeal to 'language-games' or communal 'forms of life' as the end-point of epistemological enquiry, Nelson Goodman's (1978) attack on the idea of a 'ready-made world' and emphasis on the sheer multi- plicity of 'world-versions' compatible with any given range of empirical data, Michael Dummett's (1978) logico-semantic case for anti-realism in philosophy of mathematics and other fields, certain well-known paradoxes in set-theory includ- ing the problem of mereological sums, and – not least – Putnam's own conviction that quantum mechanics posed a large obstacle to any stronger (i.e., non-frame- work-relative) version of the realist case (Putnam 1983a, 1983b). Here I shall focus mainly on this quantum-theoretical aspect of Putnam's thinking since it brings out both the depth of his engagement with issues in contemporary physical science and the extent to which – as I see it – those issues have pushed him further than need be in a sceptical-relativist direction. I shall also have more to say about recent (post-1990) Putnam and his attempt to retrieve a 'natural', 'commonsense' or 'pragmatist' version of realism that would meet all those counter-arguments – including the challenge from quantum mechanics – while making scepticism appear just a product of quaint 'metaphysical' or thinly disguised Cartesian worries about the mind/world interface. However, it is far from clear that this new approach succeeds either in dispelling those worries or providing a better – since less metaphysically burdened – defence of realism than that put forward in Putnam's early essays. Here again there is evidence that his thinking about quantum-related issues has been a large factor in Putnam's successive changes of mind on the question as to just what constitutes a valid (scientifically and philo- sophically respectable) statement of the realist case.

II

The most basic challenge to realism from quantum mechanics (QM) – at least according to the standard Copenhagen theory – is that subatomic 'particles' such as photons and electrons cannot (or should not properly) be thought of as possess- ing such attributes as definite location, continuous momentum, or discrete numerical identity. (See for instance Bohr 1958; Fine 1986; Heisenberg 1949; Honner 1987; Jammer 1974; Rae 1986.) This was the topic of a well-known exchange between Putnam and Ian Hacking which is worth summarising here since it brings out the main issues in conveniently simplified form. Hacking's argument – in brief – was that philosophy of science had run into various dead-end sceptical dilemmas through its over-concern with abstract issues (like the theory-laden character of observation-statements or the underdetermination of theory by evidence) and its strange lack of interest in what actually went on in the conduct of physical experiments (Hacking 1983). Thus sceptics might doubt the existence of (say) a recondite entity like the positron, just as Ernst Mach had once refused – on principle – to credit the existence of atoms despite the accumulating evidence from various sources in support of the atomist hypothesis. Hacking recounts how impressed he had been when a physicist colleague described the results of an experiment involving the effect of positrons (i.e., positively charged electron-counterparts) on a supercooled niobium ball. 'Now how does one alter the charge on the niobium ball? "Well, at that stage", said my friend, "we spray it with positrons to increase or decrease the charge". From that day forth I've been a scientific realist. *So far as I'm concerned, if you can spray them then they are real*' (Hacking 1983: 23). He takes this as a strong vindication of instrumental realism, that is to say, the claim that we have good warrant for asserting the existence of subatomic entities if they can actually be used – as for instance in electron micro-scopes or in experiments like that with the niobium ball – to produce observable effects that would otherwise be quite beyond reach of physical explanation.

In short, Hacking's instrumental-realist outlook has little in common with that other (e.g., Machian or orthodox quantum) instrumentalist doctrine which rules against any ontological commitments concerning a supposed subatomic 'reality' beyond or behind phenomenal appearances (Bohr 1958; Heisenberg 1949; Misak 1995). Moreover, Hacking finds support for his case – so far as it requires philosophical support – in just the sorts of argument advanced by early Putnam concerning the referential status of natural-kind terms and the truth-tracking virtue of scientific theories that contain them. However, as we have seen, Putnam now finds various reasons for thinking that position insupportable, among them (not least) the problems thrown up by quantum mechanics on the orthodox (Copenhagen) interpretation. 'What does it mean', he asks, 'to believe that "they" [i.e., the positrons] are "real"?'

> If it means that one believes that there are *distinct things* called 'positrons', then we are in trouble – a *lot* of trouble – with the theory. For the theory – quantum field theory – tells us that positrons do not in general have a definite *number*! In the particular experimental setup Hacking is describing, they do have a definite number, perhaps, but it would be quite possible to set up an experiment in which one 'sprayed' the niobium ball, not with three positrons, and not with four positrons, but with a *superposition of three and four positrons*. And elemen-tary quantum mechanics already tells us that we cannot think of positrons as having *trajectories*, or as being, in general, *reidentifiable*. (Putnam 1995: 59)

Still one may doubt that this quantum-derived argument has anything like the knock-down force that Putnam attributes to it, whether as applied to Hacking's position ('if you can spray them then they are real') or when deployed against his own earlier claims with regard to scientific realism and the truth-tracking property of natural-kind terms. To the extent that it figures crucially in Putnam's change of mind on these issues it is an argument that carries far less weight – or which is open to far more cogent objections – than he would here have us believe.

For one thing it is open to question whether orthodox QM is the best – let alone the sole possible – candidate theory for interpreting those strange phenomena (such as quantum superposition) which Putnam takes to spell the demise of any realist ontology premised, like Hacking's, on the existence of discrete particles with a continuous trajectory and objective values of position and momentum between measurements. Indeed there is a well developed alternative account – David Bohm's 'hidden-variables' theory – which can be shown precisely to match all the QM observational results and predictions while avoiding any conflict with those 'classical' realist requirements (Albert 1993; Bohm 1957; Bohm and Hiley 1993; Cushing 1994; Holland 1993). This theory adopts the hypothesis (first advanced by Louis de Broglie) according to which the particle is guided by a pilot-wave whose frequency and amplitude at any given point determine the probability of observing the particle at this or that spatio-temporal location (de Broglie 1960). In other words it still operates on the basic QM assumption that any predictive *knowledge* we can have concerning such values as particle position or momentum can only be obtained by applying the standard formalism, i.e., by use of Schrödinger's equation to calculate the wavefunction. However – most crucially – it departs from the orthodox account by taking any resultant uncertainties to be a product of our limited powers of observation/measurement rather than a matter of some deep-laid intrinsic 'strangeness' pertaining to the very nature of quantum 'reality'. On Bohm's theory the particle is none the less real – and its properties none the less objective – for the fact that those limits impose the necessity of applying a probabilistic calculus when plotting its trajectory from one moment to the next. Where the orthodox-QM error comes in – as with so many sceptical or anti-realist arguments – is at the point where theorists confuse ontology with epistemology, or the question: 'what is really and objectively the case as concerns some given phenomenon?' with the question: 'what kind of warrant can we have (observational, predictive, theoretical, etc.) for claiming knowledge of it?'.

The chief virtue of Bohm's interpretation is that it keeps this distinction firmly in view and refuses to follow the Copenhagen line of projecting epistemological dilemmas – such as the wave/particle dualism or the uncertainty-principle – onto a realm of noumenal quantum 'reality' which is thereby conceived as somehow eluding our utmost powers of conceptual grasp. Thus Bohm sides strongly with Einstein and Schrödinger – as against Bohr and Heisenberg – in maintaining the demonstrable 'incompleteness' of orthodox QM doctrine (Bohr 1935 and 1969; Einstein, Podolsky and Rosen 1935; Heisenberg 1949; Schrödinger 1967). That is to say, he proposes an alternative theory that would go beyond phenomenal appearances and explain just *why* (through what kind of underlying causal mechanism) the results and measurements should always turn out in accordance with the standard QM formalisms and predictions. On Bohm's account, therefore, there is simply no need to embrace the kinds of paradoxical consequence that many other theorists – Putnam among them – suppose to follow as a matter of strict necessity if one accepts the empirical evidence of phenomena such as quantum superposition and wave/particle dualism. Instead one can take it (on realist terms) that these problems result from our restricted observational powers or the limits of our current conceptual grasp, rather than pertaining to the very nature of objects or events in the quantum domain.

Thus, according to Bohm's hidden-variables theory, the particle *does* have definite (objective) values of position and momentum at every point in its trajectory, these values depending on the frequency and amplitude of the pilot-wave by which it is guided. When quantum physicists set out to predict results they can so only by application of the standard technique, i.e., by using Schrödinger's equation to derive the associated wavefunction and thus to assign probability values which can then be tested against the empirical evidence. However, this gives no reason to think – with Bohr and the orthodox theorists – that quantum 'reality' is itself intrinsically uncertain or probabilistic, or again, that puzzling phenomena such as quantum superposition must be accepted absolutely at face value rather than taken as reflecting the limits of our current best knowledge (Popper 1982). After all, it is a chief lesson of scientific progress to date that such problems have often arisen at the stage where some powerful new theory is on the way toward explaining some range of anomalous or problematic data, but where as yet there exists no adequate realist or causal-explanatory account. Thus, for instance, in the period before and just after Dalton's discoveries it was rational to adopt an instrumentalist outlook (or an attitude of qualified scepticism) with regard to the existence of atoms. There is a parallel here with the prolonged period of intense theoretical and often highly speculative debate that has surrounded quantum mechanics since its inception in 1900. Yet in both cases the justified refusal to accept premature ontological commitments by no means entails the kind of doctrinaire scepticism that would take such uncertainty as grounds for rejecting any possible realist outcome (Nye 1972; Perrin 1923). On the one hand such scepticism fails to acknowledge that, whatever the contested status of our current best hypotheses, their truth or falsehood is ultimately a matter of the way things stand in physical reality, rather than 'reality' itself taking on those projected doubts and uncertainties. On the other hand – more specifically – there is a strong presumption in favour of a Bohm-type hidden-variables theory in so far as it offers an intelligible picture of events in the quantum-physical domain and also avoids a drastic break with so many hitherto accepted principles of scientific thought (Holland 1993).

This was of course the main burden of Einstein's case in his series of debates with Bohr, and it has continued to divide quantum theorists down to this day. No doubt there remain certain problems with Bohm's theory, among them its highly complex mathematical structure and its need to accommodate the evidence (first established on formal-statistical grounds but since borne out by physical experiment) of superluminal 'communication' between widely separated particles that have once interacted and thereafter exhibit all the signs of remote anti-correlation or quantum 'entanglement' (Bell 1987; Cushing and McMullin (eds) 1989; Maudlin 1993; Redhead 1987). Thus the theory involves an ineluctable conflict with the basic requirement of Special Relativity that nothing – no signal or causal influence – can propagate faster than the speed of light. But, as Bohm pointed out, this anomalous finding is devoid of serious (practical) consequences since any results achieved for particle A are unpredictable before the measurement on it is actually carried out. Thus the observer stationed at a suitable point to take a measurement on particle B could have no way of decoding the 'message' since this would involve her prior possession of knowledge with regard to those results for particle A that had somehow (impossibly) been flashed even faster between the two measuring devices (Lucas and Hodgson 1990). Besides, the acceptance of remote entanglement was a small price to pay – Bohm argued – if his theory allowed a realist construal of quantum mechanics, that is to say, a consistent and empirically adequate construal that moreover (unlike the orthodox account) assigned a full range of objective values to the particle at every stage in its trajectory. For there would then be no need to accept the idea – so readily endorsed by Putnam – that quantum physics has thrown a huge set of problems into the very idea of a physical 'reality' that exists quite apart from some particular experimental set-up or localised act of observation.

Thus, in Putnam's view, it is naive in the extreme for Hacking to suppose that there are 'distinct things' called positrons, that they possess definite identity criteria, that they can somehow be counted or numerically tagged, and moreover that their progress might be tracked between one measurement and the next. Still less can we conceive such particles as 'having trajectories' in the way that macrophysical objects must be thought of as continuing to exist throughout a series of successive spatio-temporal locations irrespective of whether we happen to observe them or what kind of observation we make. Rather – Putnam thinks – it is a conclusion forced upon us by quantum field theory that at the subatomic level these criteria no longer apply and we are obliged to give up the kind of quaintly realist premises that characterise Hacking's argument. Thus (to repeat): 'it would be quite possible to set up an experiment in which one "sprayed" the niobium ball, not with three positrons, and not with four positrons, but with a *superposition of three and four positrons*' (Putnam 1995: 59). In which case Hacking's favourite example – the experiment that confirmed his particular brand of instrumental entity realism – can be seen as ironically rebounding against the lesson that he claims to draw from it. For if Putnam is right in accepting this construal of the QM evidence as regards superposed states and the non-existence of continuous particle trajectories between measurements then there would seem little hope for any theory, such as Hacking's, that stakes so much on the orthodox account's being wrong – or at any rate 'incomplete' – in some crucial respect.

However, as we have seen, there are strong counter-arguments to that orthodox construal and a rival theory (Bohm's) which effectively challenges Putnam's case point-for-point on each of the above counts. Thus according to Bohm there is no reason – doctrinal attachment aside – to take it for granted (1) that particles lack objective existence or numerical identity criteria; (2) that it is something in the nature of quantum reality (rather than our limited powers of observation) that prevents us from achieving accurate measurement values for conjugate variables such as position and momentum; (3) that such values are realised only in and through the act of measurement; and hence (4) that any naive realist talk of 'particles', 'trajectories', determinate 'location' and the like must be met with the kind of teasing rejoinder that Putnam brings against Hacking. On the contrary, Bohm argues: there is a perfectly consistent realist interpretation which rejects every one of these deeply paradoxical or counter-intuitive doctrines while never-theless producing results fully in accord with the established QM predictive-observational data. So the question remains as to just why Putnam should have banked so heavily on the orthodox quantum theory – or the presumed lack of any cogent rival account – to the point where Hacking's (after all fairly moderate) realist stance can strike him as possessing not the least plausibility in present-day scientific terms.

III

Any answer to this question must take us back to Putnam's writings on philo-sophy of logic and – in particular – his claim that quantum mechanics requires a 'deviant' (non-classical or three-valued) logic in order to accommodate such otherwise anomalous findings as wave/particle dualism (Putnam 1975[1]a, 1975[1]b, 1975[1]c and 1975[1]d). Briefly stated, this is the principle – espoused by Reichenbach, von Neumann and others – that where a conflict exists (or appears to exist) between logic and empirical evidence there is always the option of revis-ing logic rather than rejecting or reinterpreting the evidence (Reichenbach 1944; also Garden 1983; Gibbins 1987; Haack 1974; Mittelstaedt 1994). Thus the opera-tive rule in such cases is to keep the physics as simple as possible – by conserving the widest range of empirical data – and make whatever adjustments are needed when it comes to devising a logical framework (or system of inference) that finds room for those data. In the QM context this is usually taken to entail the suspen-sion of bivalence or excluded middle, that is to say, the adoption of a logic that allows certain statements – for instance, those concerning wave or particle phenomena – to possess an indeterminate truth-value or to count as true for some predictive-observational purposes and false for others. Such was at any rate Putnam's view when he argued – in company with logical empiricists like Reichenbach – that we should indeed be willing to modify the ground-rules of classical (two-valued) logic if this made it possible to avoid conflict with the findings of physical science. Quine took a similar position in 'Two Dogmas of Empiricism', adducing quantum mechanics as a handy exhibit in his case against the absolute privilege traditionally accorded to logical 'laws of thought', and his argument for holding those 'laws' to be always revisable under pressure from empirical counter-evidence (Quine 1961). However, Quine's essay is far from clear on the question as to just what could constitute such evidence, given the theory-laden character of observation-statements and the scope this offers – on his own account – for adjusting one's construal of the data so as to conserve some cherished theory or deep-laid prior commitment.

For Putnam, conversely, the chief advantage of endorsing a revisionist outlook with regard to logic was that it blocked the appeal to quantum mechanics as a source of (purportedly) decisive arguments against realism in epistemology and philosophy of science. At this stage Putnam was still committed to a causal-realist position although – as I have argued at length elsewhere – that position was increasingly subject to strain from what he saw as the conceptual resistance thrown up by problems in the quantum-theoretical domain (Norris 2000[1]). Most pressing was the issue of how one could justify abandoning the ground-rules of classical logic if this resulted in the kind of wholesale revisionist approach where nothing could effectively count as an argument – whether on empirical or logical grounds – against some proposed alteration of the rules in order to accommodate this or that favoured item of belief. Such is at any rate the widespread objection to so-called 'quantum logic', an objection voiced not only by realist philosophers of science – such as Popper (1982) – who condemn it as just another shifty device for evading the issue, but also by specialists in the field (e.g., Gibbins 1987) and even – more improbably – by a self-professed 'epistemological anarchist' like Paul Feyerabend who protests that it leaves no room for genuine, i.e., non-negotiable differences of view. 'This sly procedure', he writes, 'is only one (the most "modern" one) of the many devices which have been invented for the purpose of saving an incorrect theory in the face of refuting evidence and ..., consistently applied, it must lead to the arrest of scientific progress and to stagnation' (Feyerabend 1958: 50). Besides, there is the problem of where to draw a principled line between rules (such as bivalence or excluded middle) that can just conceivably be given up without running into manifest logical absurdity and others (such as non-contradiction) whose abandonment would clearly open the way to all manner of nonsensical results. These difficulties surface most plainly if one compares what Putnam and Quine have to say in their textbook writings on philosophy of logic with what they say about interpretative issues in quantum theory. But in Putnam's case the problems loom larger since he has been more directly concerned with those issues, and has made them altogether more central to his thinking about epistemology and philosophy of science.

They surface yet again in the course of his recent (1994) Dewey Lectures though most often obliquely or through footnote references. One such passage is worth quoting at length since it clearly exhibits the tension that exists between Putnam's new-found 'natural realist' outlook and his current (somewhat modified but still broadly orthodox) thinking on quantum mechanics. Thus:

> the quantum theories are best thought of as describing real physical things – not just the behavior of measuring instruments – but Niels Bohr and Reichenbach were right in holding that they only describe the behavior of those things *while*

they are interacting in certain ways with macroscopic things (when they are being 'measured', in quantum-mechanical jargon). How quantum-mechanical parti-cles, fields, etc., act when they are not being measured can be 'pictured' in various incompatible ways (many worlds interpretation, Bohm's hidden-variables interpretation, etc.), all of them paradoxical and none of them (at least none of the ones so far proposed) compelling. (Putnam 1994: 506n)

It should be borne in mind that the context of this footnote is Putnam's attempt to stake out a middle-ground position that would avoid the surplus ontological commitments of old-style 'metaphysical' realism while eschewing the kinds of reactive anti-realist or sceptical doctrine which he finds unacceptable. More specifically, the footnote is appended to a passage where Putnam recalls taking issue with Dummett over the latter's (as he sees it) perverse refusal to accept a realist interpretation of statements concerning unobservable, e.g., subatomic entities. Dummett's argument is similar to that of a 'constructive empiricist' like Bas van Fraassen though couched more in linguistic or logico-semantic than epis-temological terms (van Fraassen 1980, 1989). Thus, for Dummett, the case against realism with regard to unobservables rests on the claim that a word such as 'small' undergoes a crucial change of meaning when we pass from the realm of tiny objects that none the less lie within the range of perceptual verification to micro-physical entities which are way off the scale of unaided human perception. Still he agrees with van Fraassen that warranted assertability (rather than truth on a realist construal) is the relevant standard of assessment in such cases. For it follows – on Dummett's account – that we cannot be justified in asserting the existence of unobservable entities or in assigning determinate truth-conditions to various statements concerning them (Dummett 1978 and 1991). That is to say, if sense determines reference (Frege), and if the sense of a term is given by its role in some meaningful language-game or cultural life-form (Wittgenstein), then quite simply there is no making sense of statements which refer to entities beyond our current best powers of observational warrant.

Putnam understandably rejects this view as going clean against the common-sense (or 'natural-realist') conviction that what makes our beliefs objectively true or false is the way things stand in reality and not just the way they happen to appear from the epistemic standpoint of creatures like us. After all, where are we to draw the line on a scale of diminishing observational warrant that runs (say) from microbes, through molecules and atoms, to electrons, photons and quarks? Thus 'microbes are *literally* things too small for us to see ... [yet] we do not see ourselves as forcing an arbitrary new meaning on the word "small" when we so describe them' (Putnam 1994: 506). No more should we suppose – *pace* Dummett – that the truth-conditions for our referential talk undergo some drastic shift of veridical warrant when we pass from the domain of organic chemistry or molec-ular biology to that of atomic or subatomic physics. For this is once again to confuse ontology with epistemology, or the question: 'what is the objective truth-content of our current best scientific beliefs?' with the question: 'what kinds of warrant can we have for maintaining the truth of those beliefs given both the

limits of our knowledge and the problems that arise with observation or measurement on a microphysical scale?'. Early Putnam would have had no qualms
about asserting that these were indeed quite separate issues. Moreover, he would
have laid great stress on the point that ontology precedes epistemology in so far as
our beliefs are rendered objectively true or false by the way things stand in reality.
Thus the truth-value of our statements is a matter of their picking out the right
sorts of object – whether microbes, molecules, atoms or electrons – and assigning
the right properties to them, namely those properties (like molecular or subatomic
structure) which define them as objects of just that kind. Where anti-realists go
wrong – according to early Putnam – is in getting this order of priority back-to-
front and supposing that ontology is somehow dependent on our epistemic
powers or the limits of precise observation.

So it is that Dummett can deny the existence of objective truth-values for
statements belonging to the so-called 'disputed class', i.e., statements with regard
to which we possess no conclusive means of verification or determinate proof-
procedure (Dummett 1978). It is also why thinkers may feel themselves driven to
adopt some variety of 'internal' realism whereby the terms in our current-best
scientific theories are construed as referring to real entities – and our statements
as having a definite truth-value – but only in so far as they play a role in some
given descriptive framework or conceptual scheme. Yet of course this is just the
standpoint that Putnam later adopted under pressure from those various counter-
arguments which he took to have undermined his own previous realist position
(Putnam 1981). In short, he could see no means of defending that position in the
face of objections like those brought forward by exponents of orthodox QM
theory or again by critics, Wittgensteinians among them, who considered such
realist claims to be wholly misconceived – just a species of 'metaphysical' bewitchment – when viewed against the background of our communal life-forms or
shared linguistic practices. It is perhaps worth remarking that Putnam has a somewhat throwaway footnote to the Dewey Lectures which invites us to '[c]ompare
Wittgenstein's remark (I believe in *Lectures on the Philosophy of Mathematics*)
about the importance of remembering that the "particles" of modern physics are
not little billiard balls' (1994: 469n). This passage clearly picks up on his response
to Hacking and also brings out the close connection between that response and
Putnam's increasing receptiveness to a Wittgensteinian view of such matters.

It is therefore not surprising that he follows on from the argument *contra*
Hacking with a Wittgenstein-influenced paragraph which brings the issue down
to a straightforward choice between Hacking's realist view of positrons as discrete
or reidentifiable 'things' and the quantum field-theoretical approach which
supposedly rules such notions out as altogether naive or misguided. Thus:

> [i]f being a 'scientific realist' does not mean believing that positrons exist as
> distinct *things*, what content is the notion supposed to have? If, on the other
> hand, it does mean believing that they are things in the sense of having contin-
> uous identities, positions in space and time, number, etc. – and, as Wittgenstein
> reminds us, our paradigm of what is 'real' is what we can *point to*, and what we

can point to certainly has continuous identity, position, can be counted, etc. –
then being a 'scientific realist' about positrons means believing quantum field
theory is actually *false*, and not just interpreting it 'nonrealistically' (whatever
that means). But then, we lose all power to understand just the characteristic
quantum phenomena of interference, nonlocality, etc. (Putnam 1995: 59–60)

What this appeal to Wittgenstein strongly suggests is that Hacking's talk about
positrons as discrete 'things' with definite properties of number, location, spatio-
temporal continuity, etc., shows not only his attachment to classical (pre-
quantum) habits of thought but also that he is still very much in the grip of a naive
(pre-Wittgensteinian) way of thinking about language, reference, and truth. Thus
the lesson from quantum field-theory would work out as a powerful illustration
of Wittgenstein's point with regard to the fallacy of treating ostensive definition as
in any way a privileged instance of language-use or one that could possibly explain
how we come to acquire or manifest such a range of different uses in different
contexts of utterance (Wittgenstein 1958). Moreover it raises problems for any
argument – like that put forward by Strawson in his scaled-down 'descriptivist'
version of Kant – that experience cannot make sense except on the assumption of
perduring 'individuals' (persons and objects) with numerical identity-criteria and
a history of continuous spatio-temporal locations (Strawson 1959).

So the above passage marks a sizable retreat, on Putnam's part, from any
version of 'scientific realism' that would square with his earlier belief that 'terms
in a mature scientific theory typically refer' and that 'laws of a mature scientific
theory are typically approximately true' (Putnam 1975[2]d: 290). Yet it is questionable – given the interpretative problems that arise with quantum field theory
– whether Putnam is rationally justified in backing off so far from that earlier position or adopting what amounts to a line of least resistance in the face of such an
ill-defined challenge. Indeed, as I have argued elsewhere, those problems can be
seen to emerge most sharply when its advocates attempt to state the case for a
thoroughgoing field-theoretical approach that would meet the conditions laid
down by Putnam in his response to Hacking, i.e., that would avoid all reference
to 'particles' and their trajectories, spatio-temporal locations, identity criteria, and
so forth (Norris 2000[1]; Teller 1994). At least one may suspect that Putnam is
drawing premature conclusions with regard to the QM realism issue on the basis
of a theory whose conceptual foundations are as yet far from secure. This suspicion is reinforced by his few rather brief and dismissive references to Bohm's
hidden-variables theory, despite the fact – as noted above – that it provides a
consistent realist interpretation and one that is subject to none of these ontological bewilderments.

IV

All the same there are clear signs in the Dewey Lectures that Putnam is far from
happy with being cast in the role of a welcome though somewhat belated and
foot-dragging convert to the anti-realist cause. Hence his attempt to stake out the

ground for an alternative approach – so-called 'natural realism' – that would avoid any kind of 'metaphysical' commitment while blocking the retreat to a verificationist theory where objective truth gives way to the notion of warranted assertability. Thus for Dummett, as Putnam reads him, '[o]ur natural picture of what we are doing with our words and thoughts has no philosophical *weight* .... Dummett's rejection of common-sense realism about our conceptual powers is of a piece with the tradition's rejection of "naive realism" about our perceptual powers' (1994: 506). And again, Dummett's argument with regard to meaning-change in the microphysical realm – that a word such as 'small' takes on a different sense when applied (say) to molecules or subatomic particles rather than to tiny but physically visible objects – strikes Putnam as involving a straight-forward affront to our commonsense-realist intuitions. For there is something highly suspect – or distinctly anthropomorphic – about drawing the line at just that point where the powers of unaided human perception just happen to encounter their limit.

On Putnam's account, conversely, 'the words "small", "thing", "see", etc., have the same meaning in talk of "things too small for us to see" (or in the talk of particles much too small to see that figured in nineteenth-century atomic theory) that they have in describing observables' (1994: 505). From which it follows that terms such as 'molecule' and 'atom' – or indeed 'electron', 'muon' and 'quark' – should not be treated as off-the-scale for referential purposes or as applying to a range of quasi-objects whose 'smallness' is of a quite different order from that of dust-specks or needles in a haystack. Nor need we think – like van Fraassen – that anything so sheerly contingent as the limits of unaided human observation should be taken as marking the boundary between empirically warranted existence-claims and claims that are warranted solely in virtue of their instrumental yield or their role in some cherished theory (van Fraassen 1980). Rather it is a question of deciding to the best of our current scientific knowledge just how much credence we should rationally place on claims with respect to the existence of such more-or-less elusive or recondite particles. After all, as Putnam remarks, this is just the kind of progress – from speculative theory to instrumentalism and thence through stages of increasing confidence to an outlook of duly qualified realist commitment – that has characterised the history of atomic and subatomic physics. Thus there seems no reason to adopt van Fraassen's position if atoms can now be photographed through electron microscopes with striking clarity and detail, let alone moved around to create the initials 'IBM' by application of the latest nanotechnology. Nor can it be rational (as Hacking argues) to doubt the reality of positrons when their existence is so strongly borne out by the fact that they play such a central role in these and other observationally proven and instrumentally efficacious techniques. Of course there will be those of a sceptical mind – positivists or 'constructive empiricists' from Mach to van Fraassen – who maintain that we are never rationally justified in extending our ontological commitments beyond the bare minimum entailed by respect for the empirical or direct (unaided) observational evidence (Misak 1995). However this outlook must appear more a kind of *a priori* self-denying ordinance than a matter of justified scientific scruple or refusal to take on excess 'metaphysical' baggage.

So it might well seem that late Putnam – the self-styled 'natural realist' – is well along the way toward reclaiming ground first occupied by early Putnam (the strong advocate of causal realism) and only vacated by middle-period Putnam under pressure from various sceptical arguments which he now finds less than convincing. I think there is some truth in this account although it has to ignore certain clear indications in the Dewey Lectures that he is still subject to doubts and misgivings induced by those same sorts of argument. For one thing he has shifted ground only minimally with regard to quantum mechanics and its dire implications for a realist ontology premised on the existence of discrete particles with objective (observer-independent) properties of position, momentum, spin-value, and so forth. Thus he still takes it – as in the above-cited exchange with Hacking – that quantum field theory has thrown a huge paradox into any idea that we might be justified in talking of denumerable positrons rather than 'super-posed' quantum states where their number is merely a convenient *façon de parler* adopted for want of more adequate descriptive-conceptual resources. In other words he remains unconvinced by Hacking's argument – with respect to the supercooled niobium ball – that 'if you can spray them [i.e., positrons], then they are real'. Hence Putnam's claim in the Dewey Lectures that 'we no longer conceive of quantum-mechanical particles as *literally* particles', and moreover that 'at the moment we do not know how to conceive of them at all, apart from their inter-actions with the measuring instruments' (Putnam 1994: 506). Hence also his professed failure to see how these problems with the orthodox (Copenhagen) account are in any way resolved or significantly affected by adopting a Bohm type 'hidden-variables' theory. For it is one great virtue of Bohm's approach that it conserves the whole range of established QM formalisms and predictive-observa-tional data while also finding room for a causal-realist ontology which includes an account of how particles interact with the measuring apparatus.

As Putnam sees it this latter phenomenon – the effect of observation/meas-urement on the object observed – is enough to rule out any 'naive' realism with respect to particles in the subatomic domain. His present belief – to repeat – is that QM theory is 'best thought of as describing real physical things – not just the behavior of measuring instruments – but that Bohr and Heisenberg were right in holding that they only describe the behavior of those things *while they are inter-acting with macroscopic things* (when they are being "measured", in quantum-mechanical jargon)' (Putnam 1994: 506). From here he goes on to draw the conclusion that realist accounts such as Bohm's can offer no advantage over the orthodox theory since they fail to explain 'how quantum-mechanical "particles", "fields", etc., act when they are not being measured' (*ibid.*). But this is to ignore Bohm's central point: that on his theory we can perfectly well conceive of parti-cles as possessing objective values of position and momentum at every point in their trajectory *even though* we can obtain knowledge of those values only through certain (inherently limited) means of observation or measurement. That is to say, it avoids the confusion between ontological and epistemological issues that has been such a prominent feature of QM debate since Einstein's series of debates with Bohr during the 1920s and 30s (Einstein, Podolsky and Rosen 1935; Bohr 1935, 1969). What Putnam signally fails to acknowledge is the greater degree of rational warrant for accepting a theory which doesn't make 'reality' somehow dependent on our present best powers of epistemic/conceptual grasp, rather than a theory (orthodox QM) which treats them as an absolute limit on the scope of rationally warranted belief.

Thus Putnam ignores the fact that Bohm's hidden-variables account can explain the phenomenon of interaction between particle and measuring instrument (or the effect of observation on the object observed) in causal-realist terms and hence avoid any shifty retreat into talk of a 'participatory universe' or other such quasi-mystical ideas. Moreover – and perhaps most importantly – it resolves the sorts of paradox that arise with the so-called 'collapse of the wavepacket' or the notion (deeply enshrined within orthodox QM) that superposed quantum states must be thought of as assuming determinate wave or particle-form only at the moment and through the very act of localised observation/measurement (Wheeler and Zurek (eds) 1983). This is of course the chief problem that Schrödinger had in mind when he offered his cat-in-a-box thought experiment as a *reductio ad absurdum* of the orthodox theory (Schrödinger 1980). However, the idea of observer-induced wavepacket collapse is still a great source of far-fetched speculative arguments, not least among quantum cosmologists, some of whom take it as endorsing the claim that a present-day choice of measurement parameter (e.g., the orientation of a radar telescope) can retroactively 'cause' or determine the outcome of certain astrophysical events some billions of light-years distant or 'ago'. (Wheeler 1978). Such extravagant conjectures should properly be seen – even when advanced in full seriousness – as amounting to a Schrödinger-style *reductio* of orthodox QM theory, rather than as following by strict necessity when one extrapolates from the micro- to the macrophysical domain. Indeed they offer the strongest argument for supposing that theory to be 'incomplete' in at least one crucial respect, namely its failure to provide any means for fixing a boundary between what is thought to transpire at the quantum level and what we reliably know to be the case with regard to objects and events in the realm of everyday (macrophysical) experience.

So it is odd – to say the least – that proponents of the orthodox QM line should adopt an outlook of fargone scepticism with respect to the better-established portions of 'classical' physics while displaying a well-nigh fideist attachment to so deeply problematical a theory. In Putnam's case the oddness emerges very clearly if one asks what reason he can have for maintaining a 'natural realist' position which goes such complicated ways around in order to avoid that sceptical upshot while also eschewing any taint of 'metaphysical' realism. One can best understand why he feels himself forced into this awkward compromise position by recapitulating two lines of thought that figure prominently in the Dewey Lectures. The first has to do with the precise nature of his objection to Dummett-style anti-realism and the second with his curious way of approaching this issue through a discussion of Wittgenstein on rule-following and related topics. In each case – I would argue – Putnam is sidetracked from his own best course of argument by accepting the terms laid down by thinkers with a wholly different agenda, one that demonstrably weakens his case to the point where it can muster no effective resistance.

This emerges most clearly in those passages where Putnam attempts to meet Dummett on the question of realism with regard to unobservable entities by adopting Dummett's preferred idiom, i.e., by treating it as a matter of 'talk' about molecules, atoms, subatomic particles, and so forth. What this amounts to is a slide from debating the issue in realist (ontological) terms to debating it on terms quite acceptable to anyone – like Dummett – who takes the anti-realist view that we cannot intelligibly talk about anything beyond the range of objects and events whose existence or occurrence may be verified according to our best evidential criteria. Putnam's chief quarrel with Dummett is that he (Dummett) rejects the idea of revising our basic logical ground-rules and thinks it altogether more rational to adopt an anti-realist or 'strong' verificationist position with respect to those entities that figure in our current best microphysical theories (Dummett 1978a). Thus, where Putnam advises that we should simplify physics by adopting an alternative logic, Dummett takes the view that we should do much better to abandon any realist ontology and revise our logic just so far as to admit the need for a non-bivalent treatment of quantum phenomena such as wave/particle dualism. On his account these phenomena give rise to intractable philosophic problems if we think of them as possessing any kind of objective (observer-independent) reality apart from our various descriptive languages, frameworks or conceptual schemes. This fits in nicely with Dummett's programmatic anti-realist position as regards objects and events in the wider (i.e., macrophysical) domain. Putnam now finds that position unacceptable and indeed spends a good deal of time in the Dewey Lectures explaining what precisely he thinks wrong with it. Yet he still yields crucial argumentative ground by implicitly conceding (1) that orthodox quantum theory has won out against a causal-realist account such as that developed by Bohm, and (2) that this necessitates a choice between revising the ground-rules of logical thought or renouncing any kind of realist ontology.

V

Hence – I suggest – Putnam's retreat from the material to the linguistic mode, or from discussing substantive issues in philosophy of science to discussing the semantics of a term such as 'small' when applied in various (macro- and microphysical) contexts of usage. It is a retreat that seems to have been forced upon him through reflection on the strange ontology of quantum physics and the consequent need – as Putnam described it in his exchange with Hacking – to somehow envisage quantum states as involving a 'superposition' of (so-called) particles without number, determinate location, momentum, trajectories, identity-criteria, and so forth. The following passage from his Dewey Lectures makes it clear that Putnam has not shifted ground on the quantum-theoretical issue despite his general movement toward a much sturdier position concerning the reality of microphysical objects such as atoms and electrons. It is also of interest in bringing out the strong connection – as Putnam sees it – between these problems with interpreting quantum mechanics and the problem in set-theory about 'mereological sums' or the various ways in which objects may be counted under differing criteria of objecthood or group-membership. Thus:

> [t]he reason that quantum-mechanical 'particles' are not objects in the traditional sense is that in contemporary quantum mechanics 'particles' have no definite number at all (in most 'states')! But traditional objects always have a definite number. This means that, if our familiar tables and chairs (and my lamp) are 'mereological sums', it cannot be quantum-mechanical particles that they are mereological sums *of* .... Thus, quantum mechanics is a wonderful example of how with the development of knowledge our idea of what counts as even a *possible* knowledge claim, our idea of what counts as even a *possible* object, and our idea of what counts as even a *possible* property are all subject to change. (Putnam 1994: 451)

Here again, as in the dialogue with Hacking, one has the impression that Putnam is so struck by the 'wonderful' strangeness of quantum phenomena that he is willing to throw philosophical caution to the winds for the sake of pursuing their more bizarre implications. Otherwise he would surely not have made this perilous leap between the problem of numerical identity at the quantum level – i.e., the supposed lack of criteria for picking out individual particles or trajectories from one measurement to the next – and the problem of mereological sums as applied to objects (such as tables and chairs) in the macrophysical domain. What the passage seems to imply is that the two kinds of problem are somehow mutually reinforcing, or – on a bottom-up construal – that the quantum uncertainty-relations are such as to preclude by extension any confident appeal to the existence of discrete, sharply individuated items even within the perceptual range of unaided human observation. (This despite the fact that such 'traditional objects always have a definite number'.) Or again, it might be taken as suggesting rather – on a top-down construal – that the problem about mereological sums is one that extends into the quantum domain and should hence be understood as a problem which concerns all procedures of counting or identifying discrete entities, subatomic 'particles' included. However Putnam then comes flat up against the chief dilemma of orthodox quantum theory, namely that of explaining just where – and just why – the transition occurs between 'superposed' (or indeterminate) quantum states and the various well-defined objects and events that constitute the reality of our everyday macrophysical experience.

This is the dilemma that Schrödinger famously captured with his cat-in-the-box thought experiment and one that still lacks any adequate solution on the standard (Copenhagen) account (Schrödinger 1980; Wheeler and Zurek (eds) 1983). To place it in the same category as the problem of mereological sums is in effect to say that it belongs on the side of our various theories, descriptive schemes, methods for counting or picking out entities, etc. In which case it is not so much a problem 'in the nature' of quantum-physical phenomena as a problem about deciding which of those schemes or methods should be given priority in any given context of measurement or observation. This is what Bohr seems to have had in mind when he proposed the idea of 'complementarity' – i.e., that of different, strictly incommensurable but non-conflicting ontological schemes – as a means of escaping such otherwise intractable dilemmas as quantum superposition or wave/particle dualism (Bohr 1958, 1967; Folse 1985; Honner 1987). Yet Putnam (like Bohr) clearly wants to make some larger, more substantive ontological claim about the inherent strangeness of quantum phenomena and the challenge they pose to our usual way of thinking about physical objects and events. Hence – to repeat – his idea of quantum mechanics as 'a wonderful example of how with the development of knowledge our idea of what counts as even a *possible* knowledge claim, our idea of what counts as even a *possible* object, and our idea of what counts as even a *possible* property are all subject to change' (Putnam 1994: 451). But if all this is somehow taken to apply at the macrophysical as well as at the microphysical (quantum) level then there is a huge problem here – and one that Putnam conspicuously fails to confront – about resolving the issue of Schrödinger's superposed (dead-and-alive or neither-dead-nor-alive) cat or why it is that we just don't come across phenomena like that except in the realm of science fiction or quantum-theoretical conjecture. Thus Putnam seems over-willing to endorse not only the strangeness of orthodox QM but also its extension – no matter how wildly paradoxical or counter-intuitive – to the realm of macroscopic objects and events. Such is at any rate the clear implication of his argument *contra* Hacking and his appeal to the quantum-physical 'evidence' as a rejoinder to old-style realists who persist in talking about chairs and tables – let alone subatomic particles – as if they could be counted one-by-one on the basis of fixed identity criteria. Otherwise it is hard to make sense of Putnam's idea that the problem of mereological sums – or how to quantify over sets of 'objects' on whatever physical scale – is of the same basic type as the problem concerning just which particle it was that showed up as a result of successive quantum measurements. But this still leaves Putnam with the unresolved problem of accounting for the fact that 'traditional objects always have a definite number', despite all the doubts and perplexities occasioned by quantum-theoretical debate.

Yet there is no compelling reason to endorse all this – or indeed for Putnam to have started on his long retreat from causal realism – if one accepts Bohm's alternative account according to which quantum phenomena can be fully and consistently explained by means of the pilot-wave or hidden-variables theory. As I have said, Putnam gives short shrift to that theory, finding it just as 'paradoxical' as the orthodox (Copenhagen) doctrine and hence not worth all the extra complications – the excess 'metaphysical' baggage – entailed by adding a particle ontology to the wavefunction and associated QM formalisms. But this is to ignore three powerful arguments in support of Bohm's hypothesis. First, the main difficulty held to count against it is that of superluminal 'communication' between widely separated particles, a problem that was shown by J.S. Bell to be strictly inescapable given the basic QM predictive-observational data and also to follow with absolute necessity from any formulation of the hidden-variables theory (Bell 1987; Clauser and Shimony 1978; Cushing and McMullin (eds) 1989; Maudlin 1993; Redhead 1987). However this 'paradox' loses its bite if one accepts the no-first-signal principle, i.e., that such effects of instantaneous non-local interaction cannot be used to transmit information for reasons intrinsic to the nature of quantum measurement (Lucas and Hodgson 1990). Second, there is the more positive claim: that Bohm's theory yields an ontology which requires no drastic or radical break with the assumptions of classical physics, among them the existence of discrete particles with continuous trajectories between measurements and with objective (observer-independent) values of location and momentum (Holland 1993). Third, there is the fact – as I verified just recently on a visit to the cyclotron at Jyväskylä University in Finland – that this Bohmian account has the far from negligible advantage of according with physicists' own ideas of what goes on the field of applied subatomic particle research. Thus they are apt to say, when questioned, that *of course* such entities (electrons, neutrons, positrons, etc.) must be thought of as 'real' or as 'actually existing' since the whole apparatus is designed on precisely that assumption and moreover produces results – through the effect of accelerated particle bombardment – that would otherwise simply not occur or would lack any adequate explanation. In other words they come out very much in agreement with Hacking's version of entity-realism, i.e., his conclusion with regard to positrons that 'if you can spray them, then they are real'.

So there is reason to think that Putnam's retreat was forced upon him not so much by problems intrinsic to the nature of quantum-physical thought but rather by a certain questionable view of what such thinking necessarily entailed. It seems to me that he is pushed yet further in this direction by espousing a version of the 'linguistic turn' – chiefly influenced by late Wittgenstein – which leaves him effectively bereft of resources for answering the anti-realist case. The point can best be made with reference to a passage in the Dewey Lectures where Putnam at first seems committed to something very like Hacking's position but then backs off into talk about 'talk' as the baseline standard of intelligibility and the sole criterion for ascribing reality to the various posits of physical science. 'In the first lecture', he recalls,

> I remarked that the use of instruments should be viewed as a way of extending our natural powers of observation. But the use of language is also a way of extending our natural powers of observation. If I could not understand talk about 'things too small to see with the naked eye', the microscope would be at best a toy (like the kaleidoscope); what I saw when I looked through the eyepiece would mean nothing to me. (Putnam 1994: 502)

The first sentence here goes strongly against any kind of anti-realist, verificationist or 'constructive empiricist' approach which would quite arbitrarily draw a line between objects visible to the naked eye and entities (e.g., molecules, atoms or subatomic particles) requiring other, technologically assisted powers of observation. Furthermore, it supports Hacking's claim that the best source of evidence concerning the reality of 'unobservables' is the role they play not only in our best scientific theories but also in the design, construction, and employment of various scientific instruments such as electron microscopes or particle accelerators. Nor is this realist outlook in any way compromised or weakened when Putnam goes on to remark that 'the use of language' – like the use of instruments – can also serve 'as a way of extending our natural powers of observation'. After all, such claims were very much a part of Putnam's early causal-realist account of how language hooked up with the world by picking out certain objects or classes of object – paradigmatically natural kinds – which ensured sufficient stability of reference throughout any subsequent changes or refinements in our knowledge of their properties and structures (Putnam 1975[2]a, 1975[2]c). Thus there is no reason in principle why this theory should not be extended beyond such well-entrenched terms as 'molecule', 'atom' or 'electron' to encompass cases – like 'muon' or 'quark' – that have a place in the present-day standard model of subatomic structure while lacking (as yet) that degree of strong observational warrant. To preemptively deny them any claim to such status on the grounds that they lie beyond the limits of *present* observation is again to confuse ontological with epistemological issues and also to take a remarkably short-term view of both the history and the future prospects of scientific knowledge. Thus, as Putnam remarks, 'in Democritus's writings ... the notion of an "atom" was a metaphysical one, but one to which *we* can give a sense, even if Democritus himself could not' (1994: 502). And again, drawing the philosophic consequence of this: 'scientific instruments and scientific ways of talking are both ways of extending our conceptual and perceptual powers, and those ways are highly interdependent; indeed they can fuse into a single complex practice' (*ibid.*).

So Putnam appears at least half convinced that the way is still open – despite all his interim doubts and misgivings – to a realist outlook broadly consistent with his own earlier position. However this *rapprochement* turns out to have sharp limits when he goes straight on, in the above-cited passage, to claim that what makes the difference between a scientific instrument like a microscope and a toy like a kaleidoscope is chiefly our *understanding what it means* to talk about 'things too small to see with the naked eye'. On Putnam's account this is sheerly self-evident since in the absence of such understanding 'what I saw when I looked through the eyepiece [of a microscope] would mean nothing to me'. Now of course it is the case – self-evidently so – that the *meanings* we attach to object-terms across the whole range from macro- to microphysical, along with items of equipment like telescopes or microscopes, are crucially dependent on our having some grasp of their role in our current descriptive languages or means of conceptualisation. Just as clearly it is the case that without such a grasp we couldn't make a start in distinguishing the kinds of evidence provided by those various instrumental technologies from the kinds of perceptual illusion produced by kaleidoscopes and similar toys. If Putnam's argument entailed no more than this – that we need a clear sense of the difference between (say) viewing atoms through an electron microscope and seeing stars through a kaleidoscope – then one could have no quarrel with his way of stating the matter. However there are passages in his Dewey Lectures that suggest a more radical version of the linguistic turn. Here he seems pretty much in agreement with Wittgenstein on the pointlessness of pressing beyond that stage where realist arguments supposedly run out and we just have to say: 'this is how we reason, theorise, calculate, interpret the evidence (etc.) in accordance with the rules, language-games, or practices that constitute our form of life' (Wittgenstein 1958, 1969, 1976).

Such is the gist of Putnam's case – *contra* Dummett – that there is no crucial difference of meaning between 'small' as applied to tiny but macroscopically discernible objects and 'small' as applied to the range of 'unobservables' from molecules to atoms and electrons. The result is to shift the main focus of attention from first-order (substantive) issues in epistemology and philosophy of science to second-order (linguistic) issues concerning what should count as a meaningful expression or one that makes sense according to certain established communal norms. Of course the chief point of such Wittgenstein-derived arguments is to stop us from thinking in those old 'metaphysical' terms, that is, from conceiving that there is any answer to these questions aside from the appeal to our various practices and life-forms. Thus the issue about realism cannot be intelligibly raised – let alone resolved – if we carry on seeking 'grounds' or 'justifications' beyond the fact of our standardly applying certain terms in certain contexts of usage. Should the realist not take this for an adequate response – should they protest that it begs the whole question in favour of an anti-realist approach – then again they will be told: that question quite simply doesn't make sense once we acknowledge the futility of raising problems where no such problems exist. Besides, it is wrong to think that this amounts to an 'anti-realist' position or to take it as coming out on either side of that pointless and sterile debate. For if there is one thing we ought to have learned from Wittgenstein it is the lesson that philosophy leaves everything just as it is, including whatever realist assumptions may go along with our normal (communally sanctioned) practices and forms of utterance (Diamond 1991). So the only difference this lesson can make is that we won't any longer be inclined to persist in the deluded quest for 'objective' knowledge or for ultimate assurance that our language matches up with the structure of physical reality (Malcolm 1986). Otherwise – so the argument goes – we can still be as confidently 'realist' as we like about everything that figures in our various (scientific or everyday) usages.

Putnam is not alone among recent philosophers in feeling a well-nigh compulsive need to run his case through the standard Wittgensteinian review procedure and thereby ensure that it betrays no symptoms of a lingering attachment to 'metaphysical' habits of thought. Indeed I would guess that historians of philosophy a century on will consider this compulsion – and the routine deference to Wittgenstein's authority – among the most puzzling features of present-day philosophical debate (Norris 2000[2]). For Putnam it has clearly been a large factor – along with the perceived challenge from quantum mechanics – in propelling him away from causal realism to the various alternative or compromise positions that he has adopted over the past three decades. Not that Putnam is disposed to endorse the kinds of argument put forward in Wittgenstein's name by those who read him – at least with regard to epistemological matters – as a full-fledged communitarian or cultural relativist (Bloor 1983; Phillips 1977). Thus he firmly rejects the construal of Wittgenstein which has him deny 'that our knowledge claims are responsible to any reality external to communal approval or sanction', this having produced 'a swamp of misreadings too wide and boggy to wade through … without losing our thread completely' (Putnam 1994: 470). All the same it is far from clear that Putnam manages to avoid the swamp or to claim good Wittgensteinian warrant for his 'natural realist' approach while effectively disowning the pull toward cultural relativism. For the result of his taking this obligatory detour *via* Wittgenstein – like that of his longer-term engagement with quantum theory – is to undermine Putnam's realist commitments and to leave him with only the weakest of defences against the kind of 'misreading' which he thinks so wrong when applied to late Wittgenstein.

VI

There is a crucial passage in his middle-period essay 'Quantum Mechanics and the Observer' where Putnam, having canvassed the various extant QM interpretations and various problems with them, goes on to offer an alternative account which he considers the only viable option in terms of empirical adequacy and absence of internal contradiction. The passage is worth citing at length since it brings out very clearly the impact of these quantum-related problems on Putnam's thinking at just the time when he was moving away from his early causal-realist position. 'First of all', he writes,

> I now believe that the only notion of truth that makes coherent sense is the so-called 'non-realist' view that sees truth as an idealization of rational acceptability, rather than as 'correspondence to reality', where correspondence is thought of as a *non-epistemic* relation (which is why whether a statement could be justified and whether it is true are regarded as *independent* questions by metaphysical realists). On a 'non-realist' view, it is not unnatural, I think, to regard it as a deeply important question whether the verification of one statement never in principle precludes the verification of another (as was believed in Newtonian physics), or whether, on the other hand, the world is such that to verify one statement makes it impossible in principle to perform the experiment that would verify or falsify another (or makes it impossible to perform such an experiment without bringing it about that one or the other statement ceases to have any predictive import). (Putnam 1983b: 267–8)

Putnam thinks of this as an alternative to the orthodox (i.e., Copenhagen) interpretation, according to which there is no legitimate passage 'beyond' the predictive-observational data, or none that can possibly avoid giving rise to all manner of insoluble problems and paradoxes. Thus, on the orthodox view, any realist interpretation like that proposed by Bohm must defeat its own object by envisaging a quantum 'reality' which somehow has to incorporate such physically recalcitrant (non-visualisable) phenomena as wave/particle dualism or quantum superposition. I have argued already that this is not the case since Bohm's interpretation *does* in fact provide a theory consistent with all the empirical evidence and, moreover, a realist ontology which can be pictured (or modelled) by application of de Broglie's pilot-wave hypothesis to the distribution of particle positions and momenta in accordance with the standard QM formalism. By contrast, Putnam's candidate theory seems to differ from the orthodox approach only in so far as it appeals to the notion of 'idealised rational acceptability', that is to say, a purely regulative notion devoid of substantive ontological commitment and expressly opposed to anything so 'metaphysical' as a correspondence theory of truth.

This idea is prominent in many of Putnam's middle-period writings and marks the first stage of his retreat from any stronger realist conception of what renders our statements or theories objectively true or false (Putnam 1981). For the point about 'idealised rational acceptability' is that it offers a means of indefinitely postponing the issue as to whether (as early Putnam maintained) 'terms in a mature scientific theory typically refer' and 'laws of a mature scientific theory are typically approximately true' (Putnam 1975[2]d: 290). This is not just a matter of respecting the fallibilist (and realist-compatible) argument that scientific knowledge always stands under correction since our present-best theories may eventually turn out false or in need of revision as further evidence accrues. Rather, it is a matter of denying that those theories derive whatever truth-value they possess from the way things stand in reality, as opposed to their capacity for being borne out by some present or (maybe) some future-best-possible means of verification. In which case it is hard to see how Putnam's 'alternative' approach differs from the orthodox QM doctrine that likewise prohibits any talk of 'correspondence to reality' or any thought of a realist interpretation that would restore ontological content to the range of existing empirical or predictive-observational data.

Hence Putnam's insistence in the above-quoted passage that what chiefly distinguishes his own theory from the naive 'metaphysical' (correspondence-based) account is the latter's adherence to a *non-epistemic* conception of reality and truth. That is to say, it makes the truth-value of our statements and theories an issue of objective (verification-transcendent) warrant rather than an issue of their counterfactually matching up with the kinds of statement and theory that we *would* endorse under conditions of 'idealised rational acceptability'. Thus, on Putnam's favoured view, it is a 'deeply important question' whether quantum physics has shown – after Heisenberg – that we have to give up any thought of a world that exists independently of our various means of verification, or that somehow possesses a full range of determinate properties (like particle location and momentum) quite apart from our inability to obtain precise simultaneous measurement-values for such non-commuting conjugate variables. In short,

Putnam accepts a large part of the orthodox QM doctrine – not least its verificationist denial of a reality 'beyond' quantum-phenomenal appearances – while yet
holding out (in Peircean-pragmatist fashion) for some suitably 'idealised' or regulative notion of truth at the end of enquiry. However this leaves him awkwardly
placed when it comes to explaining what such truth could possibly amount to,
given the orthodox-QM claim – endorsed on his own 'non-realist' account – that
'the world is such' as to place it forever beyond hope of human attainment. For in
that case the interpretative problems with quantum physics cannot be construed
– as Bohm would argue – in terms of the epistemological limits on our present-
best or future-best-possible knowledge, and hence as posing no ultimate threat to
an ontological account that respects the crucial realist distinction between truth
and warranted assertability (Bohm and Hiley 1993; Holland 1993; Norris 2000[1]).
Rather, those problems must be thought somehow to inhere in the very nature of
quantum 'reality' and thus to foreclose any possible appeal beyond the evidential
data. In which case quantum physics would require the acceptance of a verificationist approach not only by way of acknowledging our limited powers of precise
observation/measurement but also as a matter of the way things stand with the
world once those old objectivist certitudes have broken down.

Putnam has a lengthy footnote in the same essay which credits Dummett
with having helped to overcome his resistance to this full-fledged verificationist
approach. Where he (Putnam) had once thought of it as 'virtually synonymous
with *operationism*', Dummett enabled him to see that this was not so and that one
could quite consistently adopt a verificationist stance without courting the reductionist (or hardline positivist) error of accepting as 'verifiable' only those statements that allowed of translation into a sense-datum language. Again the passage
will bear quoting at length since it shows Putnam in process of revising his earlier
realist commitments in response to what he sees as a range of pressures from
otherwise very different quarters. Thus:

> Michael Dummett has convinced me that one may hold the theory that truth is
> (an idealization of) justification without being committed to the view that state-
> ments about sense data are more basic than statements about material objects,
> and without being committed to reductionism of any kind. Indeed, as Dummett
> points out, reductionists only renounce the correspondence theory of truth for
> the statements they want to *reduce*; for statements in the *reducing* class they typi-
> cally retain the views (1) that truth and justification are independent; (2) that
> truth is determinate and bivalent; (3) that there is, in the ideal limit anyway, just
> *one* true and complete description. In short, *reductionism is a form of subjective
> idealism* (when the reducing class is the class of sense datum statements); whereas
> the 'verificationism' or 'non-realism' espoused by Dummett and myself does not
> deny the reality of any of the objects of scientific or ordinary discourse, or
> construe some of those objects as constructions out of others, but consists rather
> in a renunciation of those three assumptions about truth itself. (Putnam 1983b:
> 266n)

There are several points that are worth remarking about this passage. First, it
shows the extent of Putnam's willingness to adopt a Dummett-style verification-

ist approach by way of resolving – or attempting to resolve – the various problems thrown up by quantum mechanics on the orthodox (Copenhagen) construal. Second, it brings out his tendency at this stage to suppose that any realist theory of truth – whether at the quantum or the macrophysical level – must be committed to some kind of doctrinaire metaphysical monism or the view that there exists 'just *one* true and complete description' of any segment of reality. Third, it expresses his conviction – again in agreement with Dummett – that 'truth' and 'justification' *cannot* be independent (as the realist would have it), but rather that truth can be replaced for all practical purposes by warranted assertability or the appeal to what justifiably gains assent according to our best epistemic lights or available sources of evidence. Fourth, it concludes on the strength of this that 'reductionists' (i.e., old-style logical positivists) are wrong when they elect to conserve classical or two-valued logic in order to maintain a correspondence-theory of truth despite the anomalies which then result with respect to recalcitrant quantum phenomena such as superposition or wave/particle dualism. Fifth, it assumes that the only way out of these quantum-induced dilemmas is to give up bivalent (classically distributed) truth/falsehood values and espouse a 'non-realist' conception where statements or theories are warranted just in case they match the full range of empirical data despite any seeming contradictions that arise on a bivalent construal. In which case – sixth – Putnam's proposal can claim to be 'realist' in a different, more scientifically respectable sense, namely that it meets the conditions for empirical adequacy while renouncing only the requirements of logical consistency and truth as classically understood. And since this comes down (as he sees it) to a straight choice – since the price of respecting those requirements is to give up empirical adequacy – then there appears no rational course open except to adopt a verificationist stance with regard to both quantum-physical statements and the logical structure of quantum theory.

According to Putnam the reverse transaction carries no cost in so far as it leaves all our standing commitments firmly in place and requires only that we give up the otiose 'metaphysical' idea of truth-values that somehow transcend our utmost means of verification. Thus – to repeat – 'the "verificationism" or "non-realism" espoused by Dummett and myself does not deny the reality of any of the objects of scientific or ordinary discourse'. However, one may doubt that it comes quite so cheaply as Putnam supposes, or that the more extreme consequences of Dummett's position can be held at bay simply by denying that this kind of moderate verificationism runs into all the same problems as old-style (reductionist) logical positivism. Indeed, Putnam's way of staging the issue rather suggests an attempt to head off these awkward implications by once again shifting the focus of debate from ontology to epistemology, that is to say, from the question whether we can ever possibly be justified in asserting the existence of objective (verification-transcendent) truths to the question as to whether or under what conditions we can ever claim to know anything in particular. Hence his claim – with support from Dummett – that 'one may hold that truth is (an idealization of) justification without being committed to the view that statements about sense data are more basic than statements about material objects, and without being committed to reductionism of any kind' (Putnam 1983b: 266n). This is middle-period Putnam's solution to the stand-off between realism and anti-realism, one that purports to get over the problem by equating 'truth' for all practical purposes with what would be accepted by any rational enquirer when all the evidence was in and when nothing stood in the way of arriving at a properly informed and considered assessment of the evidence thus acquired. But it is clearly a solution which yields crucial ground on the main point at issue in the realism debate, i.e., whether we can properly (intelligibly) claim to conceive that there exist truths – in mathematics, the physical sciences, and elsewhere – that transcend *and may possibly forever transcend* our utmost powers of ascertainment. In which case Putnam's rapprochement with Dummett on the verificationist issue looks more like a straightforward caving-in under pressure from the anti-realist quarter.

VII

The *locus classicus* for this stage in Putnam's thinking is his book *Reason, Truth and History* (1981), and one passage in particular that is often cited by supporters and opponents alike. The context – in brief – is Putnam's recognition that there is something problematic about equating truth (as Dummett would have it) with 'warranted assertability' since truth is standardly taken to be timeless and unaffected by changes in our belief, knowledge, present-best state of information, etc., whereas assertoric warrant is a matter of degree and is hence always subject to revision – reinforcement or weakening – with the advent of new evidence. In short, 'truth is supposed to be a property of a statement that cannot be lost, whereas justification can be lost' (Putnam 1981: 55). However, Putnam sees this as good reason *not* for maintaining that distinction in the face of anti-realist (Dummett-type) arguments but rather for conceding the force of such arguments and redefining 'truth' in terms of *idealised* rational or warranted assertability. Thus:

> [w]e speak as if there were such things as epistemically ideal conditions, and we call a statement 'true' if it would be justified under such conditions. 'Epistemically ideal conditions', of course, are like 'frictionless planes': we cannot really attain epistemically ideal conditions, or even be absolutely certain that we have come sufficiently close to them. But frictionless planes cannot be attained either, and yet talk of frictionless planes has 'cash value' because we can approximate them to a very high degree of approximation. (Putnam 1981: 55)

Putnam is well aware of the looseness in this argument and claims only to be offering an 'informal elucidation' rather than a strict or formal definition of truth. However, the analogy with frictionless planes – and the whole idea of truth as idealised rational acceptability – gives rise to problems which the anti-realist can exploit to telling effect. Thus Crispin Wright points out that those presupposed 'ideal circumstances' might always fall short of *completeness*, that is, the condition that for any given statement either it or its determinate negation must be established beyond doubt by the best empirical evidence to hand. As Wright puts it:

'[t]here seems no good reason to impose any such completeness requirement – no particular reason why all questions which are empirical in content should become decidable under ideal conditions' (Wright 1992: 39). The analogy with frictionless planes doesn't really work because in that case – unlike the case of truth – one is considering degrees of approximation to a notional ideal that is mathematically well-defined even though no physical system can achieve it for reasons that can perfectly well be specified in causal-explanatory terms.

Wright doesn't make this particular point but it is implicit in what he has to say about the problems with Putnam's conception of truth as idealised rational acceptability. Moreover, as he does go on to remark, there is the issue as to how this approach might cope with the instance of quantum mechanics – at least on the orthodox construal – and its challenge to the very idea of a 'complete' (empirically adequate and logically consistent) interpretation of the evidence. For if one accepts that orthodox account then it follows that quantum mechanics is 'complete' in the sense proposed by Bohr and Heisenberg, that is to say, incapable of supplementation by some deep further fact or 'hidden-variables' theory that would bring it out in accordance with the dictates of a classical-realist ontology (Bohr 1935, 1969). Yet of course it was just this claim that struck other physicists – Einstein, Schrödinger, de Broglie and Bohm among them – as representing not so much an empirically warranted conclusion from the best available evidence as a dogmatic article of faith which blocked the way to a different, more 'complete' (since ontologically more adequate) interpretation (Cushing 1994; Einstein, Podolsky and Rosen 1935). At any rate, as Wright remarks, there is a problem with quantum mechanics for anyone like Putnam who adopts the completeness-requirement in its more generalised philosophical form, i.e., through holding that 'all questions which are empirical in content should become decidable under ideal conditions'. Thus:

> to take seriously the indeterminacies postulated by contemporary physical theory is to consider that there is reason to the contrary. We can suspect that an internal realist would want to suspend the principle of Bivalence for statements which would find themselves beached at the limit of ideal enquiry in this way, and ought consequently, one would imagine, to want to suspend it in any case, failing an assurance that no statements are actually in that situation. (Wright 1992: 39)

It is an odd feature of this passage that Wright claims to deduce the line of argument that Putnam 'ought' or might be expected to take when in fact he has quite explicitly taken such a line in his essays on the interpretation of quantum mechanics and on the need to adopt a non-standard (three-valued) 'quantum logic' in order to resolve precisely these problems with his own approach (Putnam 1983b). However, my main point here is that Putnam is driven to endorse this expedient very largely on account of his having adopted an epistemic theory of truth which leaves him no other option. More precisely, it is forced upon him by the conjunction of that theory with his general acceptance that orthodox QM is a 'complete' interpretation in something very like the sense propounded by Bohr and Heisenberg.

Hence his declaration in 'Quantum Mechanics and the Observer' that 'the only notion of truth that makes coherent sense is the so-called "non-realist" view that sees truth as an idealization of rational acceptability, rather than as "correspondence to reality", where correspondence is thought of as a *non-epistemic* relation' (Putnam 1983b: 267). The result is that Putnam is pushed much further in the direction of Dummett-type anti-realism than he seems altogether willing to acknowledge, as witness both the above-cited footnote – where he plays down this consequence through the contrast with old-style 'reductionist' verificationism – and his later, more overt doubts and misgivings in the Dewey Lectures. What is thus ruled out in these writings of his middle period is the alternative (ontological-realist) view that would reject Dummett's Wittgenstein-inspired arguments for the replacement of truth by 'warranted assertability', or the idea that it can make no sense to maintain the existence of verification-transcendent truths. Along with his by-and-large acceptance of the orthodox QM completeness-postulate this seems to have left Putnam deeply perplexed on the realism issue and willing to try all manner of solutions – whether pragmatist, naturalist, Wittgensteinian or framework-relativist – which offered some hope of laying the problem to rest. (See Putnam 1987, 1988, 1990, 1992.)

My own view – to repeat – is that early (pre-1975) Putnam had gone far toward laying the groundwork for a causal-realist and objectivist approach that avoided the confusion between ontological and epistemological issues and which thus held out against the various forms of sceptical doctrine that have made such a strong impression on his thinking over the past two decades. It was also an approach that helped to explain why extant problems with the interpretation of quantum mechanics should better be seen as resulting from the limits of our present-best theories, powers of observation, techniques of measurement, etc., rather than as somehow intrinsic or inherent to the very nature of quantum-physical 'reality'. On this account our use of terms such as *electron, positron* or *quark* could be taken as reliably 'truth-tracking' – or 'sensitive to future discovery' – just on condition that they picked out some viable candidate entity which played a causal-explanatory role in those present-best theories and just in case that entity existed (and exerted its causal powers) quite aside from our beliefs or the limits of our knowledge concerning it. Thus Putnam's thinking at this stage had much in common with Bohm's alternative QM interpretation and his claim that the orthodox theory was incomplete in so far as it failed to provide a credible realist ontology that made adequate sense of the observed phenomena. However, Putnam had clearly abandoned this whole way of thinking by the time of his exchange with Hacking when he took it as naive in the extreme for Hacking to attach ontological significance to talk about 'positrons' as discrete, denumerable, reidentifiable 'things' with certain causal properties such as that of reducing the charge on a supercooled niobium ball. It is a moot question whether his change of mind on this particular issue came about through Putnam's increasing openness to Wittgensteinian, Dummettian, Goodmanian and other forms of anti-realist thinking or whether – conversely – his engagement with interpretative problems in quantum theory made him more receptive to ideas of just that kind. At any rate it seems to me that Putnam has been over-willing to endorse some far from decisive arguments against the realist position so resourcefully defended in those ground-breaking essays of the early-to-mid 1970s.

References

Albert, David Z. (1993). *Quantum Mechanics and Experience*. Cambridge, MA: Harvard University Press.

Bell, J.S. (1987). *Speakable and Unspeakable in Quantum Mechanics: collected papers on quantum philosophy*. Cambridge: Cambridge University Press.

Bloor, David (1983). *Wittgenstein: a social theory of knowledge*. New York: Columbia University Press.

Bohm, David (1957). *Causality and Chance in Modern Physics*. London: Routledge & Kegan Paul.

Bohm, David and Basil J. Hiley (1993). *The Undivided Universe: an ontological interpretation of quantum theory*. London: Routledge.

Bohr, Niels (1935). 'Can Quantum-Mechanical Description of Reality be Considered Complete?', *Physical Review*, series 2, XLVII. 696–702.

—— (1958). *Atomic Physics and Human Knowledge*. New York: Wiley.

—— (1967). *The Philosophical Writings of Niels Bohr*, 3 vols. Woodbridge, CT: Ox Bow Press.

—— (1969). 'Conversation With Einstein on Epistemological Problems in Atomic Physics'. In P.A. Schilpp (ed.), *Albert Einstein: philosopher-scientist*. La Salle, IL: Open Court. 199–241.

Clauser, J.F. and A. Shimony (1978). 'Bell's Theorem: experimental tests and implications', *Reports on Progress in Physics*, XLI. 1881–1927.

Cushing, James T. (1994). *Quantum Mechanics: historical contingency and the Copenhagen hegemony*. Chicago: University of Chicago Press.

Cushing, James and Ernan McMullin (eds) (1989). *Philosophical Consequences of Quantum Theory: reflections on Bell's Theorem*. Notre Dame, IN: University of Notre Dame Press.

de Broglie, Louis (1960). *Physics and Microphysics*. New York: Harper & Row.

Diamond, Cora (1991). *The Realistic Spirit: Wittgenstein, philosophy, and the mind*. Cambridge, MA: MIT Press.

Dummett, Michael (1978). *Truth and Other Enigmas*. London: Duckworth.

—— (1978a). 'Is Logic Empirical?'. In Dummett 1978. 269–89.

—— (1991). *The Logical Basis of Metaphysics*. London: Duckworth.

Einstein, Albert, B. Podolsky and N. Rosen (1935). 'Can Quantum-Mechanical Description of Reality be Considered Complete?', *Physical Review*, series 2, XLVII. 777–80.

Feyerabend, Paul K. (1958). 'Reichenbach's Interpretation of Quantum Mechanics', *Philosophical Studies*, XX. 45–62.

Fine, Arthur (1986). *The Shaky Game: Einstein, realism, and quantum theory*. Chicago: University of Chicago Press.

Folse, Henry J. (1985). *The Philosophy of Niels Bohr: the framework of complementarity*. Amsterdam: North-Holland.

Frege, Gottlob (1952). 'On Sense and Reference'. In Max Black and P.T. Geach (eds), *Translations from the Philosophical Writings of Gottlob Frege*. Oxford: Blackwell. 56–78.

Garden, Rachel W. (1983). *Modern Logic and Quantum Mechanics*. Bristol: A. Hilger.

Gibbins, Peter (1987). *Particles and Paradoxes: the limits of quantum logic*. Cambridge: Cambridge University Press.

Goodman, Nelson (1978). *Ways of Worldmaking*. Indianapolis: Bobbs-Merrill.

Haack, Susan (1974). *Deviant Logic: some philosophical issues*. Cambridge: Cambridge University Press.

Hacking, Ian (1983). *Representing and Intervening: introductory topics in the philosophy of natural science*. Cambridge: Cambridge University Press.

Heisenberg, Werner (1949). *The Physical Principles of the Quantum Theory*. New York: Dover.

Holland, Peter (1993). *The Quantum Theory of Motion: an account of the de Broglie–Bohm causal interpretation of quantum mechanics*. Cambridge: Cambridge University Press.

Honner, John (1987). *The Description of Nature: Niels Bohr and the philosophy of quantum physics*. Oxford: Clarendon Press.

Jammer, Max (1974). *Philosophy of Quantum Physics: the interpretations of quantum mechanics in historical perspective*. New York: Wiley.

Kripke, Saul (1980). *Naming and Necessity*. Oxford: Blackwell.

Kuhn, Thomas (1970). *The Structure of Scientific Revolutions*, 2nd edn. Chicago: University of Chicago Press.

Lucas, J.R. and P.E. Hodgson (1990). *Spacetime and Electro-Magnetism*. Oxford: Clarendon Press.

Malcolm, Norman (1986). *Nothing Is Hidden: Wittgenstein's criticism of his early thought*. Oxford: Blackwell.

Maudlin, Tim (1993). *Quantum Non-Locality and Relativity: metaphysical intimations of modern science*. Oxford: Blackwell.

McCulloch, Gregory (1995). *The Mind and its World*. London: Routledge.

Misak, C.J. (1995). *Verificationism: its history and prospects*. London: Routledge.

Mittelstaedt, Peter (1994). *Quantum Logic*. Princeton, NJ: Princeton University Press.

Norris, Christopher (2000[1]). *Quantum Theory and the Flight from Realism: philosophical responses to quantum mechanics*. London: Routledge.

—— (2000[2]). *Minding the Gap: epistemology and philosophy of science in the two traditions*. Amherst, MA: University of Massachusetts Press.

Nye, Mary Jo (1972). *Molecular Reality*. London: MacDonald.

Perrin, J. (1923). *Atoms*, trans. D.L. Hammick. New York: van Nostrand.

Phillips, Derek L. (1977). *Wittgenstein and Scientific Knowledge: a sociological perspective*. London: Macmillan.

Popper, Karl R. (1982). *Quantum Theory and the Schism in Physics*. London: Hutchinson.

Putnam, Hilary (1975[1]). *Mathematics, Matter and Method* (*Philosophical Papers*, Vol. 1). Cambridge: Cambridge University Press.

—— (1975[1]a). 'Philosophy of Physics'. In Putnam 1975[1]. 79–92.

—— (1975[1]b). 'A Philosopher Looks at Quantum Mechanics'. In Putnam 1975[1]. 130–58.

—— (1975[1]c). 'Three-Valued Logic'. In Putnam 1975[1]. 166–73.

—— (1975[1]d). 'The Logic of Quantum Mechanics'. In Putnam 1975[1]. 174–97.

—— (1975[2]). *Mind, Language and Reality* (*Philosophical Papers*, Vol. 2). Cambridge: Cambridge University Press.

—— (1975[2]a). 'Is Semantics Possible?'. In Putnam 1975[2]. 139–52.

—— (1975[2]b). 'Explanation and Reference'. In Putnam 1975[2]. 196–214.

—— (1975[2]c). 'The Meaning of "Meaning"'. In Putnam 1975[2]. 215–71.

—— (1975[2]d). 'Language and Reality'. In Putnam 1975[2]. 272–90.

—— (1981). *Reason, Truth and History*. Cambridge: Cambridge University Press.

—— (1983). *Realism and Reason* (*Philosophical Papers*, Vol.3). Cambridge: Cambridge University Press.

—— (1983a). 'Possibility and Necessity'. In Putnam 1983. 46–68.

—— (1983b). 'Quantum Mechanics and the Observer'. In Putnam 1983. 248–70.

—— (1987). *The Many Faces of Realism*. La Salle, IL: Open Court.

—— (1988). *Representation and Reality*. Cambridge, MA: Harvard University Press.

—— (1990). *Realism With a Human Face*. Cambridge, MA: Harvard University Press.

—— (1992). *Renewing Philosophy*. Cambridge, MA: Harvard University Press.

—— (1994). 'Sense, Nonsense and the Senses: an inquiry into the powers of the human mind', *Journal of Philosophy*, XCI:9. 445–517.

—— (1995). *Pragmatism: an open question*. Oxford: Blackwell.

Quine, W.V.O. (1961). 'Two Dogmas of Empiricism'. In *From a Logical Point of View*, 2nd edn. Cambridge, MA: Harvard University Press. 20–46.

Rae, Alasdair I.M. (1986). *Quantum Physics: illusion or reality?* Cambridge: Cambridge University Press.

Redhead, Michael (1987). *Incompleteness, Nonlocality and Realism: a prolegomenon to the philosophy of quantum mechanics.* Oxford: Clarendon Press.

Reichenbach, Hans (1944). *Philosophic Foundations of Quantum Mechanics.* Berkeley & Los Angeles: University of California Press.

Russell, Bertrand (1905). 'On Denoting', *Mind*, XIV. 479–93.

Schrödinger, Erwin (1980). 'The Present Situation in Quantum Mechanics', trans. John D. Trimmer, *Proceedings of the American Philosophical Society*, No. 124. 323–38.

Schwartz, Stephen (ed.) (1977). *Naming, Necessity, and Natural Kinds.* Ithaca, NY: Cornell University Press.

Strawson, P.F. (1959). *Individuals: an essay in descriptive metaphysics.* London: Methuen.

Teller, Paul (1994). *An Interpretive Introduction to Quantum Field Theory.* Princeton, NJ: Princeton University Press.

van Fraassen, Bas (1980). *The Scientific Image.* Oxford: Clarendon Press.

—— (1989) *Laws and Symmetry.* Oxford: Clarendon Press.

—— (1992). *Quantum Mechanics: an empiricist view.* Oxford: Clarendon Press.

Wheeler, John A. (1978). *Frontiers of Time.* Princeton, NJ: Princeton University Press.

Wheeler, John A. and W.H. Zurek (eds) (1983). *Quantum Theory and Measurement.* Princeton, NJ: Princeton University Press.

Wittgenstein, Ludwig (1958). *Philosophical Investigations*, trans. G.E.M. Anscombe. Oxford: Blackwell.

—— (1969). *On Certainty*, ed. G.E.M. Anscombe and G.H. von Wright. Oxford: Blackwell.

—— (1976). *Wittgenstein's Lectures on the Philosophy of Mathematics*, ed. Cora Diamond. Chicago: University of Chicago Press.

Wright, Crispin (1992). *Truth and Objectivity.* Cambridge, MA: Harvard University Press.

3

Squaring with Wittgenstein: versions of 'realism' in Putnam's later philosophy

I

In this chapter I shall have more to say about Putnam's thoughts on the topic of realism in his 1994 Dewey Lectures and other recent writings. Putnam is not alone among present-day philosophers in thinking that Wittgenstein has pointed a way beyond all our worrisome obsessions in this regard, or shown them to be merely the result of misplaced 'metaphysical' doubts and anxieties (Wittgenstein 1958, 1969). Such deliverance would no doubt be welcome in Putnam's case since he, more than anyone, has worried about them and striven to produce a defence of realism that would preserve its most important philosophical commitments while meeting the objectors (anti-realists and sceptics of various hue) on the main points at issue. Hence the long trek from his early essays (1975) where Putnam took a strong causal-realist position with regard to matters of meaning, reference and truth, *via* his middle-period outlook of 'internal' or framework-relative realism (1981, 1983), to the most recent books and articles where he has canvassed a range of scaled-down pragmatist, naturalised, or 'commonsense' realist approaches (1990, 1992, 1994, 1995).

My own view – to repeat – is that early Putnam had the best of this debate and that his subsequent misgivings or concessionary moves have been largely the product of an over-readiness to accept the force of various sceptical rejoinders. However, what I want to do here is examine one particular influence on his thinking, namely that of Wittgenstein's late philosophy and its claim to have brought us out on the far side of all those delusive 'metaphysical' concerns. This is the idea of philosophy as at best a therapeutic practice whose virtue is to coax us down from the heights of giddy abstraction where scepticism gets a hold so as eventually to lead us back, as Stanley Cavell puts it, '*via* the community, home' (Cavell 1969: 94). In other words it is a matter of showing the fly of meta-physical realism how to escape the fly-bottle of that standard sceptical response which has always inexorably shadowed the realist case when it sought to explain how we could possibly *know* what by very definition lay beyond our utmost extent of knowledge (Williams 1996). Much better accept that 'realism' entails no more than a due recognition of the manifold language-games, practices or communal 'forms of life' which alone give meaningful content to our talk about everything from cabbages and kings to microbes, molecules, atoms, and electrons.

One objection to this line of argument – at least from the realist quarter – is that it opens the way to all manner of constructivist, cultural-relativist or strong-sociological approaches that find no room for the idea of objective (language-independent or non-practice-relative) truth. (See for instance Alston 1996; Devitt 1986; Leplin (ed.) 1984.) In his middle-period writings, having renounced any such 'metaphysical' conception, Putnam set out to explain how we could think of truth as always 'internal' to some given descriptive framework or conceptual scheme without thereby courting the charge of wholesale epistemological relativism. Thus the best answer to the sceptic's perennial challenge was to acknowledge the non-availability of a scheme-transcendent 'God's-eye view' while denying that this carried any dire implications for philosophy, the natural sciences, or any other branch of enquiry. On this internalist construal realism requires no more than a theory of 'idealized rational acceptability', i.e., an appeal to what we *would* (counterfactually) endorse if all the evidence were in and taking due account of our particular interests, ontological commitments, conceptual frameworks, etc. (Putnam 1981). In which case there can be no reason to endorse *either* the hardline 'metaphysical' realist doctrine which runs straight into the sceptic's trap by placing truth beyond our utmost epistemic grasp *or* the kind of fargone sceptical-relativist argument which exploits that false dilemma for its own strategic purposes. So by this stage Putnam had clearly moved a long way from his earlier causal-realist approach to issues of meaning, reference and truth even though he regarded the move as yielding no crucial argumentative ground to the sceptic. Hence his belief that one could take on board many of the arguments advanced by an out-and-out constructivist like Nelson Goodman while holding the line against cultural relativism or other, more doctrinaire varieties of anti-realist thought (Goodman 1978; Putnam 1983a).

All the same there were problems with Putnam's attempt to strike a compromise stance, among them that of defining just where and how such a line was to be drawn, given the fact that this internalist (or framework-relativist) conception of realism looked very much like Goodman-style constructivism under a different, face-saving title. Such is the case most often brought against him by philosophers who take the view that the truth-value of our various statements is a matter of objective (verification-transcendent) warrant, rather than a matter of their happening to fall square with our present-best knowledge or the regulative notion of 'idealised rational acceptability' (Alston 1996; Devitt 1986). Thus they flatly reject any argument which relativises truth to the scope and limits of human epistemic grasp, whether by conceiving it – like Goodman – as a choice among the manifold 'world-versions' that can always be devised in accordance with this or that conceptual-interpretative scheme, or again by treating it – like Dummett – as dependent on our means of verification or available proof-procedures (Dummett 1978, 1991). Middle-period Putnam was much preoccupied with defining his position *vis-à-vis* these more extreme or doctrinaire forms of anti-realist thought and with explaining why it stopped well short of such sceptical conclusions. Still, one may suspect that his worries in this regard were a major factor in Putnam's subsequent change of philosophical tack. At any rate he has published a series of books since the late 1980s which make the case for a pragmatist, naturalised or 'commonsense' approach to these issues, one that would treat them as merely the product of a misconceived hankering after old-style 'metaphysical' certitudes. Wittgenstein is a main point of reference here, along with James and Dewey, whom he takes to have likewise opened the way to a sensibly scaled-down conception of truth which gives no hold for the pointless debate between realists and sceptics (Putnam 1994, 1995).

If this argument is to work then there has to be a credible reading of Wittgenstein which brings him out on the side of realism at least in so far as it blocks the appeal to those other sorts of reading in the 'strong'-sociological or cultural-relativist mode that would undermine the whole enterprise (Bloor 1983; Phillips 1977). Such is the denial – in Putnam's words – that 'our knowledge claims are responsible to any reality external to communal approval or sanction', this idea having spawned 'a swamp of misreadings too wide and boggy to wade through ... without losing our thread completely' (Putnam 1994: 470). Putnam's favoured source-text here is the 'brilliant critique' of such misbegotten arguments offered by Cora Diamond in her book *The Realistic Spirit* (Diamond 1991). What he takes this critique to show is that Wittgenstein is in no sense a cultural relativist – as others would wrongly have it – but rather a thinker who shows us the best way forward out of all those old 'metaphysical' pseudo-problems. Moreover, Putnam thinks Dummett mistaken in claiming any kind of Wittgensteinian warrant for an anti-realist approach to the philosophy of mathematics, that is, a constructivist view of mathematical 'truth' as coextensive with our range of proof-procedures or the scope of attainable knowledge (Dummett 1978a). Thus, according to Diamond, the whole point of Wittgenstein's reflections on rule-following is to show that certain well-established procedures – such as counting objects '1, 2, 3 ...' as per the usual practice – are fully justified by their conformity with that practice, which in turn gives us warrant for claiming that anyone who doesn't so conform has made some kind of arithmetical mistake (Wittgenstein 1956, 1969, 1976). So if the subject has been told the basic rules – 'stick to the sequence of cardinal numbers', 'don't count anything twice', 'don't omit any object', 'don't confuse the order', and so forth – then it is safe to conclude that any discrepant result (like obtaining two different answers on successive operations of the 'same' procedure) must be due to their having miscounted or failed to grasp one of those agreed-upon rules.

Of course it may be that the subject is still unable see what's wrong and continues to insist – when the discrepancy is pointed out – that they had counted correctly on both occasions. But alternatively 'let us suppose that he says "Aha!" and now acts and speaks in such ways as to enable us to say that he must have made a mistake if he gets two such results' (Diamond 1991: 247). For we should then surely be entitled to claim that this was indeed a mistake and not just a case of his applying some different, to us non-standard (or plain misguided) but to him quite acceptable rule. That is to say, the discrepancy is no longer a matter of disagreement over various optional ways of proceeding but a matter of the subject's having come to accept that certain rules are constitutive of *what it means* to perform some activity like counting objects in accordance with the basic norms of arithmetical procedure. As Putnam describes it: '[a]fter his "Aha!" experience he plays [another] game … in which he is allowed to say "I have made a mistake" in these same circumstances, but also whenever two different numbers are reached in counting the same row' (Putnam 1994: 508). At this stage the subject will have taken our point that skipping items, counting them twice over, or in the wrong order is simply not to follow the rules laid down for that particular activity. And once they have demonstrably grasped what it means to be in error – out of step – with regard to the practice of counting we shall then be entitled to interpret any further such mistakes as lapses on their part rather than as instances of following some different (by our own standards inappropriate or deviant) rule.

There is a strong temptation – as witness the above paragraph – to get drawn into this strangely engrossing debate and thereby sidetracked from discussing more substantive philosophical issues. Nothing could exemplify the tendency more clearly than Saul Kripke's so-called 'sceptical solution' to Wittgenstein's rule-following paradox and the vast literature that has since built up around it (Kripke 1982; also Baker and Hacker 1984; Boghossian 1989; Holtzmann and Leich (eds) 1981). For it is hard to see any useful purpose in just rehearsing the sceptical dilemma (or pseudo-dilemma) over again and then proposing – very much in the same Wittgensteinian spirit – that the only way out is to accept that such rules have no ultimate 'foundation' except in our communal practices, language-games, acculturated life-forms, etc. This temptation is one that Putnam is likewise hard-put to resist, electing as he does to follow Diamond in her view that anti-realists (Dummett among them) have got Wittgenstein badly wrong when they recruit him for their side of the argument. So, according to Putnam,

> [b]oth sides in the debate between 'realists' and 'antirealists' about mathematical necessity believe that we are confronted with a false choice between saying either (1) that there is something *besides* our practices of calculation and deduction which underlies those practices and guarantees their results; or (2) that there is *nothing but* what we say and do, and the necessity that we perceive in those practices is a mere illusion. (Putnam 1994: 509)

Now of course it would be fine – a great philosophical service – if Wittgenstein had really shown us the way out of this false dilemma or if Diamond had really come up with a reading of Wittgenstein that showed him to have done so despite and against these gross misconceptions surrounding his work. However this seems an unduly sanguine verdict given that Diamond's own interpretation still comes down to a flat re-statement of the Wittgensteinian case along with the assurance that we need not worry – or feel ourselves driven to any sort of anti-realist conclusion – since a 'game' like counting includes among its rules the agreed-upon practice of judging people wrong when they make some mistake by our own communal lights. In other words it is just another variant of Kripke's so-called 'sceptical solution', one that presumes us to require no more in the way of objectivity or truth than what is provided by the standard Wittgensteinian appeal to shared practices or forms of life. On this account Wittgenstein is a 'realist' all right, but one whose realism consists in his steadfastly rejecting the terms in which the debate has been conducted by advocates on both sides.

Thus 'here as elsewhere … [Wittgenstein] wants to show us that it is a mistake to choose either the "something besides" or the "nothing but" horn of the dilemma' (Putnam 1994: 509). And again:

> Diamond's example brings out how both the 'realist' and the 'antirealist' (in the fashion of Dummett's Wittgenstein) share the same picture of mathematical necessity, one according to which there must be *something* forcing us – the necessity that our rules reflect, conceived of as something external to our mathematical practices and the ways of thinking internal to them. The realist tries to make sense of such a something; the antirealist concludes that no sense can be made of it, so there is no necessity either. The philosophical task here lies in seeing that giving up on the picture that both the realist and the antirealist share is not the same thing as giving up on our ordinary logical and mathematical notion of necessity. (Putnam 1994: 509)

However, this passage displays all the signs of that slippage between different senses of 'realism' that is a constant feature of commentaries on Wittgenstein, Diamond's 'realist' (or anti-anti-realist) commentary among them. Thus Putnam takes it as sheerly self-evident that mathematical rules are 'internal' to our practices of counting, calculating, theorem-proving, and so forth, and hence that the deluded ('metaphysical') realist must be in the grip of a false picture when he thinks of such rules as being somehow imposed as a matter of 'external' necessity. But this is to trade on a crucial ambiguity between (1) 'internal' = 'valid in accordance with methods and procedures that are binding upon those who properly understand a given mathematical practice', and (2) 'internal' = 'valid according to the kinds of communal warrant that effectively decide (for members of the relevant community) what shall count as proper understanding'. There is a similar ambiguity about the word 'rules', sliding across very easily as it does from the normative or regulative sense: 'rules that necessarily apply if one wants to get the right result or come up with objectively valid conclusions', and the constitutive (Wittgensteinian) sense: 'rules that define what it means to engage in some communally sanctioned practice'. And of course this equivocal usage extends to the notion of 'necessity' as Putnam deploys it, since the term can be taken as signifying either an order of objective (practice-transcendent) mathematical truth or the kind of necessity that comes of our accepting the obligatory nature of certain practices in which we customarily engage.

Since these are among the main load-bearing terms in Putnam's (and in Diamond's) argument it can hardly be counted a trivial matter that they are all systematically ambiguous as between two very different interpretations. What is involved, I suggest, is a suasive strategy that seeks to make the case for a realist construal of Wittgenstein while defining 'realism' – along with those various related lexical items – in such a way as to prevent it from getting into conflict with the communitarian theory of meaning-as-use. So it is that Diamond can present this approach as offering the best (indeed only) way forward from the sterile debate between realists and anti-realists. There is a similar move when Putnam – following Diamond – identifies the typecast 'metaphysical' realist as one who conceives necessity as something that 'forces' us against or despite our normal procedures, something 'external to our mathematical practices and the ways of thinking internal to them' (Putnam 1994: 509). For of course if this were really their avowed position – as distinct from the position wished upon them by thinkers of a Wittgensteinian persuasion – then they would be awkwardly (if not impossibly) placed to explain how we could ever manifest a competence in mathematics or any other rule-governed practice. Here again there is an easily unnoticed semantic slide from (1) 'external' = 'answering to standards of validity and truth which may on occasion conflict with established communal norms', to (2) 'external' = 'standing quite apart from those practices or rules that permit us to decide what shall count as a valid mathematical procedure'. Any realist unwise enough to maintain thesis (2) would of course fall prey to the usual line of Wittgensteinian counter-argument. But this is no reason to regard thesis (1) as open to the same objection or as likewise committed to the strictly nonsensical idea of rule-governed judgements arrived at in the absence of rules for arriving at judgements. Only by running these theses together – and treating such a composite 'externalist' view as self-evidently misconceived – can the case be made for Wittgensteinian 'realism' as the sole viable alternative.

Hence Diamond's claim that such judgements must be 'internal' to the practice in question if they are to count as meaningful or valid according to the relevant (practice-specific) criteria. However, this still begs the question as to why we should accept such a patently circular mode of argument, one that supports a 'realist' construal only in so far as it allows us to carry on talking that way without facing up to the issue as concerns the existence or non-existence of objective (i.e., verification-transcendent) mathematical truths. Thus the Wittgensteinian 'realist' is one who sensibly accepts that such talk has a prominent place in our various everyday or specialised linguistic practices but who just as sensibly refuses to be drawn into further debate regarding its pertinent truth-conditions or those objects, properties and truth-conferring states of affairs that so preoccupy 'metaphysical' realists. After all, was it not the chief lesson of Wittgenstein's later thought that philosophy should cease from its vain pursuit of these questions – as exemplified in his own early work – and should rather content itself with simply describing the various customary language-games and practices that constitute our form of life? (Wittgenstein 1961[1922], 1958; Malcolm 1986). Among these latter, no doubt, will be many that entail some commitment to a realist way of thinking about the objects and events of our everyday experience or even those other, more elusive entities (such as molecules, atoms, and electrons) that figure in our current-best scientific theories. But we shall still be at risk of metaphysical illusion if we think to justify such working beliefs through the further appeal to an 'objective' (belief-independent) reality whose nature, properties, attributes, etc., are somehow supposed to determine their truth-value. For this is just the kind of ingrained philosophical presumption which leads us to forget that philosophy 'leaves everything as it is', including the various language-games or life-forms that it finds already in place (Wittgenstein 1958).

II

It seems to me that his partial endorsement of this quietist doctrine has led Putnam to renounce some of the best and most enduring insights of his own earlier causal-realist approach, one that had the signal advantage – to my mind – of explaining the progress of scientific knowledge in terms that also made a large contribution to philosophical semantics and cognitive psychology (Putnam 1975). Just how far he has retreated from that position can be gauged from his endorsing Wittgenstein's idea of 'seeing aspects' (e.g., facial expressions) as the paradigm case of what occurs when we grasp the rules of some established practice such as counting or performing arithmetical calculations (see Wittgenstein 1958: 193–214). Here again he follows Cora Diamond who perceives no conflict between 'realism' with respect to these latter activities and the notion that they should be treated on a par with seeing the point of games like chess or Monopoly, or again with seeing how 'two picture faces have the same expression' (Diamond 1991: 249). Where the analogy comes in – for Diamond – is with the switch from an idiosyncratic view of what such games involve to an achieved understanding of the communal rules which constitute the game in question. Thus:

> Diamond points out that in the case of card games we sometimes do and sometimes do not see one game as a form of another: in particular, she contrasts someone who sees an activity as playing Hearts or chess or Monopoly by oneself, and someone who sees no relation between this activity and playing the same game with several players. She refers to this as a difference in the 'sense' that the activity has for the players. (Putnam 1994: 508)

And again, what counts as 'seeing the point' (i.e., the practice-specific character) of games such as these is very like what counts as perceiving the similar expression in two picture-faces which would elude anyone who was aspect-blind to the sorts of similarity in question. As Diamond puts it: '[t]his is not like saying the mouths are the same length, the eyes the same distance apart; it is not that kind of description. But it is not a description of *something else*, the expression, distinct from that curved line, the dots, and so on' (Diamond 1991: 249). So it is with the matter of getting things right as regards those other activities (like counting) which we are tempted to think of as involving 'something else' – some 'external' normative compulsion – beyond the appeal to shared understanding or communal warrant. For Diamond this is just a product of the false idea that we are confronted with an ultimate choice between respecting the 'rules' of correct arithmetical practice and endorsing the kind of cultural-relativist or social-constructivist argument – often foisted on to Wittgenstein – that rejects any notion of correctness or truth. If we can only read Wittgenstein aright then this dilemma simply fades away along with all the other misbegotten anxieties that have plagued philosophy (but also kept philosophers in business) since Descartes took the first of many such unfortunate wrong turns.

Putnam is more than half-way convinced by this currently widespread belief that Wittgenstein provides the wished-for deliverance from all our longstanding philosophical perplexities. Thus: '[t]he analogy between seeing the same facial expression in two different configurations of lines and dots and seeing a necessity common to different practices of counting and calculating is an illuminating one' (Putnam 1994: 509). That is to say, the problem can be made to disappear – or no longer to look very interesting – if one opts to view it in a Wittgensteinian perspective. Moreover, one can treat a whole range of kindred philosophical issues (in logic, mathematics, epistemology, ontology, philosophy of science) as so many instances of the salutary change brought about by seeing some practice under a certain agreed-upon or communally sanctioned aspect. Here again Putnam agrees with Diamond that the crucial point is not to be seduced by the idea that getting things right with respect to this or that practice must involve the appeal to 'external' (i.e., practice-transcendent) truths or validity-conditions. 'Seeing an expression in the picture face is not just a matter of seeing the lines and dots; rather, it is a matter seeing something *in* the lines and dots – but this is not a matter of seeing something *besides* the lines and dots' (Putnam 1994: 509). Where the metaphysical realist goes wrong – on this Wittgensteinian account – is in the thought that nothing can count as genuinely 'following a rule' unless that rule has 'objective' or practice-transcendent warrant. But this is a condition that self-evidently cannot be satisfied by any practice that falls within the scope of humanly attainable knowledge or competence. Thus '[f]or Diamond, the question is not one of distinguishing between the "rules" of an activity and components of the activity which are not "rules"; for Diamond – and for Wittgenstein as Diamond reads him – the question is one of our "natural reactions", of our ways of "seeing the face" of one activity in another' (Putnam 1994: 509). In other words what makes all the difference between grasping and not grasping the point of an activity such as counting or arriving at logically justified conclusions from given premises is also what makes all the difference between seeing or failing to see certain aspects of a real-life or a sketched facial expression. And if this analogy holds – if the Wittgensteinian argument goes through – then clearly 'realism' of Diamond's sort is the only sort worth defending or the only kind of realism that doesn't fall prey to the usual range of Wittgenstein-inspired objections.

Still it is hard to understand how Putnam can sustain this argument while coming out strongly – as he does elsewhere in the Dewey Lectures – against Dummett-type antirealism or deflationist accounts of truth which reduce it to a nominal or place-holder function compatible with just about any position on the realism issue (Dummett 1978; Horwich 1990). Clearly his hope is that our 'natural reactions' (and hence the outlook of 'natural' or commonsense realism) can find all the justification they need in Wittgenstein's idea of getting things right as a matter of viewing our various practices under the right (communally warranted) aspect. Yet it is a strange kind of 'realism' – from any but a Wittgensteinian standpoint – that would allow no significant distinction to be drawn between practices such as seeing aspects of a picture or construing facial expressions and practices such as counting or 'seeing the point' of a valid deductive argument. For in the end this amounts (*pace* Diamond) to a communitarian version of the standard anti-realist claim that we simply cannot make sense of any argument entailing the existence of objective or verification-transcendent truths. After all, it is on precisely these Wittgensteinian grounds that Dummett mounts his case against realism and urges a more modest approach which contents itself with 'warranted assertability' (rather than truth) as the most we can legitimately hope to achieve. Putnam rejects this case since it fails to comport with our 'natural', commonsense-realist convictions as regards the existence of manifold truths that transcend the limits of our present-best knowledge or currently available means of verification. In the end, as he somewhat wearily remarks, '[o]ur journey has brought us back to the familiar: truth is sometimes recognition-transcendent because what goes on in the world is sometimes beyond our power to recognise, even when it is not beyond our power to conceive' (Putnam 1994: 516). This catches precisely the equivocation in Dummett-type anti-realist arguments, that is, the often unno-ticed slide from an epistemological thesis ('what *we recognise* as truth may be inde-terminate in certain problematical regions of knowledge') to the full-blown ontological version ('in that case there must be certain "gaps in reality" – Dummett's phrase – corresponding to those same limits on our range of information or powers of conceptual grasp'. For such arguments are open to an obvious riposte: that the physical universe and most of its furniture, from subatomic particles to galaxies, existed long before there were sentient creatures around to observe it and will most likely continue to exist long after those crea-tures have departed.

   This has always been the realist's strongest line of argument against phenom-enalism, logical positivism, van Fraassen-style 'constructive empiricism', and other versions of the curiously anthropocentric idea that the limits of human perceptual or conceptual grasp are such as to exclude all legitimate appeal to objective or recognition-transcendent truths. (See especially Ayer (ed.) 1959; Hanfling (ed.) 1981; Misak 1995; van Fraassen 1980.) It is also the best short answer to that Dummett-style logico-semantic variant of the same basic case which denies that we could ever have warrant for asserting the bivalent (objectively true-or-false) character of statements in the 'disputed class' for which as yet we possess no adequate means of proof or ascertainment (Dummett 1978). After all, as Putnam remarks, we can now look back to earlier stages in the history of scientific thought and recognise a vast range of possible statements whose truth-value could not have been known or proven at the time, but concerning which we are now strongly placed to affirm or deny their veracity. Then again, there are statements that *have* turned out to lack any determinate truth-value, e.g., those made before 1905 and containing some assertion with respect to the absolute simultaneity of events when such statements are construed in the wake of Special Relativity and Einstein's arguments against the existence of a privileged rest-frame except relative to the speed of light (Einstein 1954; also Angel 1980). Putnam adduces this particular example in the context of discussing Tarski's logical theorem that every well-formed declarative sentence *S* must be either true or false, that is to say, that either *S* or the negation of *S* must be true (Tarski 1956). But while rejecting that claim as applied to certain statements in the discourse of pre-Einsteinian physics – since 'the use of "true" and "false" in "Such and such a sentence is *neither true nor false*" is inadmissible in Tarskian semantics' (1994: 511) – Putnam also rejects the Dummettian anti-realist thesis which attributes this strictly nonbivalent status to all sentences in the so-called 'disputed class'. For the chief point about the Einstein example is that we now have reason to treat it as a *discovery* about such sentences that they don't after all have the definite truth-value that was once (mistakenly) assigned to them, unlike other sentences that have turned out true though their truth-value was once undecidable, or others again that have turned out false although once accepted as true. In each case the advancement of know-ledge came about through discovering some aspect of the physical world – such as the speed of light as the sole measure by which to assign values of space-time location and momentum – which entailed a redistribution of truth-values in accordance with that new (presumptively more adequate) understanding.

However, this cuts clean against any Dummett-style argument from the absence of determinate 'criteria' for statements of the disputed class to the claim that such statements can possess no objective (verification-transcendent) truth-value. For in the Einstein case it is precisely the point that ascriptions of putative simultaneity were shown to have rested on a *false* (or at any rate a partial and no longer adequate) idea of what could truly be asserted with reference to objects and events in the spatio-temporal domain. Thus one result of Einstein's revolution in physics was to bring it about that thinkers with a grasp of this latest advance were able to perceive how previous thinkers had in fact been mistaken (understandably so) in assigning a determinate truth-value to sentences of the relevant kind. But this is very different from claiming – like Dummett – that whenever we lack such criteria, for whatever reason, then our sentences must always be taken as entailing a truth-value deficit not only with respect to our state of knowledge but also with respect to some putative 'gap in reality'. I had better cite chapter and verse at this point since Dummett's position is both wildly counter-intuitive and sometimes phrased in more cautious or less provocative terms. Thus: '[t]here are gaps in reality ... meaningful statements, which we can understand and whose truth or falsity we can therefore conceive of establishing but for which, nevertheless, the question whether they are true or false has no answer: they concern a region of reality which is simply indeterminate' (Dummett 1992: 146). But in that case there could be no grounds for supposing that we had actually *discovered* something false or restricted in its scope of application about the pre-Einsteinian use of such sentences, rather than having merely switched languages – somewhat in the Kuhnian or Rortian fashion – and come up with some alternative paradigm or descriptive scheme (Kuhn 1970; Rorty 1982, 1991). That is to say, the very absence of determinate 'criteria' would place them squarely within the 'disputed class' and thus remove them once and for all from the category of sentences that possessed an objective truth-value *or an objective lack of such value* quite aside from our present (or erstwhile) inability to recognise that this was the case. Indeed, Dummett on occasion quite explicitly denies the possibility of asserting even that such sentences are 'neither-true-nor-false' (Dummett 1991). From which it would follow, improbably enough, that relativity-theory could have taught us nothing about the restricted applicability of sentences embodying the classical spacetime assumptions of Newtonian physics. And this is surely enough – Putnam now thinks – to show that Dummettian anti-realism flies in the face of some powerful and valid intuitions with regard to our knowledge of the growth of knowledge in the physical sciences and elsewhere.

III

If the Dewey Lectures mark a change in Putnam's thinking compared with his work of the previous decade it has to do mainly with his overt rejection of anti-realist arguments of this sort. He also comes out very firmly against the more circumspect version of Dummett's case which would have it that certain (as yet) unverifiable sentences may none the less be counted as possessing warranted assertability 'in principle' just so long as we can form some adequate conception of what their verification might ideally involve. Thus:

> [One] aspect of the extension of our conceptual abilities brought about by the possession of words for generality is the possibility of formulating conjectures that transcend even 'ideal verifiability', such as 'There are no intelligent extra-terrestrials'. The fact that this conjecture may not be verifiable even 'in principle' does not mean that it does not correspond to a reality; but one can say what reality corresponds to it, if it is true, only by using the words themselves. And this is not deflationism; on the contrary, deflationism, by identifying under-standing with possession of verification abilities, makes it mysterious that we should find these words intelligible. Once again, the difficulty here lies with keeping what is right in verificationism (or in this case in deflationism) while throwing out what is wrong. (Putnam 1994: 503–4)

However, there is a question as to just where this line should be drawn or how far Putnam can sustain his outlook of 'natural' or 'commonsense' realism while none the less adopting a scaled-down version of the verificationist argument or the deflationary theory of truth. For it is hard to see how he can take such ideas on board – even in a heavily qualified form – and yet hold fast to the distinction between an alethic (objective and truth-based) conception of realism that entails verification-transcendence and an epistemic (knowledge-based) conception that quickly falls prey to the kinds of attack mounted by Dummett and the 'strong' deflationists. (See especially Alston [1996] for a detailed account of these tensions in Putnam's later thought.) This problem emerges most clearly in the above-cited passage when Putnam moves in the course of a single sentence from asserting the existence of objective truths beyond even 'ideal verifiability' to asserting that our only means of forming such conjectures is 'by using the words themselves', that is, through the 'extension of our conceptual abilities brought about by the possession of words for generality'. For in that case – Wittgenstein again – it can easily appear that what counts as 'truth' must in the end be a matter of veridical warrant on the terms laid down by some existing language-game or communal form of life.

There are several passages in the Dewey Lectures where Putnam proposes this idea of language as the crucial means by which human beings extend their capacity to make the kinds of inference that are shared – albeit at a more primitive level – by certain animal species. Thus we are wrong, he believes, to over-emphasise the differences ('enormous and important as they') between what goes on when a wolf forms the habit of expecting to find deers in a meadow and what goes on in the human process of arriving at valid conclusions through various kinds of inferential procedure. Even though '[t]he cognitive states of animals lack anything like the determinacy of human cognitive states' (1994: 493), still we should acknowledge this basic continuity between their and our own sorts of reasoning, one that has very often been ignored or downplayed by philosophers from Descartes to the present. 'Our highly developed and highly discriminating abilities to think about situations that we are not observing are developments of powers that we share with other animals' (*ibid.*). All the same this analogy turns out to have sharp limits when it comes to explaining what is truly distinctive about the human capacity to generalise beyond the limits of empirical self-evidence. For 'one must not make the mistake', Putnam warns,

> of supposing that language is merely a 'code' that we use to transcribe thoughts that we could perfectly well have without the 'code'. This is a mistake, not only because the simplest thought is altered (for example, rendered far more determinate) by being expressed in language, but because language alters the range of *experiences* we can have. The fact remains that our power of imagining, remembering, expecting what is not the case here and now is a part of our nature. (1994: 493)

Now in one sense this is obvious enough, that is, in the sense that we just could not frame certain kinds of conjecture (inductive, hypothetico-deductive, counterfactual-conditional, etc.) if our thinking lacked the propositional content and the structures of rational inference that have developed through our shared possession of language. Likewise there is a sense in which our range of possible 'experience' depends upon – or is 'altered by' – the various concepts, categories, and means of articulate expression that come with the ability to represent it through everyday or scientific language. Yet these arguments are often assumed to give a purchase for the stronger (Wittgensteinian) claim that *we cannot conceive* of any thought or experience aside from those that play a role in our communally sanctioned language-games, practices or forms of life. In which case there could be no explaining how – for example – the process of scientific theory-change occurs through the revision of fundamental concepts under pressure from the weight of empirical counter-evidence. Nor could any adequate account be given of how changes in our ethical outlook occur through revision of the way that we use certain morally evaluative terms under pressure from the kinds of conflict that result from trying to accommodate new perceptions to old (residual or still predominant) modes of ethical judgement. At very least such thinking tends to endorse a consensus-based theory of values and beliefs which makes it impossible to explain how such changes might come about.

Of course there is always the stock Wittgensteinian response: that our language-games are plural and multiplex at any given time, so that nothing prevents new ideas or values from emerging as the result of some shift from one to another of the currently available range. But this fails to answer the single most pertinent objection, i.e., the charge that any such linguistic-communitarian approach must finally come down to a placid endorsement of existing values and beliefs. Putnam (like Diamond) thinks to get around this problem by treating it as just another product of the false 'metaphysical'-realist idea that we can somehow – impossibly – attain a standpoint altogether 'external' to our various language-games, practices, life-forms, etc. Thus 'the source of [this] puzzlement', he writes, 'lies in the common philosophical error of supposing that the term "reality" must refer to a single super thing, instead of looking at the ways in which we endlessly renegotiate – and are *forced* to renegotiate – our notion of reality as our language and our life develop' (Putnam 1994: 452). However this passage brings out very sharply the clash between Putnam's commonsense (or 'natural') realist outlook and the necessity he feels – in common with so many others – to square that position with a Wittgensteinian acceptance that language is in some sense the ultimate horizon of humanly conceivable truth.

Still there is no reason to think ourselves impaled on the horns of this partic-ular Wittgenstein-induced dilemma. That is to say, we can accept that reality is indeed not a 'single super thing' while rejecting the idea that it must therefore be 'internal' (for which read 'relative') to this or that language or descriptive scheme. No doubt there is a sense in which '*our notion* of reality' will always involve some particular construal which in turn depends upon the range of linguistic and conceptual resources that are currently available to us. However, it is a huge argu-mentative leap – albeit one performed with deceptive ease by anti-realists of various persuasion – which leads from this moderate epistemological claim to the kind of fargone ontological scepticism that would treat *reality itself* as somehow relative to the way that 'our language and our life develop'. Putnam, as I have said, spends a good deal of time explaining how his own position avoids any such sceptical-relativist upshot and also how his reading of Wittgenstein – like Diamond's – comes out squarely against it. This he takes to be the point of Wittgenstein's dictum that philosophy 'leaves everything as it is', including our nonphilosophical (commonsense or natural-realist) beliefs with regard to the exis-tence of those various objects, events, properties, causal dispositions, etc., which figure reliably in our day-to-day dealings with the world as well as in our more specialised scientific practices. Thus: '[t]he notion that our words and life are constrained by a reality not of our own invention plays a deep role in our lives, and is to be respected' (Putnam 1994: 452). And this despite the sceptic's likely objection that 'even my employment of the term "reality" is misleading and a source of philosophical puzzlement', along with other such general terms as 'reason', 'language', 'meaning', and 'reference' (*ibid.*). Yet Putnam's response may still be felt to equivocate between a realist conviction that the truth of our beliefs is determined (or 'constrained') by the way things stand in reality and a more Wittgensteinian or Jamesian-pragmatist view according to which such an outlook 'is to be respected' since it 'plays a deep role in our lives'. For in that case realism is best treated not as a substantive thesis with regard to the objectively existent and language-independent character of physical reality but rather as a 'notion' to be judged in accordance with our communal practices or life-forms.

Hence Putnam's pragmatist hope that the 'traditional metaphysician' – that stickler for objective reality and truth – can be coaxed down from the delusory heights and brought to accept that everything is in order with those practices and life-forms just as they stand. Such a character 'is perfectly right to insist on the independence of reality and our cognitive responsibility to do justice to whatever we describe' (1994: 452). However he is always at risk of losing 'the *real* insight in James's pragmatism, the insight that "description" is never a mere copying and that we constantly add to the ways in which language can be responsible to reality' (*ibid.*). But, again, there is a crucial ambivalence here between 'responsibility' construed on the one hand as a matter of *getting things right* quite aside from communally shared norms of justified or warranted belief, and on the other as requiring respect for those norms that are taken to 'play a deep role in our lives'. It is this ambivalence that enables Putnam to avoid the more extreme position of a thinker like Rorty, according to whom the best reason for admiring the enterprise of the natural sciences is not so much their adherence to delusive ideas about truth, progress or objectivity but rather the fact that they embody certain cultural values – 'solidarity' chief among them – which we should all do well to emulate (Rorty 1991, 1998). Putnam rejects this line of thought since it swings right across from 'metaphysical' realism to a strong-descriptivist or constructivist position which finds no room for 'responsibility' in the first of those above-mentioned senses. He is also very firm in resisting what he sees as the all-too-easy slide from a minimal-ist or deflationary conception of truth – such as Rorty can accept without any trouble – to the notion that 'reality' cannot be otherwise than the way it figures in our current-best theories, descriptions, world-hypotheses, and so forth. Thus the deflationist about truth believes that it is enough to produce some purely formal definition, some variant on the standard Tarskian schema – '"snow is white" if and only if snow is white' – which covers all possible uses of the truth predicate while avoiding any further (substantive) ontological commitment (Horwich 1990; Tarski 1956). In which case truth-talk becomes quite acceptable even for a thinker like Rorty since it amounts to no more than the kind of compliment we standardly pay to sentences which 'fit the facts' as we perceive them, those 'facts' being themselves – what else? – a subset of the range of sentences currently held true within our particular (everyday or specialised) community of knowledge.

Thus formal definitions of truth after Tarski may provide us with a highly abstract grasp of how the truth predicate operates across the whole non-denumerable class of sentences that are taken to possess some determinate truth-value. However, they furnish no answer to anti-realists such as Dummett who would adopt a sharply restrictive (verificationist) criterion according to which those sentences are very few, and are still best treated not in terms of bivalent truth or falsehood but in terms of their 'warranted assertability' as given by our best current proof-procedures, observational data, documentary evidence, methods of enquiry, etc. (Dummett 1978, 1991). And from here it is no great distance to the Rortian notion that 'truth' in any given field of enquiry at any given time can only be whatever is endorsed (or warranted) according to locally prevailing habits of usage, custom or belief. For since everything that figures in our various statements is under some description or other – since we have no access to 'reality' except by way of such descriptions – then surely it follows (in Kuhnian parlance) that the world changes with every such change in our ways of describing that world (Kuhn 1970; Rorty 1991).

Putnam's most direct encounter with this radical thesis is to be found in the volume *Starmaking* where he and other symposiasts strive to make sense of Nelson Goodman's claim that we do indeed 'make' the stars – and not just the constellations – by picking them out in accordance with a certain currently favoured range of astronomical-descriptive criteria (McCormick (ed.) 1996). What is more, Goodman argues, there is no point resorting to the standard realist counter-argument, i.e., that the stars existed for aeons before there were human beings to name them and will in all probability still be there long after the extinction of sentient life-forms. For they are 'stars' just by virtue of figuring in a certain conceptual-ontological scheme – that of modern (post-Galilean) astronomy – which posits the existence of just such celestial bodies as distinct (say) from tiny light-admitting holes in the concentric spheres of the firmament. Besides, is it not the merest of uncritical (pre-Kantian) dogmatic beliefs to suppose that the stars can have somehow preexisted and could somehow outlast our presence on the scene, given Kant's surely decisive demonstration that time and space have no 'objective' existence but must rather be construed as constitutive modalities of human knowledge and experience? So we shall do much better – Goodman thinks – to give up realism as a lost cause and acknowledge that the stars, like the constellations, 'exist' only by courtesy of the fact that human beings have an urge to name them in accordance with their own descriptive and classificatory needs (Goodman 1996).

Putnam's response to Goodman leaves no doubt that he considers this a frankly preposterous belief and just the kind of thing that tends to get philosophy a bad name. (See Putnam's various contributions to McCormick (ed.) 1996.) Yet one finds the same attitude to Goodman – and the same keenness to dissociate their own views from his – in other thinkers, Rorty among them, who have travelled a long way down the same path and barely stopped short of such a full-scale constructivist or framework-relativist position (Rorty 1991; also Margolis 1991, Quine 1981). Indeed, Putnam's theory of 'internal realism' is distinguished from Goodman's ultra-nominalist stance only to the extent that it claims a kind of scaled-down (detranscendentalised) Kantian warrant for the idea that we can carry on talking about reality just so long as our frameworks are sufficiently in kilter to prevent any major misunderstanding or outbreak of wholesale Kuhnian incommensurability (Putnam 1981). However that claim will appear less convincing if one considers, first, the well-known problems that arose with Kant's attempt to somehow square 'transcendental idealism' with 'empirical realism', and, second, the still more difficult task of explaining how this might be achieved without recourse to the transcendental machinery – the appeal to those various 'conditions of possibility' for knowledge and experience in general – which find no place in the scaled-down descriptivist approach (Kant 1964; also Allison 1983, Guyer 1987). Basically what is left after all this shedding of otiose 'metaphysical' claims is the sort of naturalised Kantianism that Strawson was the first to develop and which has lately been proposed in various forms by Robert Brandom, John McDowell and others (Brandom 1994; McDowell 1994; Strawson 1966). I have written elsewhere about the problems (as I see them) with this attempt to rehabilitate Kant – to render him suitable for 'analytic' consumption – by extracting certain salient themes or concepts, like judgement-dependence, and largely ignoring their complex relationship to other parts of the Kantian system (Norris 2000). Still more worrisome is the clear presumption that this selective approach can afford to ignore (or pass over in tactful silence) not only vast tracts of Kant's text but also pretty much the entire history of post-Kantian 'continental' thought, including those critics of the system – from Fichte on – who raised issues that are scarcely acknowledged by the current exegetes (Beiser 1987). At least one may doubt that these issues have been finally resolved by a naturalised or pragmatist recasting of the Kantian project which treats them as so many needless 'metaphysical' worries.

Putnam clearly thinks that there is an answer to be found in late Wittgenstein, that is to say, in his hard-won conception of philosophy as a means of therapeutically guiding us away from such hyperinduced doubts and dilemmas. This approach would conserve what is best about the minimalist (i.e., formal or Tarskian) theory of truth – its readiness to travel light as compared with other, more traditional theories – while holding out against the overreactive drive to jettison truth altogether in favour of a 'strong' deflationist account. Thus:

> [t]he possibility that I see in Wittgenstein's writings, of doing full justice to the principle that to call a proposition true is equivalent to asserting the proposition (doing full justice to what I called 'Tarski's insight') without committing the errors of the deflationists, is a condition of preserving our commonsense realism while appreciating the enormous *difference* between that commonsense realism and the elaborate metaphysical fantasy that is traditional realism – the fantasy of imagining that the form of all knowledge claims is fixed once and for all in advance. (Putnam 1994: 514)

However this case for the curative power of Wittgenstein's later philosophy rests on a number of highly debatable assumptions. That is, it takes for granted the validity of a realist construal of Wittgenstein – as proposed by Cora Diamond – and also the claim that this approach is in no way compromised by its ultimate appeal to the criterial authority of what makes sense within some given language-game, practice, or communal life-form. But it is precisely on account of this falling-back to a communitarian conception of 'truth' and 'reality' that Putnam raises his principal objections to the other, i.e., cultural-relativist or strong constructivist reading of Wittgenstein. Thus (to repeat) he sees nothing but a morass of incomprehension – 'a swamp of misreadings too wide and boggy to wade through' – in the notion of Wittgenstein's having denied 'that our know-ledge claims are are responsible to any reality external to communal approval or sanction' (1994: 470). Yet there is plenty of evidence in late Wittgenstein – includ-ing those passages from *On Certainty* which are often adduced in support of a realist construal – that he thought it just an instance of deluded 'metaphysical' endeavour when philosophers strove to establish some concept of verification-transcendent truth or some grounds for appeal to a language-independent reality that could render our beliefs objectively true or false. On his account the furthest we could get in this quest was to arrive at certain 'hinge propositions' whose cardi-nal role in our various practices or life-forms was such as to place them beyond reach of sceptical doubt (Wittgenstein 1969). However, this is not so much an answer to the sceptic as a flat refusal to play the sceptic's game and a recourse to the kind of strong conventionalism that decrees in favour of communal warrant as our one last source of assurance. For, according to Witgenstein, such hinge propositions are distinguished from other (less basic) items of belief in much the same way that a river pursues its course to the sea very largely unaffected by the swirls and eddies that agitate its surface from time to time (Wittgenstein 1969, Sections 95–9; also Stern 1991). Yet this metaphor clearly lends itself to a reading that would emphasise the ultimate conventionality of even our deepest-laid principles and beliefs, rather than their claim to get things right as a matter of objective truth. That is to say, it leaves room for the literal-minded sceptic to remark that river-beds *do* sometimes change course – no matter how slowly or imperceptibly – and, moreover, that the depth/surface distinction is one that has force only relative to human perceptions, time-scales, spatial perspectives, and so forth.

IV

So there is a problem about Putnam's attempt – like Diamond's before him – to enlist Wittgenstein on the side of 'commonsense' realism and against those vari-eties of cultural-relativist thinking that often claim Wittgensteinian warrant. What this argument amounts to is a stipulative redefinition of 'realism', one that rejects (or strongly plays down) the idea of objective truth-values and instead locates the criteria for truth in our various received or communally sanctioned practices. Hence all the puzzles and perplexities that Wittgensteinian exegetes have felt themselves obliged to confront in relation to concepts such as 'following a rule' or performing straightforward arithmetical operations such as 'n + 2' recur-sively applied to the sequence of numbers '2, 4, 6, 8, 10 …'. For there is always a range of different possibilities consistent with alternative (non-standard) ways of interpreting the rule, e.g., as conveying the instruction: 'add 2 until the sequence reaches 10 and then add 4, 6, 8 (etc.) at each subsequent stage'. However it takes a pretty fargone degree of Wittgenstein-induced scepticism to suppose – like Kripke – that the only viable solution to this seeming conundrum is one that has recourse to entrenched practices or agreed (arithmetically accepted) ways of carrying on (Kripke 1982; also Baker and Hacker 1984, Holtzmann and Leich (eds) 1981). After all, if a mathematics teacher came across a pupil who actually interpreted the 'rule' in this way – who insisted on continuing the sequence '10, 14, 20, 28, 38' and so forth – then she would rightly conclude that the pupil was either very bad at arithmetic or indulging some arcane (maybe Kripkensteinian) joke at her expense. In other words she would be perfectly justified in counting him wrong and not just 'wrong' according to majority opinion or the orthodox consensus on such matters. Nor can this be thought merely an instance of 'naive' or 'metaphysical' realism, one that bears witness to a kind of commonsense dogmatism or a simple failure to grasp the philosophical point. For if Kripke's 'sceptical solution' to the problem from Wittgenstein were indeed the last word on that topic – if communal agreement were indeed the bottom line with respect to arithmetical truth – then this would be no 'solution' at all but a fallback strategy which merely compounded the problem and which thus opened the way to more extravagant varieties of cultural-relativist doctrine.

The same goes for other arguments in this sceptical vein, for instance Nelson Goodman's 'new puzzle of induction', involving the use of factitious predicates such as 'grue' which when applied (say) to emeralds comes out as stipulating: 'green if observed before the year 2000 and blue if observed thereafter' (Goodman 1955). (Likewise with the counterpart predicate 'bleen' as applied to sapphires: 'blue if observed up to 2000 and green if sighted at any subsequent time'.) On the face of it this offers a sharpened re-statement of the old Humean problem and one that purportedly throws a large paradox into all our accustomed modes of inductive reasoning. But here again there is not much philosophic comfort to be had from a Kripkean sceptical 'solution' which sees the only way out of this dilemma as involving an appeal to communal warrant or the various kinds of inferential practice that constitute our normal ways of carrying on. Indeed this solution represents no advance upon Goodman's idea of habitual 'entrenchment' as that which alone makes the difference between natural and non-natural predicates, just as Kripke's answer to the Wittgensteinian rule-following 'paradox' represents no advance upon Wittgenstein's talk of acculturated language-games and forms of life. In each case the argument amounts to just a simple re-statement of the same problem along with the not very helpful advice – at least from a realist viewpoint – that we desist from seeking any other solution than that which reposes on the shared standards or criteria accepted within some given interpretive community. Thus the proper (Kripkensteinian) response to anyone who drew some unwarranted pseudo-inductive conclusion from inadequate data would be to say *not* 'you have got this wrong!' but rather: 'your reasoning doesn't conform to the customary practices that define what counts (by communal standards) as good inductive warrant'. And the case is unchanged if those standards are taken to reach right down – like Wittgenstein's 'hinge propositions' – to the deepest and seemingly most permanent aspects of our cultural life-form. For this is still a conventionalist mode of argument, one that makes truth dependent on the status of those hinge propositions within that particular life-form, rather than a matter of their claim to articulate the way things stand in reality.

My point here is that Putnam has allowed himself to be pushed into a range of philosophical dilemmas by his over-readiness to acknowledge certain anti-realist arguments which in fact have nothing like the knock-down force that he takes them to possess. These include the notion of 'reality' as internal (= relative) to our various conceptual frameworks or schemes and the Wittgenstein-influenced belief that there can be no appeal to objectivity or truth beyond what is sanctioned by our communal forms of sense-making usage or practice. Where they converge is on the verificationist assumption that we cannot be justified – rationally warranted – in asserting the existence of truths that surpass or transcend our best methods of proof or procedures of rational justification. Thus the Dummett-style anti-realist takes it as simply self-evident that any such claim must reduce to manifest nonsense since it entails our somehow purporting to know that which lies beyond our utmost powers of ascertainment (Dummett 1978, 1991; also Wright 1987). For the framework-relativist this lesson is driven home by the quasi-Kantian reflection that it cannot make sense (indeed that it amounts to a straight-forward contradiction in terms) to conceive of truths that somehow obtain outside or beyond any going conceptual scheme (Putnam 1981). From a Wittgensteinian viewpoint – *pace* Diamond – it is just as nonsensical to suppose that there might be a language in which we could meaningfully assert the existence of truths that found no criteria for warranted assertability within that language. And it is then but a short step to Dummett's rehearsal of the anti-realist position in contexts ranging from mathematics to philosophy of science, history, and ethics (Dummett 1978). In each case – so the argument runs – the realist commits a blatant logical absurdity by claiming to possess knowledge of that which exceeds the limits of present-best knowledge or for which there exists no decisive evidence or adequate proof-procedure.

However this argument holds good only on the verificationist premise that the limits of truth, properly conceived, are the limits of epistemological certitude or the bounds of warranted assertability as specified on just those terms. That is, it preemptively debars any appeal to the realist conception of truths that obtain quite apart from our present-best (or even best conceivable) methods of verification. In the Dewey Lectures there are clear signs, as I have said, that Putnam now wishes to qualify this stance at least to the point where he wouldn't feel obliged to endorse the more extreme anti-realist implications that follow from Dummett's way of framing the issue or from other (e.g., deflationist) accounts of how the truth-predicate typically functions in our everyday or scientific discourse. Yet he is still sufficiently in the grip of that way of thinking to propose a Wittgensteinian 'solution' which in fact leaves all the same problems firmly in place while purporting to resolve them through a commonsense appeal to our standard (communally warranted) ideas of reality and truth. After all, what more could we seek in the way of philosophic back-up unless we were subject to the old 'metaphysical' delusion that philosophy is somehow equipped to underwrite those same communal beliefs? Yet of course it is precisely the realist's point – supported by numerous instances from the history of science – that truth is indeed 'recognition-transcendent' in the sense that many such beliefs have turned out wrong in the past and hence (through a process of meta-inductive reasoning) that a great many of our present best beliefs will most likely turn out wrong in the future (Aronson, Harré and Way 1994; Devitt 1986; Lipton 1993; Salmon 1984). So, clearly, we are able to conceive how there might be standards of objective truth and falsehood that transcend our capacity to state just what those standards are or how our current range of accepted beliefs might at length give way to other, more adequate or powerfully unified theories.

Opponents typically turn this argument around by advancing a sceptical meta-induction to the effect that certain now falsified items of belief – like the phlogiston theory of combustion or the notion of an all-pervasive ether – were at one time strongly supported by the scientific evidence and offered the best (most rational) explanation for a large range of otherwise inexplicable phenomena (Laudan 1981). In which case surely it is the merest of short-term parochial illusions to suppose that our own current theories are true or that their various purportedly referring expressions (e.g., 'atom', 'electron' or 'quark') are somehow proof against revision or abandonment as new theories emerge. But the realist can take this argument on board without the least embarrassment just so long as she accepts – in Nicholas Rescher's well-chosen words – the 'ontological non-finality of science as we have it', that is to say, the exposure of scientific knowledge to constant testing and criticism which sometimes forces a radical revision of its standing ontological commitments (Rescher 1987: 61). Thus the sceptic's argument will seem to have force only if one accepts the anti-realist premise that it can make no sense to posit the existence of objective or verification-transcendent truths. Otherwise, if one rejects that premise, then it is altogether more rational to suppose that what grounds the possibility of scientific progress – including any future progress beyond our currently accepted beliefs – is the fact that such truths are in no way dependent on any theories, hypotheses, proof-procedures, etc., that we might entertain concerning them.

For the early Putnam (up to around 1975) it would have been a fairly straightforward matter to explain how anti-realism ducked all the pertinent issues by espousing such a doctrinaire verificationist stance. Indeed a main purpose of his work in epistemology and philosophy of language during that period was to put the case for an alternative approach that could squarely address those issues by way of a causal-realist theory of reference, meaning and truth. Thus – to recapitulate briefly – reference was fixed by an inaugural act of designative naming ('this is "water"', 'this is "gold", etc.) and thereafter held firm throughout and despite any subsequent changes in the precise definition of such terms brought about by the progress of scientific knowledge ('water is H_2O', 'gold is the metallic element with atomic number 79'). (See especially Putnam 1975a, 1975b, 1975c). The chief merit of this theory, so he claimed, was that it managed to avoid certain awkward implications of the standard (Frege–Russell) descriptivist theory according to which sense determined reference, or referring expressions picked out their referents in virtue of our grasping the various salient features, properties or attributes that enabled us to make appropriate use of such terms. But in that case it seemed to follow – absurdly – that people who had referred to substances like 'water' or 'gold' at any time before the advent of our modern (post-Daltonian) conception of molecular-atomic structure must have been referring to different substances or maybe not referring to anything at all. That is to say, their notion of the relevant criteria or identifying attributes would have been something like 'under normal conditions: colourless, odourless, liquid substance that falls as rain, collects in lakes, freezes at 0° centigrade and boils at 100° centigrade', or 'soft yellow-coloured metallic substance soluble in weak nitric acid'. So the descriptivist theory would lead to the surely untenable conclusion that they just weren't talking about *water* or *gold*, that is, applying those terms in the right way or picking out the right kinds of substance.

On Putnam's account, conversely, speakers were successfully referring to these and a whole vast range of other natural kinds long before Dalton's revolution in chemistry and the various refinements in our knowledge of atomic structure that have made it possible to distinguish (say) genuine samples of gold from fool's gold, or iron pyrites. What enabled them to do so was the causal 'chain' of transmission which started out with the fixing of reference through an inaugural act of designation – '*this* is gold!' – and thereafter ensured a sufficient continuity or stability of usage despite all those subsequent advances toward a more adequate (depth-explanatory) grasp of the relevant microstructural properties (Putnam 1975a, 1975c; also Kripke 1980, Schwartz (ed.) 1977). For we should otherwise be hard put to explain why advances of this sort are precisely advances in our knowledge concerning the nature of substances like *water* or *gold*, rather than full-scale Kuhnian paradigm shifts that bring us out referring to different substances from those that figured in some previous discourse, scientific theory, or ontological scheme. In the same way the causal theory of reference allows us to explain (for example) how a term such as 'acid' has preserved sufficient continuity of reference despite successive redefinitions, from 'corrosive substance with a sour taste in dilute form', to 'substance which turns litmus-paper red under normal conditions', to 'substance which acts as a proton-donor when it reacts with certain other substances possessing the appropriate subatomic structure'. Or again, how people were talking about 'lemons' and 'tigers' with a pretty good grasp of their species-attributes – what distinguished them from other fruits or animals – long before the advent of molecular biology and the prospect of establishing a far more precise (chromosomal) basis for making such distinctions. In each case the older, more intuitive or 'commonsense' way of picking things out was greatly refined and – on occasion – subject to drastic revision, as with the instance of fool's gold or biological species that had to be reclassified as a result of unexpected discoveries concerning their genetic make-up. Even so it makes much better sense to say (on the causal theory of reference) that 'samples of X or Y should be in fact be classified under different species or assigned different slots in the periodic table', rather than concluding – as the descriptivist theory would have it – that previous ways of talk were either referentially vacuous or referred to nothing that finds any place in our current range of candidate items. And this advantage of the causal theory is even more obvious with instances – like that of 'water' – where the progress of knowledge has not so much discredited the earlier conception as offered a more detailed microphysical account of its various phenomenal attributes.

V

My purpose in this brief return visit to the arguments set forth by early Putnam was mainly to suggest how much he has given up – in my view for less than compelling reasons – in his retreat from a causal-realist theory to a variety of so-called 'internal realism', and thence to the kind of compromise position (strongly influenced by Wittgenstein) which he adopts in the Dewey Lectures. Of course Putnam is not alone among philosophers of the post-Quinean generation in having beaten this retreat under pressure from various arguments that claim to undermine any form of 'naive' (i.e., objectivist or causal-realist) approach. In a longer perspective the issue can be viewed as going all the way back to Hume's professed attitude of sceptical doubt with regard to such basic matters as causal explanation or the existence of real-world properties, attributes, causal powers, etc., that would ground explanation in something more than our habits of associative linkage or our propensity to commit the *post hoc, propter hoc* fallacy (Hume 1975). One standard line of response to Hume – from Kant on down – is to say that we can well do without such talk of objective, mind-independent reality and truth just so long as we are none the less able to establish *a priori* (universally valid) principles or conditions for human knowledge and experience in general (Kant 1964). As we have seen, there is an aspect of Putnam's later thinking – what he calls (or used to call) 'internal realism' – which goes some way along the Kantian path but which stops well short of those aprioristic claims. Thus Putnam puts the case for a framework-relativist approach where reality is always under some description or other, with no possibility of picking out one among the range of such descriptions currently on offer and treating it as somehow ontologically privileged or possessed of ultimate realist warrant (Putnam 1981). This he takes to follow from the various well-known problems – of mereological sums, rule-following, the underdetermination of theory by evidence, the theory-laden character of observation-statements, the Wittgensteinian argument from multiple language-games, cultural life-forms, and so forth – which supposedly add up to a decisive refutation of 'naive' (objectivist) realism. And indeed there is a sense – amply witnessed by the history of debate on these issues – in which scepticism will always reemerge to confront any realist argument that yields crucial ground by relinquishing the appeal to objective (verification-transcendent) truth and espousing one or another form of internal or framework realism (Stroud 1984; Williams 1996). For this opens the way for a consequent slide into just that kind of relativist or anti-realist thinking which Putnam strongly disavows in the Dewey Lectures but which none the less resurfaces to haunt his argument at every point.

However there is a different approach to these issues which declines to accept the terms laid down by a Kantian (or quasi-Kantian) idea of framework realism as the only viable line of defence in the face of Humean and other varieties of deep-laid sceptical doubt. Also – more crucially in the present context – it offers a cogent alternative to that whole Wittgenstein-inspired way of thinking which purports to resolve such dilemmas while in fact (as I have argued) merely talking them down to the level of a placidly consensus-based appeal to our everyday linguistic practices or forms of life. That is to say, it blocks the first move in the drift toward relativism or framework-realism by maintaining a firm commitment to the principle that ontology precedes epistemology, or that the truth-value of our various observations, statements, theories, etc., is decided *not* by their 'inter-nal' role in some given conceptual scheme but rather in virtue of their describing or explaining some objective feature of the world. This is what constitutes the 'truth-tracking' property of certain referential terms, those which can be said to 'track real essence' – or be 'sensitive to future discovery' – even during periods when as yet there existed no conclusive evidence to that effect (Putnam 1975a, 1975b; also McCulloch 1995). Thus, for instance, early uses of the terms 'molecule' and 'atom' – along with a whole range of statements containing those terms – can now be endorsed as having always possessed referential and veridical import despite the fact that those pre-Daltonian and just-post-Daltonian usages lacked any present means of adequate verification. Or again, the term 'electron' is prop-erly construed as having been a genuine referring expression even at the time when physicists deployed it in a kind of proleptic or attributive role to denominate that which helped to explain certain otherwise otherwise unexplainable phenomena. In the same way – according to Putnam – early uses of terms such as 'gold', 'water', 'acid' and 'lemon' should be viewed as on the track toward a better (more precise) microphysical account in so far as they most often served to denominate genuine samples of the kind in question even though the current state of scientific know-ledge precluded any adequate specification of their atomic, molecular or genetic structure. Such uses were indeed 'sensitive to future discovery' in the sense that they would at length be borne out through the advent of more precise observa-tional means or more powerful explanatory theories.

Of course this doesn't mean that the latest (scientifically accredited) theories must be taken as the last word, or as having reached the limit of microphysical description. Rather it entails that whatever the truth about muons, gluons or fermions it will have to do with (1) the fundamental issue as to whether those particles exist, and (2) a further range of questions concerning their properties, attributes, charge characteristics, modes of interaction and so forth. Thus any statement made now – in relative ignorance – with regard to their existence or properties will possess referential and veridical status just in so far as it proves to be warranted by the standards of some later (more advanced) stage of knowledge. This argument follows by direct extrapolation from the history of terms like 'molecule', 'atom' and 'electron' which are mostly agreed – except by belated Machian positivists – to have made the transition from an instrumentalist to a realist usage. Then as now such terms are 'truth-tracking' to the extent that their role in certain well-formed referential statements has been or will be justified in the long run, as opposed to their role in certain other statements – such as 'electrons don't exist' or 'the charge on the electron is positive' – which we have good reason to think demonstrably false. Of course we might yet be forced to revise even the most basic and presently undoubted items of scientific belief. But in that case – again – such revision would be warranted only in so far as it captured or tracked some hitherto unknown feature of microphysical reality.

It seems to me that early Putnam had a theory which managed to explain all this in a highly convincing way, while later Putnam has occupied a series of positions – from 'internal' quasi-realism to pragmatism and the 'natural-realist' approach of the Dewey Lectures – which lack such descriptive and explanatory power. What he now sees as the main problem with internal realism (that is to say, with the 'moderate verificationist' standpoint espoused in *Reason, Truth and History*, 1981) is its failure to give sufficient weight to the 'world-involving' character of cognitive judgements. That is to say, it courts the charge of idealism by failing to recognise the extent to which those judgements entail a condition of reciprocal interdependence between 'subject' and 'object', mind and world, or knowledge and that which provides its objective or real-world justification. Putnam thus seems to be working around to something very like John McDowell's 'naturalised' (i.e., detranscendentalised) reading of Kant as providing the basis for a theory of judgement which would overcome all those vexing idealist antinomies without any need to drag in the whole Kantian metaphysical apparatus (McDowell 1994). However, as I have argued elsewhere, this approach may be thought to give us the worst of both worlds, on the one hand removing some essential load-bearing structures in Kant's epistemology, while on the other following Kant too far toward a judgement-relative or response-dependent conception of 'objective' reality which in effect amounts to idealism under a different ('commonsense' or naturalised) description (Norris 2000). Here again, what appears to have driven Putnam to endorse such a view is the pressure exerted by various arguments – from Wittgenstein, Dummett, and Goodman among others – which he takes to have ruled out any appeal to 'naive' (objectivist) conceptions of reality and truth. (See especially the various essays collected in Putnam 1983.)

I shall cite just one further passage from the Dewey Lectures which exhibits this tension in Putnam's later thinking and its wider relevance to issues in recent philosophical debate. 'Part of what I have been trying to show in these lectures', Putnam writes, is that what we recognize as the face of meaning is, in a number of fundamentally important cases, also the face of our natural cognitive relations to the world – the face of perceiving, of imagining, of expecting, of remembering, and so on – even though it is also the case that as language extends those natural cognitive relations to the world, it also transforms them. Our journey has brought us back to the familiar: truth is sometimes recognition-transcendent because what goes on in the world is sometimes beyond our power to recognise, even when it is not beyond our power to conceive. (Putnam 1994: 515–16).

This passage comes at the end of a paragraph which opens with the question: 'If Wittgenstein was right, how should his reflections affect our view of the concept of truth?' (*ibid.*: 515). The paragraph goes on – in symptomatic fashion – to contrast our intuitive or natural-realist attitude ('to regard an assertion or a belief or a thought as true or false *is* to regard it being right or wrong') with the Wittgenstein-derived thought that 'just what sort of rightness or wrongness is in question varies enormously with the *sort* of discourse' (*ibid.*). Furthermore, the criteria (or conditions of intelligibility) for what shall count as a valid judgement of rightness or wrongness in any given case are such as may always be subject to change with some shift in the norms that standardly apply from one to another discourse. Thus: '"statement", "true", "refers", indeed "belief", "assertion", "thought", "language" – all the terms that we use when we think about logic (or "grammar") in the wide sense in which Wittgenstein understands that notion – have a plurality of uses, and new uses are constantly added as new forms of discourse come into existence' (*ibid.*: 515). I can think of no other passage in Putnam's work that seems to entail such a radical (well-nigh Foucauldian) claim for the revisability of even our most basic concepts and categories through the process of transition from one to another prevalent 'form of discourse' (Foucault 1970, 1972). What it brings out very clearly is the influence of Wittgenstein on this aspect of Putnam's late thinking, in particular that wide notion of 'grammar' as a term that somehow extends all the way from logic – loosely conceived as the 'grammar' of thought – to those various language-games or practices that make up our communal 'form of life'. Also it shows how far this has taken him from that earlier causal-realist conception whereby all the above-mentioned terms – 'statement', 'true', 'refers', 'belief', 'assertion', 'thought', and 'language' – could be taken to satisfy the criteria for valid usage not just in so far as they played a role in some received or emergent 'discourse' but rather in so far as they described and explained our knowledge-productive linguistic engagements with the world. At any rate, the Putnam of the Dewey Lectures is very far from reaffirming his earlier position, despite all the problems that he clearly perceives with various forms of present-day relativist and anti-realist doctrine.

Of course there is a sense – a realism-compatible sense – in which new discoveries do indeed alter the conditions for counting certain statements true, for ascribing full-fledged referential status to terms (such as 'molecule' or 'atom') that previously lacked such warrant, or again, for deciding just where the distinction is to be drawn between matters of perhaps well-supported and rationally justified belief and matters of genuine knowledge. Indeed, as I have suggested, this point is crucial to any realist argument that would avoid the self-defeating idea – much exploited by anti-realists – that a commitment to realism also necessarily entails a commitment to the truth of our current best theories or the beyond-doubt existence of those entities referred to by their various constituent terms (Laudan 1981). Still there is a great difference between, on the one hand, acknowledging this basic point about the non-finality of knowledge at any given time and on the other asserting – like Putnam – that changes of 'discourse' may bring about shifts in the sense we attach to such basic terms as 'statement', 'refers', 'belief', 'assertion', 'thought', 'language', etc. What this latter claim amounts to is a kind of wholesale framework-relativism that has its source not only in Wittgenstein but also in Quine's thesis of ontological relativity, Kuhn's idea of paradigm-shifts, and a range of kindred doctrines (Kuhn 1970; Quine 1961; also Hollis and Lukes (eds) 1982).

However, it is the Wittgensteinian influence that comes through most strongly in the above-cited passage where Putnam talks about our 'natural cognitive relations to the world' as somehow 'what we recognise as the face of meaning', or 'the face of perceiving, of imagining, of expecting, of remembering, and so on' (Putnam 1994: 515–16). This analogy between meaning and facial expression is one that figures constantly in Wittgenstein's later thought. (See for instance Wittgenstein 1958, I, Sections 536–9.) Most often the metaphor is deployed in order to suggest that a certain responsiveness or due sensitivity to shared (humanly meaningful) life-forms is what alone makes possible our understanding of language, experience, and even the statements of the natural sciences or the propositions of logic. It thus goes along with Wittgenstein's idea of 'seeing aspects', that is, his belief that the furthest we can get toward a proper grasp of these matters is to acknowledge that there *just are* certain ways of perceiving or interpreting the world which count as right under certain conditions or in certain experiential contexts (Wittgenstein 1958, II: 193–229). Such perceptions may vary between different observers or may change for a single observer at different times – like the famous duck-rabbit picture – but none the less belong to a shared *Lebenswelt* or realm of humanly possible experience. Of course there are those who don't take the point, who fail to interpret the 'face of meaning' with sufficient sensitivity, and who can thus be regarded as 'aspect-blind' in some particular respect. This blindness can be manifest in various ways, from a failure to grasp arithmetical rules or basic principles of scientific reasoning, to a failure of moral or imaginative insight into other people's experience, or – at the limit – a blank incomprehension of their claims upon us as responsible moral agents. In each of these cases – and others besides – Wittgenstein tends to invoke the analogy with aesthetic experience, that is, with the capacity (or lack of such capacity) to appreciate artworks in such a way as to bring out their most salient, expressive, or humanly significant aspects (1958, 1966, 1980).

Hence the many passages in late Wittgenstein which appeal to our experience of music or the visual arts by way of suggestive comparison with other instances of getting things right or wrong, such as following a rule in one or another of its possible (standard or nonstandard) interpretations, or drawing conclusions – warranted or unwarranted – on the basis of various inductive or deductive procedures. The gist of all this is that the standards involved are not so much a matter of objective, i.e., practice- or verification-transcendent truth, but should rather be seen as immanent ('internal') to those widely shared *conceptions* of 'objectivity' and 'truth' which play a role in our communal lives. It is also this idea that Putnam invokes when he talks – in Wittgensteinian fashion – about the link between our 'natural cognitive relations to the world' and our capacity to recognise the 'face of meaning' in our various language-games, practices, modes of inferential reasoning, and so forth (Putnam 1994: 515). That is to say, this capacity is one that depends upon our seeing the practice in question under the right aspect, such 'rightness' in turn having to do with our acculturated grasp of just what it means to be involved with that practice and to know it 'from inside' as one that gives significance and purpose to our lives. In which case we can only be deluded – in the grip of some grandiose 'metaphysical' theory – if we think to adopt a critical standpoint outside and above those communal norms that provide the very criteria for meaningful utterance across the whole range of discourses and practices.

VI

That Putnam is more than half-way convinced by this Wittgensteinian line of talk is plain enough in his repeated use of the 'face of meaning' analogy and also in the way that he pointedly deploys it (along with related metaphors) against the kind of causal-realist approach that characterised his own early work. Thus:

> Instead of looking for a free-standing property of 'truth' in the hope that when we find what that property is we shall know what the *nature* of propositions is and what the *nature* of their correspondence to reality is, Wittgenstein wants us to *look* at ethical language ..., to look at religious language, to look at mathematical language, which is itself, he says, a 'motley', to look at imprecise language that manages to be perfectly clear in context ('Stand roughly here'), to look at talk that is sometimes nonsensical and to look at the very same sentences when they function perfectly well ..., to look and *see* the differences in the ways these sorts of discourses function, all the very different ways in which they relate to reality. (Putnam 1994: 515)

Here again there is a realism-compatible way of taking this passage which would come out in perfect agreement with the familiar (Aristotelian) claim that we can properly apply different standards of truth, rightness, correctness, veridical warrant, etc., according to the case in hand or the degree of accuracy required. Thus – to take one stock example – the statement 'France is hexagonal' may serve well enough as a rough description or for picking out the country in a rapid skim through the atlas but clearly won't do for specialised cartographical purposes. And of course the same applies to a whole range of statements – in the physical sciences and elsewhere – that admit various degrees of exactitude depending on whether they are intended for expert or for non-expert ('popular') consumption. Yet there is a second way of taking the passage which accords more closely with Putnam's line of argument at this point and which presses much further along the path to a Wittgenstein-inspired anti-realist position. This is the idea – chiefly carried by all those injunctions to *look* at our diverse linguistic practices – that such seeing of aspects is precisely what constitutes a 'realist' approach to the various practices concerned, or what allows us to appreciate how many and varied are the kinds of 'realism' involved. Where the objectivist ('metaphysical') realist goes wrong is in thinking that there exists some paradigm-class of statements – say those of the natural sciences or mathematics – which correspond either to how things stand in reality or to a practice-transcendent standard of correct procedure that is nowise beholden to our communal agreement in such matters. And the best cure for such thinking – so the argument runs – is to recognise the sheer multiplicity of contexts (ethical, religious, aesthetic, etc.) in which our expressions have meaning or intelligible content despite their clearly not measuring up to that delusory objectivist standard. Thus, again, we must bring ourselves 'to look and *see* the differences in the way these sorts of discourse function, all the very different ways in which they relate to reality' (Putnam 1994: 515).

However, the question then arises as to just what kind of reality it is to which those various discourses relate in their strictly non-hierarchical diversity of ways. After all, if that 'reality' is construed – following Wittgenstein – as internal (or relative) to the particular discourse in question then it is hard to conceive how we could ever discriminate between the different sorts of relationship involved or the different senses of 'realism' appropriate in various contexts. This problem emerges most clearly through Wittgenstein's appeal to aesthetic experience (the perception of significant form in visual and other kinds of artwork) as an instance – even a paradigm case – of that aspect-responsiveness or experience of 'seeing-as' which typifies every form of human understanding, from mathematics and the natural sciences to our ethical mode of being-in-the-world (Wittgenstein 1958, II: 193–229). For in that case there is essentially no difference between (1) the kind of 'realism' about scientific theories which assigns an objective reference and truth-value to such statements as 'the charge on every electron is negative'; (2) the kind of 'realism' about ethical judgements which, for instance, takes the statement 'slavery is wrong' to be justified by certain well-documented facts about the conditions of life for many people in slave-holding societies; and (3) the kind of 'realism' about aesthetic judgement which takes us to perceive what is there in a figurative painting or a piece of vividly 'realised' descriptive prose despite what we recognise – unless through naivete or a willing suspension of disbelief – as an effect of skilful artistic contrivance or response to the appropriate literary-realist conventions. The trouble with Wittgenstein's aspect-relative conception of meaning and truth is that it over-extends this last (most recognition-dependent) type of case to cover all forms of perception, cognition, understanding, judgement, or conceptual-explanatory reasoning. And in so doing it leaves no room for that crucial distinction – crucial as much for the realist in ethics as for the realist in epistemology or philosophy of science – between what is truly (objectively) the case with respect to any given domain and what we think to be the case according to our current-best knowledge or methods of enquiry.

More than that, it confuses the central issue about ethics by treating all judge-ments – no matter how factually or historically well-informed – on the routine analogy with 'seeing an aspect', thus reducing them (like the duck-rabbit example) to so many different, mutually exclusive, but equally 'right' interpretations of an always-already interpreted 'reality' (Wittgenstein 1958, II: 193–7). Thus an ethical realist who claims to have substantive grounds as distinct from just communal warrant for the judgement that 'slavery is wrong' will none the less be thought of as perceiving the institution of slavery under a certain (to them) salient aspect, and hence – in effect – as saying no more than 'slavery is wrong by our current best social and ethico-political lights'. For some, Richard Rorty among them, this appeal to the consensual values and beliefs of our own cultural community is the most that we can have – and all we need hope for – in the way of moral or indeed any other (e.g., scientific) justificatory warrant (Rorty 1989, 1991). For realists, conversely, it is most often seen as opening the way to all manner of pernicious as well as self-refuting moral and epistemological relativism (Brink 1989; Lovibond 1983). What makes things so difficult for the later Putnam is that he shares many of these worries – especially with regard to the moral issue – yet still feels obliged to take a pilgrim's route through all the problems and perplexities thrown up by engagement with Wittgenstein's late philosophy.

This emerges very strikingly in the tension between two sentences, both of which occur in the passage I cited four pages above. On the one hand, according to Putnam, '[w]hat we recognise as the face of meaning is, in a number of funda-mentally important cases, also the face of our natural cognitive relations to the world' (1994: 516). On the other hand – at the close of that same paragraph – 'truth is sometimes recognition-transcendent because what goes on in the world is sometimes beyond our power to recognise, even when it is not beyond our power to conceive' (*ibid.*: 516). Now there may be some way to reconcile these two statements, as for instance by remarking that it is 'natural' to suppose that our 'cognitive relations with the world' must leave room for truths about that world unknown – or maybe unknowable – to us with our particular ('natural') powers and limits of cognitive grasp. This would be what I have called a 'realism-compat-ible' argument, and one which indeed comes out very firmly on the realist side as concerns that crucial issue with regard to the existence of objective (verification-transcendent) truths. Still there is a problem as to how Putnam can consistently espouse this position while also propounding the 'natural' (commonsense-pragmatist) view that such objectivist talk must fall into manifest absurdity – or invite the standard Wittgensteinian charge of 'metaphysical' delusion – once it claims to go beyond the kinds of evidence that count by our present best criteria of warranted assertability. Then again, maybe the crucial point is that which Putnam makes about truths that are 'recognition-transcendent' (since we lack the requisite powers of perceptual or cognitive grasp) but which are still 'not beyond our power to conceive' (since we possess the capacity for modes of hypothetical or disciplined speculative thought which permit us to range far beyond the limits of a doctrinaire verificationist approach). This would likewise be a realist-compatible position in so far as it acknowledged the non-finality of our present best empirical procedures, observational methods, experimental techniques, and so forth. Yet it then veers sharply away from that conclusion by declining to admit the further possibility that such truths may moreover be 'beyond our power to conceive'. That is to say, it draws a line at allowing the ultimate (ontological-realist) point that truth is in the end *entirely independent* of whatever we can verify, determine or conceive concerning it.

One reason why Putnam feels compelled to draw this line is that he cannot go further without transgressing the strict Wittgensteinian veto on 'metaphysical' talk that purports to transcend our 'natural' (linguistically acculturated) modes of expression and description. Early Putnam would have had no problem here since his causal-realist approach made room for the idea of truth-tracking object-terms or predicates which – like the pre-Daltonian usage of 'atom' – were 'sensitive to future discovery' and hence in no way dependent on our current-best state of knowledge. As he puts it in the essay 'Explanation and Reference':

> [l]inguistic competence and understanding are not just *knowledge*. To have linguistic competence in connection with a term it is not sufficient, in general, to have the full battery of usual linguistic knowledge and skills; one must, in addition, be in the right sort of relationship to certain distinguished situations (normally, though not necessarily, situations in which the *referent* of the term is present). It is for this reason that this sort of theory is called a 'causal theory' of meaning. (Putnam 1975b: 199)

Of course such an argument will cut no ice with Wittgensteinians, Dummett-type anti-realists, or descriptivists of various doctrinal strength. Nor – for that matter – could it find any place in the thinking of late (post-1980) Putnam, convinced as he is that any viable theory of meaning, reference, and truth must run the full gamut of likely objections from these and other quarters. However, one could also draw the lesson that there is just no answer to scepticism – whether in its 'old' epistemological or updated linguistic forms – if this debate is scripted according to rules which the sceptic has been careful to specify in advance. That is to say, there will always come a point when the choice appears to fall between an outlook of sturdy commonsense realism (like that adopted by G.E. Moore) which strikes almost everyone as missing the point – or artfully failing to grasp it – and a Wittgensteinian approach which allows us to carry on talking in a realist way just so long as we harbour no quaint 'metaphysical' illusions (Moore 1993). Among them must be counted the idea of a world that exists and exerts its causal properties and powers quite aside from our various language-games, practices or communal forms of life. Equally 'metaphysical' – on this account – is the thought that such a language-independent reality might yet determine just *which* of those linguistic practices stand in the 'right sort of relationship' for their object-terms and predicates to pick out certain 'distinguished' or salient features. Still, that position has the strong (and one might think decisive) virtue of accounting for our knowledge of the growth of knowledge in realist and objectivist terms. At least it suggests that early Putnam had some better arguments up his sleeve than might be gathered from the record of his subsequent doubts and misgvings.

References

Allison, H. (1983). *Kant's Transcendental Idealism: an interpretation and defense*. New Haven: Yale University Press.

Alston, William P. (1996). *A Realist Conception of Truth*. Ithaca, NY: Cornell University Press.

Angel, R.B. (1980). *Relativity: the theory and its philosophy*. Oxford: Pergamon Press.

Aronson, J., R. Harré and E. Way (1994). *Realism Rescued: how scientific progress is possible*. London: Duckworth.

Ayer, A.J. (ed.) (1959). *Logical Positivism*. New York: Free Press.

Baker, G.P. and P.M.S. Hacker (1984). *Scepticism, Rules and Language*. Oxford: Blackwell.

Beiser, Frederick C. (1987). *The Fate of Reason: German philosophy from Kant to Fichte*. Cambridge, MA: Harvard University Press.

Bloor, David (1983). *Wittgenstein: a social theory of knowledge*. New York: Columbia University Press.

Boghossian, Paul A. (1989). 'The Rule-Following Considerations', *Mind*, XCVIII. 507–49.

Brandom, Robert B. (1994). *Making It Explicit: reasoning, representing, and discursive commitment*. Cambridge, MA: Harvard University Press.

Brink, David (1989). *Moral Realism and the Foundations of Ethics*. Oxford: Oxford University Press.

Cavell, Stanley (1969). *Must We Mean What We Say?* New York: Oxford University Press.

Devitt, Michael (1986). *Realism and Truth*, 2nd edn. Oxford: Blackwell.

Diamond, Cora (1991). *The Realistic Spirit: Wittgenstein, philosophy, and the mind*. Cambridge, MA: MIT Press.

Dummett, Michael (1978). *Truth and Other Enigmas*. London: Duckworth.

—— (1978a). 'Wittgenstein's Philosophy of Mathematics'. In Dummett (1978), 166–85.

—— (1991). *The Logical Basis of Metaphysics*. London: Duckworth.

—— (1992). 'The Metaphysics of Verificationism'. In Hahn (ed.), 128–54.

Einstein, Albert (1954). *Relativity: the Special and the General Theory*. London: Methuen.

Foucault, Michel (1970). *The Order of Things: an archeology of the human sciences*, trans. A. Sheridan. London: Tavistock.

—— (1972). *The Archaeology of Knowledge*, trans. A. Sheridan. London: Tavistock.

Goodman, Nelson (1955). *Fact, Fiction and Forecast*. Cambridge, MA: Harvard University Press.

—— (1978). *Ways of Worldmaking*. Indianapolis: Bobbs-Merrill.

—— (1996). 'Notes on the Well-Made World'. In McCormick (ed.), 151–60.

Guyer, Paul (1987). *Kant and the Claims of Knowledge*. Cambridge: Cambridge University Press.

Hahn, L.E. (ed.) (1992). *The Philosophy of A. J. Ayer*. La Salle, IL: Open Court.

Hanfling, O. (ed.) (1981). *Essential Readings in Logical Positivism*. Oxford: Blackwell.

Hollis, Martin and Steven Lukes (eds) (1982). *Rationality and Relativism*. Cambridge, MA: MIT Press.

Holtzmann, S. and C. Leich (eds) (1981) *Wittgenstein: to follow a rule*. London: Routledge & Kegan Paul.

Horwich, Paul (1990). *Truth*. Oxford: Blackwell.

Hume, David (1975). *Enquiries Concerning Human Understanding and Concerning the Principles of Morals*, 3rd edn, ed. L.A. Selby-Bigge, rev. P.H. Nidditch. Oxford: Clarendon Press.

Kant, Immanuel (1964). *Critique of Pure Reason*, trans. N. Kemp Smith. London: Macmillan.

Kripke, Saul (1980). *Naming and Necessity*. Oxford: Blackwell.

—— (1982). *Wittgenstein on Rules and Private Language: an elementary exposition*. Oxford: Blackwell.

Kuhn, Thomas S. (1970). *The Structure of Scientific Revolutions*, 2nd edn. Chicago: University of

Chicago Press.

Laudan, Larry (1981). 'A Confutation of Convergent Realism', *Philosophy of Science*, Vol. XLVIII. 19–49.

Leplin, Jarrett (ed.) (1984). *Scientific Realism*. Berkeley & Los Angeles: University of California Press.

Lipton, Peter (1993). *Inference to the Best Explanation*. London: Routledge.

Lovibond, Sabina (1983). *Realism and Imagination in Ethics*. Oxford: Blackwell.

Malcolm, Norman (1986). *Nothing Is Hidden: Wittgenstein's criticism of his early thought*. Oxford: Blackwell.

Margolis, Joseph (1991). *The Truth About Relativism*. Oxford: Blackwell.

McCormick, Peter J. (ed.) (1996). *Starmaking: realism, anti-realism, and irrealism*. Cambridge, MA: MIT Press.

McCulloch, Gregory (1995). *The Mind and Its World*. London: Routledge.

McDowell, John (1994). *Mind and World*. Cambridge, MA: Harvard University Press.

Misak, C.J. (1995). *Verificationism: its history and prospects*. London: Routledge.

Moore, G.E. (1993). 'The Refutation of Idealism'. In *Selected Writings*, ed. Thomas Baldwin. London: Routledge. 23–44.

Norris, Christopher (2000). *Minding the Gap: epistemology and philosophy of science in the two traditions*. Amherst, MA: University of Massachusetts Press.

Phillips, Derek L. (1977). *Wittgenstein and Scientific Knowledge: a sociological approach*. London: Macmillan.

Putnam, Hilary (1975). *Mind, Language and Reality* (*Philosophical Papers*, Vol. 2). Cambridge: Cambridge University Press.

—— (1975a). 'Is Semantics Possible?'. In Putnam (1975), 139–52.

—— (1975b). 'Explanation and Reference'. In Putnam (1975), 196–214.

—— (1975c). 'The Meaning of "Meaning"'. In Putnam (1975), 215–71.

—— (1981). *Reason, Truth and History*. Cambridge: Cambridge University Press.

—— (1983). *Realism and Reason* (*Philosophical Papers*, Vol. 3). Cambridge: Cambridge University Press.

—— (1983a). 'Why There Isn't a Ready-Made World'. In Putnam (1983), 205–28.

—— (1990). *Realism With a Human Face*. Cambridge, MA: Harvard University Press.

—— (1992). *Renewing Philosophy*. Cambridge, MA: Harvard University Press.

—— (1994). 'Sense, Nonsense, and the Senses: an inquiry into the powers of the human mind', *The Journal of Philosophy*, XCI:9. 445–517.

—— (1995). *Pragmatism: an open question*. Oxford: Blackwell.

Quine, W.V.O. (1961). 'Two Dogmas of Empiricism'. In *From a Logical Point of View*, 2nd edn. Cambridge, MA: Harvard University Press. 20–46.

—— (1981). *Theories and Things*. Cambridge, MA: Harvard University Press.

Rescher, Nicholas (1987). *Scientific Realism: a critical reappraisal*. Dordrecht: D. Reidel.

Rorty, Richard (1982). *Consequences of Pragmatism*. Brighton: Harvester Press.

—— (1989). *Contingency, Irony, and Solidarity*. Cambridge: Cambridge University Press.

—— (1991). *Objectivity, Relativism, and Truth*. Cambridge: Cambridge University Press.

—— (1998) *Truth and Progress*. Cambridge: Cambridge University Press.

Salmon, Wesley C. (1984). *Scientific Explanation and the Causal Structure of the World*. Princeton, NJ: Princeton University Press.

Schwartz, Stephen P. (ed.) (1977). *Naming, Necessity and Natural Kinds*. Ithaca, NY: Cornell University Press.

Stern, David G. (1991). 'Heraclitus' and Wittgenstein's River Images: stepping twice into the same river', *The Monist*, LXXIV. 579–604.

Strawson, P.F. (1966). *The Bounds of Sense: an essay on Kant's Critique of Pure Reason*. London: Methuen.

Stroud, Barry (1984). *The Significance of Philosophical Scepticism*. Oxford: Oxford University Press.

Tarski, Alfred (1956). 'The Concept of Truth in Formalized Languages'. In *Semantics and Metamathematics*, trans. J.H. Woodger. Oxford: Oxford University Press. 152–278.

van Fraassen, Bas C. (1980). *The Scientific Image*. Oxford: Clarendon Press.

Williams, Michael (1996). *Unnatural Doubts: epistemological realism and the basis of scepticism.* Princeton, NJ: Princeton University Press.

Wittgenstein, Ludwig (1956). *Remarks on the Foundations of Mathematics*, trans. G.E.M. Anscombe. Oxford: Blackwell.

—— (1958). *Philosophical Investigations*, trans. G.E.M. Anscombe. Oxford: Blackwell.

—— (1961[1922]). *Tractatus Logico-Philosophicus*, trans. D.F. Pears and B. McGuiness. London: Routledge & Kegan Paul.

—— (1966). *Lectures and Conversations on Aesthetics, Psychology and Religious Belief*, ed. C. Barrett. Oxford: Blackwell.

—— (1969). *On Certainty*, ed. G.E.M. Anscombe and G.H. von Wright. Oxford: Blackwell.

—— (1976). *Lectures on the Foundations of Mathematics*, ed. Cora Diamond. Chicago: University of Chicago Press.

—— (1980). *Culture and Value*, 2nd edn., ed. G.H. von Wright, trans. P. Winch. Oxford: Blackwell.

Wright, Crispin (1987). *Realism, Meaning and Truth*. Oxford: Blackwell.

4

Can realism be naturalised?
Putnam on sense, commonsense and the senses

One could tell much of the story concerning Putnam's trek from a strong causal-realist position to his current 'naturalised' (or 'commonsense') realist stance by tracing the various semantic shifts undergone by that term 'natural' and its various cognates (cf. Putnam 1975, 1994). In late Putnam it tends to shift back and forth between the naturalised-epistemological sense: 'natural = that which belongs to our straightforward perceptual and cognitive dealings with the world quite aside from otiose philosophic talk about "sense-data", "intuitions", "conceptual schemes", etc.', and the Wittgensteinian sense: 'that which belongs to our "natural", shared, communally warranted ways of talking about the world' (Putnam 1994, 1995; Wittgenstein 1958). The first kind of usage is one for which Putnam claims philosophical support from various quarters, among them J.L. Austin's famous attack on the phenomenalist sense-data doctrine in his book *Sense and Sensibilia* (Putnam 1994: 455; Austin 1962). However, it also has a proximate source in Donald Davidson's well-known insouciant phrase about those 'objects and events' whose various 'antics' are enough to render our beliefs true or false by keeping us in direct, 'unmediated' touch with reality (Davidson 1984: 198).

That this claim is compatible with pretty much any position on the realism issue is evident enough from Richard Rorty's habit of invoking Davidson whenever he wants to make his point that one can be as 'realist' as one likes about the impact of sensory stimuli on our nerve-ends – e.g., the impact of photons on Galileo's eyeball – while none the less maintaining that reality is always under some description or other, in which case such an outlook of baseline 'realism' has no substantive philosophical or scientific import (Rorty 1991: 81). Thus it is readily adaptable to that other (Wittgensteinian) usage of 'natural' where the term signifies 'having a role in our communal practices, language-games or forms of life'. So when Putnam talks – *à propos* Wittgenstein – about our 'natural cognitive relations to the world' (1994: 516) the phrase seems to carry a suggestion of both senses and, moreover, to imply that they both serve the purpose of therapeutically coaxing us down from the heights of metaphysical-realist illusion. That is to say, what is 'natural' is here conceived as what properly belongs to our *naturalised* (shared or agreed-upon) ways of construing those cognitive relations, whether in everyday practical contexts or in the discourse of other, more expert communities of knowledge like those of molecular biology or particle physics. For in neither case – so the argument goes – can we intelligibly claim to occupy some practice-transcendent viewpoint beyond the range of descriptive possibilities afforded by our cognitive-linguistic dealing with the world.

There could scarcely be a sharper contrast with the position that Putnam developed in his early writings on the causal theory of reference (Putnam 1975a, 1975b, 1975c). Here the argument is carried very largely by a usage of the term 'natural' that articulates the three main premises of an objectivist and causal-realist approach. Thus it signifies (1) the existence of certain identifiable realia – paradigmatically natural kinds – whose properties, attributes, microstructural features, genetic constitutions, and so forth, are just what enable us to pick them out with increasing exactitude as samples of such-and-such a kind; (2) the status of truth-claims in the natural sciences as grounded in a process of cumulative knowledge-acquisition – of observation, experiment, theory-construction, hypothesis-testing, inference to the best (most powerful or unified) causal explanation, etc. – which alone makes it possible to account for scientific progress in 'natural', i.e., non-miraculist terms; and (3) the condign epistemological premise that our 'natural cognitive relations to the world' are such as must be thought to enable and promote such knowledge since we should otherwise have lacked the powers and capacities to find out so much about it. Taken together they amount to a full-scale statement of the realist case which extends from ontology to epistemology and thence to a strong (but non-reductive) naturalist account of how knowledge accrues through a deepening grasp of those salient real-world features and properties that justify our various truth-claims.

Of course these premises are all subject to challenge from sceptics of various persuasion. Thus (1) will be rejected *tout court* by anyone who denies the existence of natural kinds, or who views such Aristotelian talk as merely a sign of the realist's clinging to bad old 'essentialist' habits of thought which should have gone out with Locke. (For a range of views see Dupré 1993; Quine 1969; Rorty 1991.) As regards (2), there is the standard riposte that any argument for realism from the 'evidence' of scientific progress is one that is viciously circular and which besides has to ignore the awkward fact that a good many once highly reputable scientific theories contained terms – such as 'phlogiston' or 'caloric' – which we now take as devoid of referential content (Laudan 1981). The most frequent objection to premise (3) is that it likewise begs the question by equating truth or progress in matters scientific with just those kinds of presumptive evidential warrant that happen to lie within the epistemic compass of creatures like us with our particular range of sensory inputs, cognitive powers, intellectual capacities and so forth (van Fraassen 1980, 1989). These arguments have all weighed heavily in Putnam's rejection of causal realism and his efforts to devise an internalist (or framework-relativist) theory that would acknowledge their force while none the less precluding any Goodman-style resort to a wholesale constructivist outlook (Putnam 1981, 1983; Goodman 1978). In his view, they gain further support from the various conceptual dilemmas that arise with any version of 'naive' or 'metaphysical' realism, among them – not least – the unresolved problems with any realist interpretation of quantum mechanics (Putnam 1983a, 1983b; also Norris 2000[1]).

Thus there is simply no way – as Putnam now thinks – to defend an 'external'-realist position without falling into those well-laid traps that the sceptic can always spring when it comes to debating the existence of objective (i.e., non-framework-relative or verification-transcendent) truths. For at this point the sceptic will routinely remark that such truths are by very definition beyond our utmost powers of proof or ascertainment, which is also to say – in verificationist or Dummettian anti-realist terms – that they cannot meet the most basic conditions of warranted assertability (Dummett 1978, 1991). In which case the realist is stuck with the problem of explaining how anyone could logically or consistently claim to know that which exceeds the limits of knowledge or whose very statement inevitably courts the charge of downright performative self-contradiction.

Such is at any rate the standard anti-realist riposte and the main reason why – as many philosophers have claimed – every possible argument for objectivist or external realism stands under the shadow of a sceptical rejoinder which challenges that argument at source (Stroud 1984; Williams 1996). What is so strange about Putnam's later writings is that he takes this rejoinder in its various forms to have pretty much carried the day while still coming out very firmly *against* Dummett's verificationist claim that the limits of our knowledge are also, necessarily, the limiting conditions for any truth-apt statements concerning 'objective' reality. Thus on the full-strength version of Dummett's argument any 'gaps in our know-ledge' (e.g., with regard to the historical past) must also be construed as 'gaps in reality' (Dummett 1978a, 1978b, 1978c). At times Putnam's objection to this way of thinking comes across with unmistakable force. Thus for instance:

> [a] quite different aspect of the extension of our conceptual abilities brought about by the possession of words for generality is the possibility of formulating conjectures that transcend even 'ideal verifiability', such as 'There are no intelli-gent extraterrestrials'. The fact that this conjecture may not be verifiable even 'in principle' does not mean that it does not correspond to a reality; but one can say what reality corresponds to it, if it is true, only by using the words themselves. And this is not deflationism; on the contrary, deflationism, by identifying under-standing with possession of verification abilities, makes it mysterious that we should find these words intelligible. Once again, the difficulty here lies in keeping what is right in verificationism (or in this case in deflationism) while throwing out what is wrong. (Putnam 1994: 504)

One could hardly wish for a clearer statement of the realist case against deflation-ist theories which find no room for substantive (non-circular or non-tautologous) conceptions of truth (Horwich 1990), or Dummett-type theories which reduce it to a matter of warranted assertability according to our best present proof-proce-dures or agreed-upon methods of verification. However, as I have said, there is plenty of evidence elsewhere that Putnam is prepared to go much further in a Dummettian (anti-realist) direction than might appear from the above passage. That is to say, he often seems more willing to concede 'what's right in verifica-tionism' than to 'throw out what's wrong' for the kinds of reason that are here presented as a strong rebuttal of the anti-realist case. Thus one constantly has the sense that Putnam's residual realist inclinations are subject to a strong counter-vailing influence from just the kinds of argument – summarised one paragraph above – that would count realism a lost cause in any but a weakened 'internalist' form which effectively lets the whole issue go by default.

This tension emerges very sharply in a passage where Putnam spells out his idea of just how far we should properly go with the verificationist argument. What is right about that argument, he suggests,

> is that a great deal of scientific talk does depend for its full intelligibility on the provision of the kind of thick explanatory detail that is impossible if one has no familiarity with the use of scientific instruments. For example, in Democritus's writings, as we know of them, the notion of an 'atom' was a metaphysical one, but one to which *we* can give a sense, even if Democritus himself could not. Thus, scientific instruments and scientific ways of talking are both ways of extending our perceptual and conceptual powers, and those ways are highly interdependent; indeed, they can fuse into a single complex practice. (Putnam 1994: 502)

What is so odd about this passage, I submit, is that it purports to specify what is right about verificationism – and hence, presumably, what lends some credence to Dummett's anti-realist line of thought – while none the less presenting a strong case for just the kind of realist and objectivist approach that Putnam espoused in his early writings but now seems more than half-way willing to abandon under pressure from the verificationists. His chosen example of ancient Greek atomism makes the point with exemplary force. After all, the most obvious lesson to draw is that this theory indeed started out as a matter of sheerly 'metaphysical' conjec-ture, but that later developments – from Dalton to Rutherford, Einstein, Bohr and beyond – have effected its promotion first to the status of a well-formed hypothesis with strong theoretical warrant, and then to its current position as a truth borne out by all the best (i.e., observational and causal-explanatory) evidence. At any rate this has been the case since Perrin's well-known series of experiments and since Einstein established that the phenomenon of Brownian motion could only be adequately explained in terms of the molecular-atomic hypothesis (Nye 1972; Perrin 1923).

Of course there have still been sceptics – from Ernst Mach to Bas van Fraassen – who maintain as a matter of principle that we should avoid excess onto-logical commitments and therefore not admit the 'reality' of anything that lies beyond the limits of empirical evidence or unaided human observation (Mach 1960; van Fraassen 1980; also Misak 1995). However, this self-denying ordinance seems totally at odds with both the history of scientific progress to date and the fact that so many once hypothetical or unobserved entities have since shown up with the advent of later, more advanced observational techniques. Nor is it plau-sible to argue, like van Fraassen, that these sorts of evidence shouldn't properly count in support of the realist case in so far as they involve technologically assisted means of 'observation' that exceed the range of our natural (unaided) capacity. For this is to adopt a narrowly anthropocentric conception of 'reality', one that in effect equates what is 'real' with what is real-for-us according to the scope and limits of human sensory-perceptual powers.

II

As I have said, Putnam on occasion comes out very strongly against this whole line of argument, whether couched in Dummettian anti-realist or van Frassen-style constructive empiricist terms. His reasons for denying it are spelled out at various points, for instance when he argues (*contra* Dummett) that 'small' as applied to subatomic particles should not be construed as undergoing some radical meaning-shift from 'small' as applied to tiny but macrophysically observable objects. Thus: '[i]f I could not understand talk about "things too small to see with the naked eye", the microscope would be at best a toy (like the kaleidoscope); what I saw when I looked through the eyepiece would mean nothing to me' (Putnam 1994: 502). And again, when he firmly rejects the idea that certain conjectural statements – like 'there are no intelligent extraterrestrials' – must be counted as lacking an objective truth-value in so far as we human enquirers lack any present or perhaps any future-possible means of decisive verification (*ibid.*: 504). Yet Putnam's way of making these points has a constant Wittgensteinian tendency to slide into talk about 'talk' as the furthest we can get toward justifying any sort of realism with respect to molecules, atoms, or 'things too small to see with the naked eye'.

This slide is most apparent in the above-quoted passage where he suggests that we should think of 'scientific instruments' and 'scientific ways of talking' as two 'highly interdependent' ways of extending our cognitive powers, such that, indeed, 'they can fuse into a single complex practice' (*ibid.*: 502). As regards scientific *instruments* the claim comes out pretty much in accord with Ian Hacking's defence of a realist outlook premised on the evidence of causal interaction between subatomic entities and the various sorts of apparatus – electron micro-scopes, particle colliders, etc. – in or through which those entities show up (Hacking 1983). However, this agreement transpires to have sharp limits when it comes to Putnam's notion that scientific 'ways of talking' are equally a means of 'extending our perceptual and conceptual powers', since they can fuse with the kinds of extension brought about through various observational, theoretical, tech-nological, or intrumentally assisted advances. For along with this turn toward language-dependence as a condition of scientific knowledge goes a turn toward the 'strong' anti-realist argument which would have it – as in Dummett's Wittgen-steinian version of the thesis – that truth *just is* whatever we can know or justifi-ably assert on adequate evidential grounds. And from here it is but a short step to the full-fledged Wittgensteinian conclusion that those grounds *just are* the sorts of justification arrived at when one's spade hits the bedrock of communal 'prac-tice' and one is brought to accept that nothing more can be had or properly required (Wittgenstein 1958).

It seems to me that Putnam has things the right way around when he says that 'a great deal of scientific talk does depend for its full intelligibility on the provision of the kind of thick explanatory detail that is impossible if one has no famil-iarity with the use of scientific instruments' (1994: 502). That is to say, the depend-ence-relation here – as in Putnam's early causal-realist writings – is one that makes informed 'scientific talk' a result of (rather than a precondition for) the kinds of knowledge that are warranted by getting things right with respect to a belief-independent domain of physical reality. Such knowledge must therefore be acquired through the process of engagement with a range of entities – on what-ever macro- or microphysical scale – whose existence, nature, and structural features *objectively decide* what shall count as an adequate causal-explanatory theory. No doubt there is another way of interpreting Putnam's statement which may be thought to jibe more readily with the pragmatist, internalist or frame-work-relativist drift of his later writings. Thus the phrase 'thick explanatory detail' might be taken as a nod toward the kinds of ethnographic 'thick descriptivist' approach that renounce any notion of getting things objectively (trans-culturally) 'right' and proffer a context-sensitive account of what passes for 'reality' or 'truth' in various communities of belief (Geertz 1983). From this point of view – nowa-days typified by science studies and the strong sociology of knowledge – scientific explanations are just one currently and locally privileged subset of a range of diverse culture-relative 'practices', all of which require that we judge them accord-ing to their own internal criteria and none of which can claim superior descrip-tive or causal-explanatory warrant (Barnes 1985; Bloor 1976; Fuller 1988). Putnam is very often at pains to reject any construal of his own position that would bring it out in agreement with this way of thinking. Hence also his insistence – as against the 'strong' deflationists – that the idea of objective (recognition-transcendent) truth is one that plays so crucial a role in our conception of science and every other branch of human enquiry that it is simply not open to serious doubt (Horwich 1990). All the same it is hard to see what room is left for that idea – except, maybe, on Rortian terms as a matter of useful (solidarity-enhancing) belief – when Putnam yields ground to the concept of truth as 'internal' or 'rela-tive' to some given language-game, cultural life-form, or communally sanctioned practice (Rorty 1991).

My point is that philosophy will always run into these problems – and always inevitably fail to resolve them – so long as it accepts the terms laid down by tradi-tional ways of disputing the issue between realists and anti-realists. What makes Putnam's work exemplary in this regard is the fact that he has travelled such a long and tortuous path through the various alternatives on offer and been willing to shift tack in response to every obstacle encountered along the way. Thus, for instance, in the Dewey Lectures he recalls an earlier phase of his thinking – at the time of *Representation and Reality* (1988) – when he proposed to counter the veri-ficationist (or Dummett-type anti-realist) argument by equating truth with that state of belief that would justify a subject's beliefs under 'sufficiently good epis-temic circumstances', i.e., when all the evidence was in and subject to rational assessment. On this account 'the totality of actual human sense experiences does not ... determine the totality of truths, even in the long run' since after all there is no guarantee that such circumstances will ever obtain or that human knowers will ever be placed in so maximally advantageous a position' (Putnam 1994: 462). In other words it was enough to get around the problem with any argument – like Dummett's – which assimilated truth to our present-best (or even best-humanly-possible) means of ascertainment or verification. Furthermore, '[t]o the objection that this is still an "idealist" position, I replied that it certainly is not, on the ground that while the degree of confirmation speakers actually assign to a sentence may be simply a function of their sensory experiences ... the notion of sufficiently good epistemic circumstances is a "world-involving" notion' (*ibid.*: 462). That is to say, it is a notion which effectively breaks the epistemological circle – or which removes realism from the shadow of sceptical doubt – by insisting that the truth-value of our various statements, beliefs, theories, etc., is ultimately fixed by the way things stand in reality rather than the way they might appear to us even at the limit-point of human perceptual or cognitive powers.

Such is at any rate one interpretation of the phrase 'world-involving' as Putnam uses it here. It is a construal that harks back to his earlier (causal-realist) writings in so far as it entails (1) an objectivist or verification-transcendent concept of truth, and also (2) the claim that our beliefs may be thought of as reliably 'truth-tracking' just to the extent that they pick out certain real-world objects, properties, microstructural features, causal dispositions, etc. (Putnam 1975; also McCulloch 1995). Moreover, it allows for some crucial discriminations with regard to the various stages of progress in the quest for such objective truths, some of which may figure expressly in our current best theories while others may as yet – like the term 'atom' in pre-Daltonian chemistry and physics – be incapable of adequate verification and others again (for all that we can know) lie beyond the furthest reach of human enquiry. In short, it is a theory which maintains the alethic priority of ontological over epistemological issues, or – to adopt William Alston's useful terms – the necessary distinction between 'truth-makers' (those real-world objects or properties that determine the truth-value of our various statements concerning them) and 'truth-bearers' (those statements themselves considered as subject to verification under ideal epistemic conditions) (Alston 1996). Thus it does full justice to the basic realist premise – the objectivity of truth as a 'world-involving' notion that in principle transcends even our best (presently accredited) theories and beliefs – while none the less offering a viable account of how those theories and beliefs may be thought of as possessing various degrees of epistemic and causal-explanatory warrant. Which is also to say that 'world-involvement' in this sense is just what is required in order to answer the epistemological sceptic. This it does by maintaining a realist conception of truth that respects the objective (verification-transcendent) status of truth-values yet avoids the charge of irrelevance or sheer triviality by explaining how we can have reliable knowledge of the growth of scientific knowledge.

However, there is another construal of the phrase – one more in line with the thinking of late Putnam – which effectively throws these advantages away by conceding all the main points at issue. On this view the notion of 'world-involvement' (or of our 'natural cognitive relations to the world') has to be interpreted always with reference to the various conceptual frameworks, paradigms, languages, descriptive schemes, etc., which decide what shall count as an instance of 'natural' (or commonsense-realist) belief. This points back to Putnam's middle-period theory of so-called 'internal' realism, one that acknowledged the putative force of Wittgensteinian and kindred arguments for drawing the limits of intelligible discourse at the point where our 'spade is turned', i.e., where those descriptive-explanatory resources run out and we are compelled to repose on communal usage or the normative 'rules' that alone make sense of our various procedures and practices (Wittgenstein 1958, I, Section 217). But in that case, as I have said, it is hard to see how Putnam can maintain his position against the whole range of present-day arguments – Dummettian anti-realist, strong-deflationist, cultural-relativist, and so forth – which he regards as flouting our 'natural' concep-tion of an objectively existent world whose various attributes and properties stand in the relation of truth-makers to our various truth-apt statements concerning them. For this would seem an instance of wanting to have it both ways, to resist the slide into any form of overt relativism or anti-realism while taking on board all the major theses – chief among them the internalist conception of reality and truth – whose acceptance inevitably opens the way to such arguments.

I would suggest that Putnam has been pushed in this direction by his over-readiness to concede various criticisms of the objectivist and causal-realist position developed in his own early writings. His reasons for feeling thus compelled to yield ground on so many of the main points at issue can be seen most clearly in a passage from the Dewey Lectures which I shall therefore quote at some length. The 'metaphysical realist' is right, he suggests, in one respect at least: in main-taining that 'to undercut Dummett's antirealism requires challenging his account of understanding, not adopting it' (Putnam 1994: 501). However,

> what makes the metaphysical realist's response *metaphysical* is its acceptance of the idea (which it shares with the Dummettian antirealist) that our ordinary realism – for example, about the past – presupposes a view of truth as a 'substan-tive property'. The metaphysical realist, in wanting a property that he can ascribe to all and only true sentences, wants a property that corresponds to the assertoric force of a sentence. But this is a very funny property. To avoid identifying this property of truth with that of assertability, the metaphysical realist needs to argue that there is something we are saying when we say of a particular claim that it is true over and above what we are saying when we simply assert the claim. He wants truth to be something that *goes beyond* the content of the claim and to be that in virtue of which the claim is true. This forces the metaphysical realist to postulate that there is some single thing we are saying (over and above what we are claiming) whenever we make a truth claim, no matter what sort of statement we are discussing, no matter what the circumstances under which the statement is said to be true, and no matter what the pragmatic point of calling it true is said to be. (Putnam 1994: 501)

But this is to endorse a view of 'metaphysical' realism which concedes every major point of Dummett's anti-realist case, as well as renouncing any claim to make good on his own (Putnam's) earlier position with regard to truth as a 'substantive property', one that pertains to certain statements in virtue of their getting things *objectively right* quite apart from their current degree of epistemic or justificatory warrant. As Putnam now sees it this must be a 'funny' sort of property since it involves the idea of some further (again 'metaphysical') content to our truth-claims which purportedly exists 'over and above' their straightforward assertoric content and which somehow strengthens or consolidates their standing as genuine candidates for assessment in realist terms. Yet in that case there seems little to choose between Putnam's sceptical attitude and the full-fledged deflationist theory according to which truth-talk is merely redundant or, at best, just a source of added rhetorical emphasis and a useful means of open-ended generalisation, as with 'everything Rita said was true' or 'there is no truth in any government claims about an "ethical foreign policy"' (Horwich 1990; my examples). Thus Putnam is here placed in the awkward predicament of seeking to defend a stronger concep-tion of truth than anything admitted by deflationists or Dummett-type anti-realists while effectively retreating from it under pressure from just those sorts of argument. What he shares with them is the notion that it cannnot make sense to conceive some truth-related property of statements *or some property of that to which such statements refer* 'over and above' their manifest content as a matter of straightforward epistemic or evidential warrant. Yet of course this is just the point on which Putnam takes issue with those (like Dummett and Horwich) who would deny – albeit for different reasons – that truth plays any more 'substantive' role in our various statements, theories, or beliefs.

So there is a certain irony in Putnam's claim that the 'metaphysical' realist and the Dummettian anti-realist both go wrong – that is, lay themselves open to scep-tical attack – by accepting the idea 'that our ordinary realism ... presupposes a view of truth as a "substantive property"' (1994: 501). On this account the only difference between them is that the metaphysical realist endorses the idea and wants to spell out its implications in detail while the anti-realist (like the strong deflationist) regards it as a big mistake – just a form of naive 'commonsense' meta-physics – and wants to wean us off such habits of thought. However, this will seem a highly questionable way of framing the issue if one approaches it from another standpoint, one that would reject the pejorative term 'metaphysical' as applied to *any* more 'substantive' conception of truth than those allowed under the anti-realist or strict deflationist regimes. For it would then be possible to argue – with early Putnam – that what justifies the notion of truth-values 'over and above' our present best standards of assertoric warrant is precisely what accounts for the 'truth-tracking' property of certain referring expressions, and thus renders certain of our statements 'sensitive to future discovery'. That is to say, it is their character of being up for assessment in realist and causal-explanatory terms which may not be fully specifiable as yet, or that might 'go beyond' our present-best grasp of their verification conditions. More than that: there exists a whole range of statements – especially on the microphysical and astronomical scales – whose truth-value must be thought to obtain as a matter of objective, i.e., verification-transcendent fact yet which we might be incapable of *ever* coming to know in consequence of certain limits to our powers of observation or conceptual grasp.

Early Putnam was able to accommodate both sorts of case by providing an objectivist and causal-realist theory which maintained the ultimate priority of ontological over epistemological issues but which also explained the advancement of scientific knowledge as a matter of progressively more adequate depth-explanatory theories and hypotheses. Late Putnam – so I have argued – goes a long and complex way around in trying to defend an outlook of commonsense realism that would entail no such surplus 'metaphysical' commitments while yet holding out against the various forms of present-day deflationist or anti-realist doctrine. However, this attempt miscarries for several reasons, among them the fact that it retreats so far on to ground that has already been well staked out by those opposing parties. This is, Putnam takes it pretty much for granted that a disquotational account of truth in the Tarskian mode is basically all that is required, and hence that the truth-predicate cancels out for practical purposes once it has performed its heuristic role in the construction of a T-sentence biconditional ('"snow is white" is true if and only if snow is white') for every candidate sentence in a given language (Tarski 1956). Thus the 'metaphysical realist' must surely be wrong – in the grip of a transcendental illusion – if she thinks to establish some deep further property of truth, 'something we are saying when we say of a particular claim that it is true over and above what we are saying when we simply assert the claim' (Putnam 1994: 501). Yet there is widespread disagreement among commentators on Tarski – not to mention the distinct signs of uncertainty in Tarski's own writings – as to whether this purely formal definition of truth might require fleshing out in more substantive terms (perhaps through some form of correspondence-theory) in order to avoid the charge of trivial self-evidence or empty circularity. (See for instance Davidson 1990; Johnson 1992; Kirkham 1992; O'Connor 1975.) Putnam believes that this charge can be blocked by distinguishing Tarski's minimalist approach where truth still has a genuine if scaled-down role to play from deflationist theories where it simply drops out or becomes just an all-purpose term of descriptive convenience. But in fact that distinction is hard to sustain, as emerges very clearly from his own attempts to draw the line against those (like Horwich) who see no point in maintaining it (Horwich 1990).

III

I would suggest that Putnam has been led into these various quandaries by his willingness to grant the force of certain arguments which themselves involve a drastic narrowing of the relevant terms of debate. Take for instance that sentence in the above-cited passage where Putnam explains how the 'metaphysical' realist falls into error by supposing truth to be something that 'goes beyond' the straightforward assertoric 'content of the claim' and, moreover, to be 'that in virtue of which the claim is true' (1994: 501). Now of course there is a sense – a trivial sense – in which this argument necessarily holds good since the meaning (or assertoric content) of any such claim *just is* the set of truth-conditions that have be satisfied in order for that claim to pass the test of warranted assertability. But this is not to say that those truth-conditions can be adequately specified in the formal (Tarskian) mode, nor yet to deny that such claims may be 'world-involving' in so far as their truth-values are objectively dependent on certain features, properties or attributes of the physical world that find no place in any such formalised account. Here again, late Putnam seems firmly resolved to apply a self-denying ordinance, one that preemptively blocks any access to the range of philosophical resources developed in his own earlier work.

Thus it can only be a species of 'metaphysical' illusion to argue the case for realism on objectivist grounds, or to defend a causal-explanatory approach according to which the truth-content of certain (e.g. scientific) claims can indeed 'go beyond' the current best standards of warranted assertability in so far as their terms are 'truth-tracking' or 'sensitive to future discovery'. By accepting the standard anti-realist way of setting up this debate Putnam has left himself with no option but to treat all truth-talk as 'metaphysical' (= vacuous) except when it respects the conditions laid down by a Tarskian disquotational approach. Yet it is precisely *against* that restrictive approach – along with its deflationist upshot – that Putnam seeks to reassert the viability of a 'commonsense' realism duly accountable to our 'natural cognitive relations with the world'. What drops out of the picture at this stage is any notion of that world as comprising certain objects, properties, causal dispositions, microstructural attributes, and so forth, which relate to our various statements or theories concerning them as truth-makers to truth-bearers. For otherwise there is no reason why Putnam should routinely attach the label 'metaphysical' to any kind of realist approach which takes it that the concept of truth is not exhausted by a formalised meta-linguistic treatment along the standard Tarskian lines.

According to Putnam it is the realist's obsession with that otiose metaphysical 'something beyond' that leads them to think of truth as a mysterious property which cannot be expressed or interpreted in straightforwardly assertoric terms. Thus, to repeat, 'this forces [the realist] to postulate that there is some single thing we are saying (over and above what we are claiming) whenever we make a truth claim' (Putnam 1994: 501). However, this is really just a straw-man version of the realist case, one that justifies Putnam's use of the term 'metaphysical' by constructing a typecast opponent who subscribes to beliefs that would scarcely be recognised – let alone endorsed – by anyone upholding that position. Thus the 'one single thing' might just about be construed as the property possessed by all veridical statements – perhaps on a version of the correspondence-theory – in virtue of which they can properly claim to speak the truth (or to get things right) in some particular regard. This reading is quite acceptable from a realist viewpoint and indeed captures one salient aspect of the case for objective (verification-transcendent) truth as opposed to the kinds of anti-realist argument that find no room for such a concept. However, Putnam's way of presenting the issue contrives to suggest that the realist cannot have it on these terms without also buying into all sorts of highly dubious ulterior commitment, such as the existence of a 'single' Truth – a veritable truth-of-truths – which somehow stands as a last guarantee behind our various statements and claims. For it is then easy work to represent the opposing position as just another case of 'metaphysical' bewitchment, or just another cautionary instance of the power that such thinking continues to exert when we abandon the ground of 'commonsense' or 'natural' realism. All the more so if – as Putnam implies – that superordinate Truth is taken to exist in a realm of absolute ideal objectivity 'outside and above' all mere considerations of content, context and investigative method. On this view anyone who defends an objective (alethic) conception of truth must *de facto* be committed to the notion of its holding good 'no matter what sort of statement we are discussing, no matter what the circumstances under which the statement is said to be true, and no matter what the pragmatic point of calling it true is said to be' (Putnam 1994: 501). In other words it is a truth that somehow (impossibly) floats free of any anchorage in the various particular contexts of real-world-situated knowledge and enquiry.

At this point, however, the realist will want to come back and insist that the choice is not at all as Putnam presents it, i.e., between Truth conceived in such abstract 'metaphysical' terms and – on the other hand – a pragmatist approach that allows truth a place in our everyday and scientific habits of talk just so long as it claims no substantive warrant above and beyond that facilitating role. Thus she is likely to respond that a great deal depends on the 'sort of statement we are making' since the truth-value of our various statements – e.g., 'water has the molecular structure H_2O' or 'the charge on every electron is negative' – is fixed both by the meaning standardly assigned to their constituent terms *and* by the real-world objects and properties to which those terms make reference (Armstrong 1978; Devitt 1986; Leplin (ed.) 1984; Rescher 1987; Tooley 1988). Then again, it clearly matters 'what the circumstances [are] under which the statement is said to be true', since these include – among other things – the whole range of physical and causal-explanatory factors that would figure in a full-scale attempt to spell out those operative truth-conditions. This leaves us with Putnam's final challenge to the typecast 'metaphysical' realist, namely that he postulates 'some single thing we are saying ... no matter what the pragmatic point of calling it true is said to be' (1994: 501). Here the most important point is to distinguish between two different senses of the word 'pragmatic', one of them perfectly realism-compatible ('pragmatic' = 'having to do with truth-conducive modes of real-world practical-cognitive engagement'), the other tending in an opposite direction ('pragmatic' = 'good or acceptable in the way of belief quite aside from any misplaced worries about objective truth or falsehood').

As I have said, late Putnam never ventures quite so far as to embrace this second, more extreme version of the pragmatist creed, whether in its overt Rortian form or as an unacknowledged consequence of other (e.g. deflationist) theories. He rejects it chiefly in the name of some basic commonsense principles, among them the sturdy realist conviction that there must be a great many truths that we don't yet know – and indeed might never get to know – but whose objective standing is wholly unaffected by such gaps in our knowledge. Hence his rejection of Dummett's anti-realist (or strong-verificationist) argument that such gaps must be construed also as 'gaps in reality', or regions where the lack of any definite evidence or adequate proof-procedure entails that any statement concerning them will be devoid of objective truth-value (Dummett 1978). Putnam comes out very firmly against what he sees as the massive affront to our commonsense grasp of reality and truth involved in this systematic inversion of the natural order of priority between ontological and epistemological issues. Yet elsewhere, as we have seen, he runs close to endorsing it through his claim that any viable statement of the realist case will need to take to heart those various lessons – from Wittgenstein chiefly – which alone point the way toward just such a 'commonsense' or 'natural' account. Hence the deep tension that runs through all of Putnam's post-1980 writing, and which emerges most clearly in the Dewey Lectures. It is the conflict – in short – between his strong sense that realism requires *something more* (that is, a more robust and principled defence) than the pragmatist resort to what's 'good in the way of belief' and his countervailing sense that this 'something more' cannot be specified in substantive terms without falling into all manner of naive or metaphysical delusion.

This problem is compounded by Putnam's attempt – following Cora Diamond – to make out the case for a realist interpretation of Wittgenstein, one that would 'leave everything as it is' with respect to our ordinary (non-philosophical) ways of talking and thinking about reality (Diamond 1991). For here again it is always open for the Wittgensteinian to treat any strong, e.g., causal-realist or objectivist version of the case as indeed *nothing more* than a certain language-game whose validity comes of its playing a role in some communal (even if relatively specialised) range of usages and practices. Thus the advice comes down to something more like: 'by all means carry on talking just as you did before but don't suppose – on pain of metaphysical illusion – that your talk about "substantive" or "objective" truths has any warrant over and above that role'. In the Dewey Lectures Putnam rejects this widely accredited construal of Wittgenstein, one that would have him deny 'that our knowledge claims are responsible to any reality external to communal approval or sanction' (1994: 470). All the same it is a reading that finds good warrant in numerous passages of Wittgenstein's later work and whose suasive force is manifest as much in its hold over orthodox commentators as in the problems encountered by those (like Putnam) who seek an alternative realist-compatible account. (For further argument to this effect see Blackburn 1990 and Wright 1992: 203–30.)

There is a similar problem about Putnam's equivocal stance with regard to Dummett-style anti-realism and the best way of arguing against it. Thus the metaphysical realist is right to challenge Dummett's view of the relation between truth and understanding, or his idea of warranted assertability as a concept that can adequately substitute for truth in most (if not all) domains of human enquiry. However (to repeat): 'what makes [his or her] response *metaphysical* is its acceptance of the idea (which it shares with the Dummettian antirealist) that our

ordinary realism ... presupposes a view of truth as a "substantive property"'
(Putnam 1994: 501). The trouble with Putnam's usage of the term 'metaphysical'
– here as elsewhere – is that it tends to serve in a kind of all-purpose pejorative
role which readily extends from vacuous metaphysical talk about occult qualities,
dormitive virtues, etc., to realist (causal-explanatory) talk about the various
powers, properties, or attributes which are just what give 'substantive' content to
our statements or theories concerning them. Of course this usage and the problems associated with it have a long prehistory in the empiricist tradition from
Hume to the Vienna Circle. Very often it has led to the same kind of indiscrimi-
nate attack on all kinds of (so-called) 'metaphysical' thinking, as for instance in
the case of the logical empiricists – Carnap chief among them – who applied it
not only to Heidegger and other such victims of the wholesale irrationalist
'bewitchment by language' but also to any form of putative causal explanation
that went beyond the limits of logically regimented empirical observation
(Carnap 1959, 1967; also Ayer (ed.) 1959). More recently this line of thought has
been revived in a more sophisticated guise by 'constructive empiricists' such as Bas
van Fraassen and also by anti-realist thinkers like Dummett who couch it in
jointly verificationist and logico-semantic terms (van Fraassen 1980; Dummett
1978, 1991). What they have in common – again – is an anti-metaphysical bias
which extends far beyond the justified antipathy to meaningless or pseudo-
explanatory talk and which reduces the scope of legitimate enquiry to the range
of empirically warranted observation-statements plus whatever logical resources
are needed to work out their various entailment-relations. However, this precludes
any means of establishing a substantive (non-trivial) explanatory link between the
assertoric content of our statements and the various real-world entities, structures,
causal dispositions, etc., which render those statements objectively true or false
(Salmon 1984, 1989; Grünbaum and Salmon (eds) 1988).

I think that late Putnam is over-impressed by the force of these arguments,
despite his frequently expressed misgivings with regard to their ultimate tendency
and his pragmatist espousal of commonsense (or 'natural') realism as a fallback
line of defence. For there is – as I have suggested – simply no way that the realist
could ever come up with an argument that would satisfy the sceptic on terms
which have been very largely dictated in advance by the sceptical agenda. That is
to say, this whole chapter of post-Kantian philosophical debate has developed as
a kind of programmed exchange where realism is always under the shadow of
scepticism, or where any argumentative move that the realist makes will always lie
open to the standard anti-realist rejoinder (Stroud 1984; Williams 1996). In its
basic form this rejoinder goes: if truth is indeed objective or 'recognition-transcendent' as the realist asserts, then *ex hypothesi* it lies forever beyond reach of any
knowledge we could possibly acquire or manifest concerning it, and must therefore be counted just a form of empty 'metaphysical' illusion. (See Dummett 1978
and Wright 1986.) Thus there is a clearly marked line of descent from Kant's idea
of a noumenal 'reality' transcending our utmost powers of phenomenal or cognitive grasp to Dummett's anti-realist argument according to which there is no

making sense of objectivist talk about truth-values that likewise surpass our best means or methods of adequate verification (Kant 1964). All that has changed is the widespread loss of faith in any philosophy, like Kant's, that claims to bridge the gulf between transcendental idealism on the one hand and empirical realism on the other. However, this debate will appear hopelessly stalled only if one accepts the priority of epistemological over ontological questions, that is, the typically post-Kantian idea that there can be no answer to the 'problem of knowledge' except by way of certain standard moves which then play straight into the sceptic's hands. For scepticism will always have the last word – whether from a Humean or Dummettian standpoint – so long as the argument continues to run along those same familiar tracks.

IV

Modern anti-realism can thus be seen as a logico-semantic extension and refinement of issues that emerged from some suggestive though deeply problematic passages in Kant's First *Critique* (Allison 1983; Beiser 1987; Guyer 1987). Nor (as I have argued at length elsewhere) is there much hope of a solution from thinkers in the analytic line of descent – such as John McDowell – who have lately suggested a return to Kant as the best means of overcoming those problems that have dogged philosophical thought in the wake of old-style logical empiricism (McDowell 1994; Norris 2000[2]). Putnam takes a more optimistic view since he considers McDowell to have gone a long way toward breaking the hold of that false dualist picture which led us to conceive the 'problem of knowledge' as a matter of somehow reestablishing the link between mind and world, subject and object, or thought and its various 'representational' contents. This picture held us captive, McDowell believes, only on account of the notion handed down by empiricists and rationalists alike, that is, the idea of knowledge as involving an 'interface' or point of conjuncture where sense-data somehow met up with concepts of understanding, or – in the rival rationalist account – where ideas of reason were somehow brought to bear on the 'raw data' of sensory experience. What Kant most valuably enables us to grasp is the primordial role of judgement as an active intermediary power which leaves no room for that chronic dilemma since it interprets experience as *always already* shaped and informed by the mind's synthesising capacity, and concepts as *always already* possessing empirical content in virtue of that same capacity. Thus, according to McDowell, Kant's great insight was that 'empirical knowledge results from a co-operation between receptivity and spontaneity. (Here "spontaneity" can be simply a label for the involvement of conceptual capacities.) We can dismount from the seesaw if we can achieve a firm grip on this thought: receptivity does not make an even notionally separable contribution to the co-operation' (McDowell 1994: 9). And again: 'we should understand what Kant calls "intuition" – experiential intake – not as a bare getting of an extra-conceptual Given, but as a kind of occurrence or state that already has conceptual content' (*ibid.*: 9).

Thus there is simply no need to carry on rehearsing the time-honoured 'problem of knowledge' in so far as that problem is mistakenly thought of – despite Kant's lesson to the contrary – in terms of the mind/world dualism or of 'spontaneity' as belonging on the side of conceptual representation and 'receptivity' as a matter of inert or passive sensory inputs. Rather we should abandon that whole way of thinking and, along with it, the entire prehistory of dead-end philosophical debates that have pitched empiricists against rationalists and whose latest chapter is the failed enterprise of Carnap-style logical empiricism. 'In McDowell's view', as Putnam describes it, 'the key assumption responsible for the disaster is that there has to be an interface between our cognitive powers and the external world – or, to put the same point differently, the idea that our cognitive powers cannot extend all the way to the objects themselves' (Putnam 1994: 453). Thus the only way beyond this disastrous impasse is to take Kant's point about the jointly 'receptive' and 'spontaneous' character of judgement, that is to say, its role as the faculty which somehow bridges or transcends the otherwise strictly insuperable gulf between mind and world. For we shall then be more inclined to view the so-called 'problem of knowledge' as a pseudo-problem thrown up by this and other artificial (philosophically induced) habits of thought.

However it is hard to see that Putnam's case – any more than McDowell's – is much helped by having recourse to a Kantian notion of 'judgement' which is often couched in notoriously difficult (not to say obscure and evasive) terms, and whose problematic character is fully borne out by its subsequent reception-history. Thus sensuous intuitions must be 'brought under' adequate concepts, a synthesising process that defines the scope and limits of human knowledge or experience in general, since for Kant famously 'thoughts without intuitions are empty', while 'intuitions without concepts are blind' (Kant 1964: A51/B75). And again: '[t]he understanding can intuit nothing, the senses can think nothing. Only through their union can knowledge arise' (*ibid.*). Yet of course this raises a further problem in so far as intuitions and concepts belong to quite different (categorically distinct) orders of experience and thought whose 'synthesis' cannot be envisaged in terms of a straightforward one-to-one 'fit' or correspondence-relation. At this point Kant introduces the notion of 'schemata' as somehow playing the required intermediary role, or as allowing judgement to exercise its powers in accomplishing the passage from sensuous intuitions to concepts of understanding. But again there is the danger of an infinite regress since this fails to explain how 'schemata' could partake of both functions unless by invoking some further term (or pair of such terms) that would fill the conceptual gap. At any rate the Kantian theory of judgement is a great deal more problematic than might appear from McDowell's rather sanguine appeal to it as the wished-for means of escape from all our epistemological perplexities.

These problems become all the more apparent when Kant seeks to block this threatening regress with the notion of a power vested in 'imagination' which precedes and makes possible the synthesising activity of judgement. McDowell tends to play down this aspect of Kant's thought – understandably enough – but it is one that figures at a crucial point and which has since given rise to some pene-trating commentary by thinkers less convinced that Kantian 'judgement' can indeed sustain the kind of problem-solving role here required of it. Thus 'synthe-sis', in Kant's words, is 'the mere operation of the imagination – a blind but indispensable function of the soul, without which we should have no cognition whatever, but of the working of which we are seldom even conscious' (Kant 1964: A78/B103). To the extent that judgement is itself dependent on the workings of this 'blind but indispensable' power it would seem necessarily to partake of the same mysterious character and hence to resist the utmost efforts of conceptual definition or analysis. At very least Kant's description may be thought to sit awkwardly with McDowell's claim for Kantian 'judgement' as the missing term whose recovery promises to point a way forward from the doldrums of current epistemological debate.

Moreover – as I have said – this confidence must look distinctly misplaced if one reckons with the various revisionist construals of the First *Critique* which take these passages as bearing witness to the deeply problematical character of Kant's whole enterprise. These responses have ranged from Fichte's espousal of a full-fledged subjective idealist position to Schopenhauer's dark-hued metaphysical recasting of Kantian themes and Nietzsche's charge that had Kant possessed the courage of his own best insights he would surely have pressed all the way to a thoroughgoing sceptical 'transvaluation of values' in epistemology and ethics (Fichte 1980; Schopenhauer 1969; Nietzsche 1968). Then again – purporting to surpass or 'overcome' all these – there is Heidegger's depth-ontological approach that fastens on those same passages concerning the role of 'productive imagina-tion', taken as the most revealing but also the most symptomatically occluded source of insight in Kant's critical project (Heidegger 1990). Thus, according to Heidegger, it is at just these points that an attentive reading may divine the dimension of 'authentic' temporal experience that finds no place in the dominant tradition of Western post-Hellenic philosophical thought. My point is not so much to defend these revisionist construals – Heidegger's least of all – but rather to suggest that the current 'back-to-Kant' trend among thinkers in the broadly analytic tradition is one that ignores a whole range of problems about Kant's theory of judgement, chief among them its appeal to the synthesising power of 'imagination'.

It seems to me that early Putnam was right when he claimed to cut through this entire thicket of epistemological problems by locating truth in the way things objectively stand with the world quite apart from any question concerning our beliefs, knowledge, epistemic criteria, conditions of warranted assertability, or whatever. Thus – for instance – what determines the truth or falsehood of our current-best theories with regard to the atomic constitution of 'gold', or the molecular composition of 'water', or the attribute *proton-donor* as applied to 'acid' is whether or not those theories refer to existent natural kinds and whether or not our predicative statements pick out genuine properties of them (Putnam 1975a, 1975c). Such truths are verification-transcendent in so far as they hold good objectively and depend not at all on the range or depth of our current scientific knowledge. At the same time this argument is saved from the standard anti-realist riposte – i.e., that it lacks any substantive epistemological content – by its conjunction with a causal theory of reference which accounts for the progress of scientific knowledge through our acquiring an ever more detailed knowledge of those depth-ontological or microphysical properties. At the opposite extreme this case would apply equally to statements concerning large-scale phenomena – such as the rotation of the galaxies – whose objective truth-value is wholly independent of our present-best means of observation, yet which might be borne out as a result of further (more sophisticated) methods and techniques. At any rate this seems a better explanation of our knowledge of the growth of knowledge than can possibly be had from an anti-realist viewpoint which denies the existence of objective (verification-transcendent) truths, or indeed from a more moderate 'constructive empiricist' approach according to which the only statements that possess veridical or referential warrant are those that lie within the epistemic compass of unaided human observation (van Fraassen 1980).

Early Putnam again had the best response to such arguments with his account of erstwhile unobservables – like 'molecule', 'atom' or 'electron' – as 'truth-tracking' or 'sensitive to future discovery' even at a time when their existence was a matter of strictly metaphysical conjecture. Thus the realist will see no reason to doubt that this case has equal validity when applied to the kinds of more-or-less conjectural or speculative statements that are nowadays very often to be found in the discourse of subatomic particle physics. Nor will she be over-impressed by the sceptical meta-induction which argues to precisely opposite effect, i.e., that this confidence is wholly misplaced since the history of science offers many examples of theories that once apparently enjoyed a high measure of predictive-explanatory success but whose statements thereafter turned out to be false or devoid of referential content. 'Phlogiston', 'caloric' and the 'luminiferous ether' are three such standard cautionary instances which often figure in the argument against any version of the case for convergent realism or for scientific knowledge as 'truth-tracking' in the way that early Putnam describes (Laudan 1981). Yet the realist can readily turn this argument around by pointing out (1) that those terms have been dropped from later scientific discourse precisely because they were *not* 'truth-tracking' or 'sensitive to future discovery', and (2) that this strongly vindicates the claim for truth as verification-transcendent at any given stage in the history of scientific thought (Aronson 1989; Aronson, Harré and Way 1994; Rescher 1979; Smith 1981). Moreover (3), there is a crucial difference, one that the realist is best placed to explain, between terms like 'phlogiston' and the 'luminiferous ether' which are now taken as entirely obsolete – since they refer to nothing that has played any useful or constructive role in the later development of knowledge – and on the other hand terms such as 'caloric' which did play such a role, in this case leading to the theory of specific heat, even though (or indeed precisely because) the result of that subsequent advance was to deprive 'caloric' of its erstwhile status as a genuine referring expression. (See especially Psillos 1999.)

The anti-realist can make little sense of such distinctions since on his view – one that rejects any notion of progressive convergence on truth – we are never in a good (epistemically warranted) position to sort out the kinds and degrees of truth-aptitude that characterise different theories and their various component terms.

Still less can the anti-realist explain – as early Putnam could through the causal theory of reference – how some such items (like 'molecule' and 'atom') have retained their role in a progressive and continuous history of scientific thought despite passing through a series of radical changes in our conception of their nature, constituent properties, microstructural attributes and so forth. Thus one major problem with anti-realism is that it leads very quickly to a full-fledged Kuhnian paradigm-relativist position where the meaning (and hence the reference) of every term in some given scientific theory is thought to be dependent on the whole vast range of currently accepted beliefs, from basic ontological commitments to high-level theories or hypotheses (Kuhn 1970). In which case – as likewise with Quine's thesis of ontological relativity – it is hard to explain how we can possibly talk of scientific 'progress' or account for our knowledge of the growth of knowledge by comparing different ('incommensurable') theories in point of their accuracy, predictive power, or depth of causal-explanatory grasp (Quine 1961 and 1969).

Here again the early-Putnam take on these issues has the signal advantage of locating such progress in the way that certain candidates for truth – like the atomic-molecular hypothesis – have adapted and evolved through successive stages of increasing conceptual refinement as well as through exposure to various problems, anomalies, internal tensions, discrepant results produced by crucial experiments, and so forth. Indeed, another large problem with the Quinean–Kuhnian approach is that it quite explicitly leaves no room for the decisive role of such crucial experiments. Thus any problems encountered – e.g., through the conflict between observational data and standing theoretical commitments – can always be subject to a process of adjustment (or a kind of pragmatic trade-off) whereby the discrepancy is effectively explained away by redistributing predicates and truth-values over the belief-system as a whole, or invoking alternative auxiliary hypotheses, or again (at the limit) pleading perceptual hallucination (Quine 1961). This follows from the Duhem–Quine thesis concerning the underdetermination of theory by evidence and the theory-laden (hence always corrigible) character of observation-statements (Duhem 1969; Harding (ed.) 1976). However – as I have said – it is a way of thinking that if followed through consistently would render nonsensical any talk of definite progress or advancement in our knowledge of the physical world.

On the causal-realist account, conversely, it is the hallmark of progressive (truth-apt) scientific theories that their statement takes the form of sentences containing object-terms and predicates which either succeed in picking out physically existent objects and properties or have the potential for doing just that through subsequent advances and refinements. Other philosophers – notably Hartry Field – have argued against the notion of radical meaning-variance between 'paradigms' by defining the various degrees of semantic overlap that enable (say) a term such as 'mass' to retain sufficient continuity of reference despite the conceptual shifts that it has undergone in the passage from Newtonian to Einsteinian physics (Field 1973). In short, these theories can be subject to cross-paradigm assessment by separating out the various operative senses of the term – absolute mass, rest-mass, inertial mass, relativistic mass – and showing how the process of theory-change involves both the advent of new (more powerful) concepts and the conservation of earlier concepts as still valid within certain well-defined limiting conditions. Thus Field goes a long way toward explaining why the Quine–Kuhn line of argument need not pose any ultimate threat to the realist position. However, there are still certain problems with his approach, among them the fact that it tends to assume a descriptivist account of the relation or order of priority between sense and reference. To this extent Field's theory lies open to just the kinds of sceptical counter-argument that early Putnam sought to head off by developing his alternative (causal) account of how reference is fixed and thereafter holds firm throughout and despite any subsequent shifts in the range of descriptive or identifying criteria (Putnam 1975a, 1975b, 1975c; also Kripke 1980, Schwartz (ed.) 1977).

Moreover, Putnam's theory has the great advantage of linking this claim in philosophical semantics – that fixity of reference subtends and facilitates the process of descriptive-definitional refinement – to a cognate thesis in epistemology and philosophy of science. On this view the advancement of scientific knowledge comes about through our gaining an ever more detailed depth-explanatory grasp of those properties of the physical world – whether on a micro- or macrostructural scale – which render our statements objectively true or false. The crucial point here is that Putnam's account is able to explain not only how past developments have led to our present (albeit provisional) state of knowledge but also how our theories and conjectures are 'sensitive to future discovery'. Thus they are always subject to further correction or refinement in so far as our present-best construal of their various object-terms and predicates will most likely at some stage give way to yet more precise, detailed, or adequate modes of specification.

In early Putnam this case is crucially dependent on the notion of 'wide' mental content, that is, the claim that what determines the truth or falsehood of our standing beliefs cannot be confined to the epistemic realm of private 'representations' but necessarily involves certain real-world (belief-independent) objects or properties (Putnam 1975c). Hence his use of thought-experiments – like the famous 'Twin-Earth' conjecture – whose purpose is to establish this case through a range of counterfactual instances which demonstrate the reference-fixing role of those same objects or properties. So, for example, we are to imagine a Twin-Earth substance called 'water' which shares all the phenomenal attributes of Earthly water – it is colourless, odourless, liquid at certain temperatures and under certain atmospheric pressures, has just the same freezing-point, boiling-point, proneness to condense into clouds and to fall as rain, etc. – but which happens to have the molecular structure XYZ in stead of H_2O. Or again, take the case of

aluminium and molybdenum, two metallic elements of similar surface apppear-
ance which Earthling physicists are able to distinguish in virtue of their different
atomic structures, but whose names are switched around on Twin Earth so that
their physicists reliably pick out samples of 'aluminium' where ours pick out
samples of molybdenum, and vice versa. Putnam's point – quite simply – is that
space travellers from Earth would be wrong if they used the term 'water' in referring to samples of XYZ, just as travellers from Twin Earth would be wrong if they
landed on Earth and delightedly exclaimed: 'lots of water around here!'. So likewise with 'aluminium' and 'molybdenum', assuming that everyday domestic uten-
sils on each planet were made out of the same stuff (aluminium) and other, more
specialised items – such as high-precision roller bearings – made out of molybdenum. In each case the travellers would have been deceived by appearances and led
to misdescribe the liquid or metal by applying a name from their own vocabulary
that failed to get things right. This to say – on the 'wide' theory of mental content
– that truth in such matters cannot be defined in purely epistemic or descriptivist
terms but must rather take account of objective (mind- and language-independent) properties which ultimately fix the truth-conditions for statements of the
relevant kind (McCulloch 1995). What is more, it requires that those conditions
be fixed *not* by any present-best state of knowledge but by the way things stand in
reality quite aside from the issue as to whether we ourselves or indeed any future
community of enquirers might be epistemically equipped to understand them.

So when the realist describes such usages as 'truth-tracking' or 'sensitive to
future discovery' she is not suggesting that the final criterion is that of convergence on some notional ideal of truth that would inevitably find acceptance
among those who possessed all the relevant data, observational resources, or suitably enhanced powers of theoretical grasp. This argument is one that had its
classic exposition in the writings of C.S. Peirce and that Putnam adopted during
his 'middle' period in works like *Reason, Truth and History* (Peirce 1957, 1992;
Putnam 1981). It is pragmatist in the sense of identifying truth with what is ultimately 'good in the way of belief' but not in the vulgarised (arguably Jamesian)
sense of finding no use for any notion of truth that would not fit in with the interests and priorities of some presently existing *de facto* community of belief. Rather,
it appeals to what is 'fated' to be known by truth-seekers 'at the end of enquiry'
who would by very definition be ideally placed to comprehend everything that fell
within the range of humanly possible knowledge. At that time – as Putnam recalls
in the Dewey Lectures – this seemed to him the best line of response to Dummett-
style anti-realist arguments which pushed verificationism to the point of denying
that any statement could possibly be a candidate for truth or falsehood unless we
possessed some definitive proof-procedure or means of checking its accuracy.
Thus 'I proposed to identify "being true" not with "being verified", as Dummett
does, but with "being verified to a sufficient degree to warrant acceptance under
sufficiently good epistemic conditions"' (Putnam 1994: 461).

However the trouble with this – from a realist standpoint – is that it still
comes out in accord with the notion that truth is a matter of epistemic warrant or

of what can be known (no matter how 'ideally') as opposed to what obtains quite apart from any present or future-best state of knowledge. Thus it marks the first stage of Putnam's retreat from his early objectivist stance and his turn toward an 'internal-realist' position where 'true' is identified – at least for all practical purposes – with 'good in the way of epistemically warranted belief'. With this move he effectively renounces any notion of truth as verification-transcendent, that is to say, as in principle lying beyond not only our present-best powers of verification but also any future state of knowledge brought about by extension or refinement of those powers. Putnam describes himself as having been 'bothered by the excessively "idealist" thrust of Dummett's position' (especially 'his flirtation with strong antirealism with respect to the past'), and offers his own response at the time as a means of avoiding that worrisome upshot while conceding the force of anti-realist arguments on a more moderate construal. This he hoped to achieve

> by identifying a speaker's grasp of the meaning of a statement not with an ability to tell whether the statement is true now, or to tell whether it is true under circumstances the speaker can actually bring about, as Dummett does, but with the speaker's possession of abilities that would enable a sufficiently rational speaker to decide whether the statement is true in sufficiently good epistemic circumstances. (Putnam 1994: 462)

But in that case, so the 'strong' anti-realist will argue, there is simply no use for any notion of truth as verification-transcendent or as somehow exerting an objective claim quite apart from the standards of epistemic warrant – or justified assertability – presumed to obtain under just those idealised conditions. This concession is all that he (the anti-realist) requires in order to push right through with the argument that any such talk of 'objectivity' or 'truth' is a kind of transcendental illusion or metaphysical 'bewitchment by language'. For there is then no way of blocking the sceptic's standard line of response, namely that truth-claims *cannot make sense* unless they are construed as dependent on one or another (existing or ideally attainable) method of verification.

Hence the failure of Putnam's attempt to draw a firm line between Dummett's position and his own. That is to say, it makes little difference – from an anti-realist viewpoint – whether the criterion for warranted assertability is identified with a speaker's present grasp of the meaning (i.e., the verification-conditions) of some particular statement, or their ability to tell 'whether it is true under circumstances the speaker can actually bring about', or again – Putnam's preferred alternative – their idealised capacity 'to decide whether the statement is true in sufficiently good epistemic circumstances' (1994: 462). For in each case the argument starts out by yielding the main point at issue between realists and anti-realists, i.e., the existence (as the realist would have it) of objective truths that may lie beyond our utmost attainable powers of verification. What is so odd about Putnam's self-critical retrospect is that he sees this problem clearly enough but takes it as grounds for retreating yet further from his early (objectivist) position rather than supposing that it came about mainly in consequence of that same retreat. Thus:

[i]f, on the picture we have inherited from early modern philosophy, there is a problem about how, without postulating some form of magic, we can have referential access to external things, there is an equal problem as to how we can have referential or other access to 'sufficiently good epistemic conditions'. On my alternative picture (as opposed to Dummett's), the world was allowed to determine whether I actually am in a sufficiently good epistemic situation or whether I only seem to myself to be in one – thus retaining an important idea from common-sense realism – but the conception of an epistemic situation was, at bottom, just the traditional epistemological one. (Putnam 1994: 462)

However, this is *not* the kind of 'world-involvement' that figured so importantly in Putnam's early writings and which enabled him to take a much stronger line against any theory where truth was conceived as relative to (or dependent upon) our present-best or even our future-best-possible state of knowledge concerning it. On that earlier acccount – to repeat – what fixes the reference and decides the truth-value of our various terms, predicates, statements or theories is the way things stand in some portion of objective reality and not the mere fact of their happening to fall within the scope of some 'sufficiently good epistemic situation'. In other words, 'the psychological state of the speaker does *not* determine the extension (*or* the "meaning", speaking preanalytically) of the term' (Putnam 1975c: 226). Which is also to say, more pithily: 'cut the pie any way you like, "meanings" just ain't in the *head*' (*ibid.*: 227).

V

This seems to me the most decisive contribution of Putnam's work to date, at least when judged by its explanatory worth in accounting for our knowledge of the growth of knowledge with regard to the physical sciences and other branches of enquiry. Of course there is a sense – a distinctly philosophical sense – in which scepticism will always have the last word since it raises questions of a global nature that are framed in order to exclude the possibility of an 'adequate' realist response. Thus the sceptic will typically counter any argument for realism with respect to some particular domain by protesting that it simply misses the point or takes for granted that whole range of commonsense assumptions – like belief in the existence of an objective, mind-independent, or 'external' reality – which his own argument calls into doubt (Williams 1996). The best-known case is of course that of G.E. Moore who sought to convince his lecture audience that scepticism posed no genuine threat by holding up his two hands, using each to point to the other, and declaring this action a straightforward proof that there existed at least two objects whose reality could scarcely be questioned by any person with normal powers of perceptual and cognitive grasp (Moore 1993). This purported 'refutation' of scepticism (or radical idealism) is one that has struck most philosophers – including those of a strong realist bent – as almost comically wide of the mark. Yet Moore is not alone in his failure to address the philosophical point on terms and conditions that the sceptic has so carefully laid down in advance. Rather it is the case that every possible argument against scepticism will at some stage lie open to the familiar charge of evading the issue or merely presupposing what the sceptic is out to deny. For if one thing is clear from the long history of debate on this topic it is the fact that no *philosophical* answer could ever carry weight with the sceptic or offer that definitive 'proof of an external world' by which Moore hoped to win his audience over to a commonsense-realist outlook.

Thus the sceptic need only remark that if the world is indeed 'external' (or mind-independent) as the realist requires, then there is simply no way of knowing for sure that our perceptions, beliefs, or ontological commitments bear any relation to the way things stand 'in reality'. Or again, as Michael Williams puts it: 'if the world is an objective world, statements about how things appear must be logically unconnected with statements about how they are; this lack of connection is what familiar thought-experiments dramatically illustrate' (Williams 1996: 56). From which it follows – on the sceptic's account – that the realist is faced with a no-win choice between espousing a 'strong' externalist stance which places truth beyond the utmost reach of humanly attainable knowledge, or adopting the alternative (epistemic) conception where truth becomes subject to the scope and limits of human cognitive endeavour. Either way, so it seems, there is a strictly inescapable paradox in the realist position which can only be resolved by abandoning that position altogether or else coming up with some different construal which entails no such drastic dichotomy between mind and world, subject and object, or verifiable knowledge and verification-transcendent truth. It is this latter, more complicated line of response that Putnam has consistently chosen to pursue, despite the many shifts of argumentative tack in his thinking over the past three decades. As we have seen, the complications are those that arise from his attempt to hold the balance between, on the one hand, a pragmatist outlook of 'commonsense' realism that does full justice to our normal (everyday or broadly scientific) modes of thought and, on the other, a qualified acceptance – again within commonsense limits – of the anti-realist case.

Hence the long series of visions and revisions that have marked Putnam's dealing with the problem of knowledge and given his work such a protean yet also such a dogged and impressively single-minded character. Nevertheless, I would argue that early Putnam got the emphasis right when he took the self-evidence of scientific progress in our knowledge of the physical world as a yardstick or test-case for our thinking about issues of meaning, reference, and truth. Of course this is no 'answer' to the problem of knowledge on terms that would strike the sceptic – or the convinced anti-realist – as bearing much philosophical force. But then, as I have said, all the answers that philosophers have so far come up with must be seen either as begging the question from a sceptical standpoint or as offering no more than a Wittgensteinian assurance that we can carry on talking in the same realist fashion just so long as we entertain no illusions like those to which the metaphysical realist is so distressingly prone. And what counts as 'metaphysical' on this conception is any belief in the explanatory power of those real-world properties, attributes, microstructural features, causal laws, and so forth, which alone can give substance to the realist's argument for the existence of objective (verification-transcendent) truths.

In *The Many Faces of Realism* (1987) Putnam urges that any appeal to 'the scientific method' is an empty appeal since 'there is no such thing as *the* scientific method', or nothing that legitimately answers to that description once abstracted from the various specific contexts of scientific thought. 'Case studies of particular theories in physics, biology, etc., have convinced me that no one paradigm can fit all of the various enquiries that go under the name of "science"' (Putnam 1987: 72). At this point he is discussing the idea of 'scientific method' that prevailed during the heyday of logical empiricism, namely the attempt of Carnap, Reichenbach and others to formulate a rigorous account of the inductive or deductive-nomological procedures that would serve to distinguish it from other, less exacting branches of enquiry (Carnap 1959, 1967; Reichenbach 1938). This programme had been very much a part of Putnam's formative background and one can trace a good deal of his subsequent thinking – from the early 1970s on – to his keen sense of the objections raised against it by critics like Quine and Goodman. What chiefly impressed him was the difficulty of explaining how inductive logic could ever be placed on such a formal or rigorous footing, given its appeal to analogies between past, present, and future events. Thus: '[w]hen Carnap and I worked together on inductive logic in 1953-54, the problem that he regarded as the most intractable in the whole area of inductive logic was the problem of "giving proper weight to analogy"' (Putnam 1987: 73). And he goes on to give Goodman credit for having shown that there is no formal method for distinguishing 'good' from 'bad' analogies, or for separating out those inductive 'projections' which are supposed to be reliably truth-preserving from those others (involving factitious or gerrymandered predicates) which open the way to all manner of wildly counter-intuitive results. In other words he takes Mill's cautionary point that 'there is no general method [as applied to inductive reasoning] that will not give bad results "if conjoined with universal idiocy"' (Putnam 1987: 73).

One may conjecture that Putnam's early account of meaning, reference and truth was in part an attempt to overcome this problem by proposing an alternative (causal-realist) approach which firmly rejected the logical-empiricist veto on any such so-called 'metaphysical' theory. Other philosophers bred up in that tradition – Wesley Salmon among them – can be seen to have followed a similar path to the conclusion that logical empiricism was a dead-end programme, one that conspicuously failed to resolve the longstanding Humean dilemma about inductive warrant or causal explanation. Hence Salmon's call for a decisive break with that whole way of thinking and an approach that would 'put the "cause" back into "because"' by grounding the truth of our various statements, hypotheses, theories, etc., in the various causally operative powers that the physical sciences were best equipped to explain (Salmon 1984; Salmon (ed.) 1979). Hence also – as I have argued – the range of examples that Putnam comes up with in those essays of the early 1970s where he offers a causal-realist account of meaning, reference and truth. However, this is not the lesson that he draws from the failure of logical empiricism in that passage from *The Many Faces of Realism* that I cited one paragraph above. Rather, he takes the lack of any unitary 'scientific method' – such as that pursued by thinkers like Carnap and Reichenbach – as suggesting that we henceforth adopt a more constructivist view of 'truth' and 'reality', albeit one that stops well short of Nelson Goodman's decidedly *outré* variations on this theme. Thus the picture that holds us captive, he now thinks, is the idea of standards – for instance, standards of valid inductive inference – which somehow *preexist* our various practices, reasonings, scientific procedures, etc., and which objectively decide whether or not we are managing to get things right. Yet 'this is just the picture that Goodman attacked in his famous writing on induction, and that Quine attacks in his "naturalized epistemology"'. So we should do much better to renounce this delusory objectivist view-from-nowhere and accept the basic pragmatist point that the standards in question are those which we ourselves have evolved and refined in various contexts of applied investigative thought. Such is indeed Goodman's main argument in his 'deep little book on "worldmaking"', and such the conclusion that Putnam derives from Quine's (as he takes it) definitive attack on the two 'last dogmas' of old-style logical empiricism.

These reflections are a part of Putnam's generalised case in *The Many Faces of Realism* for a more flexible conception of 'method' that would allow us to break with the typecast distinction between the kinds of reasoning appropriate to the 'hard' (i.e., physical or natural) sciences and the kinds of empathetic understanding that supposedly characterise 'soft' disciplines like psychology, sociology or literary criticism. On the one hand, as he had argued in *Meaning and the Moral Sciences* (1978), it is important to maintain a due sense of this distinction since otherwise there will be no place for *Verstehen*, that is, for the claims of interpretative insight or depth-hermeneutic understanding as opposed to the claims of inductive or deductive-nomological method. For '[i]f one tries, with Ernest Nagel, to simply *assimilate* the inferences we make in history to the inferences of the physicist, the effect is not to show that history is proper "science" after all, but to make it all look like *terrible* science' (Putnam 1987: 75). On the other hand – as Putnam now wants to stress – it is wrong to suppose that these are realms apart or that the 'hard' sciences can perfectly well get along without recourse to the kinds of non-formalisable but equally valid insight that play a central role in the humanities and social sciences. After all, is this not just the lesson that we have learned (or that we ought to have learned) from the impasse of logical empiricism? Thus if it proved impossible to formulate the canons of valid inductive inference without some appeal to analogy and hence to our intuitive grasp of the difference between 'right' and 'wrong' kinds of analogy, then surely we shall have to make adjustments to our sense of what counts as scientific 'method'. In which case the problem that Carnap came up against – that of 'giving proper weight to analogy' – is one with even larger implications for philosophy of science and its cherished self-image *vis-à-vis* the 'softer' disciplines. But this is no problem for the pragmatist since '[s]tandards and practices, pragmatists have always insisted, must be developed together and constantly revised by a procedure of delicate mutual adjustment' (Putnam 1994: 79). In which case Goodman is right to this extent at least: that there is no single method – no favoured 'projection' or ontologically privileged world-version – that can claim such status simply by virtue of capturing the way things stand in reality.

So we can see, once again, just how far Putnam has travelled from his earlier causal-realist outlook according to which the truth-value of our various statements, theories, observations, etc., is a matter of their picking out objects and properties (e.g., microstructural attributes) which exist and exert their causal powers quite aside from their role in some descriptive framework or projective scheme. Where others – like Salmon – continued to develop that causal-realist approach as the best way forward from the problems with logical empiricism Putnam chose rather to abandon it in face of the various counter-arguments put up by Goodman and other sceptics. What he hoped to retrieve, nevertheless, was a pragmatist or 'commonsense' realism which would adequately meet those sceptical rejoinders while making no concession to more extreme versions of the adversary case. There is a passage in *The Many Faces of Realism* where he argues for this kind of sensible middle-ground position, one that avoids any wholesale relativist (e.g., Rortian) notion of truth as just 'a matter of what the folks in my culture believe', while also avoiding the metaphysical-realist idea of scientific beliefs as 'approximations to the Universe's Own Scientific Theory', or of moral beliefs as 'approximations to the Universe's Own Moral Truths'. Thus:

> Ruth Anna Putnam has written that we 'make' facts and we 'make' values; but the fact that we make facts and values doesn't mean that they are arbitrary, or that they can't be better or worse. She compares the situation to the making of artifacts; we *literally* make artifacts, and we don't make them according to Nature's Own Blueprint, nor is there always one design which is forced upon all designers by Natural Law (when we make knives, we don't follow The Universe's Own Design for a Knife), but it doesn't follow that the knives we make don't satisfy real needs, and knives may certainly be better or worse. (Putnam, Ruth A. 1985; cited Putnam, H. 1987: 78)

No doubt it is true – and a point worth making against the hardline 'metaphysical' realist, if any such still exist – that objects like knives cannot sensibly be thought of as approximations to an ideal of Knifehood laid down in advance of all practical uses and purposes. Still, there is a strong suspicion, here as so often, that the pragmatist is scoring easy points off a typecast opponent by presenting what amounts to a travesty of their position and then proceeding to knock it down by appealing to our straightforward 'commonsense' grasp of the issues involved. After all, the realist might well respond that we can give an adequate causal explanation of why some knives cut better than others in virtue of their sharpness, cutting-edge serrations, tensile strength, manual balance, ratio of blade-area to handle proportions, and so forth. More than that: the metallurgist can go into detail concerning the particular kinds of steel and their molecular constitution which make for an effective and long-wearing blade, or the particular kinds of material (natural or synthetic) that make for a good sturdy handle.

None of this involves any Platonist appeal to The Universe's Own Design for a Knife, or to Nature's Own Blueprint for the ideal Knife as distinct from the various different sorts of knife that 'satisfy real needs' in various real-world practical contexts. But it does cast doubt on the pragmatist tendency to draw the line at this point and suggest that any further causal-explanatory hypotheses must involve some appeal to occult qualities or some commitment to 'metaphysical' realism in one or another form. As usual Richard Rorty offers an instructive (cautionary) lesson by pushing right through with this line of argument. Thus: '[t]he notion of reality as having a "nature" to which it is our duty to correspond is simply one more variant of the notion that the gods can be placated by chanting the right words' (Rorty 1991: 80). And again: '[t]he source of realist, antipragmatist philosophy of science is the attempt … to make "Nature" do duty for God – the attempt to make natural science a way of conforming to the will of a power not ourselves, rather than simply facilitating our commerce with the things around us' (*ibid.*: 87). Of course Putnam is very far from endorsing such a strong-constructivist or relativist stance since he wants to make the case for a common-sense realism that would have no truck with this old debate between 'metaphysical' realists and their sceptical opponents. Still he leans pretty far in a Rortian direction with his talk of 'Nature's Own Blueprint' or 'The Universe's Own Design', as if these notions are always (surreptitiously) somewhere in the background when realists appeal to 'scientific method' as a means of extending and refining our knowledge of the physical world.

Nicholas Rescher has a nice example which may help to clarify this point with regard to the knife and its various properties as viewed from a causal-realist or a late-Putnam-style pragmatist standpoint (Rescher 1987: 61). Julius Caesar didn't know – had no means of knowing – that his sword was so effective because its blade contained a high proportion of tungsten carbide which allowed it to be honed to a high degree of sharpness and moreover to retain that property despite long and hard use. What gives us a decided advantage in this respect is the fact that we can now offer a more adequate causal explanation as the result of advances in our modern understanding of metallurgy, molecular chemistry and subatomic physics. In other words we now possess what early Putnam – following Richard Boyd – calls a 'mature scientific theory', one in which terms 'typically refer' and in which laws are 'typically approximately true', that is say, true subject to correction as further such advances come about and those terms and theories undergo progressive refinement (Putnam 1975d: 290; Boyd 1984; also McMullin 1984). And again:

> As language develops, the causal and noncausal links between bits of language and aspects of the world become more complex and more various. To look for any one uniform link between word or thought and object of word or thought is to look for the occult; but to see our evolving and expanding notion of reference as just a proliferating family is to miss the essence of the relation between language and reality. The essence of the relation is that language and thought do asymptotically correspond to reality, to some extent at least. A theory of reference is a theory of the correspondence in question. (Putnam 1975d: 290)

While this offers no solution to the 'problem of knowledge', philosophically conceived, and certainly no answer to the sceptic on his or her chosen ground it does provide the best explanation of how science makes progress with regard to particular regions of applied investigative thought.

Thus Putnam is right when he concludes – some twelve years on – that there is 'no such thing as *the* scientific method' and that 'case studies of particular theories in physics, biology, etc., have convinced me that no one paradigm can fit all the various enquiries that go under the name of "science"' (1987: 72). However, I would suggest, the lesson is not so much (after Wittgenstein) that our use of such terms belongs to a 'proliferating family' of language-games nor again (after Rorty) that talk of 'correspondence' is talk about some 'occult' or mysterious relation which amounts to just a form of primitive word-magic. Rather, it is the lesson that our best source of guidance with respect to these philosophic issues is one that looks beyond them to just the kinds of detailed case-study that provide the only possible counter-argument to an outlook of global scepticism. This was early Putnam's most distinctive contribution to issues in philosophical semantics, epistemology, and philosophy of science. Whatever his subsequent doubts under pressure from a range of adversary quarters it is still – I would argue – a viable approach and one that offers a powerful challenge to prevalent forms of anti-realist and sceptical thought.

References

Allison, H. (1983). *Kant's Transcendental Idealism: an interpretation and defense*. New Haven: Yale University Press.

Alston, William P. (1996). *A Realist Conception of Truth*. Ithaca, NY: Cornell University Press.

Armstrong, D.M. (1978). *Universals and Scientific Realism* (2 vols). Cambridge: Cambridge University Press.

Aronson, R. (1989). 'Testing for Convergent Realism', *British Journal for the Philosophy of Science*, XL. 255–60.

Aronson, J., R. Harré and E. Way (1994). *Realism Rescued: how scientific progress is possible*. London: Duckworth.

Austin, J.L. (1962). *Sense and Sensibilia*. Oxford: Clarendon Press.

Ayer, A.J. (ed.) (1959). *Logical Positivism*. New York: Free Press.

Barnes, Barry (1985). *About Science*. Oxford: Blackwell.

Beiser, Frederick C. (1987). *The Fate of Reason: German philosophy from Kant to Fichte*. Cambridge, MA: Harvard University Press.

Blackburn, Simon (1990). 'Wittgenstein's Irrealism'. In Brandt and Haller (eds), 13–26.

Bloor, David (1976). *Knowledge and Social Imagery*. London: Routledge & Kegan Paul.

Boyd, Richard (1984). 'The Current Status of Scientific Realism'. In Leplin (ed.), 41–82.

Brandt, J. and R. Haller (eds) (1990). *Wittgenstein: towards a reevaluation*. Vienna: Holder-Pitchler-Tempsky.

Carnap, Rudolf (1942). *Introduction to Semantics*. Cambridge, MA: Harvard University Press.

—— (1959). 'The Elimination of Metaphysics through Logical Analysis of Language'. In Ayer (ed.) (1959), 60–81.

—— (1967). *The Logical Structure of the World and Pseudoproblems in Philosophy*, trans. R. George. Berkeley & Los Angeles: University of California Press.

Davidson, Donald (1984). 'On the Very Idea of a Conceptual Scheme'. In *Inquiries into Truth and Interpretation*. Oxford: Oxford University Press. 183–98.

—— (1990). 'The Structure and Content of Truth', *Journal of Philosophy*, LXXXVII. 279–328.

Devitt, Michael (1986). *Realism and Truth*, 2nd edn. Oxford: Blackwell.

Diamond, Cora (1991). *The Realistic Spirit: Wittgenstein, philosophy, and the mind*. Cambridge, MA: MIT Press.

Duhem, Pierre (1969). *To Save the Phenomena: an essay on the idea of physical theory from Plato to Galileo*, trans. E. Dolan and C. Maschler. Chicago: University of Chicago Press.

Dummett, Michael (1978). *Truth and Other Enigmas*. London: Duckworth.

—— (1978a). 'Can an Effect Precede its Cause?'. In Dummett (1978), 319–32.

—— (1978b). 'Bringing About the Past'. In Dummett (1978), 333–50.

—— (1978c). 'The Reality of the Past'. In Dummett (1978), 358–74.

—— (1991). *The Logical Basis of Metaphysics*. London: Duckworth.

Dupré, John (1993). *The Disorder of Things: metaphysical foundations of the disunity of science*. Cambridge, MA: Harvard University Press.

Fichte, Johann Gottlieb (1980). *The Science of Knowledge*, trans. and ed. Peter Heath and John Lachs. Cambridge: Cambridge University Press.

Field, Hartry M. (1973). 'Theory-Change and the Indeterminacy of Reference', *Journal of Philosophy*, LXX. 462–81.

Fuller, Steve (1988). *Social Epistemology*. Bloomington, IN: Indiana University Press.

Geertz, Clifford (1983). *Local Knowledge: further essays on interpretive authority*. New York: Basic Books.

Goodman, Nelson (1978). *Ways of Worldmaking*. Indianapolis: Bobbs-Merrill.

Grünbaum, Adolf and Wesley C. Salmon (eds) (1988). *The Limitations of Deductivism*. Berkeley & Los Angeles: University of California Press.

Guyer, Paul (1987). *Kant and the Claims of Knowledge*. Cambridge: Cambridge University Press.

Hacking, Ian (1983). *Representing and Intervening: introductory topics in the philosophy of natural science*. Cambridge: Cambridge University Press.

Harding, Sandra G. (ed.). (1976) *Can Theories Be Refuted? essays on the Duhem-Quine thesis*. Dordrecht: D. Reidel.

Heidegger, Martin (1990). *Kant and the Problem of Metaphysics*, trans. Richard Taft. Bloomington, IN: Indiana University Press.

Horwich, Paul (1990). *Truth*. Oxford: Blackwell.

Johnson, Lawrence E. (1992). *Focusing on Truth*. London: Routledge.

Kant, Immanuel (1964). *Critique of Pure Reason*, trans. N. Kemp Smith. London: Macmillan.

Kirkham, Richard L. (1992). *Theories of Truth*. Cambridge, MA: MIT Press.

Kripke, Saul (1980). *Naming and Necessity*. Oxford: Blackwell.

Kuhn, Thomas S. (1970). *The Structure of Scientific Revolutions*, 2nd edn. Chicago: University of Chicago Press.

Laudan, Larry (1981). 'A Confutation of Convergent Realism', *Philosophy of Science*, XLVIII. 19–49.

Leplin, Jarrett (ed.) (1984). *Scientific Realism*. Berkeley & Los Angeles: University of California Press.

Mach, Ernst (1960). *The Science of Mechanics: a critical and historical account of its development*, trans. T.J. McCormack. La Salle, IL: Open Court.

McCulloch, Gregory (1995). *The Mind and Its World*. London: Routledge.

McDowell, John (1994). *Mind and World*. Cambridge, MA: Harvard University Press.

McMullin, Ernan (1984). 'A Case for Scientific Realism'. In Leplin (ed.) (1984), 8–40.

Misak, C.J. (1995). *Verificationism: its history and prospects*. London: Routledge.

Moore, G.E. (1993). 'Proof of an External World'. In *Selected Writings*, ed. Thomas Baldwin. London: Routledge. 147–70.

Nietzsche, Friedrich (1968). *The Will to Power*, trans. Walter Kaufmann. New York: Vintage Books.

Norris (2000[1]). *Quantum Theory and the Flight from Realism: philosophical responses to quantum mechanics*. London: Routledge.

—— (2000[2]). *Minding the Gap: epistemology and philosophy of science in the two traditions*. Amherst, MA: University of Massachusetts Press.

Nye, Mary Jo (1972). *Molecular Reality*. London: MacDonald.

O'Connor, D.J. (1975). *The Correspondence Theory of Truth*. London: Hutchinson.

Peirce, C.S. (1957). *Essays in Philosophy of Science*. New York: Bobbs-Merrill.

—— (1992). *Reasoning and the Logic of Things*, ed. K.L. Ketner. Cambridge, MA: Harvard University Press.

Perrin, Jean (1923). *Atoms*, trans. D.L. Hammick. New York: van Nostrand.

Psillos, Stathis (1999). *Scientific Realism: how science tracks truth*. London: Routledge.

Putnam, Hilary (1975). *Mind, Language and Reality* (*Philosophical Papers*, Vol. 2). Cambridge: Cambridge University Press.

—— (1975a). 'Is Semantics Possible?'. In Putnam (1975), 139–52.

—— (1975b). 'Explanation and Reference'. In Putnam (1975), 196–214.

—— (1975c). 'The Meaning of "Meaning"'. In Putnam (1975), 215–71.

—— (1978). *Meaning and the Moral Sciences*. London: Routledge & Kegan Paul.

—— (1981). *Reason, Truth and History*. Cambridge: Cambridge University Press.

—— (1983). *Realism and Reason* (*Philosophical Papers*, Vol. 3). Cambridge: Cambridge University Press.

—— (1983a). 'Possibility and Necessity'. In Putnam (1983), 46–68.

—— (1983b). 'Quantum Mechanics and the Observer'. In Putnam (1983), 248–70.

—— (1987). *The Many Faces of Realism*. La Salle, IL: Open Court.

—— (1988). *Representation and Reality*. Cambridge, MA: MIT Press.

—— (1994). 'Sense, Nonsense, and the Senses: an inquiry into the powers of the human mind', *Journal of Philosophy*, XCI:9. 445–517.

—— (1995). *Pragmatism: an open question*. Oxford: Blackwell.

Putnam, Ruth Anna (1985). 'Creating Facts and Creating Values', *Philosophy*, LX. 187–204.

Quine, W.V.O. (1961). 'Two Dogmas of Empiricism'. In *From a Logical Point of View*, 2nd edn. Cambridge, MA: Harvard University Press. 20–46.

—— (1969). *Ontological Relativity and Other Essays*. New York: Columbia University Press.

Reichenbach, Hans (1938). *Experience and Prediction*. Chicago: University of Chicago Press.

Rescher, Nicholas (1979). *Scientific Progress*. Oxford: Blackwell.

—— (1987). *Scientific Realism: a critical reappraisal*. Dordrecht: D. Reidel.

Rorty, Richard (1991). *Objectivity, Relativism, and Truth*. Cambridge: Cambridge University Press.

Salmon, Wesley C. (1984). *Scientific Explanation and the Causal Structure of the World*. Princeton, NJ: Princeton University Press.

—— (1989). *Four Decades of Scientific Explanation*. Minneapolis: University of Minnesota Press.

Salmon, Wesley C. (ed.) (1979). *Hans Reichenbach: logical empiricist*. Dordrecht: D. Reidel.

Schopenhauer, Arthur (1969). *The World as Will and Representation*, trans. E.F.J. Payne (2 vols). New York: Dover.

Schwartz, Stephen (ed.) (1977). *Naming, Necessity, and Natural Kinds*. Ithaca, N.Y.: Cornell University Press.

Smith, Peter J. (1981). *Realism and the Progress of Science*. Cambridge: Cambridge University Press.

Stroud, Barry (1984). *The Significance of Philosophical Scepticism*. Oxford: Oxford University Press.

Tarski, Alfred (1956). 'The Concept of Truth in Formalized Languages'. In *Semantics and Metamathematics*, trans. J.H. Woodger. Oxford: Oxford University Press. 152–278.

Tooley, M. (1988). *Causation: a realist approach*. Oxford: Blackwell.

van Fraassen, Bas (1980). *The Scientific Image*. Oxford: Clarendon Press.

—— (1989). *Laws and Symmetries*. Oxford: Clarendon Press.

Williams, Michael. (1996). *Unnatural Doubts: epistemological realism and the basis of scepticism*. Princeton, NJ: Princeton University Press.

Wittgenstein, Ludwig (1958). *Philosophical Investigations*, trans. G.E.M. Anscombe. Oxford: Blackwell.

Wright, Crispin (1986). *Realism, Meaning, and Truth*. Oxford: Blackwell.

—— (1992). *Truth and Objectivity*. Cambridge, MA: Harvard University Press.

5

How many positrons make five?
Science, scepticism and the 'ready-made world'

I

We have now seen something of the long and complicated path that Putnam has travelled from the causal-realist approach to issues in philosophical semantics, epistemology and philosophy of science which typified his writings of the early 1970s to the 'naturalised' or commonsense-pragmatist outlook developed in his work during the 1990s. What first led him to embark on this path was his acceptance of certain arguments that appeared to pose a large obstacle to realism on any strong (objectivist or non-framework-relative) construal. Among them were the problem of mereological sums – the possibility of counting objects in different ways, e.g., one-by-one or in various superadded group configurations – and, more generally, that of drawing any sharp line between properties we 'discover' in the world and properties we 'project' on to it according to some given conceptual scheme or descriptive-explanatory purpose. (See especially Putnam 1978, 1981, 1983.) These doubts about realism were further reinforced by Putnam's engagement with Wittgenstein on the topic of rule-following; his encounter with the paradoxes of set-theory and kindred problems in the conceptual foundations of mathematics; his work on the philosophy of quantum mechanics; and – above all – his protracted effort to salvage some workable theory of truth from the difficulties raised by Michael Dummett and other exponents of a refined verificationist approach (Putnam 1983, 1987, 1988). So it was that Putnam gave up the hopeless attempt – as he now saw it – to vindicate the truth-claims of physical science by appealing to a 'world' whose existence, nature and intrinsic properties were conceived as 'objectively' transcending the scope and limits of our knowledge. From then on his chief endeavour was to show how we could still claim to be 'realists' in a meaningful sense of that term while renouncing the deluded (metaphysical and self-contradictory) idea that what justified this claim was our somehow having access to just such a realm of objective or non-epistemic truths (Putnam 1994[1], 1995).

Stage One was the phase of 'internal realism' which Putnam offered as a kind of scaled-down (naturalised or detranscendentalised) Kantian approach that retained the idea of an objective reality beyond phenomenal appearances while denying that we could ever have knowledge of it except under some framework-relative description. However, this argument soon came to strike him as just another version of the same old subject–object or mind-world dualism that had plagued philosophy from Descartes, through Kant, to Carnap and the logical empiricists. That is to say, it did nothing to close the gap between 'objective' truth-values conceived as existing beyond our furthest epistemic reach and whatever counts as knowledge (or warranted belief) for creatures equipped with our partic-ular range of sensory inputs, cognitive capacities, powers of rational inference, and so forth. Middle-period Putnam saw a means of overcoming this dichotomy in the idea of truth as what knowledge would amount to – counterfactually speak-ing – when all the evidence was gathered in and subject to a process of rational appraisal under 'ideal epistemic circumstances' (1981). Still this left an opening for sceptics to make their standard anti-realist point, namely that truth is verification-dependent *even at the ideal limit* and hence not 'objective' in any sense that the realist could see fit to endorse. It was mainly in response to such arguments – very often of his own devising – that Putnam moved on from 'internal realism' to a standpoint of 'moderate verificationism' which supposedly retained the best features of a commonsense-realist approach while acknowledging the force of such sceptical challenges (1987). However, it remained far from clear how one could possibly defend a realist position on which truth came out as ultimately subject to the scope and limits of human understanding. Putnam's strategy at this stage was to give up the notion of 'ideal epistemic circumstances' and in stead bring the argument back down to earth by talking in more homely pragmatist terms of our 'natural cognitive relations with the world' (1994[1]). Even so, it is hard to see how this could resolve the age-old philosophic problem – going back at least to Plato's *Theaetetus* – concerning the criteria for genuine knowledge as opposed to 'natural' (or naturalised) commonsense belief. For if one thing stands out from the history of scientific progress to date it is the fact that advances have often been achieved through a radical break with what had previously counted as truths self-evident to reason or beliefs so integral to our commonsense-intuitive grasp of the world that they seemed secure beyond rational doubt.

Such was the process – to take the most obvious examples – that led from Ptolemaic to Copernican astronomy, from Euclidean to non-Euclidean geo-metries, and from Newtonian to Einsteinian conceptions of spacetime physics. In each case it involved a challenge to received ways of thinking whose truth had previously been taken as a matter of *a priori* warrant or as borne out by the entire range of our perceptual and cognitive experience. In each case, moreover, it entailed some far-reaching revisions or adjustments to our sense of where the boundary should properly be fixed between the various orders of necessary and contingent truth, analytic and synthetic statements, or *a priori* and *a posteriori* knowledge. (See Putnam 1983 for further discussion.) Thus there is general agree-ment (at least among philosophers of science) that Kant's epistemology is seriously weakened by his arguing that certain presumptive truths – like those of Euclidean geometry and Newtonian physics – are synthetic *a priori* and hence unrevisable since they constitute the very conditions of possibility for human knowledge and experience (Kant 1964).

Of course this is not to say that philosophy should always be science-led to the point of renouncing all its normative claims or its entitlement on occasion to

criticise certain forms of scientific reasoning. Still less is it to argue that philosophers can never be justified when they object to the kinds of far-fetched metaphysical or speculative theorising that scientists – physicists especially – are
sometimes prone to indulge on the basis of large extrapolations from minimal or
dubious evidence. Indeed, it seems to me that a large factor in Putnam's retreat
from his early causal-realist position was his tendency to be somewhat over-
impressed by conceptual problems in various fields – such as quantum mechanics
– where realism was not so much ruled out by conclusive reasoning on the
evidence as subject to the kind of orthodox veto that flatly rejected any realist
construal (Putnam 1975[1]a, 1975[1]b, 1975[1]c, 1975[1]d), 1983a, 1983h). Thus
Putnam is the last thinker of whom it might fairly be claimed that he – like Kant
– allows certain deep-laid philosophical preconceptions to dictate what should or
could properly count as a valid scientific truth-claim. However, it is possible for
philosophers to lean too far in the opposite direction, that is, toward a science-led
treatment of issues in epistemology and philosophy of language which fastens
selectively on just those problematic topoi that seem *within the limits of our
present-best conceptual grasp* to support an anti-realist conclusion. Then the way
appears open to a generalised statement of the case which takes such instances to
challenge or subvert any argument for scientific realism as the best theory by
which to explain the steady advancement in our powers of predictive and depth-
explanatory grasp.

Putnam's engagement with quantum theory is one clear example of this
marked preference for problem-areas or unresolved dilemmas in the more
advanced theoretical quarters of present-day physical science. Thus, in brief, he
accepts the widely held notion of quantum mechanics as requiring nothing less
than a wholesale transformation in our 'classical' framework of causal-explanatory
concepts and – beyond that – an equally drastic revision to such ground-rules of
classical logic as bivalence or excluded middle. Hence Putnam's outright denial, in
response to Ian Hacking, that positrons can be 'counted' or thought to possess
any kind of discrete numerical identity, let alone objective (measurement-
independent) values of position and momentum (Putnam 1995: 59; Hacking
1983). On the contrary, he argues: we must think of them as somehow existing in
a 'superposed' quantum state which prohibits the assignment of such classical
values until the system is momentarily measured and the wave-packet thereby
reduced or 'collapsed' into one or another macrophysically observable condition.
In which case surely we should give up the naive objectivist belief that the truth-
value of our various statements is fixed by the way things *actually are* – i.e., by
some standard of non-observer-relative or verification-transcendent truth – quite
apart from the particular descriptive framework or ontological scheme that we
bring to bear in the process of observation/measurement. For if this is the message
from quantum mechanics – a theory whose conceptual problems are far
outweighed by its high (indeed overwhelming) degree of predictive-observational
success – then, according to Putnam, it is one with much wider implications for
science and philosophy of science in general.

However, this raises a number of questions which I have discussed elsewhere at some length and will here rehearse in summary form (Norris 2000). First, it ignores the two major problems – those of 'Schrödinger's cat' and 'Wigner's friend' – which result from the idea that the wave-packet is collapsed only through an act of conscious or sentient observation, thus requiring not only that the cat must remain in a superposed (dead-and-alive) state until the box is opened for inspection, but also that the observer be likewise suspended between the two possible outcomes until observed by another sentient being, and so on through an infinite regress (Schrödinger 1980; Wheeler and Zurek (eds) 1983). This was why Schrödinger considered his parable a *reductio ad absurdum* of the orthodox theory, whatever the 'strange but true' response that it has often evoked among popularising commentators. Second, there is the failure of orthodox quantum theory to come up with any adequate solution to the measurement problem, that is to say, the problem of explaining just where – at what point on the micro- to macro-physical scale – this collapse comes about and thereby ensures that we live in a world of determinate objects and events that don't display such unnerving properties as that of showing up in two places at once or only when and where we happen to look (Rae 1986; Squires 1994). Third, it is hard to make sense of any claim for the virtues of a so-called 'quantum logic' which aims primarily to 'keep the physics simple' (i.e., to minimise conflicts with the range of observational-predictive data) even if this means renouncing classical two-valued logic in response to phenomena like superposition or wave/particle dualism. For then – as with Quine's kindred suggestion – there could be nothing to prevent one from redistributing truth-values across the whole 'web' of existing beliefs on a 'vaguely pragmatic' principle of least resistance that simply ruled out any conflict between theory and evidence or prior commitments and empirical results which would otherwise count decisively against them (Quine 1961). Thus the adoption of a full-fledged 'quantum-logical' approach would amount to a vote of no confidence in the very possibility of assessing rival theories or interpretations on rational comparative grounds (Gibbins 1987; Haack 1974; Mittelstaedt 1994).

This leads on to the fourth main problem with orthodox QM thinking, namely its lack of any adequate *explanation* for just those advances in a range of applied technological fields – at the macro as well as the microphysical level – which are perfectly in line with established QM predictive-observational results but which the orthodox theory tells us to regard as inherently beyond reach of any such deeper causal-explanatory account. In which case – fifth – it is a curious (not to say scandalous) feature of this whole debate that, at least until recently, so few physicists have been willing to consider David Bohm's proposals for an alternative theory that perfectly matches all the standard QM formalisms, predictions, and empirical measurement-data but which renders them compatible with a realist interpretation (Bohm 1957; Bohm and Hiley 1993; Cushing 1994; Holland 1993). Thus, according to Bohm, we can think of particles as possessing a full range of objective values for location, momentum, or spin *at every point in their trajectory* and hence irrespective of whether or not they happen to be 'measured' at some

given point or with respect to some given parameter. Any uncertainty can therefore be placed on the side of our limited knowledge or restricted powers of observation, rather than requiring that it somehow pertain to the very nature of
quantum-physical 'reality'. In short, Bohm's approach has the signal merit of
offering a causal-explanatory account which effectively resolves the measurement
problem, avoids the kinds of paradox (or infinite regress) that result from the
orthodox theory, and moreover provides an intuitable picture of events and trans-
actions at the quantum level. This is not to deny that the Bohmian account has
its own share of problems and conceptual difficulties when worked out in
adequate detail. Among them are the complex mathematics involved, the elusive
character of the force-field (or 'quantum potential') that defines the overall state
of the system, and above all the fact – as Bohm readily concedes – that it has to
take on board the evidence of remote faster-than-light interaction or 'entanglement' between widely separated particles. But if one sets these problems against
its strengths as a theory that conserves and extends the body of existing scientific
knowledge then they are likely to appear somewhat less than decisive in any
rational weighing of the evidence.

My point – once again – is that Putnam's allegiance to the orthodox interpretation of quantum mechanics is not so much a matter of respecting the present
best state of scientific knowledge but rather a distinct philosophical *parti pris*
which predisposes him toward an anti-realist stance on this and wider issues of
ontology and epistemology. More precisely, quantum theory figures in his thinking as yet another instance – perhaps the most crucial – of the way that naive
('metaphysical') realism has lately come up against intractable problems which
cannot be resolved without a large-scale revision to those old-style 'objectivist'
conceptions of knowledge and truth (Putnam 1975[1], 1983). Yet there is something decidedly odd about a theory that draws such extreme revisionist lessons
from a branch of physics so rife with as-yet unresolved conceptual dilemmas and
so much given over to speculative theories that run far ahead of the available
evidence. This oddity is all the more striking, as I have said, if one considers the
full implications of Putnam's proposal for revising the ground-rules of classical
logic – and along with them the most basic standards of evidential reasoning – in
response to various quantum anomalies such as superposition and wave/particle
dualism. What that proposal amounts to is a technique for effectively transposing
these conceptual problems from the domain of quantum theory to the domains
of ontology, epistemology, and philosophy of logic. That is to say, it shifts the
burden from physics – or one interpretation of certain quantum-physical
phenomena – to philosophy conceived as a second-order discourse whose main
purpose is to clear the way for whatever transformations physics might require in
our concept of knowledge or even (at the limit) our hitherto accepted canons of
logical thought.

However, one then has to ask what could possibly count as evidence for or
against some given theory or as rational grounds for revising one or other of our
standing doxastic commitments where conflicts arise within the overall Quinean

'fabric' of beliefs (Haack 1974). On this view such conflicts could only be a matter of short-term localised strain since any major anomalies – or logical problems – would be smoothed out as soon as they appeared by making suitable coherence-preserving adjustments elsewhere in the fabric. Moreover, there is nothing – 'pragmatic inclination' aside – that could settle the issue as between different kinds of adjustment, whether at the observational periphery (where one might always doubt the evidence of the senses or the accuracy of one's observational equipment in order to protect some cherished theory), or again at the so-called logical core (where the ground-rules can always be revised or suspended in order to conserve conflicting items of empirical evidence). Quine is fully prepared – at least in 'Two Dogmas of Empiricism' – to endorse this full-scale holistic approach and (presumably) the various problematic consequences that flow from it, among them the thesis of radical paradigm-incommensurabilty and the relativisation of truth-values to whatever descriptive framework or conceptual scheme one happens to adopt (Quine 1961). In Putnam's case things are more complicated since, as we have seen, he has never gone quite so far along this path as to endorse such a wholesale framework-relativist approach. Indeed, his main reason for proposing an alternative (three-valued) quantum logic was that this seemed the only viable option if one wished to respect the empirical evidence of phenomena such as wave/particle duality and yet to maintain a qualified realist outlook that avoided the resort to phenomenalism, instrumentalism, or other such face-saving strategies (Putnam 1975[1], 1983). Nevertheless, it may be thought that Putnam's chosen solution was one that ironically played a large part in his subsequent embrace of an 'internal' (framework-relativised) realism and thereafter in the various compromise positions that he has taken up in recent years. For this choice left him open to the kind of anti-realist objection brought against him by Dummett who argued – in the context of quantum-theoretical debate – that any such proposal to revise the ground-rules of classical (two-valued) logic was an option that must either turn out to be incoherent or else require that one assert no claim regarding the existence of objective (verification-transcendent) truths (Dummett 1978a).

II

I have written elsewhere about this issue between Putnam and Dummett and the way that Dummett-type anti-realism can always trump any argument premised on the revisability of logical 'laws' in response to empirical anomalies such as those thrown up by quantum mechanics on the orthodox construal (Norris 2000). My main point here is that Putnam's choice was dictated not so much by the proven or empirically established necessity of interpreting QM phenomena in this way but rather by a certain preconceived view which already ruled out any realist solution along alternative (e.g., Bohmian) lines. The same can be said about Putnam's engagement with issues in other fields, among them – most importantly – the conceptual foundations of mathematics and elementary number theory. Briefly stated, his position here is that we just don't have any working conception of these matters that would manage to explain (1) how mathematical truths can be 'objective' and therefore in principle transcend our present-best and even best-possible methods of proof or ascertainment, and (2) how we can gain knowledge concerning such truths since on this account – by very definition – they must lie beyond our furthest conceptual grasp (Putnam 1975[1]). Among his most-favoured arguments to this effect are the 'Polish logicians' problem about counting objects either one-by-one or in various combinatorial arrangements and the Löwenheim–Skolem theorem according to which there is no possible formalisation of set-theory that would provide an adequate (consistent and paradox-free) foundation for mathematics (Putnam 1987). Thus, on Putnam's account, there is an inbuilt contradiction in the claim that mathematical truths are both objective and knowable, i.e., that they hold good independently of our theories, methods, or proof-procedures yet can somehow be *known* to possess this status by use of (what else?) those same theories, methods or procedures.

In short, Putnam agrees with the sceptical verdict pronounced by Paul Benacerraf in his well-known essay 'What Numbers Could Not Be', namely that 'nothing works' in the philosophy of mathematics since objectivity is bought at the cost of knowledge and knowledge at the cost of giving up any claim to objective (verification-transcendent) truth (Benacerraf 1983; Putnam 1994[2]a). Of course it is always open for the thoroughgoing naturalist – in mathematics as elsewhere – to grasp the second horn of this putative dilemma and say, in effect, 'so be it: let us do without that whole abstract ontology of numbers, sets, truth-values, etc., and bring the debate down to earth by simply quantifying over concrete objects with some definite space-time location'. (See for instance Maddy 1990.) On this view the quarrel between realists and anti-realists is just a product of the same old Platonic hang-up which compels philosophers to seek something more – some ultimate truth-behind-appearances – that would serve as a bulwark or last guarantee against the threat of sceptical doubt. Thus the realist (or Platonist) about numbers and sets is merely one who has been over-impressed by the strength of that threat and who has failed to see how mathematicians – like physicists and everybody else – can carry on perfectly well once relieved of these pointless metaphysical worries. What is required, therefore, is a naturalised approach that finds no room for such hyperinduced philosophic problems and which takes a lead from thinkers like Quine in treating epistemology as a branch of empirical psychology whose methods and interests are continuous with those of the natural sciences. That is to say, it is a matter of observing how physically constituted creatures like ourselves when subject to various sorts of incoming sensory stimuli will set about the business of individuating objects, counting, adding, multiplying, assigning those objects to sets, and so forth (Quine 1969a). Strangely enough Quine himself professes to be a Platonist with regard to mathematical entities such as numbers and sets. Yet this Platonism has sharp limits when it comes to epistemological issues and the need – as he sees it – to adopt a naturalistic standpoint from which those issues can be made to appear just a residue of our misplaced attachment to old forms of 'metaphysical' thought.

Still there is an obvious problem here and one that Putnam is acutely aware of despite the clear signs, in his later work, of a movement away from objectivist realism and toward some form of naturalised epistemology. It is the problem of explaining – if one accepts this view – how we could ever make sense of those various 'abstract' entities whose status may indeed be problematic yet whose strictly indispensable role in our thinking cannot be denied without producing further (and yet more intractable) problems. After all, as Jerrold Katz very pointedly asks,

> How can numbers and sets be naturalised? How can it even be meaningful to ascribe physical location to a number or a set? How can there be enough natural objects for all the numbers and sets? Where is the null set? Is it in more than one place? What explanation can be given for the special certainty, if not the necessity, of mathematical and logical truths? (Katz 1998: 18)

One could tell much of the story of Putnam's thinking over the past three decades as an attempt to answer these questions in a way that would acknowledge their force – thus granting something more to mathematical truth than can be captured in purely naturalistic terms – while treating them as *ultimately* pseudo-problems which should lose much of their anxiety-provoking power once subject to reinterpretation along broadly naturalistic (or pragmatist) lines. What has made this attempt so difficult is Putnam's awareness of the problems that ensue from any approach, such as Quine's, which adopts a thoroughgoing physicalist standpoint and which thereby excludes the normative dimension bound up with all claims to distinguish veridical knowledge from belief-states or 'assenting dispositions'. For on the Quinean account this distinction drops out in favour of a naturalised epistemology that leaves no room for such normative talk except (maybe) in so far as it figures in the kinds of response that subjects typically produce when prompted to offer some justification for their various reasoning practices. In which case 'normative' is just another word – like 'knowledge' and 'truth' – whose utterance on this or that occasion can best be explained through their acquired disposition to talk like that in certain contexts or under certain physically specifiable conditions.

Here it is worth recalling the familiar passage where Quine puts his case for this naturalised approach in the strongest possible terms. I cite it mainly in order to suggest both the extent to which Putnam has been influenced by this way of thinking and the extent to which he has held out against it for just the kinds of reason canvassed above, i.e., that it altogether fails to explain the normative or justificatory dimension of mathematics and other truth-seeking disciplines. Thus, according to Quine,

> [e]pistemology, or something like it, simply falls into place as a chapter of psychology and hence of natural science. It studies a natural phenomenon, viz., a physical human subject. This human subject is accorded a certain experimentally controlled input – certain patterns of irradiation in assorted frequencies, for instance – and in the fullness of time the subject delivers as output a description of the three-dimensional world and its history. The relation between the meager

input and the torrential output is a relation that we are prompted to study for somewhat the same reasons that always prompted epistemology; namely, in order to see how evidence relates to theory, and in what ways one's theory of nature transcends any available evidence. (Quine 1969a: 82–3)

Putnam has never gone anything like so far in a reductive physicalist direction or exhibited anything like this degree of studied insouciance with regard to normative issues. Indeed it is one of his chief objections to naturalised epistemology in the Quinean mode that it utterly fails to explain how we could ever achieve the kind of knowledge – in mathematics, logic, or the more theoretical branches of the physical sciences – that by its very nature 'transcends any available [at any rate empirical] evidence'. (See Putnam 1983b, 1983c, 1983d, 1983g.) Thus Putnam would be quick to point out that it remains a total mystery, on Quine's account, how the 'meager input' of sensory data or surface irritations should somehow give rise to the 'torrential output' of theories, conjectures, rational hypotheses, inferences to the best (most adequate) explanation, and so forth. That is to say, Quine's resolutely physicalist approach leaves him with a yawning gulf between 'evidence' and 'theory', and with no means of explaining their 'relation' except through the appeal to a process of *ad hoc* belief-adjustment which offers least resistance to entrenched (stimulus-conditioned and reinforced) habits of response. At any rate there seems little substance to his claim that this project is undertaken 'for somewhat the same reasons that always prompted epistemology'. For the result – if Quine's programme were carried right through – would be a drastically reductive behaviorist version of epistemological enquiry that lacked any normative or justificatory grounds.

One can therefore see why Putnam has been at such pains to distinguish his own understanding of pragmatism – and also his conception of 'naturalised' epistemology – from anything that too closely resembles the Quinean approach. He finds the same problem with Davidson's idea that one can do without talk of 'conceptual schemes' or other such gap-filling devices just so long as one accepts a straightforward causal theory whereby the 'content' of our various statements and beliefs is determined directly through the impact of physical stimuli on our sensory receptors (Davidson 1984). According to Davidson this approach has the signal merit of putting us back in 'unmediated' touch with those real-world circumambient objects and events whose 'antics' are just what make our sentences about them determinately true or false (*ibid.*: 198). It thus provides a ready means of resolving all those pseudo-dichotomies – mind and world, subject and object, conceptual scheme and empirical content – that have exerted such a baneful influence on philosophy from Descartes and Kant to the logical empiricists and even (albeit in residual form) on Quine's approach in 'Two Dogmas'. However, Putnam argues, the 'real worry' with any such causal account is that 'sentences cannot be true or false of an external reality if there are no justificatory connections between things we say in language and any aspects of that reality whatsoever' (Putnam 1995: 65). And again: 'if "the cause" is supposed to be something non-conceptual, something simply "built into" the extra-linguistic world, then we get a monstrously unrealistic view of causation' (*ibid.*: 65). 'Unrealistic', that is, in the sense that it over-extends a certain kind of narrowly physicalist causal-explanatory account to the point where this leaves no room for normative criteria or the exercise of rational judgement.

So it is that a professed Davidsonian like Richard Rorty can claim to be a 'realist' for all practical purposes, i.e., in so far as he can happily endorse the claim that the impact of photons on Galileo's eyeball *via* the telescope was what convinced Galileo with respect to the moons of Jupiter (Rorty 1991: 81). Yet it is also what enables him to argue that this kind of 'realism' is perfectly compatible with the claim that interpretation goes 'all the way down', or so far down as to leave it finally an open question whether Galileo was right or wrong in maintaining their existence as against the more orthodox (theologically motivated) astronomers of Padua. For at the baseline level of unmediated sensory 'inputs' there is nothing to distinguish the two interpretations of those incoming sensory data. Rather the disagreement arises only at the stage where – in Davidson's parlance – stimuli are always 'under some description' or other, and thus become subject to variant construals in line with different (in this case sharply conflicting) doctrinal allegiances. Thus the end-point of Quine's physicalist epistemology is a theory of belief-fixation which on the one hand reduces knowledge to a product of unmediated causal 'impacts' while on the other it affords maximum scope for all manner of interpretive adjustments or revisions. What is conspicuously lacking on this account is any means of explaining how *some* interpretations (e.g., Galileo's) turned out to possess a more adequate degree of jointly empirical and theoretical warrant while others (e.g., that of the orthodox-minded astronomers) eventually ran up against intractable problems in just that regard. Once again, it is the absence of a normative or justificatory dimension which prevents such a theory from making just the kinds of discriminative judgement that are surely required of any adequate approach to the philosophy and history of scientific thought.

As I have said, Putnam is fully alive to these problems and indeed takes them as a chief reason for rejecting 'naturalised epistemology' in the wholesale Quinean or physicalist mode. To this extent he agrees with other critics of Quine – Jaegwon Kim among them – who have raised similar objections. In Kim's words, '[i]f justification drops out of epistemology, knowledge itself drops out of epistemology. For our concept of knowledge is inseparably tied to that of justification .... Knowledge itself is a normative notion. Quine's nonnormative, naturalised epistemology has no room for our concept of knowledge' (Kim 1993: 232). However, Putnam is often deflected from making this case with equivalent force by his reluctance to espouse any version of realism that requires the existence of objective or verification-transcendent truths. Hence his advice – following Wittgenstein – that by far the best cure for these needless metaphysical anxieties is simply to acknowledge the 'primacy of practice' and the fact that such issues can have no bearing on our normal (everyday or scientific) forms of life. Thus: '[t]o know under what conditions a statement ... is assertable is to know under what conditions it is true or liable to be true …. "Assertability" and "truth" are internally related notions: one comes to understand both by standing inside a language-game, seeing its point, and *judging* assertability and truth' (Putnam 1995: 48–9). In which case, he thinks, we shall do best to acknowledge that 'internal' realism is the only version that makes any sense or that doesn't run up against the standard range of objections from a sceptical or anti-realist quarter. That is to say, it avoids the trap that 'metaphysical' realists lay for themselves when they claim access to a realm of objective truth which by very definition (their own definition) tran-scends whatever can be known concerning it.

However, to repeat, this leaves Putnam in an awkward – not to say impos-sible – position from which to accuse anti-realists like Dummett of flouting our 'natural' or 'commonsense' attitude with regard to such matters. For it is precisely Dummett's Wittgensteinian point that we can replace truth-talk with talk about 'warranted assertability' and then carry on just as before with all our practices, language-games, and rule-following activities where the 'rules' in question are those that possess communal warrant and therefore require no further appeal to notions of objective (practice-transcendent) truth (Dummett 1978; Wittgenstein 1958, 1969). Yet despite apparently endorsing this argument – in the passage cited above – Putnam elsewhere takes issue with Dummett on the grounds that it mani-festly fails to explain how we can *know* (in some appropriate sense of the term) that there exist a great many mathematical, scientific, historical and other kinds of truth which exceed our furthest capacities of knowledge (in a different – epis-temic or verificationist – sense). Thus the problem with Dummett's 'global anti-realist' approach, as likewise with deflationist accounts, is that they 'cannot properly accommodate the truism that certain claims about the world are (not merely assertable or verifiable but) *true*' (Putnam 1994[1]: 501). But in order to make this criticism stick Putnam needs to specify just where the difference lies between his own position – that 'assertability and truth are internally related notions' – and the more overt strain of anti-realist thinking which he finds unac-ceptable in Dummett and others. For if 'one comes to understand both by stand-ing inside a language-game' then this leads straight back, *via* Wittgenstein again, to the idea of truth as internal – or relative – to our various communal life-forms, practices, or modes of acculturated being-in-the-world. In which case – to adopt one of Putnam's favoured Jamesian pragmatist criteria – the difference would be one that effectively 'makes no difference', thus bringing him out pretty much in agreement with the anti-realist position.

This problem emerges most clearly when Putnam invokes Wittgenstein in the context of describing what it means to say of someone – for instance, an expe-rienced electrician – that they have grasped the 'point' of some practical activity such as measuring the flow of electrical current. His main quarry here is the old-style positivist (or logical-empiricist) account, exemplified by Carnap, according to which 'the electrician understands this sentence ['current is flowing through a wire'] by knowing that, e.g., it is assertable if the voltmeter needle is deflected, and he recognises that something is a voltmeter by recognising that it has a certain appearance (and it has VOLTMETER printed on it, perhaps)' (Putnam 1995: 46–7; Carnap 1956). Putnam quite rightly objects to this account as failing to describe what it truly means for us to say that the electrician *knows what she is doing* when she measures the current, as distinct from just going through the motions and getting the right result. But instead of arguing that she (and we) have need of a more detailed descriptive and causal-explanatory account Putnam chooses to take the Wittgensteinian path and suggest that we consider 'the language-game of a good electrician' in order to grasp what is involved. For in such cases 'someone who does not see the "point" of the language game, and who cannot imaginatively put himself in the position of an engaged player, cannot judge whether the "criteria" are applied *reasonably* or unreasonably here' (Putnam 1995: 47). Just as, in other contexts, we often feel the need to distinguish between genuine expressions of feeling and those that are feigned or merely 'put on' for effect, so likewise – in matters of practical expertise – we often want to tell the difference between genuine knowledge and the mechanical or rote-like application of methods that could as well be performed by a factory robot. And what alone makes this possible – according to Putnam – is our shared capacity (like that of the 'good' electrician) to grasp those criteria whose proper application is sufficient to manifest a genuine grasp of the practice or activity concerned.

Now in one sense this is plainly sensible advice since the electrician might, by attentive listening, come to learn a great deal about currents, conductivity, voltage differentials, the design and function of voltmeters, and even – if she has an interest in such matters – the theory of electrical charge and transmission through the flow of free electrons. Such is at any rate the kind of explanation that Putnam would most likely have given during his early causal-realist phase. 'Consider [he invites us] the following description of the use of "electricity is flowing through the wire"':

> one uses a voltmeter, etc., to tell if electricity is flowing through the wire. A voltmeter is constructed in such and such a way —— (here, imagine an explanation of how a voltmeter "works" – *not* in observation language). In using a voltmeter it is important to be sure that no electromagnetic fields be present which might affect the accuracy of its readings. (Putnam 1995: 48)

Now undoubtedly this would give reason to conclude not only that the electrician knew what she was talking about – and doing – but also that she counted as an expert in the field, one with an uncommon depth of theoretical knowledge. For it would show that she had grasped a whole range of causally operative mechanisms, properties and features that most effectively *explained* what was going on when the pointer was deflected to a certain number on the scale (or, nowadays, when the digital read-out more accurately registered a certain voltage level). In other words such understanding – realistically construed – offers the best possible grounds for trusting her competence whether as a physicist, a lab technician, or a somewhat over-qualified electrical repairs agent.

However it is Putnam's Wittgensteinian notion of 'language-games', 'practices', and 'life-forms' that leads him to treat this particular case as a paradigm instance of just what it means to manifest 'genuine' knowledge according to shared norms of assertoric warrant. Thus:

> knowing the 'use' of 'current is flowing through the wire' is knowing things like *this*. Of course, much else is presupposed; in fact, acculturation in a technical society, with all that this entails. *Understanding a language game is understanding a form of life.* And forms of life cannot be described in a fixed positivistic meta-language, whether they be scientific, religious, or of a kind that we do not have in Western societies today. (Putnam 1995: 48)

This passage nicely catches the ambivalence of Putnam's argument, that is to say, the marked tension that exists between his residual realist leanings and his Wittgenstein-influenced tendency to equate knowledge (understanding, practical grasp, expertise, competence, theoretical acumen and so forth) with the capacity to manifest that knowledge through forms of expression that play a role in some communal form of life. After all, it is precisely this latter line of thought that motivates Dummett's expressly anti-realist position (Dummett 1978). Thus there is simply no question of taking statements to possess definite (objective and bivalent) truth-conditions except in so far as (1) we have a fully adequate grasp of their meaning as given by those same conditions, and (2) we are in a position either to verify them now through our best current methods and procedures or at any rate to know what would count as verification under improved (humanly attainable) epistemic circumstances. For, according to Dummett, '[i]t is an essential feature of any theory of meaning that will yield a semantics validating classical [i.e., bivalent] logic that each sentence is conceived as possessing a determinate truth-value, independently of whether or not we know it or have at our disposal the means to discover it' (Dummett 1977: 371). However, he thinks, this argument breaks down – and the entire realist structure of assumptions along with it – on the manifest impossibility that we could *know what it meant* for some candidate sentence to be true or false quite apart from our knowing what could or might serve as a means of decisive verification. Thus '[t]he solution is to abandon the principle of bivalence, and suppose our statements to be true just in case we have established that they are' (*ibid.*: 375). Or on Dummett's alternative, more cautious construal: just in case we possess an adequate grasp of what exactly that would entail. And it is but a short step from this anti-realist position (meaning = truth-conditions = method or procedure of verification) to the Wittgensteinian argument that the standards or criteria for warranted assertability are those that consensually count as such within some given language-game or communal form of life. For if objective truth drops out in favour of evidential warrant and if such warrant is conceived as attributable only to those – like Putnam's good electrician – who manifest it in linguistically appropriate ways then indeed it must appear that the relevant criteria can be decided only by reference to communal norms.

Whence, as I have said, the tension that runs through much of Putnam's later writing and which emerges very clearly in the passage cited one paragraph above. The Wittgensteinian influence is there at full strength in his statement that '[u]nderstanding a language game is sharing a form of life', and when he equates the kind of knowledge possessed by the good electrician with her 'knowing the "use" of [expressions such as] "current is flowing through the wire"' (Putnam 1995: 48). On the other hand Putnam is still enough of a realist to concede that '[o]f course, much else is presupposed', including 'acculturation in a technical society, with all that that entails'. Yet even here the concession is quickly withdrawn – or given an implied Wittgensteinian gloss – by the idea that what counts is not so much (as early Putnam would have argued) a grasp of certain real-world properties and causal powers but rather the duly 'acculturated' sense of how to talk about topics in this or that 'technical' register. (Cf. Putnam 1975[2]a, 1975[2]b, 1975[2]c.) No doubt it is the case – as he goes on to claim – that 'forms of life cannot be described in a fixed positivistic meta-language', i.e., through the kind of formalised approach that Carnap and others took as their basis for distinguishing valid (scientifically verifiable) from invalid ('metaphysical' or downright vacuous) statements and pseudo-statements. For one need not follow Quine all the way to his radically holistic conclusion in order to show how that claim ran aground on the problem of producing any version of the verification-principle that came out valid (or meaningful) according to its own specified criteria. Nevertheless one may doubt whether Putnam's disenchantment with this hardline positivistic approach necessarily entails his acceptance of the Wittgensteinian view that 'language-games' or 'forms of life' must always be interpreted from inside, or in keeping with their own *sui generis* standards of rational accountability.

III

It is significant that his main point of reference here is Peter Winch's book *The Idea of a Social Science and its Relation to Philosophy*, a work that pushes further than most with the cultural-relativist interpretation of Wittgenstein's late thought (Winch 1958). Thus on Winch's account, as Putnam construes it, 'the use of the words in a language cannot be described without using concepts which are related to the concepts used *in* the game' (Putnam 1995: 46). For Winch the most interesting test-cases are those – like anthropological attempts to make sense of 'primitive' customs and rituals – where the typical approach (at least until recently) was to draw a sharp contrast between 'their' irrational beliefs and our own, presumptively more adequate ways of describing or explaining those beliefs. Thus Winch takes a strong relativist line in asserting that this is just a form of cultural arrogance and one, moreover, that prevents us from achieving any insight into the various practices involved since it condemns us to a wholly 'external' standpoint with regard to their culture-specific meaning or their role within some particular communal life-form.

This lesson can also be applied – Putnam thinks – to scientific contexts or to cases (like that of the good electrician) where there is also a need for the kind of understanding that only comes with an 'acculturated' grasp of the relevant concepts and expressions. Where critics of Wittgenstein very often go wrong, he believes, is in concluding that this must lead to a doctrine of full-scale cultural relativism since the 'criteria' for knowing what to make of some candidate utterance are thought of as wholly internal to the life-form or language-game concerned, and therefore (in effect) as precluding any challenge from a standpoint outside that system of beliefs. Their criticism could only have force if one took it – like the early positivist exegetes – that Wittgenstein's notion of 'criteria' was such as to imply that 'the use of words can be described in terms of what speakers are allowed to say and do in observable situations' (Putnam 1995: 46). What makes all the difference, he thinks, is the experiential context in which such sayings and doings typically occur, and the extent to which that context inherently transcends any description that we could offer in terms of directly observable behaviour or rule-governed practice. Thus:

> a good electrician relies on 'criteria' in this [i.e., positivistic] sense, to be sure; but when things go wrong (and anyone who has ever repaired his own appliances or fixed a car knows how much can go wrong when one is dealing with the real world) he also knows to distrust the criteria, and the knowledge of when to distrust the criteria is not something that is learned by rules. (*ibid.*: 47)

Rather we should take Wittgenstein's cardinal point that there may indeed be 'rules' in a certain sense, but that 'they do not form a system', and that 'only experienced people can apply them right' (Wittgenstein 1958: 227). However this appeal to 'experience' cannot do the work that Putnam requires of it, any more than the stock Wittgensteinian appeal to 'language-games' or 'forms of life'. That is to say, it offers no support for the case – which he finds best argued by Cora Diamond – that one can take this approach fully on board and still be as realist as one likes about electrical currents, voltmeters, car ignition systems, and so forth (Diamond 1991). After all, if philosophy (in Wittgenstein's famous phrase) 'leaves everything as it is', then it does so only on certain conditions, among them the requirement that we cease raising issues that cannot be resolved by a straightforward recourse to our customary practices and modes of expression. From this point of view 'realism' is itself just another language-game, one that deploys a whole range of internally related concepts and which makes good sense – indeed seems simply incontrovertible – for anyone who shares those same criteria. But there can then be no resisting the cultural-relativist conclusion that other beliefs might go clean against that entire (as we think it) 'realist' worldview and yet possess an equal claim to truth on their own self-validating terms.

Here again Putnam seems torn between this *echt*-Wittgensteinian approach and his realist (minus the quote-marks) conviction that 'criteria' can always be revised or abandoned in the face of recalcitrant evidence. Hence his appeal to the kinds of knowledge that can only be gained through hands-on experience of 'how much can go wrong when dealing with the real world', or to cases like that of the good electrician who knows far more than could ever be captured by a merely observational, behavioural, or rule-based account. Yet he follows Winch in stressing precisely those passages in Wittgenstein's later work which go furthest toward an outright denial that there exists any difference – in point of veridical status –

between the 'language-game' of (say) electrical engineering and that of (say) Zande magical practices or witchcraft beliefs. Thus, according to Putnam, '[t]he value of a form of life is not, in general, something one can express in the language games of those who are unable to share its evaluative interests' (1995: 51). And again: 'Wittgenstein makes it clear that he, standing outside religious language (or affecting to), cannot say that religious language is cognitive or non-cognitive; all he can say is that, from the "outsider's" perspective, the religious man is "using a picture"' (*ibid.*: 49-50). But since *every* language-game – science included – involves some 'picture' or some aspect-relative view of the world then of course it follows (on Wittgenstein's account) that there is no standpoint from which one could rightfully or intelligibly judge between them.

Nor can the appeal to 'experience' be of much use if one wants to distinguish modes of scientific or technical expertise from those other kinds of acculturated belief that characterise religious practices or life-forms. For despite the different 'criteria' involved – such that (for instance) one would scarcely think to evaluate statements of religious belief on empirical or verificationist grounds – still these language-games may all be assessed by at least one common standard, namely the extent to which they manifest a genuine depth of experiential grasp. Thus '[t]he question, the one that we are faced with over and over again, is whether a form of life has practical or spiritual value' (Putnam 1995: 50–1). Putnam's phrasing here is crucially ambiguous as between (1) 'practical *or* spiritual' in a sense that would keep these language-games firmly apart, and (2) 'practical or spiritual' in a sense that stresses not so much their disjunctive character as their manifestation under different 'aspects' according to the various life-forms or practices involved. The former construal is what Putnam needs if he is to make out a plausible case for Wittgensteinian realism. That is, it allows for an interpretation whereby certain (e.g., scientific) language-games are valid just in case they express a working knowledge of objects and events in the real-world physical domain, while others – like statements of religious belief – are subject to no such constraint. Early Putnam could perfectly well have accepted this position since it falls square with his objectivist ontology and his strong causal-realist approach to issues in episte-mology and philosophy of science (Putnam 1975[2]). Nor would he have found anything remiss in the claim that expressions of religious belief make sense – at any rate for those who accept them – according to quite different criteria. What he *would* surely have rejected outright is the second construal of that ambiguous sentence which I cited above. After all, it was a chief tenet of the early-Putnam theory of reference that 'meanings just ain't in the head' since – for a fairly large class of statements – referential content and truth-conditions are fixed by the way things stand in reality, rather than by our present-best state of knowledge concerning them. But in that case it won't do to suggest, after Wittgenstein, that we can get all the realism we need by giving up the delusory appeal to a 'private' realm of meanings, senses, mind-states, etc., and accepting that justification runs out – strikes bedrock – at the point where we invoke communal norms of practico-linguistic 'experience'. For this leaves the problem firmly in place if one goes on to ask why those norms should be thought of as necessarily possessing any greater degree of veridical warrant or authority. The only change, in effect, is a shift from the kind of private-individualist solipsism that Wittgenstein attacked in a number of well-known passages to a collectivised or communitarian version which appeals to the shared understanding of a given cultural life-form.

So for Putnam, to repeat, '"assertability" and "truth" are internally related notions: one comes to understand both by standing inside a language game, seeing its "point"' (1995: 49). But this is already to concede the anti-realist case (as in Dummett's construal of Wittgenstein) that it cannot make sense to posit the existence of truths that exceed our cognitive grasp or for which we possess no presently conceivable means of verification. Take for instance the two contradictory assertions (which I borrow from Scott Soames): (1) 'There is a duplicate of the sun in an inaccessible region of space', and (2) 'There is not a duplicate of the sun in an inaccessible region of space' (Soames 1999: 32). For Dummett these would figure as paradigm cases of statements belonging to the so-called 'disputed class', i.e., statements whose truth-value is epistemically undecidable and which must therefore be counted as not falling under the logical regime of bivalent truth/falsehood (Dummett 1978). Early Putnam, conversely, would have had no problem in declaring that each of these statements possessed an objective truth-value (i.e., was definitely *either* true or false), despite the *de facto* impossibility of our ever getting to know which way around those predicates applied. Late Putnam would, I think, be loth to relinquish that position altogether – or without a struggle – since he sees how quickly its abandonment leads, *via* Dummett-style anti-realism, to the kind of wholesale 'constructivist' outlook espoused by thinkers such as Nelson Goodman (Goodman 1978). What is not so clear is whether Putnam can hold the line against arguments of this sort while also maintaining some version of the Wittgensteinian or internalist approach that purports to defeat the sceptic at first base by giving up all that hopelessly problematic talk of 'objective' truth and reality. (See also Putnam 1983e, 1983f.)

It may help to get these issues into sharper focus if we take a brief return visit to the volume *Starmaking* where Goodman defends his constructivist theses against a number of sceptical or downright incredulous commentators, Putnam among them (McCormick (ed.) 1996). Thus, for Goodman, not only do we 'make' the constellations by grouping stars into various humanly recognisable shapes and patterns but we also 'make' the stars by picking them out, giving them names, and assigning them properties in accordance with our own favoured method of projection. To which his critics routinely respond – in tones ranging from wry amusement to sheer exasperation – that Goodman surely *cannot* mean what he says or, if so, that his argument amounts to just a zany update on well-worn solipsist or Berkeleian idealist themes. Most likely (they suggest) it is a colourful way of making the milder Kantian point that our knowledge of the world is confined to phenomenal appearances and cannot give access to the noumenal reality behind or beyond those appearances. This would at least save

Goodman from his own worst rhetorical excesses, or from the charge that he has simply blundered by confusing ontological with epistemological issues. After all, is it not self-evidently the case that the stars existed long before there were human beings around to observe them, and moreover that they will continue to exist long after the extinction of life on earth or even of our own solar system? No, Goodman answers: just go off and read Kant if you need convincing that space and time are not objective (mind-independent) attributes of some extra-human reality but are rather the very forms – 'external' and 'internal' – under which experience presents itself *to us* as creatures with our particular range of pheno-menal intuitions or world-making concepts and categories. So his critics had better not appeal to Kant if they want to press the point about stars and space-time, especially in view of the ease with which subsequent thinkers – German idealists and modern anti-realists alike – have managed to exploit the problematic gap between Kant's professed doctrines of 'empirical realism' and 'transcendental idealism'.

If this is not enough, then they might consider the evidence from current astrophysics where – according to the quantum cosmologist John Wheeler – the results of certain delayed-choice experiments showing remote faster-than-light 'entanglement' between particles on a laboratory scale can be extended to an arbi-trary distance of spacelike separation, thus entailing the possibility of retroactive causation across billions of light-years as reckoned according to the standard (rela-tivistic) framework. In which case we can somehow – through the act of observa-tion or momentary choice of radio-telescope setting – bring about events which, on a human time-scale, must be thought of as having occurred long 'before' our appearance on the cosmic scene (Wheeler 1978). I have written elsewhere about what I take to be the various philosophical confusions that typify such large-scale extrapolative treatments of the quantum-physical data (Norris 2000). My point is that Putnam has spent much of his time over the past four decades attempting to steer a difficult path between realism of one or another variety and the sorts of challenge that are pushed to an extreme by arguments like those summarised above. Nor is Goodman the only philosopher to have drawn extravagant conclu-sions on the basis of orthodox quantum theory and its various paradoxical aspects. In Dummett's case there is no explicit connection between his thinking on quantum-related issues and his idea that past events can indeed be 'brought about' through our present state of knowledge concerning them, or the kinds of evidence we are able to acquire by the best means at our disposal (Dummett 1978b, 1978c, 1978d). All the same this connection is strongly implied since Dummett's anti-realism informs every part of his work, from philosophy of science and mathe-matics to epistemology, historiography, and issues in ethical theory. Thus, on his account, there is simply no denying that 'gaps in our knowledge' are also 'gaps in reality', that is to say, lacunae which cannot be filled by any self-refuting realist appeal to truth-claims for which *ex hypothesi* we lack any possible means of verifi-cation. And this would lend weight – philosophical weight – to all manner of strong-revisionist claims regarding the knowledge-dependent character of historical events or (at the limit) their status as constructions out of our own present interests, values, and concerns.

This is just the aspect of Dummett's thought which Putnam finds most bothersome, requiring as it does – if taken literally – that *those events themselves* should somehow be thought of as somehow retroactively revisable, rather than as subject to variant interpretations with the passage of time, the discovery of new information-sources, or the shift from one to another ideological viewpoint. Indeed it is a thesis that provokes anxiety in Dummett himself, not least since it might be construed as underwriting such extreme revisionist claims with regard to historical events like the Holocaust. So there is often some doubt – through ambiguities of phrasing – as to whether Dummett intends the argument to be taken at full ontological strength or whether he would accept the more moderate (interpretativist) version which accords pretty much with the working belief of most historians who have resisted infection by the virus of postmodern scepticism. However, this reading is one that encounters strong resistance from other passages in Dummett's work and which goes against the logic of his anti-realist argument when applied to mathematics and the physical sciences. Thus – despite the more technical (logico-semantic) character of Dummett's case – it is always at risk of seeming to endorse a Goodman-type wholesale constructivist outlook that would push right through with the idea that there exist as many worlds as projectible 'world-versions', each with an equal claim to get things right on its own self-validating terms (Goodman 1978). And this idea gains credence from various kinds of cultural-relativist thinking, among them the Wittgenstein-derived argument that language-games and life-forms cannot be compared – much less criticised or adjudicated – from some 'objective' standpoint outside or above their different *sui generis* criteria.

It is clear enough from Putnam's rather bemused response to Goodman that he doesn't know quite how to take this notion that the entire universe – at every scale from the subatomic to the astrophysical – somehow depends on the existence of sentient creatures like ourselves with our particular range of sensory inputs, perceptual modalities, powers of conceptual grasp, and so forth. (See Putnam's various contributions to McCormick (ed.) 1996.) In the end he seems inclined to treat it as a *reductio ad absurdum* of the strong-descriptivist line which others – like Rorty – manage to present in a somewhat more plausible guise. However, one could argue that the whole development of Putnam's thought since the mid-1970s has been moving toward a position that leaves him ill-equipped to counter such arguments. In *Reason, Truth and History* (1981) he is already well along the road to an internalist or framework-relativist approach whereby it can make no sense to single out certain (e.g. scientific) descriptions as somehow more 'objective' or truer to the way things stand 'in reality' than other (e.g., phenomenological) descriptions. After all,

> [i]f we take the physicist's rainbow to be the rainbow 'in itself', then the rainbow 'in itself' has no *bands* (a spectroscopic analysis yields a smooth distribution of frequencies); the red, orange, yellow, green, blue and violet bands are a feature

of the *perceptual* rainbow, not the physicist's rainbow. The perceptual rainbow depends on the nature of our perceptual apparatus itself, on our visual 'world making', as Nelson Goodman has termed it. (The physicist's 'objects' also depend on our worldmaking, as is shown by the plethora of radically different versions physics constructs of the 'same' objects.) ... Vision is certified as good by its ability to deliver a description which fits the objects *for us*, not metaphysical things-in-themselves. (Putnam 1981: 146)

This passage is notable both for its seeming endorsement of Goodman's wholesale constructivist argument and also – what amounts to the same thing – for its readiness to give up that entire 'metaphysical'-realist way of thinking that Putnam had once put forward as the only means of securing reference and explaining our knowledge of the growth of scientific knowledge (Putnam 1975[2]). Thus the sentence in parenthesis – with its scattering of quote-marks – takes it as a simply inescapable conclusion that the physicist's 'objects' are constructed in accordance with some favoured 'way of worldmaking', just as we 'make' the perceptual rainbow (pick out its various salient colours) quite apart from what present-day physics has to tell us concerning what is truly or 'objectively' the case. By the same token – Putnam goes on – 'mathematical intuition is good when it enables us to see mathematical facts "as they are" – that is, as they are in the mathematical world which is constructed by human mathematical practice (including the application of mathematics to other subject matters)' (Putnam 1981: 146). For the only alternative, as he now thinks, is an objectivist (practice-transcendent) conception of mathematical truth which fails to explain how we could ever gain knowledge of that which inherently eludes or exceeds our furthest powers of apprehension.

What emerges very clearly from this passage – and others like it – is the extent to which Putnam has accepted the terms and adopted the logic of anti-realism despite his express misgivings in that regard. Thus he agrees with Benacerraf in thinking that realism (or objectivism) about mathematics must give rise to a strictly insoluble paradox since if truth in such matters is indeed objective then it is not the kind of thing that we could ever get to know or that could possibly play a role in our various reckonings, procedures, scientific practices, and so forth (Benacerraf 1983; Putnam 1994[2]a). However, this assumes that mathematical knowledge can properly or usefully be thought of by analogy with those other kinds of knowledge that involve perceptual acquaintance or – as with the rainbow example – a trade-off between perceptual appearances and the dictates of scientific method. Anti-realism is often made to look plausible by exploiting precisely this idea, i.e., that the realist about mathematics must be a Platonist in the full-blown sense of supposing that we can somehow have epistemic access to abstract entities such as numbers or sets through a process of quasi-perceptual apprehension, a knowledge (like that of the Platonic 'forms') which purports to transcend mere sensory acquaintance while covertly taking it as a model. In which case, of course, the realist position would come out as contradictory or self-refuting in just the way that its critics standardly maintain.

However their arguments will appear less forceful if one acknowledges that other thinkers – Gödel among them – have espoused a realist (and indeed an expressly Platonist) standpoint while not buying into anything like this impossible compromise deal. Thus, as Gödel writes,

> mathematical intuition need not be conceived of as a faculty giving an *immediate* knowledge of the objects concerned. Rather it seems that … we *form* our ideas also of those objects on the basis of something else which is immediately given. Only this something else is *not*, or not primarily, the sensations … . It by no means follows, however, that the data of this second kind, because they cannot be associated with actions of certain things on our sense organs, are something purely subjective, as Kant asserted. Rather, they, too, may represent an aspect of objective reality; but, as opposed to sensations, their presence in us may be due to another kind of relationship between ourselves and reality. (Gödel 1983: 484)

No doubt there are deep philosophical problems when it comes to explaining just what this relationship is or what grounds we can have for claiming knowledge of objective or verification-transcendent truths. These problems have been central to Putnam's thinking from the outset and it would clearly be absurd to suggest that he has not taken account of Gödel's way of framing the issue in the above passage and others like it. Indeed one reason that Putnam often gives for renouncing his early 'metaphysical'-realist position is the belief that it is impossible to endorse such an outlook on account of Gödel's Incompleteness Theorem, that is, his celebrated proof that any system sufficiently complex or powerful to generate the sentences of elementary arithmetic will also contain sentences that cannot be proved within the system but which have to be accepted as axioms (Gödel 1962). For Putnam this constitutes yet further evidence – along with the 'Polish Logicians' problem about mereological sums, the argument from quantum mechanics, and the case of non-Euclidean geometries – for maintaining that we simply cannot have access to an order of *a priori* truth that would hold firm against empirical revision or against any challenge from alternative theories. Hence his long retreat from stage to stage in a progress of deepening scepticism with regard to such presumptive and (as he now sees them) scientifically unwarranted claims.

IV

There is another way of thinking about Gödel's proof, one that has lately been proposed with great vigour by the mathematician and quantum physicist Roger Penrose (1990, 1994). On this account what truly follows from the Incompleteness Theorem is that we *must* be capable of grasping the existence of verification-transcendent truths, i.e., truths for which we possess no existing or finitely computable proof-procedure but which can none the less somehow be known to obtain as a matter of strict necessity. For we could otherwise have no possible reason to accept the Theorem as valid given the impossibility – on Gödel's account – of establishing that its own methods are fully consistent or its conclusion capable of rigorous (axiomatic-deductive) proof. Thus Penrose interprets Gödel's Platonism as involving (1) the assertion that certain kinds of mathematical truth-claim cannot be verified on a straightforward recursive or computational basis, and (2) the assertion – *contra* anti-realists like Dummett – that this gives no reason to think them inherently undecidable or lacking objective content. In other words there are truths that we are capable of grasping despite the fact that they elude any algorithmic method of determination, even with the aid of a maximally powerful computer-run proof procedure.

Penrose derives some far-reaching implications from this argument, among them the claim that artificial intelligence – at least as conceived in computational or functionalist terms – could never in principle come close to reproducing the full scope and capacities of human intelligence. To this extent he agrees with the later Putnam (e.g., in *Representation and Reality*, 1988) who presses a similar case against his own previous espousal of a functionalist theory of belief-content, propositional attitudes, rational-choice procedures, and so forth. However, there is a crucial difference between Putnam's way of making this point – his Wittgensteinian appeal to a context of socialised 'practices' or 'life-forms' that inherently elude any narrowly mentalist conception of meaning and truth – and Penrose's claim for the existence of truths whose objective character is such as to place them beyond the limits of straightforward (computable) verifiability. More precisely, Putnam has two such arguments, one of them deriving from his early causal-realist theory of reference, the other from his subsequent turn toward a broadly pragmatist or Wittgensteinian standpoint. The first maintains – as in his various 'Twin-Earth' thought-experiments – that meanings 'just ain't in the head' since reference is fixed by the way things stand (e.g., at the molecular or subatomic level) with respect to a mind- and language-independent reality (Putnam 1975[2]). This he takes to confute the functionalist thesis that belief-content can be specified in terms of a mental language – Jerry Fodor's 'mentalese' – whose semantic content is subject to various deep-level computational processes (Fodor 1983, 1994; Putnam 1988: 1–56). The second pretty much gives up on this line of thought in favour of a socialised conception where there is still an appeal – as in early Putnam – to the 'linguistic division of labour' but where this is conceived not so much in terms of having experts around who can be relied upon to know the subatomic constitution of 'gold' or the molecular composition of 'water', but rather in terms of a communal warrant that rests on shared language-games, practices, and cultural forms of life. My point is that Putnam has been moving steadily away from any theory that could possibly accommodate Gödel's realist account, that is, his claim that certain truths can be objective (verification-transcendent) and yet accessible to human knowers even when – as with Gödel's Incompleteness-Theorem – they have to do with the absolute limits placed upon our powers of computational proof. For on Putnam's later account, to repeat, what makes mathematical intuitions 'good' is that they enable us to see 'mathematical facts "as they are" – that is, as they are in the mathematical world which is constructed by human mathematical practice' (Putnam 1981: 146). And in this respect they are like our perception of distinct colour-bands in the rainbow, namely, ways of seeing that cannot be denied – rejected as 'incorrect' or objectively false – by some higher-level theory (in mathematics or physical science) which claims access to an order of reality beyond such merely practice-based or 'commonsense' beliefs.

It is evident from various passages in Putnam that he interprets Gödel's 'Platonism' as involving just the sorts of problem that arise from the idea of mathematical knowledge as a kind of quasi-perceptual contact with abstract entities like numbers or sets. Thus:

> Kurt Gödel believed that 'mathematical intuition' was analogous to *perception*: mathematical objects (which he called 'concepts') are *out there*, and our intuition enables us to intellectually perceive these Platonic entities; but few mathematicians would commit themselves to such a Platonic metaphysics. Gödel's comparison of mathematical intuition to perception reveals an over-simple idea of perception. (Putnam 1981: 145–6)

At which point Putnam goes on to develop his argument about the rainbow and the fallacy of thinking that scientific modes of description (e.g., through spectroscopic analysis) should be thought of as somehow displacing or supplanting our everyday perceptual experience. However this analogy will seem distinctly forced if we recall the passage from Gödel cited above and its insistence that mathematical 'intuition' should not be confused with the kinds of 'immediate' knowledge that result from sensory perception or from 'the actions of certain things on our sense organs'. Putnam's proposal – very much in line with his later way of thinking – is that we give up that 'over-simple idea of perception' (a kind of direct realism with regard to mathematical truths) since it runs into all the familiar problems pointed out by critics of Plato from Aristotle down. Rather we should take a much-needed lesson from recent advances in cognitive psychology and the theory of perception, among them – most importantly – lessons concerning the extent to which our 'immediate' perceptual experience is shaped and conditioned by our various modes of sensory and cognitive processing. Thus: '[v]ision does not really give us direct access to a ready-made world, but gives us a description of objects which are partly structured and constituted by vision itself' (Putnam 1981: 146). What the rainbow analogy helps to bring out is this reciprocal dependence between mind and world such that it simply *cannot make sense* to postulate a realm of objective truths that we are somehow mysteriously capable of knowing through a kind of intellectual intuition. All that is needed in order to resolve this otherwise intractable problem is an acceptance that the truths of mathematics – like those of the physical sciences or our everyday perceptual dealing with the world – are products of a complex interactive process which puts us reliably in touch with 'reality' so far as we can know or perceive it. Where the Platonist typically goes wrong – in company with objectivists and hardline realists of various stripe – is in supposing that *something more* is required (some appeal to a mind-independent world or a realm of practice-transcendent mathematical truths) if we want to avoid the slide into relativism or a wholesale constructivist outlook. Much better just acknowledge, in Putnam's laconic formulation, that 'the mind and the world jointly make up the mind and the world' (1981: xi). Or again, 'to make the metaphor even more Hegelian, [that] the Universe makes up the Universe, with minds – collectively – playing a special role in the making up' (*ibid.*).

Thus Putnam's internal-realist approach extends to mathematics – as well as the physical sciences – since mathematical truths must likewise be conceived as dependent on those various knowledge-constitutive practices (computational methods, proof constructions, rule-following procedures, etc.) which decide what shall count as an instance of valid mathematical thought. This is why Putnam rejects the idea that such truths could be 'objective' in Gödel's sense, that is, possess a character of absolute ideal objectivity that is somehow within our intuitive reach while none the less transcending the scope and limits of accustomed mathematical practice. It is also – I have suggested – why he sets aside Gödel's reiterated claim that mathematical knowledge involves a *different kind* of 'intuition', one that has to be clearly distinguished from sensory-perceptual experience. What Putnam finds so implausible about this claim is the fact that it appeals to a realm of *a priori* truths which are self-evident to reason and which can therefore be grasped even where they exceed our best available methods of verification. It is just this point that Penrose stresses in his construal of Gödel's Incompleteness Theorem as proving the power of mathematical thought to yield objectively valid insights which could not be arrived at by application of a rigorous (recursive and fully axiomatised) proof-procedure since they concern precisely the inbuilt limits of any such formal approach (Penrose 1994). For Putnam, conversely, the limits in question are those that philosophy must always encounter when it strives to establish some ground of *a priori* self-validating knowledge which purports to transcend the various practices that 'make up' its very conditions of intelligibility. Thus it follows – on Putnam's account – that one cannot consistently argue the case for realism with respect to mathematical truths without falling back on the Platonist idea that we can access such truths through a form of 'intellectual intuition', or a quasi-perceptual mode of contact with abstract entities such as numbers and sets. Hence (to repeat) his alternative suggestion: that 'mathematical intuition is good when it enables us to see mathematical facts "as they are" – that is, as they are in the mathematical world that is constructed by human mathematical practice' (1981: 146).

Now there are various ways of taking this passage and others to broadly similar effect. Indeed one could argue that Putnam himself has taken most of them at one or another stage, and that the chief value of his later writings is their constant willingness to revise 'old' positions in the quest for some adequate approach. Thus a great deal depends on the idea of 'practice' and on whether his appeal to a practice-based conception of knowledge and truth is understood (after Wittgenstein) in communitarian terms or else according to some other, more objectivist construal. There is textual evidence for both interpretations – sometimes within the space of a page or two – and I think it is fair to say that Putnam never succeeds in resolving the conflict between them. What he does try to do in a number of passages is nudge Wittgenstein toward a middle-ground position that would find room for a notionally 'realist' approach while retaining the idea of communal 'practice' – of language-games, life-forms, agreed-upon ways of proceeding – as a means of deliverance from all these vexing dilemmas. On the one hand, Putnam somewhat ruefully concedes, 'Wittgenstein thought that it was some subset of our institutionalized verification norms that determines what it is right to say in the various "language games" we play and what is wrong, and that there is no objective rightness or wrongness beyond this' (1981: 108). Such a reading is borne out by Wittgenstein's idea that 'agreement in our judgements' is the precondition for having concepts at all, since otherwise we should lack any means of expressing those concepts in a language that made sense to others or indeed to ourselves. Yet surely this cannot be the end of the matter, Putnam muses, since 'it is just too vague who the "we" is in Wittgenstein's talk of "our" judgements; and I don't know whether his "forms of life" correspond to the institutionalized norms I have mentioned' (*ibid*.: 108). What he (Putnam) wants from those 'institutionalized norms' is a practice-based approach to epistemological issues that avoids the Scylla of wholesale cultural relativism while managing to steer successfully around the Charybdis of so-called 'metaphysical' realism. In other words it is a theory which takes full account of Wittgenstein's communitarian arguments but which also makes room for the role of more specialised (e.g., scientific or mathematical) communities in fixing the criteria by which we make sense of various particular truth-claims.

What is not so clear is whether this wished-for solution can be had on anything like such mutually accommodating terms. Thus, for instance, it would have to get around such problems as Wittgenstein's verificationist insistence that the Darwinian theory of species evolution by natural selection through random mutation was widely accepted on inadequate grounds since it lacked anything like the requisite degree of empirical verification (see Putnam 1981: 109n). It is typical of Putnam's intellectual honesty that he cites this passage in a long footnote even though it involves him in yet more strenuous and wire-drawn exegetical endeavours. Thus Wittgenstein: 'Did anyone see this process happening? No. Has anyone seen it happening now? No. The evidence of breeding is just a drop in the bucket' (Wittgenstein 1966: 26). As an argument against evolutionary theory – or even for reserving judgement on the matter – this could scarcely go further in its downright refusal to apply the appropriate criteria, i.e., those of inference to the best (most conceptually adequate) long-term explanatory theory. In fact Putnam goes straight on to cite a passage from the molecular biologist Jacques Monod which convincingly explains why it is far more rational to accept than to reject the basic tenets of Darwinian theory, above all since its claims have been strongly borne out – and its details progressively refined – by the rediscovery of Mendelian genetics (Putnam 1981: 109n). To which one might add, *contra* Wittgenstein, that the process can indeed now 'be seen happening' in the case of bacteria which very quickly respond and adapt to changes in their physical environment. Yet Putnam still takes it that any adequate solution to the problem of scientific realism will have to go by way of a settlement with Wittgenstein on terms that Wittgenstein has pretty much laid down in advance. That is to say, it must at all costs renounce the appeal to an objectivist (practice-transcendent) theory of truth or an external-ist epistemology – like that proposed in his own early writings – that would account for such advances in scientific theory through the fact of their providing more detailed kinds of depth-explanatory knowledge. This despite Putnam's express misgivings with regard to the strongly marked cultural-relativist tendency that he finds in Wittgenstein's later thought and also that strain of doctrinaire verificationism which leads Dummett to narrow down the range of admissible truth-claims to a point where some of the best-supported theories are considered to lack adequate evidential warrant.

One reason why Putnam has been so susceptible to these Wittgenstein-induced quandaries is that he accepts at least one basic tenet of anti-realism, namely the idea that any claim for objective truth-values' – whether in mathe-matics or the physical sciences – is wholly incompatible with any claim for our ability to know or recognise such values. However, his arguments, unlike Dummett's, tend to focus not so much on the logic of anti-realism – i.e., the presumed illogicality of claiming to know what transcends the limits of verifica-tion – as on various particular cases in the history of science and mathematics where different theories can be seen to have entailed a different range of putative realia along with all their likewise disparate imputed properties. It is this line of thought that brings Putnam close – sometimes uncomfortably close – to Goodman's wholesale constructivist claim that we 'make' the stars, just as we 'make' the constellations, through a choice among the manifold world-versions that cannot be ranked on any scale of correctness but must rather be judged according to internal (framework-relative) criteria (McCormick (ed.) 1996). As I have said, Putnam often shies away from endorsing the implications of this argu-ment when pushed to their 'logical' extreme. However, from the mid-1970s on, it figures as a constant point of reference for his case against 'metaphysical' realism and in favour of various internalist, pragmatist, or scaled-down 'commonsense' alternatives. For it is now Putnam's conviction – like Goodman's before him – that any realist case with regard to (say) numbers, sets, microphysical entities, macroscopic objects, or the properties and powers thereof will always come unstuck when it seeks to explain how these can be thought of as somehow exist-ing 'objectively' despite being subject to a wide range of descriptions, theories, conceptual schemes, set-theoretical orderings, causal-explanatory hypotheses, etc. Thus, in Putnam's view, 'metaphysical realism collapses' since it has to assign an objective status and also a truth-preserving interpretation to numerous claims – such as those about 'electrons' at various stages of pre- and post-quantum physics – that can only be subject to meaningful comparison on condition that we give up defending such a view. All the same, he continues, we need not worry too much since 'internal realism ... doesn't collapse' but rather comes out consider-ably strengthened by the demise of its erstwhile rival. For '[m]etaphysical realism was only a *picture* anyway. If the picture is, indeed, incoherent, then the moral is surely *not* that something is wrong with realism *per se*, but simply that realism *equals* internal realism. *Internal realism is all the realism we need* (Putnam 1978: 130).

V

Still one may suspect that his assurance on this point is not so much a matter of our really having left all those old 'metaphysical' problems behind as of Putnam's hope that an adequate solution is somewhere in the offing. Moreover, it will seem distinctly optimistic if one recalls the various unresolved problems and tensions in his later work. Chief among them is the fact that 'internal realism' is a highly unstable theory, offered as a remedy for sceptical doubt and as 'all we need' by way of effective counter-argument, yet tending very often – despite this claim – toward a strong anti-realist position. Such is the following (fairly typical) passage from *Reason, Truth and History* in which Putnam draws what he takes to be the strictly unavoidable consequence from cases, like that of the term 'electron', where theory-change must be thought to bring about a radical shift in meaning and reference. '"Objects" do not exist independently of conceptual schemes. *We* cut up the world into objects when we introduce one or another scheme of description. Since the objects *and* the signs are alike *internal* to the scheme of description, it is possible to say what matches what.' (Putnam 1981: 52) But if this is 'all the realism we need' – in Putnam's sanguine view – then it is also just what the sceptic needs in order to press her argument home. That is, she has only to repeat Putnam's point: that any notion of correctness (of 'what matches what') must be framework-internal or theory-relative, along with all the various object-terms, predicates, imputed properties, and so forth, which make up a given ontological scheme. Of course there is a possible saving ambiguity in the quote-marks around 'objects', in so far as this might suggest either (1) that *our talk* about them is scheme-relative (even though they belong to a scheme-independent or real-world object-domain), or (2) that the very idea of 'objectivity' is one that we shall have to give up with the shift to an internal-realist perspective. Putnam never quite brings himself to break altogether with the first (realist) construal, since it offers an escape-route from the various kinds of fargone sceptical or cultural-relativist doctrine which he finds unacceptable. Yet he strongly implies that any talk of 'objects' as existing apart from our various descriptive schemes must be counted a mere 'metaphysical' delusion which collapses as soon as one reflects on the evidence of theory-change in the physical sciences.

To the extent that causal explanations play a role in Putnam's thinking at this time they do so very often in a curiously roundabout fashion which he takes to strengthen the internalist case and to constitute an argument against any form of objectivist realism. The above-cited passage from *Reason, Truth and History* comes after a discussion of the way that theoretical terms like 'electron' are introduced into the discourse of science and thereafter undergo radical changes which – on Putnam's internalist account – entail that they must be construed as referring to different 'objects' and different ontological schemes. A causal theory simply won't

work, he declares, since 'the dominant cause of my belief about electrons is probably various *textbooks*', even though – despite this causal connection – 'the occur-
rences of the word "electron" I produce … do not *refer* to textbooks' (1981: 51). At
this stage Putnam is at the furthest point of retreat from the kind of causal-realist
thinking that had been a chief feature of his early work. Hence – I would suggest
– the somewhat ludicrous idea that a causal explanation of our usage of a term like
'electron' might involve no more than the word's having prompted some reflex
response through our having come across it in our reading around on the topic.
What drops completely out of sight on this account is the kind of causal-explanatory approach that Putnam (along with Kripke) had once developed to a high
point of philosophical refinement (Putnam 1975[2]; Kripke 1980; also Schwartz
(ed.) 1977).

Thus – to recapitulate – such terms have their reference fixed by an initial act
of designative naming and thereafter retain sufficient continuity or stability of
usage despite various theory-related shifts in our conception of 'atoms', 'molecules', 'electrons', etc. It is a causal account firstly in the sense that this property
can only be explained by assuming the existence of a series of links – a continuing
'chain of transmission' – which enables us to use or apply those terms in a reference-preserving way. So even in cases of radical theory-change (like those which
occurred between pre- and post-Daltonian chemistry or pre- and post-quantum
concepts of 'electron') it makes good sense to claim – *contra* Kuhn and other advocates of wholesale incommensurability – that scientists who used the same terms
under different theoretical descriptions can properly be held to have been talking
about the same things (Kuhn 1970). But it is also, secondly, a causal account in
the sense that it explains such theory-changes through our acquisition of a more
advanced (e.g., depth-structural or microphysical) knowledge of the various items
and properties concerned. On this view it is simply an error to suppose that the
causal 'fixing' of reference for a term like *electron* might just as well be a result of
our encountering the term in a textbook and thus wholly unrelated to the physical existence of particles answering that description. On the contrary: what
decides the truth-value of statements concerning electrons is the way things stand
in subatomic reality and the current stage of progress in our scientific knowledge
with regard to microphysical entities of just that kind. Thus it is possible to
combine a causal account of how reference passes down through the 'chain of
transmission' with a realist and causal-explanatory account of how terms refer
with increasing precision to objects whose existence and distinctive properties –
mass-charge ratio, subatomic structure, molecular configuration, etc. – are in no
way contingent upon states of belief brought about through the encounter with
text-book descriptions or other such largely serendipitous causal factors. After all,
it is a crucial point for early Putnam that reference may at first be fixed in a vague
or scientifically inadequate way (as with the cases of 'gold' and 'water') and yet be
'sensitive to future discovery' through progressive refinements in our knowledge
of their various microphysical structures and attributes. Thus the relevant 'chain'
is one that passes down through a history of expert or qualified investigation, a

process whereby – as in Putnam's idea of the 'linguistic division of labour' – it is enough that some people (maybe physicists or chemists) should possess the relevant specialised knowledge while others can reliably defer to their judgement in disputed cases (Putnam 1975[2]a, 1975[2]c).

This is also, I would suggest, a more than adequate response to late-Putnam's worry about aberrant causal chains, or about the possibility that our knowledge of electrons might be directly explained by some personal encounter with a text-book treatment of the topic. For that encounter would qualify as knowledge-conducive only on condition that the textbook offered an informed and scientifically up-to-date account of how electrons figured in the current-best findings of subatomic particle research. Yet so convinced is Putnam that there *must* be something wrong with the causal theory that he now regards this as just another means of evading the issue with regard to theory-change and the problem of reference. Thus three years later (in *Meaning and the Moral Sciences*, 1978) he offers the same example – 'electron' as construed in different theoretical contexts – and draws much the same lesson.

> As soon as one tries to broaden the causal theory so as to cover, say, theoretical terms in science ('electron'), then the principle of the benefit of the doubt comes in, in some version or another – the principle that says that to find out what Bohr referred to by 'electron' in 1904 we must see what would be reasonable reformulations of the descriptions he gave which failed to refer (because, for example, they violated the principle of complementarity that Bohr himself enunciated thirty years later); and giving any *precise* analysis of the notion of a *reasonable* reformulation of a definite description is, if anything, *more* hopeless than giving a precise list of constraints on translation. And the problems are very similar: both reference-assignment and translation depend on choosing 'reasonably' to pair up not-exactly-matching sets of beliefs. To simulate (or even precisely to define) 'reasonableness' is to simulate (or at least define) full human capacity. In short, [this] is a species of scientific *utopianism*. (Putnam 1978: 57–8)

I should note that Putnam doesn't see this as a straightforward repudiation of his own or Kripke's causal theory of reference (what he now prefers to call the 'social co-operation plus contribution of the environment theory of the *specification* of reference' [*ibid.*: 58]). On the contrary, he argues that theory was on the right track in so far as it rejected the descriptivist approach of thinkers like Frege and Russell, an approach that he still regards as producing all manner of highly counter-intuitive or downright unacceptable results. Nevertheless, 'a theory of how reference is *specified* isn't a theory of what reference *is*; in fact it *presupposes* the notion of reference' (1978: 58). Hence Putnam's argument in the above-cited passage: namely, that any attempt to *define* reference in terms of causal chains will always run aground on problem cases – like Bohr's two models of subatomic structure – since in order to construct an intelligible story (one that makes allowance for theory-change while preserving sufficient continuity of reference) it will need to invoke such vague criteria as that of achieving a 'reasonable' match between different conceptual schemes or 'sets of beliefs'.

Yet here again it may argued that these problems arise – despite Putnam's protests to the contrary – through his having abandoned the most important insights of his own earlier causal-realist approach. For what he now demands of that approach is something it could never be expected to provide, that is to say, a theory of 'what reference *is*', rather than a working account of 'how reference is *specified*'. However this criticism – that a causal analysis '*presupposes* the notion of reference' – is one that would cut no ice from the standpoint of Putnam's earlier theory. Indeed, the main purpose of that theory was to offer an alternative way of addressing these issues, that is, an approach that specified reference in terms of whatever we can know to have a proven explanatory role in our current best scientific theories, or again, whatever we can properly (reliably) refer to so long as there are specialists around with the required expertise. So the element of 'presupposition' is a genuine problem *only if* one maintains – like Putnam here – that any adequate causal theory of reference must also meet a whole range of further (incompatible) demands, such as that of providing a translation-scheme for terms or 'definite descriptions' as they figure in rival scientific theories, or explaining how we could 'reasonably' pair up 'not-exactly-matching' sets of beliefs. Otherwise these arguments will look rather more like a strange reversion, on Putnam's part, to just the kind of descriptivist approach that he once rejected precisely on account of its creating such unnecessary problems. At any rate the causal theory of reference in its full-fledged (early-Putnam) form has by far the strongest claim to resolve those problems and to block the kinds of sceptical challenge that loom so large in his later work.

References

Benacerraf, Paul (1983). 'What Numbers Could Not Be'. In Benacerraf and Putnam (eds). 272–94.

Benacerraf, Paul and Hilary Putnam (eds) (1983). *The Philosophy of Mathematics: selected essays*, 2nd edn. Cambridge: Cambridge University Press.

Bohm, David (1957). *Causality and Chance in Modern Physics*. London: Routledge & Kegan Paul.

Bohm, David and Basil J. Hiley (1993). *The Undivided Universe: an ontological interpretation of quantum theory*. London: Routledge.

Carnap, Rudolf (1956). *Meaning and Necessity*. Chicago: University of Chicago Press.

Cushing, James T. (1994). *Quantum Mechanics: historical contingency and the Copenhagen hegemony*. Chicago: University of Chicago Press.

Davidson, Donald (1984). 'On the Very Idea of a Conceptual Scheme'. In *Inquiries Into Truth and Interpretation*. Oxford: Oxford University Press. 183–98.

Diamond, Cora (1991). *The Realistic Spirit: Wittgenstein, philosophy, and the mind*. Cambridge, MA: MIT Press.

Dummett, Michael (1977). *Elements of Intuitionism*. Oxford: Oxford University Press.

—— (1978). *Truth and Other Enigmas*. London: Duckworth.

—— (1978a). 'Is Logic Empirical?'. In Dummett (1978), 269–89.

—— (1978b). 'Can an Effect Precede its Cause?'. In Dummett (1978), 319–32.

—— (1978c). 'Bringing About the Past'. In Dummett (1978), 333–50.

—— (1978d). 'The Reality of the Past'. In Dummett (1978), 358–74.

Fodor, Jerry A. (1983). *The Modularity of Mind*. Cambridge, MA: MIT Press.

—— (1994). *The Elm and the Expert: mentalese and its semantics*. Cambridge, MA: MIT Press.

Gibbins, Peter (1987). *Particles and Paradoxes: the limits of quantum logic.* Cambridge: Cambridge University Press.

Gödel, Kurt (1962). *On Formally Undecidable Propositions of* Principia Mathematica *and Related Systems*, trans. B. Meltzer. New York: Basic Books.

—— (1983). 'What Is Cantor's Continuum Problem?'. In Benacerraf and Putnam (eds), 470–85.

Goodman, Nelson (1978). *Ways of Worldmaking.* Indianapolis: Bobbs-Merrill.

Haack, Susan (1974). *Deviant Logic: some philosophical issues.* Cambridge: Cambridge University Press.

Hacking, Ian (1983). *Representing and Intervening: introductory topics in the philosophy of natural science.* Cambridge: Cambridge University Press.

Holland, Peter (1993). *The Quantum Theory of Motion: an account of the de Broglie–Bohm causal interpretation of quantum mechanics.* Cambridge: Cambridge University Press.

Kant, Immanuel (1964). *Critique of Pure Reason*, trans N. Kemp Smith. London: Macmillan.

Katz, Jerrold L. (1998). *Realistic Rationalism.* Cambridge, MA: MIT Press.

Kim, Jaegwon (1993). *Supervenience and Mind.* Cambridge: Cambridge University Press.

Kripke, Saul (1980). *Naming and Necessity.* Oxford: Blackwell.

Kuhn, Thomas S. (1970). *The Structure of Scientific Revolutions*, 2nd edn. Chicago: University of Chicago Press.

Maddy, Penelope (1990). *Realism in Mathematics.* Oxford: Oxford University Press.

McCormick, Peter J. (ed.) (1996). *Starmaking: realism, anti-realism, and irrealism.* Cambridge, MA: MIT Press.

Mittelstaedt, Peter (1994). *Quantum Logic.* Princeton, NJ: Princeton University Press.

Norris, Christopher (2000). *Quantum Theory and the Flight from Realism: philosophical responses to quantum mechanics.* London: Routledge.

Penrose, Roger (1990). *The Emperor's New Mind.* London: Vintage Books.

—— (1994). *Shadows of the Mind: a search for the missing science of consciousness.* London: Vintage Books.

Putnam, Hilary (1975[1]). *Mathematics, Matter and Method* (*Philosophical Papers*, Vol. 1). Cambridge: Cambridge University Press.

—— (1975[1]a). 'Philosophy of Physics'. In Putnam (1975[1]), 79–92.

—— (1975[1]b). 'A Philosopher Looks at Quantum Mechanics'. In Putnam (1975[1]), 130–58.

—— (1975[1]c). 'Three-Valued Logic'. In Putnam (1975[1]), 166–73.

—— (1975[1]d). 'The Logic of Quantum Mechanics'. In Putnam (1975[1]), 174–97.

—— (1975[2]). *Mind, Language and Reality* (*Philosophical Papers*, Vol. 2). Cambridge: Cambridge University Press.

—— (1975[2]a). 'Is Semantics Possible?'. In Putnam (1975[2]), 139–52.

—— (1975[2]b). 'Explanation and Reference'. In Putnam (1975[2]), 196–214.

—— (1975[2]c). 'The Meaning of "Meaning"'. In Putnam (1975[2]), 215–71.

—— (1978). *Meaning and the Moral Sciences.* London: Routledge & Kegan Paul.

—— (1981). *Reason, Truth and History.* Cambridge: Cambridge University Press.

—— (1983). *Realism and Reason* (*Philosophical Papers*, Vol. 3). Cambridge: Cambridge University Press.

—— (1983a). 'Possibility and Necessity'. In Putnam (1983), 46–69.

—— (1983b). 'Two Dogmas Revisited'. In Putnam (1983), 87–97.

—— (1983c). 'There Is At Least One *A Priori* Truth'. In Putnam (1983), 98–114.

—— (1983d). 'Analyticity and Apriority: beyond Wittgenstein and Quine'. In Putnam (1983), 115–38.

—— (1983e). 'Reflections on Goodman's *Ways of Worldmaking*'. In Putnam (1983), 155–69.

—— (1983f). 'Why There Isn't a Ready-Made World'. In Putnam (1983), 205–28.

—— (1983g). 'Why Reason Can't be Naturalized'. In Putnam (1983), 229–47.

—— (1983h). 'Quantum Mechanics and the Observer'. In Putnam (1983), 248–70.

—— (1987). *The Many Faces of Realism.* La Salle, IL: Open Court.

—— (1988). *Representation and Reality.* Cambridge, MA: MIT Press.

—— (1994[1]). 'Sense, Nonsense, and the Senses: an inquiry into the powers of the human mind', *Journal of Philosophy*, Vol. XCI:9. 445–517.

—— (1994[2]). *Words and Life*, ed. James Conant. Cambridge, MA: Harvard University Press.

—— (1994[2]a). 'Philosophy of Mathematics: why nothing works'. In Putnam (1994[2]), 499–512.

—— (1995). *Pragmatism: an open question*. Oxford: Blackwell.

Quine, W.V.O. (1961). 'Two Dogmas of Empiricism'. In *From a Logical Point of View*, 2nd edn. Cambridge, MA: Harvard University Press. 20–46.

—— (1969). *Ontological Relativity and Other Essays*. New York: Columbia University Press.

—— (1969a). 'Epistemology Naturalized'. In Quine (1969), 69–90.

Rae, Alasdair I.M. (1986). *Quantum Physics: illusion or reality?* Cambridge: Cambridge University Press.

Rorty, Richard (1991). *Objectivity, Relativism, and Truth*. Cambridge: Cambridge University Press.

Schrödinger, Erwin (1980). 'The Present Situation in Quantum Mechanics', trans. John D. Trimmer, *Proceedings of the American Philosophical Society*, No. 124. 323–38.

Schwartz, Stephen (ed.) (1977). *Naming, Necessity, and Natural Kinds*. Ithaca, NY: Cornell University Press.

Soames, Scott (1999). *Understanding Truth*. Oxford: Oxford University Press.

Squires, Euan (1994). *The Mystery of the Quantum World*, 2nd edn. Bristol and Philadelphia: Institute of Physics Publishing.

Wheeler, John A. (1978). *Frontiers of Time*. Princeton, NJ: Princeton University Press.

Wheeler, John A. and W.H. Zurek (eds) (1983). *Quantum Theory and Measurement*. Princeton, N.J.: Princeton University Press.

Winch, Peter (1958). *The Idea of a Social Science and its Relation to Philosophy*. London: Routledge & Kegan Paul.

Wittgenstein, Ludwig (1958). *Philosophical Investigations*, trans. G.E.M. Anscombe. Oxford: Blackwell.

—— (1966). *Lectures and Conversations on Aesthetics, Psychology and Religious Belief*, ed. C. Barrett. Oxford: Blackwell.

—— (1969). *On Certainty*, ed. G.E.M. Anscombe and G.H. von Wright. Oxford: Blackwell.

6

The 'many faces' of realism:
reference, meaning and theory-change

I

We have seen how Putnam started out as a strong causal realist concerning issues in philosophical semantics, epistemology and philosophy of science and then – from the mid-1970s on – produced a whole range of arguments for thinking that position untenable. (Cf. Putnam 1975[2], 1978, 1981, 1983, 1987, 1990, 1995.) Hence the long series of books in which he has striven to steer a course between the opposed temptations of old-style 'metaphysical' realism (his own previous work included) and those varieties of downright anti-realist or cultural-relativist thinking which he finds equally unacceptable. In the process he has tried out various alternative theories – internal-realist, framework-relativist, or common-sense-pragmatist – which struck him as achieving the right sort of balance and avoiding any such false dilemma. That is to say, what we need – on Putnam's account – is an approach that conserves our basic realist intuitions while having no truck with objectivist talk which would make 'reality' entirely independent of our various beliefs concerning it, and would thus give a hold for the sceptic's claim that we can have no knowledge of any such 'external' (epistemically inaccessible) world. Such was at any rate the view he adopted in *Meaning and the Moral Sciences* where Putnam declared that 'internal realism' is 'all the realism we want or need', since causal theories – whether in philosophy of science or philosophical semantics – are metaphysically over-committed and hence an easy prey to sceptical attack (Putnam 1978: 130).

A decade later – in *Representation and Reality* – he has clearly undergone another change of mind, not least (one suspects) as a result of having witnessed the widespread trend toward forms of anti-realist or 'strong' social-constructivist thinking. We can best pick up the thread by examining a passage from that book where Putnam returns to a topic that had long been central to his thinking – continuity of reference under theory-change – and offers what he takes to be a realist-compatible but metaphysically unburdened account. His example is that of the term 'electron' as it figures in the two very different theories of subatomic structure offered by Niels Bohr before and after his conversion from a classical to a quantum-physical way of thinking (Bohr 1934, 1958; also Honner 1987). In *Meaning and the Moral Sciences* Putnam had taken this as a prime instance of the problems created for any realist approach by the fact that such a term could undergo radical shifts of meaning (i.e., of descriptive or theoretical content) to the point where continuity of reference became the merest of metaphysical dogmas.

In which case the realist is confronted with yet another version of the 'old sceptical "argument from error"', namely: 'What if *all* the theoretical entities postulated by one generation (molecules, genes, etc., as well as electrons) invariably "don't exist" from the standpoint of later science?' (Putnam 1978: 24). For we shall then be forced to acknowledge that 'truth' and 'reference' are otiose notions since any truth-values that we presently assign to statements containing theoretical terms must be taken as either referentially void or – what amounts to much the same thing – almost certain to turn out referentially void with the next major change in scientific thinking about 'genes', 'molecules', 'electrons', etc. Thus 'the following meta-induction becomes overwhelmingly compelling: *just as no term used in the science of more than fifty* (or whatever) *years ago referred, so it will turn out that no term used now* (except maybe observation terms, if there are such) *refers*' (Putnam 1978: 25; italics in the original). And of course if this argument goes through then it places a large obstacle in the way of any case for scientific realism – such as that espoused by Putnam in his earlier writings – which assumes (1) sufficient continuity of reference through and despite theory-change, and (2) the existence of various real-world entities (electrons included) whose nature, properties, charge-characteristics (and so forth) are what render our various statements about them objectively true or false. In short it blocks any version of the twofold realist claim that Putnam had once approvingly cited from Richard Boyd, i.e., that 'terms in a mature scientific theory typically refer' and that 'laws of a mature scientific theory are typically approximately true' (Putnam 1975[2]: 290; also Boyd 1984).

As I have said, this marks a phase in Putnam's thinking – roughly the period from 1978 to the mid-1980s – when he was maximally impressed by sceptical arguments that appeared to rule out any appeal to our knowledge of the growth of scientific knowledge or to science as a progressive enterprise grounded in the ever more detailed (microstructural or depth-explanatory) knowledge of physical realia. Thus it also marks his furthest point of retreat from the causal-realist theory of truth, meaning and reference which had occupied such a prominent role in his earlier writings. However, to repeat, there is a shift of emphasis by the time of *Representation and Reality* (1988), where he goes back to the paradigm case of Bohr's two models of subatomic structure. Thus:

> [t]he 1900 theory said that electrons go around the nucleus just as planets go
> around the sun, i.e., electrons have trajectories, whereas the 1934 theory (which
> is, in essence, the present quantum theory) says that an electron never has a
> trajectory – in fact, it never has a position and a momentum at the same time.
> Yet a physicist might well describe the development of the later theory from the
> earlier in this way: in the nineteenth century we discovered that electrons have a
> certain mass-charge ratio by deflecting electron beams in a magnetic field; later
> we discovered by another experiment what the electron charge is (and hence
> what the value of the electron mass must be); we discovered that electric current
> is a stream of electrons; we discovered that every hydrogen atom consists of one
> electron and one proton; we thought for a time that electrons had trajectories,
> but then we discovered the Principle of Complementarity; and so on. In short,

he would tell the story as a story of successive changes of belief about the same objects, and not as a story of successive 'changes of meaning' ... . In fact, treating 'electron' as preserving at least its *reference* intact through all of this theory change and treating Bohr's 1934 theory as a genuine *successor* to his 1900 theory are virtually the same decision: the decision described once as as a decision about the meaning or reference of a term and once as decision about the familial relations of research programs. (Putnam 1988: 12–13)

I have quoted the passage at length since it shows how Putnam had by this time reverted to a theory which strongly endorsed the need for continuity of reference despite and across radical changes in the 'meaning' (or theoretical content) assigned to a term like 'electron'. Of course this is not to say that it marks a full-circle return to the causal-realist position which had characterised his early work in epistemology and philosophy of language (Putnam 1975[2]). Thus the argument is explicitly presented as the kind of *story* that a physicist would most likely tell if seeking to explain the progress of particle physics from the late nineteenth century to Bohr's quantum-theoretical account of subatomic structure. Hence the numerous subjunctives, conditionals, and phrases like 'might well describe ...', along with other clear signals ('we thought for a time ...') that each stage in this progress was quickly overtaken by some startling new discovery. Moreover, the story is told from the standpoint of our present-best candidate theory – 'in essence' that which Bohr proposed in 1934 – and must therefore be counted strictly provisional, especially given its large burden of unresolved conceptual-interpretative problems. Lastly, there is the fact – in Putnam's view – that this can only be a matter of *decision* between alternative accounts, the choice being settled (here at least) by the need to 'keep reference intact' across changes in theory and resultant shifts in the meaning of constituent terms, thus preserving what he calls 'the familial relations of research programs'. In short, it is primarily a matter of pragmatic expedience or a means of ensuring that the story comes out in accordance with our need to make sense of such episodes in terms of a continuing process of discovery with respect to some (notionally) theory-independent or real-world object domain.

On this account, contrary to Putnam's early thinking, it is not so much the *intrinsic properties* of electrons – such as their always bearing a negative charge or producing certain repeatable effects through interaction with other particles – which justifies our referring to the 'same' entities from one theory to the next. Rather it is a generalised principle of 'charity' (or 'benefit of the doubt'), adopted with a view to explaining how Bohr could view his second theory as marking a definite advance over the first, and also how we – with benefit of hindsight – can fit them both into a coherent (reference-preserving) 'story' which links up with our own present stage in the history of scientific thought. Thus:

When we interpret Bohr in 1900 as referring to what *we* call 'electrons', we are thereby making at least some of his 1900 beliefs come out 'true' by our lights, whereas interpreting him as referring to nonexistent objects would be to dismiss all of his 1900 beliefs as totally wrong. And, of course, Bohr in 1934 extended the

same 'charitable' attitude toward his 1900 self that we do (which is why he
continued to use the term 'electron' in all those papers). (Putnam 1988: 13)

Still there are problems with this Davidsonian 'principle of charity', especially
when extended to issues in the history and philosophy of science (Davidson 1984).
Chief among them is its decidedly *over*-charitable premise that we have no choice
but to consider most theories (beliefs, explanations, worldviews, etc.) as containing more truth than falsehood – or as 'coming out true by our lights' – since otherwise we couldn't make a start in understanding where they converge with or differ
from our own. No doubt this is a useful premise to adopt when confronted with
the kinds of argument – Whorfian ethnolinguistic relativism, Quinean talk about
diverse ontological schemes, Kuhn's idea of incommensurable scientific paradigms, and so forth – which ignore the extent to which we can (and often do)
achieve a good measure of shared understanding across wide differences of scientific, historical, or socio-cultural context (Kuhn 1970; Quine 1961; Whorf 1956).
However, it is less helpful – indeed highly misleading – when applied (as here) to
particular cases in the history of scientific thought. For there is no generalised
argument of this sort, that is, no wholesale 'principle of charity' that could be of
much use in deciding the issue as between (say) the phlogiston-based and the
oxygen-based theories of combustion, or theories of electro-magnetic propagation
through space involving the existence or non-existence of a luminiferous ether,
or descriptions of subatomic structure – from Thomson and Rutherford to
Einstein, Bohr and beyond – which entail different ontological claims and
conflicting construals of the evidence. Indeed, when applied in this way, the principle comes out – ironically enough – as endorsing just the kind of paradigm-relativist approach and giving rise to just the kinds of conceptual problem with
inter-paradigm translation that Davidson sought to avoid. (See Newton-Smith
1981; Papineau 1979.) That is to say, it pushes 'charity' to the point of requiring
that other (e.g., earlier scientific) theories be interpreted on a truth-optimising
strategy which allows us to treat them, in Putnam's phrase, as coming out true 'by
our lights'. However, this gain is bought at the cost of obscuring how crucial terms
in some of those theories (like 'phlogiston' or the 'luminiferous ether') have
proven entirely devoid of referential content while others – such as 'electron' in
Bohr's 1900 model of subatomic structure – may still be assigned such content
despite subsequent shifts in their meaning or theoretical role.

So there are problems, as I have said, if we choose this strategy for saving
ourselves – and the Bohr of 1934 – from the surely unpalatable conclusion that his
previous (1900) 'self' was 'referring to nonexistent objects' and was therefore
'totally wrong [in] all his beliefs'. Where the strategy miscarries is in swinging right
across to the opposite 'charitable' extreme according to which past theories, along
with their various constituent terms, must always be given the 'benefit of the
doubt' by our current best interpretative lights. It seems to me that Putnam adopts
this principle because he still wants to offer some viable account of how progress
occurs – and can be known to occur – in the physical sciences yet no longer thinks
that this account can be given in causal-realist or 'strong' reference-preserving

terms. All the same, if one turns back to the long passage cited two paragraphs above (beginning 'The 1900 theory said …'), then it soon becomes clear – despite all the cautionary nuances and qualifying phrases – that the strong theory is doing most of the crucial explanatory work. So, for instance, '[i]n the nineteenth century we *discovered* [Putnam's italics] that electrons have a certain mass-charge ratio by deflecting electron beams in a magnetic field' (1988: 12). No doubt this is a part of the 'story' typically told by physicists and historians/philosophers of science when they seek to make sense of that particular episode in terms of scientific progress to date. Yet in order to play that credibilising role it must be taken as recounting a genuine *discovery* as concerns the mass-charge ratio of electrons and one that consequently opened the way to further such progress-enabling episodes. Thus: 'later we discovered by another experiment what the electron charge is (and hence what the value of the electron mass must be)' (*ibid.*).

My point – *pace* the later Putnam – is that none of this could make any kind of explanatory sense except on the realist premise that there exist such objects as 'electrons', objects that were indeed *discovered* through a range of applied experimental techniques, and which at this stage acquired full-fledged ontological status as distinct from their earlier heuristic or speculative role as appearance-saving theoretical posits. The same goes for 'mass-charge ratio' as a likewise objective (i.e., experimentally determined) relationship between two measurable quantities which enables electrons to be picked out as microphysical objects of just that kind. And it is only on the basis of a realist account that the subsequent episodes in Putnam's 'story' make sense, from the discovery that 'electric current is a stream of electrons' to the discovery that 'every hydrogen atom consists of one electron and one proton'. To be sure, certain complications arise at this point since it brings us to the advent of quantum mechanics – as in Bohr's 1934 model of the atom – and hence to a stage where object-talk (at least on the orthodox Bohr-derived theory) becomes highly problematic. Indeed, it is just these quantum-theoretical problems about wave-particle dualism, superposition, the need for 'complementary' state-descriptions, and so forth, which have played a large role in motivating Putnam's retreat from his earlier causal-realist position. (See the various essays on this topic collected in Putnam 1975[1] and 1983). Yet there is something odd about taking what is, on his own account, a deeply paradoxical and counter-intuitive theory as grounds for rejecting another theory which possesses such strong and well-tried explanatory scope except in that particular (far-from-decisive) case. Besides – as I have argued at length elsewhere – it is by no means established that orthodox quantum mechanics is a 'complete' theory in the sense of ruling out any alternative account that would match the established predictive-observational results while restoring a realist ontology with objective values of particle location and momentum between measurements (Norris 2000; also Bohm and Hiley 1993; Cushing 1994; Holland 1993).

This may remind us of Putnam's exchange with Ian Hacking and his claim that Hacking must be in the grip of a naive (pre-quantum) ontology if he hopes to justify realism by recounting the experiment – described by a physicist colleague – in which a supercooled niobium ball was sprayed with positrons in order to increase or decrease its charge (Hacking 1983: 23). More precisely, Hacking takes the view that 'we ought to be nonrealists with respect to theories (which are just calculating devices, according to him) and realists with respect to what we can "manipulate", either literally or with the aid of instruments' (cited in Putnam 1995: 59). So the positrons are *real* – not notional items adduced in support of some favoured theory – to the extent that their charge-altering effects can actually be brought about and observed in some given experimental set-up. To which Putnam responds with the standard range of arguments: that 'particles' should properly be thought of as possessing neither definite position nor momentum, that they cannot be reidentified from one measurement to the next, and moreover – according to quantum field theory – that one could just as well set up an experiment 'in which one "sprayed" the niobium ball, not with three positrons, and not with four positrons, but with *a superposition of three and four positrons*' (Putnam 1995: 59). But in that case, he asks, what becomes of Hacking's cardinal distinction between the realist outlook that we are warranted in taking with regard to 'manipulable' entities and the anti-realist outlook enjoined with regard to theories and (presumably) those notional entities that figure only as heuristic posits or terms of theoretical convenience? For this distinction surely collapses when confronted with the quantum-field-theoretical claim that there is just no way of resolving the problem about particle 'superposition' except by acknowledging the range of possible outcomes for any given act of observation/measurement and the fact that any outcome will always be subject to a range of possible (theory-related) interpretations. Thus, on the one hand, '[i]f being a "scientific realist" does not mean believing that positrons exist as distinct *things*, what meaning does that notion have?' On the other, if it *does* mean believing that particles have definite location, momentum, continuous identity, etc., then 'being a "scientific realist" about positrons means believing quantum field theory is actually *false*, and not just interpreting it "nonrealistically" (whatever *that* means)' (Putnam 1995: 60). And it is clear enough from the knock-down rhetorical tone of Putnam's argument that he considers this a price that no self-respecting philosopher of science would or should be willing to pay. From which he concludes – on a strange version of the principle of charity – that 'in Hacking's prose, "real" is just a comforting *noise*, stripped of all its conceptual connections with reidentifiability, countability, locatability, etc.' (*ibid.*).

II

Still, I think that we should not be over-impressed by an argument that raises these conceptual dilemmas about quantum mechanics into a case for doubting the basic tenets of scientific realism and inference to the best explanation. After all, the chief problem – as Putnam sees it – is how to explain the so-called 'collapse of the wavepacket', that is, how and when the transition occurs between superposed quantum microphysical states and the realm of macrophysical phenomena where those states are always resolved into one or another determinate (e.g., wave or particle) form. (See especially Putnam 1975[1] and 1983: 248–70). In other words, it is the famous problem of Schrödinger's cat and the sheer impossibility of thinking that the cat is somehow both alive and dead – or neither-alive-nor-dead – until the box is opened up for inspection by a sentient or conscious observer (Schrödinger 1980; Wheeler and Zurek (eds) 1983). At any rate this parable serves the purpose of forcing the issue for anyone, like Putnam, who is tempted to derive far-reaching philosophical lessons from the 'evidence' of quantum mechanics. What it brings home – in dramatic if simplified fashion – is the strictly *unresolvable* conflict between a realist ontology premised on our normal (scientific and everyday-commonsense) knowledge of the world and a quantum-theoretical perspective wherein that knowledge must be counted partial at best and perhaps the merest of illusions.

Putnam is inevitably tugged both ways since he considers quantum physics the most advanced (hence standard-setting) field of present-day scientific thought yet can never quite bring himself to give up the belief that there *must* be some alternative construal that would resolve the measurement-problem and thus fall square with our realist convictions regarding the existence of an objective (observer-independent) physical domain. The result is a constant oscillation in his later work between passages that tend toward a markedly sceptical or anti-realist position and passages that set such doubts temporarily aside by reasserting the claims of a commonsense or pragmatist realism which often takes a lead from William James in managing without delusive 'metaphysical' guarantees (Putnam 1994, 1995). Still, there is a question as whether this approach can do the kind of problem-solving work that Putnam requires of it, or whether it amounts to just another variant on the anti-realist theme whereby the whole issue is conveniently shelved in favour of a therapeutic appeal to what counts as 'truth' or 'reality' by our present-best communal lights. While such answers have an obvious appeal for mid-to-late-period Putnam they are also apt to strike him – on occasion – as a means of evading philosophical problems which cannot be so easily set aside.

This tension is most pronounced at various points in the collection *Realism and Reason*, especially the chapter 'Why There Isn't a Ready-Made World' (Putnam 1983: 205–28). The title echoes Nelson Goodman, whose influence is by now clearly visible in Putnam's deepening scepticism with regard to his own earlier position on the existence of natural kinds and our ability to pick them out through a knowledge of their essential features, microstructural properties, causal dispositions, transworld necessary attributes, and so forth (Goodman 1978). It is likewise evident in Putnam's doubts – inherited from Hume *via* Goodman – as concerns the possibility of providing any adequate (philosophically cogent) justification for our practices of inductive reasoning in the natural sciences and elsewhere. At this stage Putnam is more than half-way convinced that any such attempt will always run up against Goodman's 'new puzzle' of induction, i.e., his use of factitious or gerrymandered predicates – such as 'grue' and 'bleen' – in order to demonstrate the open-ended range of possible truth-conserving 'projections' from some given body of observational data (Goodman 1955). Thus, in Putnam's words: 'Nelson Goodman has shown that no purely formal criterion can distinguish arguments which are intuitively sound inductive arguments from unsound arguments, [since] for every sound inductive argument there is an unsound one of the very same form' (1983: 214). From the standpoint of early (causal-realist) Putnam it would have been an easy matter to show just where this sceptical thought-experiment went wrong, namely in assuming that artificial predicates – like 'grue = green if observed before the year 2000 and blue if observed thereafter' – were somehow (absurdly) on a par with natural or straightforwardly projectible predicates like 'green' and 'blue'. And if this might be thought to raise certain well-known problems concerning the objective status of secondary qualities such as colour then those problems would surely not apply to cases – like 'water = H_2O' or 'gold = the metallic element with atomic number 79' – where we are enabled to distinguish true from false samples on the basis of 'projecting' from known (scientifically established) properties of the kind in question (Putnam 1975[2]). Moreover, there can be no reason in principle for doubting that the same argument applies to subatomic particles (protons, electrons, or positrons) that are picked out by reference to certain intrinsic features – such as electrical charge – which in turn make it possible to explain the higher-level properties of atoms and molecules.

However, Putnam now takes the sceptical view that causal-realist explanations of this sort are fatally weakened by their reliance on induction and by the lack of any 'formal' method for distinguishing valid from invalid modes of inductive inference. In short, such distinctions must always result from some formally undecidable *choice* as to which predicates we treat as 'projectible' and which we regard as non-natural and hence as unworthy of playing a role in our various inductive and causal-explanatory practices. As he writes:

> [i]f we think of explanation as relation in 'the world', then to define it one would need a predicate which could sort projectible from non-projectible properties; such a predicate could not be purely formal for then it would run afoul of Goodman's result, but it could not involve the particular fundamental magnitudes in *our* world in an essential way for then it would be open to counterexamples in other possible worlds. (Putnam 1983: 214)

Yet of course it was a main plank in the Kripke/early Putnam causal theory of reference that such properties and predicates were transworld projectible – that they applied *necessarily* across a range of possible worlds – just so long as those alternative worlds were like our own *in all the relevant physical respects* (Putnam 1975[2]; Kripke 1980; also Schwartz (ed.) 1977 and Wiggins 1980). So a statement such as 'heat = the mean kinetic energy of molecules' is one that holds good as a matter of necessity for all instances of heat in our particular world and also in others where heat can be described or explained for scientific purposes as having that same constitutive feature. Putnam called this the 'synthetic identity of properties', while Kripke spoke in somewhat stronger modal-logical terms of 'epistemically contingent necessary truth' or truths which, though not *a priori* (since discovered through various kinds of empirical investigation) are none the less 'metaphysically necessary' in transworld applicable terms. Yet they both made a chief point of insisting that there were other possible (i.e., conceivable or logically consistent) worlds where those properties didn't obtain and which were characterised by different physical attributes, microstructural features, or causal-explanatory laws. Thus:

> if someone describes a logically possible world in which people have sensations of hot and cold, in which there are objects that feel hot and cold, and in which these sensations of hot and cold are *explained by a different mechanism than mean molecular kinetic energy*, then we do *not* say that he has described a possible world in which *temperature is not mean molecular translational kinetic energy*. (Putnam 1983: 54)

It is a similar point that Putnam makes through his examples of Earthian and Twin-Earth 'water' (molecular constitutions H₂o and XYZ respectively), or 'aluminium' and 'molybdenum' where the names of those elements are systematically switched by denizens of the two planets, a fact that can only be established by investigation of their subatomic structures or properties (Putnam 1975[2]: 139–52, 215–71). Here again it is the case that 'metaphysically necessary' truths may yet be 'epistemically contingent' – or subject to empirical discovery – since they concern the way things stand in our particular world and in others that resemble it closely enough with regard to those salient features. Or, as Kripke says, they are a matter of *a posteriori* necessary truth which holds for just that range of possible worlds which don't depart from our own in the relevant (physically specifiable) respects.

Thus the causal theory of reference is one that deploys the resources of modal logic in order to justify a realist approach to issues in semantics, epistemology, and the history and philosophy of science. Yet in *Realism and Reason* (1983) Putnam is to be found casting doubt on that whole approach and doing so, moreover, from a sceptical standpoint that endorses Goodman's 'strong' constructivist view. On this account there is no 'ready-made world' since we can always devise as many world-versions as there exist different ways of picking out objects – or kinds of object – and projecting the various properties or predicates associated with them (Goodman 1978; Putnam 1983: 205–28). In short, Putnam has given up the modal-realist claim that *some* such objects and properties must be thought of as enjoying privileged status – and *some* such predicates treated as possessing genuine projectibility – since they pertain to certain necessary features of our own and other 'nearby' (physically congruent) worlds. Just how far he has shifted from that way of thinking can be gauged by his statement elsewhere in the same essay that 'salience and relevance are attributes of thought and reasoning, not of nature', and hence that '[t]o project them into the realist's "real world", into what Kant called the *noumenal* world, is to mix objective idealism (or, perhaps, medieval Aristotelianism) and materialism in a totally incoherent way' (Putnam 1983: 215). Above all he now thinks – again following Goodman – that there is simply no defending the idea of causal explanation if that idea is supposed to come equipped with some means of picking out the salient causal factor(s) in a given context from the background conditions or the range of possible alternative explanatory hypotheses. Rather we should see that this is just a form of old-style 'metaphysical' realism which collapses into manifest incoherence as soon as one appreciates how many and varied are the properties, attributes, or causal powers that might plausibly be adduced.

This is why Putnam devotes some fairly withering commentary to Richard Boyd's claim that causality is a 'primitive' concept, one that plays so basic a role in our everyday and scientific thinking that it cannot be considered to require any further philosophical justification (Boyd 1984). What he finds altogther unacceptable here is just the kind of causal-explanatory argument that had once figured so prominently in his own work and which still – as we have seen – exerts a residual appeal at other points in this same volume (1983) when Putnam rehearses the details of that earlier approach. His chief argument against Boyd is that talk of causation is often (and he thinks quite wrongly) construed as involving a *de re* notion of causal powers – tendencies, capacities, latent dispositions, etc. – that are somehow inherent in the objects themselves, rather than belonging to the space of reasons or the *de dicto* realm of explanatory theories and hypotheses. Moreover, Putnam thinks, it tends to suggest an idea of 'total' (monocausal) explanation which falls apart as soon as one examines the range of potentially relevant factors in any given case. Thus:

> [w]hen Boyd, for example, says that a certain micro-structure is a 'causal power' (the micro-structure of sugar is a 'causal power' in Boyd's sense, because it *causally explains* why sugar dissolves in water) he does not mean that the micro-structure in question is the *total cause* of the explained events (sugar will not dissolve in water if the water is *frozen*, for example, or if the water is already saturated with sugar, or if the water-cum-sugar is in an exotic quantum mechanical state). 'Causal powers' are properties that *explain* something, given background conditions and given standards of salience and relevance. (Putnam 1983: 215)

In Putnam's view, those conditions and standards are set by excluding such a wide range of possible alternative acccounts – among them bizarre quantum-physical conjectures – that 'salience' and 'relevance' must likewise be construed as relative (or internal) to this or that preferred system of explanatory concepts. Nothing could be further from his early approach wherein what counted as an adequate causal explanation was ultimately fixed by just those salient properties (like the molecular structure of sugar) which provided a depth-ontological account of phenomenal attributes like solubility in water (Putnam 1975[2]). Nor is this approach shown up as naively 'metaphysical' by the sorts of counter-argument that Putnam brings to bear in the above-cited passage. After all, the physicist or chemist will hardly be stuck for an answer – that is to say, for another causal explanation – if asked why sugar fails to dissolve in frozen water or in a mixture of water and sugar that has already reached saturation-point. For it is a standard and much-discussed feature of all such reasoning – from J.S. Mill to J.L. Mackie – that it has to admit certain *ceteris paribus* clauses or make due allowance for complicating factors, among them the absence of certain necessary background conditions or the presence of others which may alter the outcome from one situation to the next (Mackie 1974; also Harré and Madden 1975; Leplin (ed.) 1984; Salmon 1984; Tooley 1988).

Early Putnam had plenty of examples to make this point and also, as I have argued, a well-developed theory which managed to account for them in realist and causal-explanatory terms. That he later felt obliged to retreat from this position under pressure from various philosophic quarters is, I think, more a sign of the sceptical times than a sure indication that something is wrong with that entire so-called 'metaphysical' way of thinking. How else should one explain Putnam's readiness to summon up even the most 'bizarre' quantum-theoretical conjectures when they afford an opportunity for casting further doubt on the claims of scientific realism and inference to the best causal explanation? Thus it is certainly conceivable – indeed a strict consequence of quantum mechanics – that the water-cum-sugar might happen to exist in some 'exotic' superposed state which arrested or suspended the molecular process by which sugar normally dissolves in water. Yet there is surely something odd about a theory which requires that we expand the range of *ceteris paribus* clauses to include not only 'provided the water is not frozen', or 'provided it is not already saturated', but also – as the case might be – 'provided it has not been subject to supercooling under controlled laboratory conditions that result in a quantum-coherent state with some highly unusual effects'. At any rate, that theory would involve a large departure from the norms of causal-explanatory reason that apply in every area except that of quantum-theoretical debate. And there are, as I have suggested, problems enough with the interpretation of quantum mechanics to warn against deriving any such generalised lessons as regards our knowledge of objects and events in the macrophysical domain.

The same goes for Putnam's other example in this context, that of a match in perfect physical condition which, rather than being struck, is broken into pieces and thrown in a river. According to one fairly standard line of argument such cases are best analysed in counterfactual-conditional terms, i.e., by stating that had the match been struck in the appropriate way and with nothing to impede or divert the usual course of physical events then ignition would surely have occurred. However, Putnam asks, 'what does the statement actually assert?' (1983: 216). On his construal it asserts almost nothing, or nothing with substantive causal-explanatory import when examined with a view to the various concessions or *ceteris paribus* clauses that need to be added if the statement is to survive rigorous critical scrutiny. Thus:

> [a] first stab at an explication might go as follows: the statement is true if it follows from physical laws (assume these to be given by a list – otherwise there are further problems about 'laws') that if the match is struck (at an average [for me?] angle, with an average amount of force) against that striking surface, then, it ignites. But this doesn't work: even if we describe the match down to the atomic level, and ditto for the striking surface and the angle and force involved, there are still many other relevant variables unmentioned .... If no oxygen mole-

cules [sic] happen to be near the top of the match, or if the entire match-cum-striking-surface-cum-atmosphere system is in a sufficiently strange quantum state, etc., then the match *won't* ignite (even if struck with that force, at that angle, etc.). (Putnam 1983: 216)

Here again there is a sense – a 'sufficiently strange' quantum-theoretical sense – in which Putnam's argument may be thought to hold good and to throw a whole series of strictly unsurmountable problems into the very idea of causal explanation. On this view, it stands as perhaps the most 'exotic' (but none the less conceivable) case on a scale of such problematic instances which leads back – *via* the case where no oxygen molecules happen to exist in the immediate vicinity – to the relatively humdrum case of the match being broken into pieces and plunged in water. As so often it is Goodman's influence that emerges most clearly when Putnam mounts these objections to any kind of causal-explanatory account which relies on counterfactual-supporting arguments and a certain necessarily limited range of *ceteris paribus* clauses. Thus he cites Goodman's essay 'The Problem of Counterfactual Conditionals' to the effect that no such theory can possibly work, given the strictly *un*limited scope for variation in the causal factors that operate or the background conditions that apply from one instance to the next (Goodman 1947). In Putnam's words, '*everything* else *couldn't* be as it was at the time if the match were struck. The gravitational fields, the quantum mechanical state, the place where there were oxygen molecules in the air, and infinitely many other things, *couldn't have been* "as they actually were at the time" if the match had been struck' (Putnam 1983: 217). In which case – Putnam concurs with Goodman – one cannot rest the argument for causal explanation on a mode of counterfactual-conditional reasoning which fails to acknowledge this open-ended range of alternative possibilities.

However Putnam's argument will appear less compelling if one questions the strangely inverted order of priorities that leads him to draw such a sceptical lesson with regard to our knowledge of macrophysical causes and effects from a theory (like orthodox quantum mechanics) which remains so heavily burdened with unresolved problems and conceptual paradoxes. Thus there is no difficulty – from a causal-realist standpoint – about explaining why the match won't ignite if struck with insufficient force, or at the wrong angle, or if thrown into water. Nor do any great problems arise under the somewhat more *outré* supposition of its being struck when there is no oxygen around to support combustion. Things get really difficult only at the subatomic level where one has to reckon with 'exotic' states which – at least on the orthodox quantum theory – must forever elude the best efforts of causal explanation (Bohr 1934, 1958). Even so, it seems little short of absurd to present such cases as a clinching rejoinder to *any* kind of counterfactual-supporting argument, that is to say, any argument of the general form: 'the match *would have* lit under certain specifiable conditions, and barring certain others, on account of its physical constitution, the chemical properties of phosphorus, the presence of sufficient oxygen, the friction-generated heat (mean kinetic energy of molecules) created by the act of striking it', and so forth. Certainly there will always be a practical limit to the range of necessary conditions and *ceteris paribus* clauses that one could write down or keep in mind when elaborating any such argument. But this is no reason for counting it a hopeless endeavour since some of those clauses – like the ones involving bizarre quantum states or disturbances in the gravitational field – are so utterly remote from the practical business of explaining why combustion does or does not occur that they are better treated as belonging to the realm of speculative fancy rather than the realm of genuine (real-world) counterfactual possibility.

One is tempted to suggest that Putnam has been misled by forgetting all those crucial distinctions in the nature of causal-explanatory argument that he and Kripke had once raised to a high point of conceptual refinement. Besides, as I have argued, there is no compelling reason – orthodox prejudice aside – to suppose that quantum physics *necessarily* excludes any Bohm-type causal-realist interpretation. And even if that possibility were firmly ruled out by some future, decisive experiment then there would still be some huge problems to confront, among them – most crucially – that of explaining how and where the transition occurs from the quantum 'world' of superposed states to the world of macro-physical objects and events where these states are never observed, or only in certain highly specialised and hard-to-replicate laboratory conditions (Wheeler and Zurek (eds) 1983; also Norris 2000). So it is, to say the least, a questionable move on Putnam's part to adduce such admittedly 'bizarre' and 'exotic' quantum-mechanical states with a view to raising problems about causal explanation at the macrophysical level. Moreover, one theory (along with Bohm's) which claims to resolve these quantum dilemmas is the idea – derived from thermodynamics – that non-local 'entanglement' effects between vast numbers of superposed systems are such as to bring about an overall collapse into discrete states and hence to explain why the transition occurs quite apart from any act of observation/meas-urement (Rae 1986). Thus there do exist genuine, scientifically respectable alter-natives to orthodox quantum thinking which entail nothing like such a range of paradoxical or counter-intuitive consequences but which – perhaps for that reason – Putnam declines to entertain.

III

Indeed, his most striking argument from thermodynamics is to be found in a passage from *The Many Faces of Realism* (1987) where Putnam takes it as yet further evidence *against* any theory of causal explanation premised on the exis-tence of real-world properties, powers, dispositions, microstructural attributes, etc. Thus he begins by distinguishing 'strict' dispositions – like that of bodies with non-zero rest-mass to travel at velocities less than the speed of light – from other dispositions, such as the tendency for sugar to dissolve in water, which are subject to the usual range of *ceteris paribus* clauses. This distinction might itself seem damaging (even fatal) to Putnam's case since after all, as he concedes, 'the notion of a "strict disposition" presupposes the notion of "physical necessity"', which can scarcely be had without letting that case go by default. Still, '[t]his is a notion I am allowing the "scientific realist", at least for the sake of argument' (Putnam 1987: 10). What interests him more is the sugar-in-water example and the question as to whether this can be counted an instance of 'strict' disposition when due allowance is made for the standard counter-instances (frozen water, saturated water, the presence of chemical impurities, etc.). No indeed, Putnam answers, and for various reasons, among them one from the theory of thermodynamics:

> Suppose I drop a sugar cube in water and the sugar cube dissolves. Consider sugar which is in water, but in such a way that while the situation is identical with the situation I just produced (the sugar is dissolved in the water) with respect to the position of each particle, and also with respect to the numerical value of the momentum of each particle, all the momentum vectors have the exactly opposite directions from the ones they now have. This is a famous example: what happens in the example is that the sugar, instead of staying dissolved, simply forms a sugar cube which leaps out of the water! Since every normal state (every state in which sugar dissolves) can be paired with a state in which it 'undissolves', we see that there are infinitely many physically-possible conditions in which sugar 'undissolves' instead of staying in solution. Of course, these are all states in which entropy increases; but that is not impossible, only extremely improbable! (Putnam 1987: 10)

Putnam's liberal use of exclamation-marks, here and elsewhere, is a clear sign that he knows such bizarre counter-instances to be simply irrelevant from one point of view, that which holds – as he himself once held – that the proper business of causal explanation is with just those real-world operative attributes, structures or causal dispositions that actually *explain* what typically *occurs* under *normal* (or not wildly abnormal) physical conditions. To be sure, such instantaneous large-scale reversals of vector-state might conceivably occur according to the theory of thermodynamics, just as – to revert to our previous example – it is within the range of quantum-theoretical possibility that the match might not light if the entire system of match, striking surface, and atmosphere happened to be in some 'sufficiently strange' quantum state. But in each case the argument proceeds by taking such bizarre hypotheses from the realm of theoretical physics and treating them as knock-down evidence against any form of counterfactual-conditional reasoning that assumes the existence of *de re* causal properties, powers or dispositions. So it is that Putnam adduces the second law of thermodynamics *not* with a view to its possible explanatory yield – as applied (say) to the measurement-problem in quantum mechanics – but rather with the aim of blocking such arguments at source by raising all manner of extravagant hypothetical counter-instances.

No doubt, he concedes, these instances are far-fetched to the point where the chance of their actually occurring – as distinct from existing in the realm of conceptual possibility – must be thought of as vanishingly small. Thus the probability that dissolved sugar might reconstitute itself into cuboid form and jump out of the water is pretty much on a par (as such reckonings go) with the probability of a macrophysical system, like Schrödinger's cat, turning up in a superposed quantum state between life and death. In the former case – classically envisaged by James Clark Maxwell with his fable of the molecule-sorting demon – it would involve a decrease of entropy and hence a reversal of the thermodynamic law that explains (among other things) the passage of time and the unidirectional nature of most causal processes. All the same, Putnam thinks, this is 'not impossible, only extremely improbable', and must therefore count as a decisive argument against the idea that causal explanations can take the form of counterfactual-supporting hypotheses plus whatever is needed in the way of normalising *ceteris paribus* clauses. Granted, '"causal powers" are properties that *explain* something, given background conditions and given standards of salience and relevance'. On the other hand, '[b]e that as it may, salience and relevance are attributes of thought and reasoning, not of nature' (Putnam 1983: 215). To suppose otherwise, in Putnam's view, is a form of metaphysical delusion – even a kind of 'medieval Aristotelianism' – which conflates the attributes of mind and nature in a thoroughly promiscuous way.

Still less can such a causal-realist argument claim 'materialist' credentials, or present itself as the sole philosophical approach consistent with scientific method and rigour. For what it asks us to accept (he infers) is the curious claim that 'materialism is *almost* true: the world is completely describable in the language of physics *plus* the one little added notion that some events intrinsically *explain* other events'. Putnam thinks this a manifest absurdity which demonstrates the hopeless character of any such attempt to vindicate scientific realism in objectivist and causal-explanatory terms. After all,

> [i]f events *intrinsically* explain other events, if there are saliences, relevancies, standards of what are 'normal' conditions, and so on, built into the world itself independently of minds, then the world is in many ways *like* a mind, or infused with something very much like reason. And if *that* is true, then materialism *cannot* be true. One can try to revive the projects of speculative metaphysics, if one wishes; but one should not pass *this* sort of metaphysics off as (future) physics. (Putnam 1983: 215–16)

This seems to me an extraordinary passage and one that very clearly brings out the impact on Putnam's later thinking of those various sceptical arguments which have led him not only to renounce his earlier causal-realist position but to view it as a reenchantment of the world totally at odds with any outlook informed by scientific methods and principles. Thus the idea that causal explanations are warranted just in so far as they describe something *in the nature* of physical reality – some 'intrinsic' disposition or causally operative power – must be viewed as merely a recrudescence of 'speculative metaphysics', one that can have no legitimate place in a 'materialist' (physics-based) ontology or epistemology. That is to say, it implies a well-nigh Hegelian commitment to the notion that 'the real is the rational', or that normative attributes such as 'salience' and 'relevance' can somehow be located – like 'reason' itself – in the realm of material objects, processes, and events. Worse still, so the above passage implies, there is the covert hint of an animist or panpsychist appeal to causal 'powers' that are supposedly exerted within that material realm but which in fact merely populate the physical world with projected mental attributes. In which case causal explanations of this sort revert to a kind of naively anthropomorphic thought which even Hegel consigned to the earliest stages of emergent human consciousness.

These claims are all the more remarkable for the fact that Putnam can be found elsewhere in the same volume (*Realism and Reason*) continuing to offer a strong defence of his own earlier causal-realist theory. (See for instance Putnam 1983: 46–68, 69–75.) That he chose to gather such discrepant views between a single set of book-covers is a tribute to Putnam's intellectual courage and willingness to let the reader in on his emergent doubts and misgivings. Yet it does raise the question as to whether this change of mind represents an advance toward greater clarity as regards certain intractable problems with causal realism or whether – on the strength of that earlier account – they should not rather be seen as artefacts of a philosophic culture that has pushed him in that direction, perhaps against his own better judgement. Thus the issue still turns principally on such paradigm instances as those which Putnam and Kripke first offered in support of their case for an order of 'objective, nonepistemic, metaphysical necessity' (Kripke's phrase) that secured adequate stability of reference despite even the most radical episodes of scientific theory-change (Kripke 1980). This is the position that Putnam upholds in the chapter 'Reference and Truth' (1983: 69–86) where he cites a range of familiar examples, among them – prototypically – 'gold' and 'water' as natural-kind terms whose reference was fixed at a time when their constituent (subatomic and molecular) structures were as yet unknown but were none the less 'sensitive to future discovery' through the process of advancing knowledge-acquisition. Or again, he invites us,

> consider the kind *lemon*. There are lemons which are green rather than yellow; and there could well be a citrus fruit which was yellow and *not* a lemon. What makes something a lemon is having the same nature (e.g., the same DNA) as paradigm lemons, and not fulfilling some set of criteria (yellow colour, thick peel, tart taste, …) laid down in advance. Natural kinds do not have analytic definitions. (Putnam 1983: 73)

My point is that this passage occurs in a local context of argument where it is clearly intended to carry demonstrative and causal-explanatory force yet where it sits alongside passages from other chapters – like those cited above – that are just as clearly intended to subvert its claim to validity or truth. In all fairness, Putnam's Introduction to *Realism and Reason* makes a point of acknowledging the book's transitional character and the fact that it records a decisive change in his thinking about these matters (1983: vii–xviii). Still, it is far from self-evident that the tension between his early (causal-realist) and his subsequent (at this stage 'internal-realist') approach to these issues is one that could only be resolved by adopting some version of the latter approach. For there are, as I have suggested, reasons to think that Putnam's case for abandoning that earlier position results more from a kind of *a priori* scepticism backed up by 'bizarre' or 'exotic' counter-instances than from any inherent weakness in the argument for causal realism.

From this point of view it is absurd to claim that the idea of 'intrinsic' causal powers (i.e., dispositional properties pertaining to real-world objects, processes, and events) is merely a species of quaint animistic projection harking back to medieval or scholastic notions of 'essence', 'substantial form', 'intellectual intuition', and so forth. On the contrary, it is just the kind of depth-explanatory grasp that comes of advances in scientific knowledge like that which enables us – with the benefit of modern physics – to improve upon a Lockean agnostic account of 'secondary qualities' like colour. For Locke, such qualities consisted in a 'power' to produce certain distinctive sensations in human observers, but a power whose nature or causal mechanism lay beyond reach of any adequate explanatory account (Locke 1959; also Ayers 1981). For Putnam, as late as *Reason, Truth and History* (1981), this example can be taken as supporting his claim that we *have* made genuine progress in the physical sciences and, moreover, that it is just the kind of progress which allows us to regard Locke's scepticism as no longer justified. In short, '[t]his power has an explanation, which we did not know in Locke's day, in the particular micro-structure of the piece of cloth which leads it to selectively absorb and reflect light of different wave-lengths' (Putnam 1981: 58). So we have good reason – scientific reason – to think ourselves better placed than Locke in this regard, and hence better able to resist his sceptical conclusion that there could be no knowledge of 'real' as opposed to 'nominal' definitions or essences.

The same applies to other Lockean 'secondary qualities', as for instance in the case of heat, which can now be defined – with benefit of modern thermodynamic theory – as 'mean kinetic energy of molecules', and thereby brought within the compass of an adequate causal-explanatory account. Moreover this explanation can be given in terms of a Kripkean modal-logical approach that deploys counterfactual or 'possible-worlds' reasoning in order to establish the existence of truths that are not *a priori* – since discovered through a process of empirical enquiry – yet which hold as a matter of necessity for any world where the relevant (this-world-operative) physical laws apply. Thus – to repeat – in the case of a logically possible world where the inhabitants feel hot or cold on occasion but where the explanation involves some mechanism other than mean kinetic energy of molecules we wouldn't all the same be justified in saying 'yes, they feel *heat* all right, but their kind of heat has nothing to do with molecular kinetic energy'. Rather, we should say that our informant has described a world in which 'heat' doesn't exist, or where sensations that closely resemble our own sensations are in fact caused by some other (to us unfamiliar) physical process. As with the paradigm cases of 'water' and 'gold' what fixes the reference and ensures the stability of such natural-kind terms is their having once been used – in a relatively ill-defined way – to pick out certain objects, substances, or properties which thereafter prove capable (through advances in scientific knowledge) of more precise definition or depth-explanatory grasp. 'To belong to a natural kind', Putnam writes, 'something must have the same composition, or obey the same laws ... as model members of the class, and this composition or these laws are not usually known when the natural kind term is introduced, but require an indeterminate amount of investigation to discover' (Putnam 1983: 74). Thus the theory has a strong explanatory claim not only with respect to the history of science and the process of cumulative knowledge-acquisition but also with respect to problems in philosophical semantics such as that of explaining – *contra* sceptics, anti-realists, or framework-relativists like Kuhn – how continuity of reference for certain crucial terms is preserved across and despite episodes of radical paradigm-change (Kuhn 1970; also Field 1973; Hacking (ed.) 1981; Pearce and Maynard (eds) 1973).

Yet it is just these signal advantages of the causal-realist theory that Putnam seems intent upon throwing away in pursuit of certain 'exotic' or 'bizarre' counter-instances which purport to demonstrate its unworkability on the strictest philo-sophical terms. Take for instance the essay 'Possibility and Necessity' (1983: 46–68) where he raises just such objections to Kripke's claim that the statement 'water is H_2O' is one that of necessity holds good in all physically compossible worlds, that is, in all worlds where the name 'water' is applied to the substance which has just *that* molecular constitution, whether or not this fact is yet known to users of the term. 'Consider', Putnam writes,

> a possible world in which water exists only in the form of H_6O_3 molecules. Kripke may object that this example is not fair: 'Water is H_2O' is oversimplified even in the actual world (such molecules as H_4O_2, H_6O_3 actually exist), and his theory is that the composition of water in the actual world determines its composition in all possible worlds. But even if, say, $H_{20}O_{10}$ could not exist in the actual world, I think we would call a substance with similar properties which consisted of $H_{20}O_{10}$ molecules in some possible world 'water'. (Putnam 1983: 63)

This argument strikes me as valid, intuitively speaking, up to a point although I cannot see that it possesses the intended argumentative force against Kripke's conception of transworld necessary properties and identity-conditions. Thus one might think it strongly borne out by the existence of various istotopes or (more exotically) of transuranic elements whose fleeting existence can only be achieved through the use of supercolliding particle accelerators. Of course those elements have different subatomic structures from any that exist under normal conditions and are therefore called by different (newly invented) names and assigned a new place in the extended periodic table. In this sense they are not like the variant form of water (molecular composition $H_{20}O_{10}$) which Putnam takes as his counter-Kripkean example. Yet that example surely works against his argument in so far as it postulates a substance whose resemblance to ordinary H_2O goes beyond its phenomenal attributes, i.e., those which it shares with Twin-Earth 'water' despite the latter's consisting of molecules with the structure XYZ. Where the difference comes in is at the isotopic level – as with 'heavy water' – where it does make sense (in scientific terms as well as for the sake of reference-preserving usage) to apply the same name to such substances despite their not being paradigm samples of the kind.

Of course there is still the problem for Kripke – as Putnam sees it – that mole-cules of the kind $H_{20}O_{10}$ might not exist or be physically possible (i.e., capable of molecular bonding) 'in the actual world' and yet compose a substance properly describable as 'water' in some other possible world where the laws of physics were different in just that respect. However, this begs the whole question – from Kripke's as well as from early-Putnam's viewpoint – as to what constitutes a 'possible world' in the context of causal-explanatory arguments that restrict the range of counterfactual possibility to worlds that are relevantly (physically) compossible with ours, rather than extending to the far wider class of thinkable, conceivable, or logically consistent alternative worlds. My point is that Putnam's various counter-examples – from H_4O_2 to $H_{20}O_{10}$ – must be thought of as occupying different positions on a scale that runs from instances of 'actual' possibility to hypothetical cases which no longer have any but a notional or speculative bearing on issues of real-world causal explanation. Putnam effectively concedes this point in a subsequent passage which is also of interest for its reference to quantum mechanics. Thus:

> What Kripke wants to say that is correct is that science does more than discover mere correlations. Science discovers that certain things *can* be, that certain things *must* be, etc. And once we have discovered the chemical composition of water in the actual world to be H_2O (actually to be a quantum-mechanical superposition of H_2O, H_4O_2, H_6O_3, ...), we do not call any other actual or hypothetical substance 'water' unless it is *similar in composition* to this. (Putnam 1983: 63)

To be sure, Putnam goes on to remark that '"similar in composition" is a somewhat vague notion', and therefore that the claim that '"Water is H_2O", or any such sentence, is "true in all possible worlds" seems an oversimplification' (*ibid.*). But the main force of his argument here is that what counts as a genuine sample of water – as opposed to a sample of some other (maybe Twin-Earth or merely 'hypothetical') water-substitute – is the fact of its possessing the relevant *kind* of molecular structure even if our understanding has to be revised in response to discoveries like that concerning the superposition of discrete quantum states. For in order to qualify as genuine *discoveries* they must have reference to real-world existent microphysical properties and powers, rather than belonging to an abstract realm of purely hypothetical possibility. Thus, granted that the existence of $H_{20}O_{10}$ is ruled out by the physics of molecular bonding, we can take it as likewise off-the-scale for any argument concerned with the nature and scope of causal explanation. Moreover, in this case – unlike the other instances from Putnam which I cited earlier – quantum physics comes in not so much as a means of confuting scientific realism but rather as showing how the existence of 'superposed' quantum states can in principle be reconciled with just such a realist account. For there could otherwise be nothing to distinguish the range of physically possible molecular or subatomic structures from those that lie at some point on the speculative scale beyond the limit of actual or potential real-world instantiation.

IV

I have pressed rather hard on these passages from *Realism and Reason* because they bring out the tension that exists at this stage between Putnam's residual attachment to some version of causal realism and – at other points – his deepening scepticism with regard to any such approach. Thereafter, the development of his thought can be mapped in terms of a constant effort to steer some middling course that would avoid the twin perils, as he sees them, of a hardline 'metaphysical' realism on the one hand and, on the other, an equally hardline anti-realist or paradigm-relativist outlook which lapses into incoherence when challenged to explain the progress of science or our knowledge of the growth of knowledge. By the time of *The Many Faces of Realism* (1987) Putnam has swung pretty far toward thinking that the greater of these temptations – and the one that requires more resistance – is the pull toward a realist philosophy of science which ignores or underrates the strength of opposing arguments. Thus '[t]he deep systematic root of the disease, I want to suggest, lies in the notion of an "intrinsic" property, a property something has "in itself"', apart from any contribution made by language or the mind' (Putnam 1987: 8). So he has now moved just about as far as possible from his earlier (pre-1975) causal-realist position. Yet compare this with the passage from *Realism and Reason* (cited above) where Putnam charges the causal realist – the believer in 'intrinsic' properties, saliences, 'standards of what are "normal" conditions, and so on, built into the world independently of minds' – with indulging a quaint animist belief in 'causal powers' which in fact emanate from the human mind but which the realist deludedly projects on to nature through a form of naive quasi-mystical or participatory thought (Putnam 1983: 215–16). That passage is one of the few in Putnam that could come straight out of one of Rorty's essays in the wholesale realist-debunking mode. Thus it puts one in mind of Rorty's mischievous claim that philosophers who talk about properties, dispositions or 'causal powers' might just as well be uttering some chant to placate the gods or engaging in some sadly belated form of primitive word-magic. (See Rorty 1991: 80.) However, this invites the obvious realist rejoinder: that by denying the existence of 'intrinsic properties' – and hence the possibility of *de re* causal explanations – philosophers are led to embrace the idea that reality cannot be thought of as existing and exerting its causal powers 'apart from any contribution made by language or the mind'. In short, the Rortian charge comes back like a boomerang: if there is one trend in recent philosophy that has tended to promote such vaguely animistic ideas it is the widespread attraction to various kinds of anti-realist, relativist, or social-constructivist thinking.

It seems to me that much of Putnam's work since the early 1980s has been strongly marked by this trend while none the less striving to resist its more extreme or doctrinaire manifestations. The tension emerges in his various protracted engagements with quantum mechanics (on the orthodox construal); with Wittgenstein-influenced linguistic and social philosophy; with Kuhn's paradigm-relativist approach to the history of science; with Quine's ideas about theory-change and ontological relativity; with Goodman's *ne plus ultra* version of the strong-constructivist argument; and with various kindred currents of thought that run strongly counter to the realist position developed in his early writings. For Putnam never *quite* lets go of that position or renounces his belief that the physical sciences provide our best source of guidance when confronted with problems in epistemology and philosophical semantics. Indeed, he can still be found as late as 1987 – in *Representation and Reality* – rehearsing the causal-realist argument with respect to natural kinds and offering a similar range of examples to make his point that reference is fixed by the naming of just those salient kinds which thereafter may be specified with increasing precision through advances in physics, chemistry or molecular biology. Thus 'Twin Earth water violates (and always violated) two conditions for being called "real" water: it neither has the same ultimate constitution as "our" water nor exhibits exactly the same behavior' (Putnam 1988: 35). And again: '[i]f Twin Earth "cats" were never able to mate with Earth cats (and produce fertile offspring), then not only biologists but laymen would say that Twin Earth cats are another species' (*ibid.*). All that has changed in the interim – since Putnam's first use of these and kindred examples – is that he now places greater emphasis on the 'linguistic division of labour', that is to say, the cooperative aspect of language whereby we can talk about (e.g.) 'beeches' and 'elms' in the confident knowledge that those names refer to different kinds of tree even though we may not be able to tell them apart by visual inspection, let alone through the ability to specify their difference in up-to-date scientific terms. It is enough that there are experts (maybe arborologists) around who could – if required – come up with the relevant criteria and thus settle any lay dispute or any doubt in the mind of those (like Putnam) who just don't know the difference. (See especially Putnam 1988: 22–6.) Yet this is not to say, in Wittgensteinian fashion, that what counts as 'knowing the difference' is a matter of sufficiently widespread agreement among speakers who share some particular language-game or cultural 'form of life' (Wittgenstein 1953). For it is still a main plank in Putnam's argument that stability of reference depends not only on such communal sense-making norms but also on the input of specialists who possess a more adequate scientific knowledge and can thus sort out any problems that arise with deviant samples or borderline cases.

Indeed, so far is Putnam from simply abandoning this whole line of thought that he produces some additional refinements in response to critics who had objected to it on various grounds, as for instance by maintaining that if Twin-Earth 'water' is to serve in this thought-experimental role then it must display *all* the same physical properties as water on planet Earth. However, this is 'simply a mistake', Putnam argues, since it takes no account of the progressive and open-ended nature of scientific enquiry, and hence the likelihood that future advances – like those in the past – will provide some adequate investigative means of distinguishing the two kinds of substance. Thus:

> [e]ven the chemists in 1750 were aware of only a limited range of properties. They knew, for example, the boiling point of water (although not with present-day accuracy). They knew the density of water. They certainly did not know of all the chemical reactions into which water enters. However, H_2O and XYZ are supposed to be different compounds. Thus, there has to be some third substance S such that H_2O chemically reacts with S in one way (perhaps in the presence of

catalyst C, or in the presence of heat, etc.). For example, it may be that when water is mixed with S and then C is added and the mixture is heated, then the mixture turns green and drops a yellow precipitate, whereas when Twin Earth water is mixed with S and C is added and the mixture is heated, then one gets a tremendous explosion. (Or it might simply be that Twin Earth water fails to react with S at all, or reacts only with a different catalyst.) This phenomenon (and many other similar ones) would show that Earth water and Twin Earth water are two different substances. (Putnam 1988: 32–3)

I have quoted this passage at length because it shows how the Putnam of 1988 – despite all his doubts with regard to any form of counterfactual-supporting causal explanation – is still strongly drawn to just such arguments when confronted with criticism of them. Nor is this by any means the only passage in Putnam's later work where he adopts a decidedly realist position as concerns the truth-content of scientific statements or theories and the possibility of ranking them on a scale of progressively more adequate descriptive and causal-explanatory knowledge. For instance, he compares the ancient Greek idea of water ('not only the substance that we drink, but ... also the name of an element, ... a universal principle of liquidity') with later theories that marked stages on the road to our modern post-Daltonian conception (Putnam 1988: 48). Thus it was thought by scientists like Newton and Boyle that all matter consisted of atoms but that these were identical in every substance, so that what made the difference between (say) gold and lead was the specific *arrangement* of atoms, rather than the various subatomic configurations that distinguish those elements one from another. This 'intermediate' theory – Putnam's term – explains why 'so great a scientist as Boyle held that any substance can, in principle, be transformed into any other'. And again: 'Boyle would not have seen any sense in saying that ice is water "in a frozen state". According to him, ice and water are as different as water and lead; freezing water is *transmuting it into* ice' (1988: 48).

My point is that Putnam is here assuming certain standards of scientific knowledge, progress and causal-explanatory warrant that simply *wouldn't be available* if one treated them according to the sceptical view adopted elsewhere in his later work, and indeed at other points in this very same book. Of course there is always the Kuhnian option (sometimes with backing from Wittgenstein) which purports to resolve the issue by holding that each of these various theories – water as one of the four primal elements, water and ice (like gold and lead) as different arrangements of identical atoms, water as a certain molecular structure of atomic constitution H_2O – must be viewed in relation to the 'paradigm', 'language-game', or communal scientific 'life-form' which prevailed at some given time (Kuhn 1970; Wittgenstein 1953). However there are numerous signs in the above-quoted passage that Putnam would firmly reject such a wholesale cultural-relativist approach. Among them is the clear implication that these theories represented definite *stages of advance* in our knowledge of the physical world, and also his remark that *even* 'so great a physicist as Boyle' was led to believe in the transmutability of elements through his holding an 'intermediate' theory – half-way between the ancient-Greek and post-Daltonian views – which appeared to support that belief. So likewise, Putnam argues, with names such as 'phlogiston', 'caloric', and 'ether', names that were once thought to designate real-world occurrent substances with a range of observable properties and effects, but which then turned out – on further investigation – to be devoid of referential content. All the same we should surely not wish to say that these different terms must be treated as strictly synonymous since they all possess the same (i.e., empty) extension. In such cases we can best have recourse to a descriptivist account of 'conceptual roles' which explains how each of them once played a part in some accepted scientific theory, even though that theory was later discredited, along with its constituent ontology and range of quasi-referential terms. Thus: '[n]ot having an extension (that is, lacking a *nonempty* extension) to constitute the, so to speak, individuality of the word, one naturally falls back on the conceptual role. Indeed, the conceptual role theory comes closest to being true in the case of words with an empty extension' (Putnam 1988: 50). All the same, the paradigm instances – whether in history/philosophy of science or philosophical semantics – are those where purportedly referring expressions have indeed turned out to designate objects, kinds, properties, causal dispositions, etc., and where reference thus determines 'conceptual role' rather than the other way around.

Here again quantum physics is the big problem case where Putnam thinks that such arguments encounter their limit. For as yet – he believes – there is no interpretation in sight that would permit us to distinguish between properly referring and empty terms, or those that pick out genuine objects of reference and those that either fail altogether in this regard or whose referential status must be viewed as strictly indeterminate. If one goes back to the essays collected in *Mind, Language and Reality* (1975[1]) – the high point of Putnam's causal-realist phase – one finds him taking a strong line on this issue and declaring firmly against any talk of radical meaning-change or indeterminacy of reference brought about by shifts of theoretical perspective with regard to terms like 'electron'. Thus:

> there is nothing in the world which *exactly* fits Bohr's description of an electron. But there are particles which *approximately* fit Bohr's description: they have the right charge, the right mass, and, most important, they are responsible for key *effects* for which Bohr thought 'electrons' were responsible; for example, electric current (in a wire) is flow of these particles. The Principle of Reasonable Doubt dictates that we treat Bohr and other experts as referring to *these* particles when they introduced and when they now use the term 'electron'. (Putnam 1975[2]: 275)

This is just the kind of argument that typifies Putnam's thinking, early and late, when his concern is chiefly with defending a realist approach to general issues in philosophy of science, rather than addressing more specific problems in the interpretation of quantum mechanics. That is to say, it is an argument that implicitly endorses those principles – stability of reference, convergent realism, inference to the best (counterfactual-supporting) causal explanation – which Putnam once took as strongly borne out by the evidence of scientific progress to date.

Moreover, the 'Principle of Reasonable Doubt', as Putnam applies it here, is one that judges certain kinds of doubt *unreasonable* since they generate problems – like that of explaining how such progress could occur or could ever be known to have occurred – whose very lack of any possible adequate solution on their own terms is enough to suggest that they are misconceived or out of place in the scientific context. In short, 'we should give the dubber, or the relevant expert, if the person at the other end of the chain of transmissions or cooperations isn't the original dubber, the benefit of the doubt ... by assuming he would accept reasonable modifications of his description' (Putnam 1975[2]: 275). What justifies this precept – with Bohr's use of 'electron' as likewise with Putnam's other case-studies from the history of science – is a realist position with respect to (1) the objects of scientific knowledge, (2) the continuity of reference to them across changes of scientific theory, and (3) their possession of distinctive properties (structures, attributes, causal dispositions, generative powers, etc.) that belong to them *necessarily* as objects of just that kind yet which have to be *discovered* through an ongoing process of empirical enquiry. Thus there is no reason in principle – as distinct from reasons having to do with the limits of present understanding – why causal explanations should not be extended to the realm of subatomic or quantum-physical phenomena. That this is also the position espoused by David Bohm and other advocates of the heterodox 'hidden-variables' theory is yet further grounds for counting it a viable option, despite Putnam's curious lack of interest in pursuing that particular path (Bohm 1957; Bohm and Hiley 1993; Holland 1993; Norris 2000). At any rate, we shall fail to grasp the full complexity of Putnam's thinking about these issues if we view his philosophical development to date as a straightforward or unilinear retreat from any version of the causal-realist approach that characterised his early writings.

References

Ayers, M.R. (1981). 'Locke *versus* Aristotle on Natural Kinds', *Journal of Philosophy*, LXXVII. 247–72.

Bohm, David (1957). *Causality and Chance in Modern Physics*. London: Routledge & Kegan Paul.

Bohm, David and Basil J. Hiley (1993). *The Undivided Universe: an ontological interpretation of quantum theory*. London: Routledge.

Bohr, Niels (1934). *Atomic Theory and the Description of Nature*. Cambridge: Cambridge University Press.

—— (1958). *Atomic Physics and Human Knowledge*. New York: Wiley.

Boyd, Richard (1984). 'The Current Status of Scientific Realism'. In Leplin (ed.), 41–82.

Clark, Peter and Bob Hale (eds) (1993). *Reading Putnam*. Oxford: Blackwell.

Cushing, James T. (1994). *Quantum Mechanics: historical contingency and the Copenhagen hegemony*. Chicago: University of Chicago Press.

Davidson, Donald (1984). 'On the Very Idea of a Conceptual Scheme'. In *Inquiries Into Truth and Interpretation*. Oxford: Oxford University Press. 183–98.

Field, Hartry (1973). 'Theory-Change and the Indeterminacy of Reference', *Journal of Philosophy*, LXX. 462–81.

Goodman, Nelson (1947). 'The Problem of Counterfactual Conditionals', *Journal of Philosophy*, XLIV. 113–28.

—— (1955). *Fact, Fiction and Forecast*. Cambridge, MA: Harvard University Press.

—— (1978). *Ways of Worldmaking*. Indianapolis: Bobbs-Merrill.

Hacking, Ian (1983), *Representing and Intervening: introductory topics in the philosophy of natural science*. Cambridge: Cambridge University Press.

Hacking, Ian (ed.) (1981). *Scientific Revolutions*. Oxford: Oxford University Press.

Harré, Rom and E.H. Madden (1975). *Causal Powers*. Oxford: Blackwell.

Holland, Peter (1993). *The Quantum Theory of Motion: an account of the de Broglie–Bohm causal interpretation of quantum mechanics*. Cambridge: Cambridge University Press.

Honner, John (1987). *The Description of Nature: Niels Bohr and the philosophy of quantum physics*. Oxford: Clarendon Press.

Kripke, Saul (1980). *Naming and Necessity*. Oxford: Blackwell.

Kuhn, Thomas S. (1970). *The Structure of Scientific Revolutions*, 2nd edn. Chicago: University of Chicago Press.

Leplin, Jarrett (ed.). (1984). *Scientific Realism*. Berkeley & Los Angeles: University of California Press.

Locke, John (1959). *An Essay Concerning Human Understanding*. 2 vols. New York: Dover.

Mackie, J.L. (1974). *The Cement of the Universe*. Oxford: Clarendon Press.

Newton-Smith, W.H. (1981). *The Rationality of Science*. London: Routledge & Kegan Paul.

Norris, Christopher (2000). *Quantum Theory and the Flight from Realism: philosophical responses to quantum mechanics*. London: Routledge.

Papineau, David (1979). *Theory and Meaning*. Oxford: Oxford University Press.

Pearce, G. and P. Maynard (eds) (1973). *Conceptual Change*. Dordrecht: D. Reidel.

Putnam, Hilary (1975[1]). *Mathematics, Matter and Method* (*Philosophical Papers*, Vol. 1). Cambridge: Cambridge University Press.

—— (1975[2]). *Mind, Language and Reality* (*Philosophical Papers*, Vol. 2). Cambridge: Cambridge University Press.

—— (1978). *Meaning and the Moral Sciences*. London: Routledge & Kegan Paul.

—— (1981). *Reason, Truth and History*. Cambridge: Cambridge University Press.

—— (1983). *Realism and Reason* (*Philosophical Papers*, Vol. 3). Cambridge: Cambridge University Press.

—— (1987). *The Many Faces of Realism*. La Salle, IL: Open Court.

—— (1988). *Representation and Reality*. Cambridge, MA: MIT Press.

—— (1990). *Realism With a Human Face*. Cambridge, MA: Harvard University Press.

—— (1994). 'Sense, Nonsense, and the Senses: an inquiry into the powers of the human mind', *Journal of Philosophy*, XCI:9. 445–517.

—— (1995). *Pragmatism: an open question*. Oxford: Blackwell.

Quine, W.V.O. (1961). *From a Logical Point of View*, 2nd edn. Cambridge, MA: Harvard University Press.

Rae, Alastair I.M. (1986). *Quantum Physics: illusion or reality?* Cambridge: Cambridge University Press.

Rorty, Richard (1991). 'Texts and Lumps'. In *Objectivity, Relativism, and Truth*. Cambridge: Cambridge University Press. 78–92.

Salmon, Wesley C. (1984). *Scientific Explanation and the Causal Structure of the World*. Princeton, NJ: Princeton University Press.

Schrödinger, Erwin (1980). 'The Present Situation in Quantum Mechanics', trans. John D. Trimmer, *Proceedings of the American Philosophical Society*, No. 124. 323–38.

Schwartz, Stephen (ed.) (1977). *Naming, Necessity, and Natural Kinds*. Ithaca, NY: Cornell University Press.

Tooley, M. (1988). *Causation: a realist approach*. Oxford: Blackwell.

Wheeler, John A. and W.H. Zurek (eds) (1983). *Quantum Theory and Measurement*. Princeton, NJ: Princeton University Press.

Whorf, Benjamin Lee (1956). *Language, Thought and Reality*. Cambridge, MA: MIT Press.

Wiggins, David (1980). *Sameness and Substance*. Oxford: Blackwell.

Wittgenstein, Ludwig (1953). *Philosophical Investigations*. Oxford: Blackwell.

7

Is logic revisable?
Putnam, Quine and 'contextual apriority'

I

In this chapter I propose to examine some unresolved tensions in Hilary Putnam's thinking that have resulted from his lengthy engagement with issues in the philosophy of science, mathematics and logic. More specifically, I shall focus on two such issues: on the problem of scientific realism as Putnam conceives it (can science legitimately claim to provide us with knowledge of a mind-independent or objective reality?) and on questions concerning the nature, scope, or very possibility of *a priori* knowledge. These topics are closely related in Putnam's work, not least through his involvement – early and late – with conceptual problems in the interpretation of quantum mechanics (Putnam 1975[1]; 1983). Thus his best-known proposal in this regard is that we give up certain classical 'laws' of logic (i.e., bivalence or excluded middle) which have hitherto most often been taken to possess *a priori* warrant in order to accommodate certain otherwise paradoxical phenomena such as wave/particle dualism or quantum superposition. In short, we should aim to 'keep the physics simple' – empirically adequate and paradox-free – by conserving the full range of established quantum predictive-observational data and revising our logic so as to avoid the various dilemmas (conflicts, contradictions, anomalies) which result on a bivalent construal of those same empirical data. In this way it is possible, Putnam thinks, to resolve the longstanding interpretative problems with quantum mechanics through adoption of a 'deviant' or three-valued logic while retaining bivalent truth/falsehood values for statements concerning macrophysical objects or events where no such problems normally arise. Thus '[t]he whole difference between classical and quantum logic lies in this: that propositions do not form a distributive lattice according to quantum logic, whereas according to classical logic they do' (Putnam 1975[1]: 194). And again: 'quantum mechanics itself explains the *approximate* validity of *classical* logic "in the large" just as non-Euclidean geometry explains the *approximate* validity of *Euclidean* geometry "in the small"' (*ibid.*: 184). In both cases – so the argument runs – there is a need to revise certain hitherto existing 'classical' conceptions of logic or *a priori* warrant in response to anomalies thrown up in the course of empirical investigation. (See also Beltrametti and van Fraassen (eds) 1981; Garden 1983; Gibbins 1987; Haack 1974; Mittelstaedt 1994.)

Not that Putnam is by any means satisfied with the orthodox (Copenhagen) construal of quantum mechanics or willing to accept the standard instrumentalist line, that is (in brief): 'don't worry about the "reality" behind or underlying quantum phenomena just so long as the formalism works and the measurements or predictions turn out right'. (See for instance Bohr 1958, 1987; also Cushing 1994, Home 1998, Honner 1987, Jammer 1974, Squires 1994.) For this answer merely shelves all the unresolved dilemmas, among them the notorious measurement-problem or the impossibility – for orthodox QM – of explaining just how and at just what stage the transition occurs from superposed quantum states to the realm of observed (macrophysical) objects and events where we simply don't witness any such weird phenomena (Wheeler and Zurek (eds) 1983). Putnam is very firm in counting this a genuine problem and in refusing what he sees as the evasive line of least resistance espoused by Bohr, Heisenberg, and the orthodox school. Still less is he convinced by ontologically extravagant theories which purport to get over this problem by adopting a 'many-worlds' or a 'many-minds' approach, i.e., by asserting that *every possible* outcome of *each and every* wave-packet 'collapse' is realised in one or another of the multiple realities (or experiential lifelines) that branch off from moment to moment in an endlessly proliferating series. On the contrary, Putnam writes: '[t]he result we wish is that although micro-observables do not have definite numerical values at all times, macro-observables do. And we want this result to come out of quantum mechanics in a natural way. We do not want simply to add it to quantum mechanics as an *ad hoc* principle' (Putnam 1975[1]: 157). Yet he quickly came around to the verdict that his own attempt to provide a solution by way of three-valued logic was very far from having achieved that wished-for outcome. For 'a defect of my interpretation is that it does not *explain* just why and how measurement (construed as a physical process, on my interpretation) causes a "reduction of the wave packet"' (*ibid.*: 165). That other proposals were no more successful in this regard gave all the more reason to think that any eventual solution to the measurement-problem must entail some fairly drastic changes to our sense of what counts as an adequate scientific theory or inference to the best explanation.

A footnote to his later essay 'Why There Isn't a Ready-Made World' puts the case in typically forthright terms. 'I ignore', Putnam writes, 'my *own* past attempts at a realist interpretation of quantum mechanics (using non-standard logic) for two reasons: they have never found much acceptance, and (more importantly) I no longer think quantum logic enables one to reconcile quantum mechanics with realism.' (Putnam 1983: 205–28; 211n.) What is worth stressing here – in connection with the issue about scientific realism – is that Putnam's quantum-related arguments for adopting a non-standard (three-valued) logic were proposed as part of a wider attack on the idea that there existed certain *a priori* truths which by very definition could not be abandoned or revised in response to conflicting empirical evidence. The standard example is that of non-Euclidean geometry and its requirement that we give up the axiom of parallels, i.e., the 'self-evident' geometrical truth that any two straight lines which are both perpendicular to a third straight line will extend to infinity without diverging or ever meeting at any point. According to Euclid – and also Kant, for whom this served as a prime example of synthetic *a priori* knowledge – there could simply be no doubting such truths since they formed the very 'conditions of possibility' for knowledge and experience in general (Kant 1964). Yet of course non-Euclidean geometry is now conceivable not merely as a matter of abstract *logical* possibility, which Kant was himself quite willing to concede, but also as possessing a far better claim to describe the structure of physical reality in post-Einsteinian terms. Thus: '[a]ccording to the physical theory we accept nowadays, ... [l]ight passing near the sun behaves as it does not because the light travels in curved lines, but because the light continues to travel in straight lines and the straight lines behave in that way in our non-Euclidean world' (Putnam 1981: 83). In this case – as in a good many others – Putnam comes out very strongly against any conventionalist or operationalist account whereby the meaning of a term like 'straight' must be taken as undergoing some crucial change in the process of transition from one theory to another. On the contrary, he argues: this is just another evasive strategy which shifts the whole burden of explanation from substantive issues in science and philosophy of science to trivial issues in semantics. Rather we should take such challenges at full force and accept that they require some drastic re-thinking of what constitutes rational self-evidence or *a priori* truth.

This is the predominant tenor of Putnam's arguments in *Mathematics, Matter and Method*. Thus he remarks that many early – and some more recent – advocates of non-Euclidean geometry 'sought to minimise the impact of their proposals (or, rather, to make them more palatable) by adopting an extreme operationist style of presentation' (1975[1]: 78). In the same way, proponents of a non-standard quantum logic tend to suggest that it only holds good – or only has valid application – for a certain 'precisely specified operational meaning of the logical connectives', thus precluding any awkward implications outside or beyond the quantum domain (*ibid.*). On this view classical logic would retain its validity not only as applied to our methods of inference with regard to macrophysical objects and events but also in certain quantum-related contexts where the paradoxes of superposition and wave/particle dualism can safely be ignored and there is hence no need for redefinition of the logical connectives 'and' and 'or' so as to save empirical appearances. However, as I have said, Putnam rejects this whole operationist line of argument. 'In my opinion, whatever their intentions, [these theorists] *are* challenging logic.' And again:

> [j]ust as the almost unimaginable fact that Euclidean geometry is false – false of *paths in space*, not just false of 'light rays' – has an epistemological significance that philosophy must some day come to terms with, no matter how long it continues to postpone the reckoning, so the fact that Boolean logic is false – false of the *logical relations between states of affairs* – has a significance that philosophy and mathematics must come to terms with. (Putnam 1975[1]: 78)

In which case, he thinks, we shall have to accept some far-reaching and philosophically disturbing consequences, among them questions with regard to the standard propositional calculus which is still used for most scientific purposes (including the more speculative branches of particle physics), and also with regard to the conceptual foundations of set theory. Moreover, we shall need to get used to the idea that any progress in these or other fields may turn out to require a radical break with one or other of our deeply entrenched *a priori* commitments or truths now taken as self-evident to reason. For such ideas can no longer be a guide – or, if so, then a strictly fallible guide – when it comes to evaluating rival theories, fixing limits to the scope of counter-intuitive hypotheses, or weighing the force of empirical evidence as against some cardinal precept of logic. What emerges from the cases of non-Euclidean geometry, relativity theory and quantum mechanics – not to mention previous episodes like the shift from Ptolemaic to Copernican astronomy – is the fact that no degree of intuitive self-evidence or assumed *a priori* warrant can ever be sufficient to exclude the prospect of some challenge arising in the subsequent course of enquiry.

This applies just as much to mathematics and logic as to instances in the more empirical branches of applied scientific endeavour. Here also, Putnam argues, it might transpire that what had hitherto counted as a strictly indubitable statement, axiom, or 'law' of logic came up against a range of recalcitrant data that forced its revision or abandonment. So the case with mathematics and logic is essentially no different from the case with geometry, since there is nothing *in the nature* of these disciplines – no appeal to an order of sheerly self-validating truth – that could render them proof against conceptual change under pressure from conflicting evidence. (See especially Putnam 1983.) To this extent he agrees with Quine: that if we find it hard to dispense with such notions then the reason is to be sought in their deep entwinement with our various existing beliefs, theories, conceptual schemes, canons of valid inference, etc., rather than their status as necessary truths secure beyond rational doubt (Quine 1961). Thus in answer to the question: 'could some of the "necessary truths" of logic ever turn out to be false *for empirical reasons?*', he responds that this might indeed be the case since 'logic is, in a certain sense, an empirical science' (1975[1]: 174). On the other hand – as so often with Putnam – he is uneasy about endorsing this argument at full Quinean strength since it seems to controvert some powerful intuitions that are held not only by specialist philosophers of logic and mathematics but also by a good many lay thinkers when pondering the same sorts of question. Indeed, one could devote a good deal of commentary to Putnam's various changes of mind on the issue as to whether there exist (or can be known to exist) any strictly *a priori* or necessary truths. (See especially the essays on this topic collected in Putnam 1975[1] and 1983.) For the consequence of rejecting that thesis outright is to raise large problems about the conduct of enquiry in every field of thought, from mathematics to philosophy of logic and thence to the pure and applied scientific disciplines. That is to say, if one accepts that 'logic is empirical' – that the ground-rules (or 'necessary truths') of reason might always conceivably be subject to change – then it is hard to explain how any such revision can claim adequate warrant or be justified by a process of inference to the best (most rational) explanation.

II

This issue receives its fullest treatment – though also (typically) its least conclusive – in Putnam's essay 'There Is At Least One *A Priori* Truth', collected in the volume *Realism and Reason* (1983: 98–114). That the essay comes equipped with a postscriptum 'Note' and a further 'Supplementary Note', plus a cautionary memo ('I no longer agree with the conclusion for a number of reasons, but I still think the arguments are still of interest' (110)) gives some indication of his doubts on this score but also of his strong countervailing sense that if the thesis doesn't hold then we are in bigger trouble than Quine, for one, seems willing to admit. Putnam starts out by running through a range of candidate statements – from empirical generalisations (like 'the leaves always turn in October') to Euclidean geometry as a theory of actual space and thence to the 'laws' of pre-quantum physics – which can be all be shown to admit of possible disconfirmation and thus to have failed the test. Nevertheless, he now seeks to defend the claim that 'there is at least one *a priori* truth in exactly the sense that Quine and I denied, i.e., at least one truth that it would never be rational to give up' (1983: 100). This will be what Putnam calls a 'weak version of the law of contradiction', that is to say, one that is 'weak' enough to accommodate the various counter-instances (like those from non-Euclidean geometry and the presumptive failure of bivalence with respect to quantum mechanics) while avoiding the kinds of logical conundrum which result – as he now thinks – from denying that claim.

Thus in its classical form the law holds simply that 'no proposition is both true and false', or as expressed in the notation of modern symbolic logic, $\sim (p \, \& \, \sim p)$. A stronger version might hold $\forall p$ True $\sim (p \, \& \, \sim p)$ where the universal quantifier $\forall$ specifies that p is to be taken as ranging over all propositions, statements, or sentences. According to Aristotle this is indeed a necessary truth – one that stands firm against revision – since its denial entails the truth of every proposition along with the truth of its contrary. More precisely, for Aristotle it is a logical impossibility that anything (any attribute or predicate) should hold good and not hold good of the same object and in the same respect. However, Putnam argues, it might be maintained that the principle *does* need revising or require that some limit be placed on its scope of application, as for instance in the case of quantum-physical phenomena like wave/particle dualism where '"the electron is a particle" is both true and false, or "the electron is a wave" is both true and false' (1983: 100). Perhaps one could get around this problem by invoking 'the *typical* principle of contradiction', one that applied only to the class of bivalent (true-or-false) statements concerning macrophysical objects or events, and which thus excluded such atypical cases as superposed quantum states. But Putnam prefers to avoid having recourse to this kind of *ad hoc* solution. Rather, he will present the 'weakest pos-sible' or 'minimal' version of the principle of contradiction, namely that 'not every statement is both true and false'. For if there might just conceivably be counter-instances to the stronger (classical or Aristotelian) version then in this form at least the principle appears beyond reach of coherent or intelligible doubt. That is to say, any future theory T that denied the weak version – perhaps as the result of some as-yet inconceivable result thrown up by empirical research – would be a theory that 'consisted of every statement and its negation', not only in a specified (anomalous) domain such as that of quantum mechanics but across the whole range of statements in the physical sciences and elsewhere. In which case clearly it would be quite incapable of proof or falsification – hence devoid of genuine empirical content – since any 'evidence' adduced would count for nothing on either side of the argument.

Putnam runs through various possible objections or sceptical rejoinders and argues – to my mind convincingly – that they fail to answer his point, i.e., that the acceptance of theory T would amount to a wholesale repudiation not only of the single most basic principle of logic but also of any empirical grounds one could have for entertaining such a drastic revisionist move. In particular he comes out strongly against the conventionalist idea that an *a priori* truth of the kind under review might possess this character of seeming logical necessity (in modal terms: of holding good across all possible worlds) solely by virtue of its central role in our system of beliefs or accepted practices of justificatory reasoning. This is also where Putnam takes issue with his own earlier argument that such truths can best be treated as instances of 'contextual a priority', that is to say, propositions or logical axioms which are so deeply entrenched and bound up with so many of our standing assumptions, theories, ontological commitments, and so forth, that we are simply *unable* to conceive of their yet being open to revision or replacement. (Cf. Putnam, 'It Ain't Necessarily So', 1975[1]: 237–49.) On this 'moderate Quinean' view, as Putnam describes it, 'what we mistake for absolute apriority is a status which some propositions truly have, a status which is truly different from ordinary, garden-variety contingency, but which is not an absolute apriority' (1983: 101). So might it not be the case – he now asks – that the weak version of the principle of contradiction – 'not every statement is both true and false' – is itself another instance of contextual apriority, one that we are strongly inclined to endorse as possessing 'absolute' status, but which seems to enjoy that unique privilege only on account of our sheer inability to think what could constitute evidence against it? However, this idea runs up against all the difficulties mentioned above, chief among them the fact that we cannot deny the weak version without thereby affirming the truth of every statement and its contrary, in which case the argument collapses into manifest nonsense.

It seems to me that Putnam is right about this – 'absolutely' and not just 'contextually' right – since the weak version of the principle of contradiction is one that stands proof against counter-argument precisely by virtue of its logical form and the strict impossibility that we should ever find evidence that forced us to revise or renounce it. That is to say, we are unable to specify conditions under which some well-formed predictive hypothesis with definite (i.e., verifiable or falsifiable) content might be subject to test and shown to be both true and false, thus proving an exception to the rule. Such would be the case if, for instance, one predicted that on opening a box that contained a sheet of paper the sheet would turn out to be both red and not-red, rather than possessing a primary colour that had never been seen before. Should the latter finding apply then this would certainly involve some considerable upset to a branch of physical theory, 'namely the physical theory that says that colour is determined by lambda, the wavelength of the light reflected from the paper' (1983: 104). Indeed, we might find it hard to accept this evidence – to believe our eyes – in so far as it presented such a massive (well-nigh incredible) affront to our standing beliefs with regard to what could possibly *count* as a veridical perception. After all, 'if that theory is true, and it is also true that we have correctly mapped out which lambdas correspond to which colours, and which lambdas the human eye is sensitive to, then there is no room, in the sense of no room in the theory, for another major colour' (*ibid.*). Still there is some doubt – according to the latest research – as to whether that theory *is* in fact true, or whether there might be other factors (such as variable reflectance across sharp edges) of which it takes no account. In any case Putnam's general point is that we can at least conceive -- if not intuit – what it would mean for the prediction to be borne out by our opening the box and discovering the sheet to possess some hitherto undreamt-of primary colour. But the case is quite different with his other example, that of our predicting that the sheet will be both red and not-red, and of *this* forecast turning out true when the box is opened for inspection. For when we try (and fail) to envisage such an outcome '[t]he kind of inconceivability that is relevant is not mere unintuitability'. Rather, it is a question of our not being able to make the least sense of a flatly contradictory pair of predictive hypotheses, let alone frame any adequate idea of what might count as a confirmatory sighting.

Then again, 'it isn't that "the sheet of paper is red" and "the sheet of paper is not red" is literally unintelligible in the way in which "wa'arobi besnork gavagai" is literally unintelligible, even though some philosophers have tried to assimilate the unintelligibility of contradictions to the unintelligibility of what is literally without sense in the language' (1983: 105). If this were the case then one could argue – in Wittgensteinian fashion – that the criteria for apriority (and likewise for instances of logical contradiction) are only to be grasped in the context of our various communal language-games, life-forms, rule-following practices, etc. (Wittgenstein 1953) However, there is a crucial difference, as Putnam remarks, between the failure to grasp what somebody means by uttering a string of linguistically deviant or downright nonsensical sounds and the failure to assign any meaningful predictive or assertoric content to their words on account of their having flouted some basic principle of logic. In the latter case – where the language itself is no problem – we can at least figure out the intended gist of their utterance by applying a shared range of phonemic, lexical and grammatical resources. Indeed, it is precisely on this basis that we know them to have uttered two contradictory statements and are hence at a loss to construe their words in any rational or logically sense-preserving manner. As Putnam puts it:

> '[t]his sheet of paper is red and this sheet of paper is not red' isn't unintelligible
> at all. It simply asserts what cannot be the case. And the reason that *when I open*

the box you will see that the sheet of paper is red and the sheet of paper is not red does not count as a prediction, is that we know – know *a priori* – that it can't possibly turn out to be the case. (Putnam 1983: 105)

Thus it cannot be classed with instances – like that of Euclidean geometry – where what had previously counted as a paradigm case of 'absolute apriority' turned out to be no such thing, or rather, to possess only the kind of 'contextual apriority' which came of its playing a central role in the thought of mathematicians, logicians and philosophers over a long period. Nor can it be placed in the same category as the prediction that, when the box is opened, it will be found to contain a cloth of some hitherto unknown primary colour. For here also we are able to conceive – i.e., spell out in non-contradictory and logically intelligible terms – what this discovery would entail, even though it would constitute a massive shock to our standing beliefs and perceptual expectations, as well as a drastic upheaval in the field of scientific colour-theory. Rather these comparisons bring out the main point about 'absolute' *a priori* truths as Putnam construes them: i.e., that such truths are simply not open to any kind of challenge, revision, adjustment, or change of status in response to empirical counter-evidence or to new ways of thinking (like non-Euclidean geometry) which might require that they henceforth be reclassified as 'contextually' *a priori*. Thus 'to explain the special status of the principle of contradiction, or at least of the minimal principle of contradiction, in terms of contextual apriority, is a loser' (1983: 105–6).

In which case philosophers like Quine must be wrong – or pushing the argument much too far – when they claim to have deconstructed the very distinction between analytic and synthetic orders of statement, or *a priori* truths self-evident to reason and empirically warranted 'matters of fact' that are always, in principle, open to challenge from the kinds of evidence periodically thrown up by new discoveries in the physical sciences. Of course, Quine can say that 'centrality' (his near-equivalent of Putnam's 'contextual apriority') is all that is required in order to preserve our strong intuitions in this matter, that is, our sense that some such truths – like the principle of contradiction – are so central or basic to our whole way of thinking as to stand beyond challenge for all practical purposes (Quine 1961). However, Putnam counters,

we should be clear about what the centrality argument does not show. It does not show that a putative law of logic, for instance the principle of contradiction, could not be overthrown by *direct observation*. Presumably, I would give up the principle of contradiction if I ever had a sense datum which was both red and not red, for example. And the centrality argument sheds no light on how we know that this could not possibly happen. (Putnam 1983: 110)

In fact there is some room for doubt as to whether Quine would push this far with his logical-revisionist case, inclined as he is – at least in his text-book writings on philosophy of logic – to countenance revision of other principles (such as bivalence and excluded middle) while drawing a line at the principle of contradiction (Quine 1970). Nor is this in any way surprising, given the fact – pointed out by

Aristotle – that any joint assertion of two contradictory statements entails the simultaneous truth and falsehood of *each and every* well-formed or meaningful statement that could possibly be uttered (Aristotle 1941, Book IV, Chapter 4, 1007b). Also there is the further Aristotelian point, as Putnam remarks, that 'if anyone pretends to disbelieve one of the laws of logic and undertakes to argue with us, we can easily convince him that his own argument presupposes the very laws of logic that he is objecting to' (Putnam 1983: 109–10). Of course it might be questioned – as, for instance, by anti-realists like Dummett or proponents of an alternative (many-valued) quantum logic – whether this applied to other logical 'laws' such as bivalence or excluded middle. Yet they would surely not wish to invite the above sorts of charge by extending this revisionist line of argument to the principle of contradiction.

Now I think – to repeat – that Putnam is right ('absolutely' right) in all this and that his case for the existence of at least one *a priori* truth – that 'not every statement is both true and false' – is made out to convincing effect. What is more remarkable, given its sheer self-evidence, is that Putnam should have felt the need to defend this position at such length, and also that his essay comes attended with so many doubts, second thoughts, and qualifications, including those raised in the two supplementary Notes. I won't go into any great detail on these and thereby risk straining my reader's patience. Sufficient to say that they touch on a number of issues – from set-theory, mathematical intuitionism, quantum mechanics, and so forth – which Putnam has himself, on other occasions, taken as plausibly requiring some more-or-less drastic change to our idea of what counts as a necessary (analytic) truth or an *a priori* (hence unrevisable) statement of logical principle (Putnam 1975[1]). These doubts emerge in a passage toward the end of his December 1977 'Note to supersede (supplement?) the preceding note' where Putnam asks: 'just how important is it that Quine is wrong in his *total* rejection of the *a priori*?'. After all, he goes on,

> [i]n one way it is not very important. We do not have a good *theory* of rational-ity, and are unlikely to have one in the foreseeable future. Lacking the 'rigid designator' of rationality, the theoretical definition which tells us what rational-ity is in every possible world (as 'water is H_2O' tells us what water is in every possi-ble world) it is virtually hopeless to show with any semblance of good argument that any specific statement is such that it would be irrational to ever give it up (apart from special examples, such as the one I constructed). (Putnam 1983: 113–14)

Yet this comment seems oddly (even perversely) off-the-point if one considers that Putnam's 'special example' – his minimalist variant of the principle of contradic-tion – is a case that doesn't stand alone but which, if valid, has wider implications for the status of a great many other such instances. Among these latter would be truth-claims (whether in logic, mathematics or the physical sciences) that are indeed capable of more 'specific statement' in terms of their meaning, content, truth-conditions, or predictive-explanatory warrant. For otherwise there could be little point to his argument concerning that one special case, devised as it was –

on the minimalist principle – to meet all comers and therefore to yield as few hostages as possible to any kind of counter-argument. Rather it stands (somewhat in the manner of Descartes' *cogito, ergo sum*) as a rock-bottom basis for meeting the sceptics on their own ground and then going on to derive proper standards – of truth, rationality, warranted inference, etc. – for application in other (more specific or substantive) contexts of debate.

No doubt there is a sense in which Putnam really does want to treat it, at least for the purposes of his argument here, as the sole instance of an *a priori* truth which we could never – under any conceivable circumstances – be justified in rejecting or revising. This is why, as we have seen, he spends a lot of time explaining how it differs from cases (like the passage from Euclidean to non-Euclidean geometry or the emergence of a new primary colour) that belong to a quite distinct category even though they once involved – or might yet involve – some hitherto unthinkable drastic revision to our standing habits of belief. For these latter would thenceforth have to be regarded as instances of 'contextual apriority', whereas no such revision could possibly affect the status of an absolute *a priori* truth like the (weak or minimal) principle of contradiction. Even so – as I have said – there is no good reason to conclude from Putnam's strategic choice of example that this very 'weakness' is such as to preclude its having any bearing on other cases that would involve something more definite in the way of substantive philosophical content. That he himself appears tempted to take it that way is I think another sign of Putnam's chronic uncertainty as to just how far – and in just what respects – logic may have to be thought of as revisable under pressure from empirical counter-evidence. There is a nice passage in the supplementary 'Note' which concedes all this with typically disarming candour. Thus:

> we philosophers are frequently torn in just the fashion that I am now torn between opposing considerations, but we very infrequently show it *in print*. What we do is let ourselves be torn in private until we finally 'plonk' for one alternative or the other; then the published paper only shows what we plonked for, and not the being torn. For once, the present paper-plus-potentially-infinite-series-of-notes *will* show the 'being torn'. (Putnam 1983: III–12)

All the same I would want to argue – with support from Putnam in his own more sanguine moments – that the minimal version of the principle of contradiction goes a lot further than he gives us to believe when making those various concessionary statements. That is to say, it is more closely tied up with other principles of 'classical' logic (such as bivalence and excluded middle) which Putnam, like Quine, is occasionally willing to consider as possible candidates for revision.

Take for instance the passage cited two paragraphs above where Putnam appears to yield crucial ground by conceding that 'in one way' his argument *contra* Quine is 'not very important' since we don't at present possess 'a good *theory* of rationality' and are unlikely to get one in the near future (1983: 113–14). More precisely, what we lack in this regard is a Kripkean 'rigid designator' which would pick out just those instances of rationality that applied across all possible worlds, and which thus possessed the status of necessary truths as opposed to contingent (or this-world-relative) matters-of-fact (Kripke 1980). Still, there is something very loose and *ad hoc* about Putnam's use of the argument here, at least when compared with his own earlier writings on the causal theory of reference (Putnam 1975[2]). What drops out completely is the crucial distinction between analytic truths whose necessity (or transworld validity) derives from their purely logical character and those other instances of *a posteriori* necessary truth – such as 'water is H_2O' – which possess that status in virtue of their having been discovered through a process of empirical discovery or reference-fixing that applies to all genuine samples of the kind across worlds that resemble our own in the relevant physical respect. After all, it was just this distinctive feature of the Kripke/early Putnam theory of reference that was claimed to represent a signal advance over other (i.e., descriptivist) theories which failed to explain how scientific progress came about through an ever more detailed depth-explanatory knowledge of the various structures, properties, or attributes involved (Putnam 1975[2]: 139–52, 196–214, 215–71). That this approach doesn't work for a concept such as 'rationality' is scarcely surprising given its role in Putnam's argument here, that is to say, his case for the existence of at least one (albeit 'minimal') *a priori* truth that would hold good against the various counter-arguments put up by Quine and others. For it was just Kripke's point – like Putnam's – that it could work only if one drew a clear distinction between *a priori* truths whose necessity inheres in their purely logical transworld character and *a posteriori* truths (like those concerning the subatomic structure of gold or the molecular structure of water) whose necessity inheres in the way things stand in our own and relevantly similar worlds (Kripke 1980; also Wiggins 1980). To conflate these distinct orders of necessity is to conjure doubt not only with regard to the status of empirical truth-claims in the physical sciences but also with regard to the status and validity of logical reasoning in general.

Hence – I suggest – Putnam's doubt in the above-cited passage as to whether we possess (or are likely to achieve 'in the foreseeable future') any workable criterion for *a priori* truth with the same kind of transworld validity that holds for statements such as 'water is H_2O'. That is to say, this involves just the kind of category-mistake that Kripke and early Putnam sought to reveal with their various examples of *a posteriori* necessary truth, i.e., cases where the truth in question was a matter of *de re* necessity discovered through a process of empirical investigation rather than a matter of rational self-evidence. Their chief point in making that distinction – more explicitly in Putnam's case – was to show how fixity of reference was maintained despite and across those signal advances in scientific knowledge that had often effected a radical change in the specification of various physical properties or attributes. Yet clearly this cannot apply in the case of *a priori* truths, such as the principle of contradiction, whose character of transworld necessity derives solely from their logical form. For that character has nothing to do with the existence of certain natural kinds whose microstructural features are such as to determine the truth-conditions for any statement concerning them either with respect to the actual world or else with respect to any other world which may or may not contain objects of just those kinds.

Thus – to repeat – it is a matter of *a posteriori* necessity that water will indeed be H_2O wherever such stuff is to be found, just as (counterfactually) Twin-Earth 'water' would always be identified by its possessing the distinctive molecular structure XYZ (Putnam 1975[2]: 223–35). But these truths are in no sense *a priori* since we can well conceive of other *logically* possible worlds where the laws of subatomic structure were different, so that (for instance) atoms were not held together by the opposed (positive and negative) charges on protons and electrons. Perhaps those charges would turn out to be reversed – with Twin-Earth physicists referring to 'electrons' where Earthian physicists refer to 'protons' – or perhaps there might exist a whole different range of Twin-Earth subatomic particles with other (to us highly strange or exotic) forces acting between them. Yet of course we should simply be wrong to conclude – on the descriptivist theory of reference – that 'Twin-Earth electrons have a positive charge', just as Putnam's space-travellers would be wrong to announce that 'Twin Earth water is XYZ and not H_2O'. Rather, we and they should draw the conclusion that 'electrons (and water) don't exist on Twin-Earth' owing to the different physical laws that obtain on that deceptively Earth-like planet where phenomenal appearances are apt to mislead any Earthian visitor. For this is just Putnam's and Kripke's point: that reference is fixed by the way things stand with respect to what *we* take as paradigm samples of the kind, along with their essential properties and attributes, like molecular structure in the case of water and negative charge in the case of electrons. Thus Earthian physics would collapse at a stroke if the travellers returned with the news that 'electrons on Twin-Earth have a positive charge', and if this were taken by the physics community as a genuine counter-instance to the law that 'the charge on every electron is negative'. What they (the physicists) would more likely say, perhaps with help from Earthian logicians and philosophers of language, is that 'people in the Twin-Earth physics community use the term "electron" where we use "proton"'. Or again, if the laws of Twin-Earth physics were *really* so very different, then they would have to conclude that *nothing corresponded* to the phrase 'Twin-Earth electron' and hence that they required a *whole different theory* – one with a whole new range of elementary particles – in order to account for the subatomic structure and properties of Twin-Earth matter. Otherwise there could simply be no making sense of the space-travellers' report, any more than with the case of Twin-Earth water turning out to be XYZ and not H_2O.

III

My point is that the force of such arguments depends on maintaining a firm sense of the modal-logical distinction between various orders of counterfactual possibility. These range all the way from possible worlds which depart from our own in some minor (e.g., historically contingent) respect to worlds, such as Putnam's Twin-Earth, where different molecular structures show up, and thence – *via* worlds that entail some change in the laws of subatomic physics – to the limit-case instance of a notional world in which (just conceivably) we might be forced to renounce or at any rate to drastically revise certain ground-rules of rational inference. Even so there are some such rules – like the 'weak' or 'minimal' principle of contradiction – that could not be abandoned without falling into manifest nonsense or absurdity. In early Putnam this argument is chiefly deployed in support of a causal-realist approach to issues in philosophical semantics, epistemology, and the logic of scientific explanation. Thus it offers a strong response to those sceptical thinkers – from Hume to Goodman – who have questioned the validity of inductive reasoning on account of its failure to meet the strict requirements of deductive warrant (Hume 1975; Goodman 1955). J.S. Mill was among the first to challenge such scepticism as involving a misapplication of standards that were perfectly valid (indeed indispensable) elsewhere but which had no place in the context of inductive inference to the best, most adequate causal explanation (Mill 1973–74). His challenge finds support in the Kripke/early Putnam theory of reference since it shows that inductive procedures have a lot more to go on than Humean observed regularity or 'constant conjunction'. What provides this additional warrant is the fact that we *can* reasonably claim to have a better (more detailed or depth-explanatory) knowledge of those various objects, properties, causal powers, dispositional attributes, microphysical structures, and so forth, than earlier thinkers – like Hume and Locke – who felt themselves driven to a sceptical verdict by reflection on the limits of scientific knowledge in their time. Thus, for instance, Locke's rather vague talk of colour as a 'secondary quality' or dispositional 'power' to produce certain kinds of subjective sensation in the observer can nowadays be given a more adequate scientific explanation, namely one that involves 'the particular micro-structure of [e.g.] a piece of cloth which leads it to selectively absorb and reflect light of different wave-lengths' (Putnam 1981: 58; Locke 1959).

I take this example from *Reason, Truth and History* (1981), a book that in many ways marks a crucial stage in his long-haul retreat from causal realism, but where clearly that outlook still exerts a strong countervailing pull. What is so strange about Putnam's later development is the constant resurfacing of arguments like this alongside the constant appeal to arguments – from quantum physics, non-Euclidean geometry, deviant (many-valued) logics, mereological sums, Quinean ontological relativity, Goodman's 'new puzzle' of induction, Gödel's Incompleteness Theorem, or the Löwenheim–Skolem Theorem with respect to conceptual problems in set-theory – which he takes to undermine the case for realism except in a suitably scaled-down 'internal-realist' guise. Thus by the time of *Meaning and the Moral Sciences* (1978) he has moved so far in this latter direction that it becomes difficult to explain how the sentence '"cow" refers to cows' can be capable of even an internal-realist (let alone a stronger 'metaphysical' realist) construal. That is to say, it stands open to just the sorts of challenge that I have listed above, among them the impossibility of assigning any 'unique *intended* interpretation' to the sentence, or picking out just one among the 'non-denumerably many interpretations (in the sense of satisfaction-relations) which would render true an *ideal* theory', or basing that theory on the 'set of all true sentences' that ranged over all and only instances of the bovine kind (1978: 135). At this point, Putnam suggests, the internal realist will be best advised to respond along the following lines:

> '"Cow" refers to cows' follows immediately from the definition of 'refers'. In fact, '"cow" refers to cows' would be true even if internal realism were false: although we can revise '"Cow" refers to cows' by scrapping the theory itself (or at least scrapping or challenging the notion of a *cow* – and this is how the fact that '"cow" refers to cows' is not *absolutely* unrevisable manifests itself – *relative to the theory*, '"Cow" refers to cows' is a logical truth. (Putnam 1978: 136)

Even so, the anti-realist can still come back with a series of arguments purporting to show that this sentence may indeed be analytic – or a 'logical truth' – but only relative to the theory in question, that is to say, by certain theory-specific criteria of meaning or definitional equivalence. Thus the sentence 'is true in all admissible interpretations of the theory – but that isn't at issue' (*ibid.*: 136). To which (predictably) Putnam responds that this rejoinder misses the internal-realist point: that there is *just no way* of deciding or intelligibly raising such issues except from one or another theory-relative (or internal) viewpoint. So the sceptic can now best be answered by remarking: (1) that '"the way the theory is understood" can't be discussed within the theory', and (2) that 'the question whether the theory has a *unique* intended interpretation has *no* absolute sense' (*ibid.*). For it is an irony lost on the sceptic – Putnam thinks – that his or her challenges to the internal realist are couched in such a way that they could not possibly be satisfied except by some version of strong ('metaphysical') realism. Thus '[t]he critic's "how do you know?" question assumes a theory-independent fact of the matter as to what a term in a given theory corresponds to – i.e., assumes the picture of metaphysical realism; and this is a picture the *internal* realist need not – and better not – accept' (*ibid.*).

Now it seems to me that the irony here works the other way around and that Putnam's internal-realist argument cannot be upheld against the kinds of criticism that he attributes to the token interlocutor. For by this stage he has yielded so much ground – as compared with his earlier realist position – that the sceptic has only to exert a little pressure and insist that there is really no difference (in pragmatist terms: no difference that makes any difference) between Putnam's theory and the sceptic's outlook of full-fledged anti-realism. If any further proof were needed – so the sceptic might claim – then consider the following passage where Putnam lays out his response to this challenge in terms that he thinks quite adequate to meet it on all the main points at issue. 'What I am saying', Putnam writes,

> is that, in a certain 'contextual' sense, it is an *a priori* truth that 'cow' refers to a determinate class of things (or a more-or-less determinate class of things – I neglect ordinary vagueness). Adopting 'cow talk' is adopting a 'version', in Nelson Goodman's phrase, from within which it is *a priori* that the word 'cow' refers (and, indeed, that it refers to cows). (Putnam 1978: 137)

No doubt some further specification is required in order to head off sceptical rejoinders, as for instance by explaining that 'cow' is to be treated as a word (or lexical item) rather than a three-letter string. All the same what is remarkable here is that Putnam should feel himself obliged to adopt this extreme 'contextualist' position as regards not only such recondite entities as electrons or protons but also as regards such lifesize objects as those that one often encounters on walks in the country grazing or chewing the cud. I put it like this – rather flippantly, some may think – in order to emphasise just how far Putnam has departed from anything that could plausibly be claimed to constitute a realist approach to such matters. For if the only argument that now strikes him as carrying weight against the sceptic is one that involves a 'contextual *a priori*' standard of necessary truth then it is scarcely surprising that Putnam ends up by endorsing a Goodman-type sceptical position on which 'cow-talk' can indeed be taken as referring to cows but only within the particular scheme – or world-version – that finds room for such talk. After all, it is a very odd notion of *a priori* truth that would accommodate sentences like '*this* is a cow' or 'animals of *that* sort are cows'. No doubt it is *a priori* in a narrower, purely analytic sense that '"cow" refers to cows is a logical truth', since this follows as a matter of straightforward definitional or logico-semantic warrant. But on any stronger (i.e., non-circular) understanding of *a priori* truth it is absurd to suppose that our justification for referring to certain kinds of animals as 'cows' can be aprioristically grounded. If this were the case then we could never be wrong in making such judgements or statements since they would be strictly unrevisable – synthetic *a priori* – come what may in the way of empirical counter-evidence.

Of course it might be said that Putnam very sensibly concedes this point by allowing that they are *a priori* only 'in a certain "contextual" sense', that is, relative to what we normally take (on the best evidence to hand) as adequate warrant for applying the name 'cow' in this or that particular instance. However, the thesis then becomes trivial since the truth-condition for ascriptions of cowhood can entail nothing more than a certain way of talking that merely counts as '*a priori*' by the standards, conventions, or accepted criteria which characterise that kind of talk. In which case, the whole argument collapses into manifest circularity and does nothing to meet the objections raised by Putnam's imagined interlocutor. Thus the above passage goes an odd way around in answering the sceptic and refuting the idea that we might have problems with fixity of reference (or criteria for kind-membership) even as regards familiar objects like cows. That is to say, it conspicuously *doesn't* take the Kripke–early Putnam line according to which there is a certain kind of animal that we standardly refer to under just that name, whose visible features most often serve for the purpose of reliable identification, and whose membership in the bovine species can always be decided – should appearances not suffice – by consulting some expert source, whether farmer, zoologist, or (if need be) specialist in genetic science (Kripke 1980; Putnam 1975[2]). On this Kripkean account it is a matter of *a posteriori* necessity that the creature thus referred to should possess certain reference-fixing attributes such as a distinctive DNA profile or chromosome sequence. So if Twin-Earth 'cows' were seemingly perfect replicas of their Earthian counterparts yet turned out to be silicon-based rather than organic (carbon-based) life forms then the space-traveller from Earth would simply be wrong – misled by deceptive appearances – in applying that familiar name. But of course this has nothing whatever to do with the issue about *a priori* truths, whether 'absolute', 'contextual', or rock-bottom 'minimalist' in Putnam's favoured form. Rather, it is a question of the way things stand – *necessarily* stand – with regard to certain natural kinds and their various intrinsic features, properties, genetic or molecular constitutions, etc. And this in turn is a matter of its having been established *a posteriori* through a range of well-proven scientific methods and techniques that possession of just those distinctive features is sufficient to identify the item concerned as an instance of just that natural kind. (See also Schwartz (ed.) 1977.)

It seems to me that the above-cited passages go a long way toward explaining why the later Putnam started out on his long voyage of retreat from causal realism. For if there is any sense in which it is known *a priori* that the name 'cow' must be taken as referring to 'a determinate class of things' (i.e., cows), then this can only be construed in analytic terms, or as a merely definitional 'truth of reason' that follows from the meaning of the word 'refers' when used in this or any number of related contexts. Of course Putnam wants his argument to do more serious philosophical work, since otherwise the sceptic will rightly point out that the claim is circular and hence wholly trivial. Yet he then has to specify just what that alternative construal might be, given the patent absurdity of thinking that our grasp of the relevant features, attributes, or membership-conditions for the species 'cow' could somehow be known *a priori* or without the least benefit of previous cow-related knowledge by acquaintance or description. Thus we are advised to take his claim 'only in a certain "contextual" sense', that is to say, as involving what counts *for us* as a matter of self-evident (presuppositional) truth since it holds for all contexts in which we would have reason to use or apply that name. But this concession once again leaves his case wide open to the sceptic's line of attack, namely that 'contextual' (or 'internal') realism amounts to no more than a face-saving strategy or a means to keep up realist appearances while covertly adopting a relativist or 'strong' anti-realist position. Why else would Putnam go on to remark – in the very next sentence – that '[a]dopting "cow talk" is adopting a "version", in Nelson Goodman's phrase, from within which it is *a priori* that the word "cow" refers (and, indeed, that it refers to cows)'? (Putnam 1978: 137) For by now it has become quite evident that Putnam is unable to hold the line against anyone who asks what difference there is – practically speaking – between a 'realist' theory of reference that is *a priori* 'in a certain "contextual" sense' and a full-blown constructivist theory (such as Goodman's) that can just as well claim *a priori* warrant if one defines apriority in suitably vague or world-version-relative terms (Putnam 1978). Thus the passage slides from the claim that our cow-talk refers to a 'determinate class of things', *via* the claim that such talk is 'more-or-less-determinate' (so long as one neglects 'ordinary vagueness'), to the point of acknowledging that it is only within some particular world-version that one can have any grip on the context-related notions of cowhood, reference, or indeed apriority. In which case – so the sceptic will surely remark – Putnam might as well drop this pretence of upholding a distinctive 'internal-realist' position and accept that there is nothing more to such talk than its making sense by the interpretative lights of some particular language-game, conceptual scheme or preferential world-version.

So there is certain irony about his then going on – in the next paragraph – to attribute these problems to the 'metaphysical realist', one whose mistake (as Putnam now sees it) is to think that we could ever have grounds or warrant for adopting a stronger position. Thus: '[o]ne of the puzzling things about the meta-physical realist picture is that it makes it unintelligible how there can be *a priori* truths, even contextual ones, even as a (possibly unreachable) limit. An *a priori* truth would have to be the product of a kind of direct 'intuition' of the things themselves' (Putnam 1978: 137). However, this is only a puzzle if one takes realism to involve some wildly implausible claim such as the idea that we can know *a priori* – by direct intuition – what constitutes the essence of the bovine kind, and thus what makes it a necessary truth that any instance of genuine (veridical) cow-talk refers to cows and nothing but cows. Otherwise the puzzle will be not so much a problem for the so-called 'metaphysical' realist as a matter of explaining why Putnam should think that this issue has anything to do with apriority, whether 'absolute', 'contextual', or world-version-relative. After all, he had once – and not so long before: in *Realism and Reason*, 1983 – explained very clearly how the 'new' theory of reference, as developed by Kripke and himself, made it pos-sible to set such problems aside by introducing a more adequate set of terms and distinctions. 'What Kripke is suggesting', in Putnam's words,

> is that (1) the old idea that science discovers necessary truths, that science discov-ers the essence of things, was, in an important sense, right not wrong; [and] (2) that the necessity in question, 'metaphysical necessity', or truth in all possible worlds, is *not* the same as apriority; epistemic necessity and metaphysical neces-sity have been unwarrantedly conflated. (Putnam 1983: 55)

However, these distinctions can have no place in Putnam's later thinking. For he is now convinced – under pressure from various sceptical quarters – that the choice falls out between, on the one hand, a naive 'metaphysical'-realist theory of reference which claims 'direct "intuition" of the things themselves' and, on the other, a theory which makes reference a matter of *a priori* warrant though only 'in a certain "contextual" sense'. And from here, as we have seen, it is no great distance to Goodman's claim that there exist as many right world-versions as there exist alternative referential schemes or ways of projecting words on to worlds (Goodman 1987). In which case one might be forgiven for thinking that the world pretty much drops out of this argument and that contextualism (or 'internal realism') amounts to no more than a figleaf variant of the sceptical-relativist position.

IV

I have suggested that one main reason for Putnam's dilemma is the relative neglect, in his later work, of those cardinal distinctions from modal logic that offered such a powerful explanatory resource when applied to issues in philosophical semantics, epistemology, and philosophy of science. Hence his rejection of the so-called 'metaphysical' realist approach that takes the reference and the truth-value of our various terms, observation-sentences, statements, theories, etc., to be fixed by the way things stand in reality rather than by the internal criteria which count as *a priori* within some given descriptive scheme or Goodmanian world-version. On the one hand, this weakens the notion of *a priori* truth to the point where it becomes just a product of contextual definition or a matter of self-evident (analytic) warrant for anyone who shares that particular scheme. On the other, it excludes any notion of science as discovering *a posteriori* necessary truths, that is to say, truths about 'the essence of things' – atomic weights, molecular structures, chromosomal properties, etc. – that serve to fix the reference of certain terms and also the operative truth-conditions for statements concerning them. But this was just the point of Putnam's early theory: to prevent the otherwise inevitable slide from a sceptical standpoint with regard to the existence of certain synthetic *a priori* truths (such as those once attributed to Euclidean geometry or Newtonian celestial mechanics) to an outlook of generalised scepticism as regards the very possibility of finding out truths about the physical world through investigation of its salient properties and attributes. What is more, such truths are informative (i.e., not tautologies or analytic truths-of-reason) precisely in so far as they involve knowledge of the physical world and its constituent, e.g. microstructural, features rather than a merely definitional knowledge of the various terms that happen to figure in our current-best theories and descriptions. Thus, for instance,

> if I describe something as a *lemon*, or as an *acid*, I indicate that it is likely to have certain characteristics (yellow peel, or sour taste in dilute water solution, as the case may be); but I also indicate that the presence of those characteristics, if they are present, is likely to be accounted for by some 'essential nature' which the thing shares with other members of the natural kind. What that essential nature is is not a matter of linguistic analysis but of scientific theory construction; today we would say it was chromosome structure, in the case of lemons, and being a proton-donor, in the case of acids. (Putnam 1975[2]: 140–1)

Of course, we might yet turn out to be wrong in taking these as the ultimate reference-fixing properties that render our statements objectively true or false, or that decide whether or not our current-best theories are 'truth-tracking' with respect to the way things stand in physical reality. (See also McCulloch 1995.) Yet this is not to grant the sceptical meta-induction which thinks to refute realism by arguing from the falsehood of so many past scientific beliefs to the strong probability that most of our current beliefs will likewise be falsified or at any rate – as with Euclidean geometry or Newton's laws of celestial motion – be shown to hold good only within certain limited frames of references. On the contrary: it is just such cases that provide the strongest possible warrant for scientific realism in so far as they require that the truth-value of any given statement or theory is dependent on certain objectively existing features of the physical world – say, the chromosome structure of lemons or the subatomic properties of acids – rather than our current state of knowledge or belief concerning them.

Hence early-Putnam's crucial point, as against that widespread neo-Lockean tendency in present-day thought which denies any prospect of our ever advancing from 'nominal' to 'real' definitions, or from notions of 'essence' that merely satisfy existing definitional criteria to a knowledge of essences that captures the depth-ontological nature of things. Such scepticism results – in his view – from an over-readiness to shift discussion from the *de re* level, where reference and truth are determined by real-world objects and their properties, to the *de dicto* level, where talk about 'objects', 'properties', 'reference' and 'truth' is merely a function of the way those terms figure in some given context of usage. Nor can this upshot be avoided, as late Putnam believes, by making it a matter of necessary (*a priori*) truth that 'lemon' refers to lemons, or 'acid' to acids, just so long as the apriority in question is construed in context-relative rather than 'absolute' terms. For in that case there is nothing that could possibly explain how science has advanced beyond periods of relative ignorance or confusion (such as the prevailing state of knowledge with regard to chemistry in Locke's time) when nominal definitions were indeed the best that could be hoped for, to periods such as the present when we possess a far better scientific grasp of what constitutes the essence – or defining property – of lemons, acids and so forth. Still, there is a sense in which scientists at Locke's time were referring to the same range of natural kinds when they used some term that picked out a sample of the kind in question despite their lacking any adequate grasp of its essential nature. This is what enables the realist to claim that the usage of natural-kind terms is 'sensitive to future discovery', i.e., that their reference is fixed for all time and across all physically compossible worlds by their denoting just those salient properties even if (say) enquirers are still at the stage of identifying lemons by their yellow peel or acids by their corrosive properties and sour taste when diluted in water. For it is precisely the hallmark of advances in scientific knowledge that they accommodate the discovery of counter-instances such as green lemons, or acid that doesn't taste sour in water since the water contains a high proportion of dissolved sugar, or, again, zebras that don't have stripes like most members of their species. That is to say, such anomalies can henceforth be treated as belonging to a range of strictly *non*-essential attributes whose variations from one sighting to the next are irrelevant when it comes to deciding what counts as a genuine sample of the kind.

Another great strength of the early-Putnam theory is its ability to explain how reference is fixed in various cases by appealing to different levels or degrees of micro-structural description. Thus it is not just a question – as some physicists would claim – of applying the most 'fundamental' (e.g., subatomic) theory of matter that is currently to hand and taking this as our benchmark standard for purposes of natural-kind attribution. After all, as Putnam points out, even if I have a description in, say, the language of particle physics of what are in fact the chromosomal properties of a fruit, I may not be able to tell that it is a lemon because I have not developed the theory according to which (1) those physical-chemical characteristics are the chromosomal structure-features (I may not even have the notion 'chromosome'); and (2) I may not have discovered that chromosomal structure is the *essential* property of lemons. (Putnam 1975[2]: 141–2)

In short, there is a patent fallacy involved in arguing from the 'fundamental' character of particle physics – since this is the science that investigates the ultimate depth-structural properties of matter – to the claim that physics alone bids fair to provide an ultimate 'theory of everything', at which stage presumably the other sciences (molecular biology, chemistry, solid and fluid mechanics, etc.) would thenceforth assume ancillary status or else be consigned to the pre-history of scientific thought. (See for instance Weinberg 1992.) Thus early Putnam's realism about natural kinds goes along with a highly discriminating sense of the different priorities or salience-conditions that apply in various well-defined contexts of enquiry. However, this is crucially *not* to endorse the idea – as in later Putnam – that reference is fixed (or rendered 'more or less determinate') only 'in a certain contextual sense', that is, relative to one or another among the going range of referential schemes, frameworks, projections or alternative world-versions. Rather, it is to say that the properties in question – subatomic, molecular, chromosomal, etc. – are such as to fix not only the reference of natural-kind terms but also the *precise level of description* at which science can properly claim to know what it is in the nature of things that marks them out as things of just that kind.

Here again, one consequence of Putnam's retreat from a causal-realist position is to deprive him of any resources for distinguishing between those among the sheer multiplicity of Goodmanian 'worlds' which are kindred to ours in some particular (physically salient) respect and those that belong to the various orders of counterfactual, hypothetical, or merely fictive possibility. By this stage Putnam has plainly despaired of defending any such argument against the massed ranks of anti-realists, framework-relativists, Wittgensteinian adepts of 'language-game' talk, and – not least – advocates of the view that natural-kind theories can only be redeemed from hopeless 'metaphysical' naiveté by reformulation in a language that eschews all essentialist terms and predicates. Hence his resort to a theory of reference where what counts as a sample or instance of the kind in question is settled by the role that referring expressions play in some given theory or with respect to some 'more-or-less determinate' paradigm-class (Putnam 1978). It would then be *a priori* (analytic, more like) that our talk about 'lemons' or 'acids' *just is* talk about lemons or acids since that is what we and our communal peers standardly mean or intend by using such terms. On this account there is no longer any question of our usage being subject to real-world constraints that involve the nature and properties of the objects concerned, or of our statements having their truth-value fixed by those same objective (i.e., language-independent) constraints. Still less could our talk be considered 'truth-tracking' or 'sensitive to future discovery', as for instance if scientists should one day produce a more adequate depth-ontological account which makes our present theories of subatomic or molecular structure seem to them just as primitive as we now think the sour-taste theory for identifying acids or the colour-based criterion for picking out lemons. For it is hard to see what could possibly *count* as a better (more adequate) means of identification if the only relevant standard is the role that such criteria are taken to play in some given context of descriptive, theoretical or causal-explanatory discourse. Nor can it make much difference if one elects – like the later Putnam – to substitute talk of 'more-or-less determinate classes of things' for that old (presumptively discredited) talk of 'natural kinds' and their various essential properties or salient attributes. For one is then stuck with the problem of explaining why some such 'classes' have a claim to embrace all and only those items that are relevantly similar while others must be thought of as promiscuous sets or zany compilations without any genuine organising principle. And from here it is but a short step to Goodman's far-out constructivist doctrine of multiple world-versions or – at the limit – Michel Foucault's fantastical Borges-derived anecdote about the Chinese encyclopaedia with its crazily heterodox classification of animal kinds (Putnam 1978; Foucault 1970: 2).

There are plenty of passages in early Putnam that come out strongly against this sceptical-nominalist line and which deploy the explanatory resources of causal realism (along with those of modal logic in the Kripkean possible-worlds idiom) in order to make their point. I select the following as a representative example and one that pinpoints exactly these problems about the strategy of replacing natural-kind talk with talk about 'classes', internal realism, contextual definition, and so forth. Thus:

> [e]ven if we *could* define 'natural kind' – say, 'a natural kind is a class which is the extension of a term P which plays such-and-such a methodological role in some well-confirmed theory' – the definition would obviously embody a theory of the world, at least in part. It is not *analytic* that natural kinds are classes which play certain kinds of roles in theories; what *really* distinguishes the classes we count as natural kinds is itself a matter of (high level and very abstract) scientific investigation and not just meaning analysis. (Putnam 1975[2]: 141)

This seems to me a cogent piece of argument which contrasts very sharply with the nominalist or sceptical-relativist turn in Putnam's later thinking about issues in epistemology, philosophical semantics, and philosophy of science. Above all, it anticipates the problems that result when he gives up arguing the case for causal realism and, along with it, the basic realist distinction between analytic truths-of-definition (arrived at through meaning analysis) and truths about the nature or structure of physical reality (arrived at through a process of *a posteriori* scientific investigation). Thus his point in the above passage is that one cannot get far with any formalised or logico-semantic approach that substitutes talk of 'classes' for talk of 'natural kinds', since the latter is taken to involve all manner of naively metaphysical or essentialist beliefs. Such a strategy will end up either by renouncing any claim to get things objectively right – as distinct from just 'right' according to certain theory-specific standards – or else by accepting that it does, after all, embody a substantive 'theory of the world' whose truth-conditions are determined by the world (by its constituent kinds, features, properties, causal dispositions and so forth) and not by the theory itself. That is to say, any move toward higher levels of abstraction had better be one that involves more powerful (explanatorily adequate) forms of scientific reasoning, rather than one that merely explicates the meaning of observation-sentences or covering-law statements.

This latter doctrine of semantic ascent – from first-order 'material' languages to higher-order formal or meta-linguistic levels of discourse – is among the chief legacies of logical empiricism, as classically exemplified in Tarski's work. (See Tarski 1956; also Carnap 1956.) For early Putnam it is a doctrine that manifestly fails to explain how we could ever have knowledge of the growth of knowledge, or grounds for asserting that such progress consists in a better (more adequate) explanatory grasp of those real-world objects and intrinsic properties that determine what counts – or should ultimately count – as a genuine referring expression or veridical statement. However, by the time of *Reason, Truth and History* (1981), he has backed off so far from this realist position as to class it among the most extravagant examples of old-style 'metaphysical' talk. Thus: 'believing that some correspondence intrinsically just *is* reference (not as a result of our operational and theoretical constraints, or our intentions, but as an *ultimate* metaphysical fact) amounts to a magical theory of reference' (Putnam 1981: 47). Still, one may think that Putnam's retreat has more to do with the problematic legacy of logical empiricism and its sceptical-relativist aftermath than with anything inherently wrong or naive about his earlier causal-realist position. This suspicion is borne out when he goes on to say that, according to the realist view, '[r]eference itself becomes what Locke called a "substantial form" (an entity which *intrinsically* belongs with a certain name)' (*ibid.*). Yet, as I have noted already, there are passages elsewhere in which Putnam accepts that we are now better placed than Locke to talk about intrinsic (reference-fixing) properties for natural-kind terms since we now possess a more detailed knowledge of those salient (e.g., microstructural) properties that constitute the real essence of the kinds in question.

Late Putnam will of course have none of this, convinced as he is that no such argument can possibly fend off the sceptic's objections. Thus:

> [e]ven if one is willing to contemplate such unexplainable metaphysical facts, the epistemological problems that accompany such a metaphysical view seem insuperable. For, assuming a world of mind-independent, discourse-independent entities (this is the presupposition of the view we are discussing), there are, as we have seen, many different 'correspondences' which represent possible or candidate reference relations (infinitely many, in fact, if there are infinitely many things in the universe). (Putnam 1981: 47)

However, this passage makes a number of crucial assumptions – crucial, that is, to the case against 'naive' or 'metaphysical' realism – which the sceptic will regard as simply self-evident but which the realist will surely wish to challenge for just the sorts of reason that were once put forward by Putnam himself. After all, it is only on the sceptical (late-Putnam) view that one has to treat talk about real-world existent objects, properties, microstructural features, and so forth, as involving an appeal to 'unexplainable metaphysical facts', or as betraying a hopelessly misguided attachment to essentialist notions of objecthood, species identity, or natural-kind membership. Likewise, it is only if one takes it for granted that such notions cannot stand up to sceptical scrutiny that one will see no warrant for the realist belief in 'a world of mind-independent, discourse-independent entities' whose various distinctive attributes are discovered through a process of *a posteriori* scientific investigation which in turn enables us to pick them out with increasing precision. Nor will the realist be over-impressed by any Goodman-style argument that adduces the variety of different 'correspondences' or 'candidate reference relations' in order to vindicate its claim that the entities concerned – together with their kinds and classes – must be thought of as strictly relative (or 'internal') to some given conceptual scheme. This is simply to deny – in nominalist fashion – that we could ever advance beyond the Lockean stage where descriptive criteria of a non-essential kind are the best that can reasonably be hoped for, and where is there nothing that fixes reference aside from the fact that certain terms and associated properties have a role in our currently accepted range of theories, practices, or working definitions. It is just that denial – as I have argued above – which leads Putnam to adopt his analytic (meaning-based) criterion for necessary truth in such matters and hence to abandon the whole idea of *a posteriori* necessary truth as applied to the real-world object domain and its various constituent properties.

Least of all will it seem to clinch the case when Putnam suggests that reference-relations may indeed be 'infinitely many ... if there are infinitely many things in the universe'. For on the realist account it is a straightforward fallacy to argue from the fact that those objects may be infinite in number to the claim that they must be thought of as possessing no distinctive real-world features or attributes. What this shows at most is that our knowledge has limits – whether now or at the Peircean epistemic 'end of enquiry' – as compared with the sheer multiplicity of 'things' which make up the physical universe. Hence Putnam's claim that 'the epistemological problems that accompany such a [realist] metaphysical view seem insuperable'. But this is once again to ignore one of his own (and Kripke's) cardinal points, namely that issues of metaphysical necessity should not be confused with issues of epistemological warrant. (See Kripke 1980; Putnam 1975[2]; also Loux (ed.) 1979; Schwartz (ed.) 1977; Wiggins 1980). Putnam goes some way toward acknowledging this in the previous paragraph where he writes: 'Kripke's view, that "water is H_2O" is true in all possible worlds, could be right even if reference in the actual world is fixed only by operational and theoretical constraints' (1981: 47). But he then promptly withdraws this concession by remarking that, while the Kripkean view 'presupposes the notion of reference', it still 'does not tell us whether reference is determinate or what reference is' (*ibid.*). Yet of course this is *just* what Kripke claimed to do – and early Putnam likewise – by offering a range of examples (from electrons, atoms and molecules to acids, gold, water, elms, tigers and so forth) where reference was 'fixed' in both senses, that is, as a matter of picking out natural kinds and doing so in virtue of a reference-relation whose nature could be specified in adequate detail from case to case.

V

That he ceased to find such claims in the least degree convincing – that they came to strike him as 'metaphysically' profligate and 'epistemologically' insupportable – is no sufficient reason, I would suggest, for accepting Putnam's verdict or endorsing his adoption of an internal-realist position that generates so many problems of its own. In my view the causal theory of reference is quite simply the best to be had if one's main requirements are (1), that any theory in this field should be judged by its capacity to make good sense of our regular (everyday or specialised) linguistic practices; (2), that it should do so without falling back on Wittgensteinian or other conventionalist doctrines which treat such 'practices' as the bottom line of justificatory warrant; (3), that it should offer an adequate account of how terms acquire increasing specificity of reference through a process of ongoing scientific enquiry; (4), that it should also explain how such terms preserve continuity of reference across changes of theory or paradigm-shifts; (5), that it should capture what is *essential* about both the physical items referred to and the reference-relation involved; and (6) that it should meet the whole current range of sceptical or anti-realist arguments in a convincing, i.e., philosophically cogent and scientifically informed manner. It seems to me that the causal theory of reference comes out with high marks on each of these counts and that we should not be swayed into thinking otherwise by Putnam's subsequent doubts and misgivings. What this amounts to in more general terms is a case for inference to the best explanation, whether as applied to issues in the philosophy and history of science or to issues in philosophical semantics. That is to say, it holds that we cannot be rationally justified in adopting a sceptical theory which creates huge problems for our basic understanding of science, language, or human experience in general if there exists a well-tried alternative theory – such as causal realism – which has a strong *prima facie* claim to resolve those problems that are raised by the opposing (sceptical) view. (See also Harman 1965; Kornblith 1993; Lipton 1993; Salmon 1967, 1984.)

No doubt the sceptic will come straight back and say that this argument is completely off-the-point in so far as it merely takes for granted everything that scepticism calls into doubt. Thus the realist's talk of 'inference to the best explanation' will strike the sceptic as a plain case of begging the question since it assumes that we possess objective criteria for deciding what should count as inductive warrant or adequate causal-explanatory grounds. Yet of course this belief has been challenged by philosophers – from Hume to Goodman – who argue that it lacks any semblance of logical justification and comes down to mere force of ingrained psychological habit. Thus inductive reasoning and causal explanation must likewise be viewed as entailing a version of the *post hoc, propter hoc* fallacy, that which involves an unwarranted leap from observed regularity or Humean 'constant conjunction' to some putative causal nexus which is taken as adequate grounds for supposing that the future will resemble the past in all relevant respects. Such an argument is purely circular – so the sceptic maintains – since it purports to vindicate induction by invoking just those principles (like the uniformity of nature or the existence of causal powers) that both rely upon inductive reasoning and provide its prerequisite means of support. Hence Goodman's 'new riddle' of induction, one that sharpens the Humean challenge by effectively re-stating it in present-day semantic or logico-linguistic terms. On this view the problem is that of explaining how we could ever be justified in singling out certain so-called 'natural' predicates like *blue* or *green* in preference to other factitious predicates – such as *grue* or *bleen* – whose truth-conditions can always be specified in counterfactual though logically consistent and (to this extent) perfectly acceptable terms (Goodman 1955).

Thus the upshot of Goodman's argument – like Kripke's 'sceptical solution' to Wittgenstein's rule-following paradox – is to make it a matter of entrenched communal practice that we *just do* carry on reasoning, calculating, or drawing inductive inferences in the standardly accepted way, quite aside from any issue of 'ultimate' (practice-transcendent) justification (Kripke 1982). In which case there seems very little to choose between downright scepticism or anti-realism and those various hard-put compromise positions which end up by yielding all the main points at issue. However, as we have seen, early Putnam had arguments in plenty – from modal logic as well as from the history and philosophy of science – for treating Goodman-type counterfactual instances as strictly irrelevant with regard to issues about reference, truth, and the growth of knowledge. If his later thinking has been characterised chiefly by a swing toward scepticism on just these points then the reason is to be sought, I suggest, in his over-readiness to grant the force of such arguments. At any rate there is much to be said for a theory which falls square with the evidence of scientific knowledge and progress to date even if (necessarily) it does so on terms that the sceptic will be quick to challenge.

References

Aristotle (1941). *Metaphysics*, trans. W.D. Ross, ed. Richard McKeon. New York: Random House.

Beltrametti, Enrico G. and Bas van Fraassen (eds) (1981). *Current Issues in Quantum Logic*. New York: Plenum.

Bohr, Niels (1958). *Atomic Physics and Human Knowledge*. New York: Wiley.

—— (1987). *The Philosophical Writings of Niels Bohr*, 3 vols. Woodbridge, CT: Ox Bow Press.

Carnap, Rudolf (1956). *Meaning and Necessity*. Chicago: University of Chicago Press.

Cushing, James T. (1994). *Quantum Mechanics: historical contingency and the Copenhagen hegemony*. Chicago: University of Chicago Press.

Foucault, Michel (1970). *The Order of Things: an archaeology of the human sciences*, trans. A. Sheridan. London: Tavistock.

Garden, Rachel W. (1983). *Modern Logic and Quantum Mechanics*. Bristol: Adam Hilger.

Gibbins, John (1987). *Particles and Paradoxes: the limits of quantum logic*. Cambridge: Cambridge University Press.

Goodman, Nelson (1955). *Fact, Fiction and Forecast.* Cambridge, MA: Harvard University Press.
—— (1987). *Ways of Worldmaking.* Indianapolis: Bobbs-Merrill.
Haack, Susan (1974). *Deviant Logic: some philosophical issues.* Cambridge: Cambridge University Press.
Harman, Gilbert (1965). 'Inference to the Best Explanation', *Philosophical Review*, LXXIV. 88–95.
Home, Dipankar (1998). *Conceptual Foundations of Quantum Mechanics: an overview from modern perspectives.* New York: Plenum.
Honner, John (1987). *The Description of Nature: Niels Bohr and the philosophy of quantum physics.* Oxford: Clarendon Press.
Hume, David (1975). *Enquiries Concerning Human Understanding and Concerning the Principles of Morals*, 3rd edn, ed. L.A. Selby-Bigge, rev. P.H. Nidditch. Oxford: Clarendon Press.
Jammer, Max (1974). *Philosophy of Quantum Mechanics: the interpretations of quantum mechanics in historical perspective.* New York: Wiley.
Kant, Immanuel (1964). *Critique of Pure Reason*, trans. N. Kemp Smith. London: Macmillan.
Kornblith, Hilary (1993). *Inductive Inference and its Natural Ground.* Cambridge, MA: MIT Press.
Kripke, Saul (1980). *Naming and Necessity.* Oxford: Blackwell.
—— (1982). *Wittgenstein on Rules and Private Language: an elementary exposition.* Oxford: Blackwell.
Lipton, Peter (1993). *Inference to the Best Explanation.* London: Routledge.
Locke, John (1959). *An Essay Concerning Human Understanding*, 2 vols. New York: Dover.
Loux, M. (ed.) (1979). *The Possible and the Actual.* Ithaca, NY: Cornell University Press.
McCulloch, Gregory (1995). *The Mind and Its World.* London: Routledge.
Mill, J.S. (1973–74). *A System of Logic Radiocinative and Inductive: being a view of the principles of evidence and the methods of scientific investigation*, ed. J.M. Robson. London: Routledge & Kegan Paul.
Mittelstaedt, Peter (1994). *Quantum Logic.* Princeton, NJ: Princeton University Press.
Putnam, Hilary (1974). 'How to Think Quantum-Logically', *Synthèse*, XXIX. 55–61.
—— (1975[1]). *Mathematics, Matter and Method* (*Philosophical Papers*, Vol. 1). Cambridge: Cambridge University Press.
—— (1975[2]). *Mind, Language and Reality* (*Philosophical Papers*, Vol. 2). Cambridge: Cambridge University Press.
—— (1978). *Meaning and the Moral Sciences.* London: Routledge & Kegan Paul.
—— (1981). *Reason, Truth and History.* Cambridge: Cambridge University Press.
—— (1983). *Realism and Reason* (*Philosophical Papers*, Vol. 3). Cambridge: Cambridge University Press.
Quine, W.V.O. (1961). 'Two Dogmas of Empiricism'. In *From a Logical Point of View*, 2nd edn. Cambridge, MA: Harvard University Press. 20–46.
—— (1970). *Philosophy of Logic.* Englewood Cliffs, NJ: Prentice-Hall.
Salmon, Wesley C. (1967). *The Foundations of Scientific Inference.* Pittsburgh, PA: Pittsburgh University Press.
—— (1984). *Scientific Explanation and the Causal Structure of the World.* Princeton, NJ: Princeton University Press.
Schwartz, Stephen (ed.) (1977). *Naming, Necessity and Natural Kinds.* Ithaca, NY: Cornell University Press.
Squires, Euan (1994). *The Mystery of the Quantum World*, 2nd edn. Bristol and Philadelphia: Institute of Physics Publishing.
Tarski, Alfred (1956). 'The Concept of Truth in Formalized Languages'. In *Logic, Semantics and Metamathematics*, trans. J.H. Woodger. Oxford: Oxford University Press. 152–278.
Weinberg, Steven (1992). *Dreams of a Final Theory.* New York: Pantheon.
Wheeler, John A. and W.H. Zurek (eds) (1983). *Quantum Theory and Measurement.* Princeton, NJ: Princeton University Press.
Wiggins, David (1980). *Sameness and Substance.* Oxford: Blackwell.
Wittgenstein, Ludwig (1953). *Philosophical Investigations*, trans. G.E.M. Anscombe. Oxford: Blackwell.

8

The Platonist fix: why 'nothing works' (according to Putnam) in philosophy of mathematics

I

Putnam has written extensively about issues in the philosophy of mathematics and their bearing on wider philosophical debates with regard to the status of scientific truth-claims, theories and hypotheses. (See especially Putnam 1975[1].) In that wider context his position has shifted – famously so – from a strong causal-realist to an 'internal'-realist (or framework-relativist) approach, and thence to an outlook of pragmatist or 'commonsense' realism which treats such debates as largely irrelevant once we have learned a few much-needed lessons from William James and the later Wittgenstein. (Cf. Putnam 1975[2]; 1981, 1983, 1987, 1994[1], 1995.) What I propose to do here is examine the development of Putnam's thinking in light of his engagement with problems in the conceptual foundations of mathematics, set-theory, and philosophy of logic. There are several reasons for adopting this approach, among them its centrality to Putnam's own interests over the past three decades, his uncommonly expert knowledge of mathematics and the physical sciences, and the fact that his change of mind on the realism issue has given rise to such widespread discussion. (See for instance Clark and Hale (eds) 1993.) Thus it seems worthwhile to look in detail at some of those passages in Putnam, early and late, where that issue is raised specifically in relation to mathematical realism (under various construals) and the arguments brought against it from a range of dissenting viewpoints. This will also provide an interesting angle on the reasons for Putnam's growing scepticism as regards the prospects for a viable realist approach to philosophical semantics, epistemology, and philosophy of science. That is to say, there are certain crucial ambiguities about his understanding of what 'realism' entails in the philosophy of mathematics which can be seen to exert an unsettling influence on his larger philosophical project. So this approach may help to explain both the direction that project has taken during recent years and the strong sense – to my mind at least – of its having ruled out some distinctly promising alternative resources, among them the kinds of argument developed by early (realist) Putnam.

We can perhaps best start by recalling a much-cited passage from his essay 'What Is Mathematical Truth?' which offers a succinct statement of the case for scientific realism as a matter of inference to the best causal explanation (Putnam 1975[1]: 60–78). Thus:

> [t]he positive argument for realism is that it is the only philosophy that doesn't make the success of science a miracle. That terms in mature scientific theories

refer (this formulation is due to Richard Boyd), that the theories accepted in a mature science are typically approximately true, that the same term can refer to the same thing even when it occurs in different theories – these statements are viewed by the scientific realist not as necessary truths but as part of the only scientific explanation of the success of science, and hence as part of any adequate scientific description of science and its relation to its objects. (*ibid.*: 73; also Boyd 1984)

What is even more striking about this passage is the fact that it occurs in the context of an argument for *mathematical* realism, that is, for the existence of mathematical entities (numbers, sets, classes, functions, tensors, vectors, etc.) which – according to Putnam – have to be construed in objective or verification-transcendent terms. Here he comes out strongly against any kind of Dummett-type anti-realist theory that would make mathematical truth dependent on our various rules, definitions or proof-procedures, and hence on our state of mathematical knowledge at any given time (Dummett 1978, 1991). In Putnam's view the main reason why philosophers and mathematicians have been driven to endorse this idea is their belief that it offers the only alternative to a Platonist conception which locates mathematical truth in a realm of ideal 'forms' or 'essences' that by very definition exist beyond reach of human epistemic grasp. On this account there is simply no means of explaining how we could ever gain access to such truths through certain well-defined discovery procedures or why the various results thus obtained should have shown such an otherwise 'miraculous' power to advance our knowledge of objects and events in the real-world physical domain. Thus Platonist realism creates more problems than it solves for anyone – like Putnam – who is chiefly impressed by the extent to which mathematics has proved an indispensable resource in the progress of the natural sciences, above all in the history of applied and theoretical physics from Galileo to Newton, Einstein and beyond. For it is precisely through the increasing mathematisation of nature – the discovery of ever more powerful means of expressing physical quantities and laws in relatively abstract mathematical terms – that modern science has been able to break with earlier, intuitive or 'commonsense' notions concerning the physical world.

Thus there is no making sense of that history unless we grant (*contra* the conventionalists and Dummett-type anti-realists) that mathematical truths are objective and verification-transcendent but also (*contra* the Platonists) that they cannot be divorced from our various activities of real-world empirical enquiry and investigation. In Putnam's words:

> [t]he important thing is that the mathematician is studying something objective, even if he is not studying an unconditional 'reality' of non-material things, and that the physicist who states a law of nature with the aid of a mathematical formula is abstracting a real feature of a real material world, even if he has to speak of numbers, vectors, tensors, state-functions, or whatever to make the abstraction. (Putnam 1975[1]: 60)

Putnam's chief example here – and in other writings of the same period such as his 1971 book *Philosophy of Logic* – is Newton's Law of Universal Gravitation, which he takes as offering decisive support for a realist as opposed to a nominalist or conventionalist interpretation of mathematics. That is to say, the only means of explaining why Newton's law should hold good (within certain specified limits) with respect to the physical world is by taking its 'pure' mathematical form:

$$F = \frac{gM_aM_b}{d^2}$$

as an equation whose terms, functions, formal structure, numerical values, and so forth, are such as must apply (again within certain specified limits) to the way that gravitational forces can actually be measured and predicted on just that basis (Putnam 1971: 36). In its simplest expression, the law states categorically that the force of attraction between two bodies will be directly proportional to the product of their two masses and inversely proportional to the square of the distance between them. Or again: the magnitude of that force F is given by the above equation, where a and b are the two bodies, g a universal constant, M_a the mass of body a, M_b the mass of body b, and d the distance that separate those bodies at the time of measurement.

Putnam's point is that we cannot make sense of this law or explain its overwhelming degree of observational-predictive success – at least for non-relativistic purposes – except on the assumption that its formal structure expresses a relation between quantities and forces that exist and operate in the physical world. For otherwise, again, it would be nothing short of a 'miracle' that the law should have held good for such a range of theoretical and practical purposes, and should moreover have remained valid for most such purposes even after its absolute status was challenged – or its compass restricted to a certain spatio-temporal framework – by the advent of General Relativity. I must now quote Putnam at greater length since the argument is crucial to his case for realism in mathematics, philosophy of logic, and the physical sciences. It is also a passage of particular interest for stating very clearly those realist premises which Putnam will later qualify to the point where he seems more in agreement with conventionalist or nominalist approaches like those which he here decisively rejects. Thus:

> [t]o say that [Newton's] Law is true – even to say that it is approximately true at nonrelativistic distances and velocities – one has to quantify over such nonnominalistic entities as forces, masses, distances. Moreover, to account for what is usually called 'measurement' – that is, for the numericalization of forces, masses, and distances – one has to quantify not just over forces, masses, and distances construed as physical properties … but also over *functions from* masses, distances, etc. *to* real numbers, or at any rate to rational numbers. In short … a reasonable interpretation of the *application* of mathematics to the physical world *requires* a realistic interpretation of the mathematics. Mathematical experience says that mathematics is true under some interpretation; physical experience says that that interpretation is a realist one. (Putnam 1975[1]: 74)

Again this works out as a version of the argument from inference to the best explanation, that is to say, the claim that if a realist construal of forces, masses, state-functions, numerical values, and so forth, is manifestly required by our best scientific theories then it is futile – a kind of perverse self-denying ordinance – to reject that construal in favour of some other theory with no such impressive explanatory yield. (See also Harman 1965; Lipton 1993; Salmon 1967 and 1984.) To be sure, there are limits on the range of mathematical entities that Putnam would regard as prime candidates for realist treatment on account of their central role in the genesis and structure of those present-best theories. Thus his argument for realism admits certain qualifications, extending as it does to 'sets of things, real numbers, and functions from various kinds of things to real numbers', and stopping short of 'sets of very high type or very high cardinality' (Putnam 1975[1]: 74). With respect to these latter it is Putnam's view that 'they should today be investigated in an "if-then" spirit', that is, treated as candidates for full-fledged realist status but candidates whose worth has yet to be proved beyond reasonable doubt. In such cases the best attitude – Putnam thinks – is something much closer to the verificationist (though *not* the doctrinaire nominalist or anti-realist) line. All the same, '[o]ne day they may be as indispensable to the very *statement* of physical laws as, say, rational numbers are today; the doubt of their "existence" will be as futile as extreme nominalism now is' (*ibid.*).

This is the position that Putnam takes in his short book *Philosophy of Logic*, where again his chief quarry is the nominalist claim that logicians and mathematicians had best avoid any needless metaphysical commitment to the 'real' (objective) existence of numbers, sets, functions, or other mathematical entities. But then, he asks, what are we to make of the fact that physical theories such as those of Galileo, Newton, or Einstein have always involved quantification (or the assignment of specific ontological values) over just those 'abstract' features and properties that the nominalist wishes to treat as mere products of formal definition? After all, if this has proved strictly indispensable for the purposes of physical science then there is surely no reason – prejudice apart – why a similar requirement should not hold for our thinking about issues in logic, mathematics, and other such formal branches of enquiry. For here also it is typically the case that any results thus achieved will be closely bound up with developments in physical science, whether as a matter of proving their validity through tests of observational-predictive yield or establishing their worth by opening the way to some decisive scientific advance. At any rate, '[t]here is no reason in stating logical principles to be more puristic, or more compulsive about avoiding reference to "nonphysical entities", than in scientific discourse generally' (Putnam 1971: 14). Thus the burden of proof rests squarely with the nominalist since he or she is proposing a large-scale revision to the way we talk and think about entities – numbers, sets, classes, etc. – which have proved not only useful but downright indispensable to the advancement of scientific knowledge. If the nominalist wishes us to make such a change, then in all honesty 'he must provide us with an alternative mode of speech which works just as well, not just in pure logic but also in such empirical sciences as physics (which is full of references to such "nonphysical" entities as state-vectors, Hamiltonians, Hilbert space, etc.)' (*ibid.*).

What Putnam sets out to show is the current non-availability of any such adequate alternative and the sheer unlikelihood of its being achieved despite the best efforts of nominalists, fictionalists, conventionalists, and other sceptical parties.

II

So the question remains: why should Putnam have felt himself obliged to renounce this position and opt instead for a compromise settlement (so-called 'internal' realism) which yields so much argumentative ground to the nominalist case? It seems to me, on the evidence of his later writing, that the answer is to be found in Putnam's attempt to steer a path between mathematical realism in the Platonist sense – the notion of numbers, sets, classes, functions, etc., as existing in a realm of absolute ideal objectivity – and the need to bring those entities back to earth in the various practices that constitute our methods of achieving mathematical and scientific knowledge. This tension comes out in numerous passages, but never more plainly than when Putnam remarks – albeit at risk of appearing to 'strain after smartness' – that 'there *are* necessary truths in physics, but that they can be revised if necessary!' (1975[1]: 88). For it is a consequence of Putnam's empiricist stance with regard to truth-claims in logic, mathematics, and the more theoretical (mathematics-led) branches of physical science that they *must* be open to challenge or revision should the empirical evidence require it. This pushes him into a very tight corner when it comes to deciding what can ultimately stand as an instance of *a priori* knowledge, since on Putnam's account the only candidate sentence that emerges unscathed by counter-examples (such as non-Euclidean geometry and quantum physics) is the trivial assertion: 'not every statement is both true and false'. (See especially 1983: 98–114, 115–38.) This follows from Putnam's belief that any viable defence of a realist position in mathematics and theoretical physics must give up the illusion of synthetic *a priori* truths – like those which Kant mistakenly attributed to Euclid and Newton – and acknowledge the in-principle revisability of all such claims when confronted with empirical counter-evidence.

If Platonist realism is not an option – since it places truth beyond our cognitive reach – then neither is the Kantian epistemological appeal to a realm of truths which supposedly constitute the 'conditions of possibility' for knowledge and experience in general (Kant 1964). As he puts it in *Reason, Truth and History*:

> since our notions of rationality and rational revisability are the product of our all too limited experience and all too fallible biology, it is to be expected that even principles we regard as 'a priori', or 'conceptual', or whatever, will from time to time turn out to need revision in the light of unexpected experiences or unanticipated theoretical innovations. (Putnam 1981: 83)

Hence Putnam's recourse at this stage to the notion of 'contextual apriority', adopted for want of any stronger ('absolute') conception that would not fall prey to these and other instances of large-scale theory change. However, it is then hard to see what could count as an argument for realism in mathematics, logic, or the more theoretical branches of physical science, given the sheer impossibility – as Putnam now thinks – of drawing any firm or principled line between truths that are presumed to hold firm against revision under pressure from empirical counter-evidence and truth-claims that are strongly borne out by all the evidence to hand yet which might just conceivably be subject to revision should conflicting evidence turn up. After all, it follows from this Quinean doctrine of across-the-board revisability that the realist can have no ground to stand on – 'conservatism' or 'pragmatic convenience' apart – if she wishes to argue that *some* such truths (e.g., the ground-rules of deductive inference) are intrinsic to any kind of rational procedure for weighing up the evidence in this or that particular case (Quine 1961). Putnam has devoted many long discussions to this aspect of Quine's think-ing, most often with no very definite result save a sense that it cannot be altogether right since there *must* be certain standards of logical thought which cannot be treated as *wholly* context-relative, even if the only instance that he is able to produce – after much casting around – is the rock-bottom minimalist principle of contradiction (i.e., 'not every statement is both true and false'). (See especially Putnam 1983: 87–97, 98–114, 115–38.) Yet of course this falls far short of establish-ing the case for other, more substantive (non-trivial) truths that would explain why our processes of logical inference – as well as our various mathematical pro-cedures – possess such a singular degree of empirical (or observational-predictive) warrant when applied in the physical sciences.

Thus Putnam is frankly worried by Quine's proposal that '[t]he laws of logic are as empirical as the laws of geometry, only more abstract and better protected'. Nor can he find much comfort in Quine's concession that '[l]ogic is the *last* thing we shall ever revise', since even so 'it is not *immune* from revision', and may indeed require such revision should this prove the best (most scientifically acceptable) way of interpreting the various anomalies with quantum mechanics (Putnam 1983: 51). Hence – as I have suggested – Putnam's increasingly hard-put endeavour to save at least one (albeit minimal) counter-instance that could hold out against the Quinean thesis of wholesale revisability. After all, 'no-one has proposed revis-ing the principle of contradiction', since 'what would it mean to give up the state-ment that "No statement is both true and false"?' (*ibid.*). Yet Putnam himself goes a long way toward abandoning – or at any rate revising – this putative 'law' of logic in response to Quinean and other objections from the strong-revisionist quarter. Thus his scaled-down version comes out in the form: 'Not *every* statement is both true and false', which he takes to provide a sufficient basis for refuting the more extreme varieties of holistic or contextualist doctrine. In which case, accord-ing to Putnam, '[t]he scope of the *a priori* is indeed shrinking; but the claim that every truth is empirical is still far from being an acceptable or even a coherent thesis' (1983: 51). Yet there is a marked tension – if not perhaps a flat contradiction – between his argument here (and in other passages to similar effect) and his argu-ment elsewhere that the best case for realism, whether with respect to mathemat-ics or the physical sciences, is one that acknowledges the revisability of logic and the extent to which our standing *a priori* convictions might always be subject to challenge from empirical counter-evidence. Above all, it creates large problems for Putnam's realist (or anti-nominalist) outlook with regard to those various mathematical entities – numbers, sets, classes, functions, etc. – which he thinks of as playing a strictly indispensable role in the physical sciences. For on this realist view it is well-nigh inconceivable – or 'miraculous' – that they should somehow have managed to play such a role while existing merely as Quinean 'posits' or convenient fictions, adopted in order to 'expedite our dealings' with the incoming barrage of sensory stimuli (Quine 1961). That is to say, it is impossible to square Putnam's case for a realist construal of those entities with his case for treating them – or the truth-value of any statement or theory that concerns them – as subject to revision on empirical grounds should the evidence turn out to require it.

This throws a different light on Putnam's claim (in the passage cited above) that 'the physicist who states a law of nature with the aid of a mathematical formula is abstracting a real feature of a real material world, even if he has to speak of numbers, vectors, tensors, state-functions, or whatever to make the abstraction' (1975[1]: 60). On the one hand it offers a strong counter-statement to those various forms of conventionalist or nominalist doctrine which effectively sever the link between mathematical truth and the 'real material world'. But on the other it makes such truth always dependent on our present-best (always revisable) knowledge of the features, properties, causal dispositions, etc., which constitute that physical world and which might turn out – with some future advance in scientific theory – to require that we revise or abandon even our most basic conceptions of mathematical (or logical) truth. It is this possibility that Putnam can never quite bring himself to accept even though he sometimes runs close to endorsing it when engaging with issues in philosophy of science (e.g., non-Euclidean geometry and quantum mechanics) or with the strong-revisionist approach of thinkers – Quine chief among them – who take it on board with no such philosophical qualms. His dilemma emerges with particular force in the essay 'What Is Mathematical Truth?' where Putnam puts the case for a realist theory that eschews any kind of Platonist appeal to verification-transcendent truths by redefining the 'abstract' nature of mathematical entities as a matter of their standing at a certain remove – a formal or procedural remove – from methods of empirical enquiry in the physical sciences. Thus he asks: '[i]s there any reason, other than a sociological one, why quasi-empirical methods should not be used in mathematics?' (Putnam 1975[1]: 62). And again: '[i]f it turned out that the Martians do use quasi-empirical methods, and their mathematical practice is highly successful, could we say that they are irrational?' (*ibid.*). Putnam's point is that a good many signal advances in mathematics *have* in fact come about through the application of such 'quasi-empirical' methods, that is to say, proof-procedures or forms of reasoning which at some point depend upon experience, intuition, or the evidence of achieved 'success' in arriving at some useful or desired result. And if it is asked what should count as 'success' in this context then the best short answer – so Putnam thinks – is 'success as measured by their proven usefulness or even (in some cases) their necessity for the purposes of physical science'.

Thus he offers the example of Zermelo's Axiom of Choice which holds, as a matter of intuitive self-evidence, that every set can be well-ordered despite the lack of any formal proof to this effect and indeed the demonstrable impossibility that any such proof could be achieved. Putnam cites a passage from Zermelo's response to those 'logical purists' – Peano among them – who objected to his argument on just these grounds, i.e., that it was 'merely' intuitive and could not be derived by any formal logico-deductive procedure from the basic principles of set-theory as laid out in more rigorous fashion by Peano himself. But such objections are beside the point, Zermelo argues, if the Axiom of Choice can be shown to have played a decisive (indeed indispensable) role in the development of set-theory, even though it had never been spelled out explicitly or 'formulated in a textbook system'. On the contrary,

> [s]uch an extensive use of a principle can be explained only by its self-evidence, which, of course, must not be confused with its provability. No matter if this self-evidence is to a certain degree subjective – it is surely a necessary source of mathematical principles, even if it is not a tool of mathematical proofs, and Peano's assertion that it has nothing to do with mathematics fails to do justice to manifest facts. (Zermelo 1967: 187)

Now this might be construed – though Putnam doesn't make the point – as an endorsement of mathematical intuitionism, and hence as a case for giving up talk of objective truth in favour of Dummett-style 'warranted assertability', or truth within the limits of our present-best knowledge, proof-procedures, or means of verification (Dummett 1978; also 1977). The way would then be open to extend this anti-realist argument from mathematics to the physical sciences and every field of enquiry where 'gaps in knowledge' could plausibly be treated – again following Dummett – as 'gaps in reality' or areas of doubt where bivalence fails since they are simply not amenable to judgements of determinate truth or false-hood. In his later work, Putnam is drawn to this way of thinking – or at least feels compelled to admit its logical force – even though he holds out against its more extreme and (in his view) philosophically disabling consequences. (See Putnam 1994[1].) However, this is *not* what he finds so compelling about the passage from Zermelo cited above, that is to say, in the context of his (Putnam's) thinking about issues in the philosophy of mathematics. Rather, it is the fact that, according to Zermelo, the Axiom of Choice is so deeply built into the working methods and assumptions of present-day mathematics-based science that it simply *must* be taken as proof against doubt for all practical purposes. Thus '[i]t is noteworthy that what Zermelo characterises as "objective" is not the "self-evidence" of the axiom of choice but its *necessity for science*. Today it is not just the axiom of choice but the whole edifice of modern set theory whose entrenchment rests on great success in mathematical application – in other words, on "necessity for science"' (Putnam 1975[1]: 67). This clearly involves an inference to the best explanation, i.e., the kind of argument which holds that if an axiom is (1) possessed of great intuitive force or strength of rational self-evidence, and (2) prerequisite to a great range of successful scientific practices, then we are justified in regarding its truth as secure beyond reasonable doubt (Harman 1965; Lipton 1993). What is more, as Putnam goes on to remark, one can strengthen this argument by adducing the success of other sciences – physics preeminent among them – which depend heavily on the axiomatisation of set-theory, and which therefore presuppose the Axiom of Choice as a matter of logical necessity. So there would seem little hope for any line of counter-argument which rejected that axiom while still seeking some plausible (i.e., non-miraculist) explanation for the role of mathematics as a strictly indispensable resource in the advancement of scientific knowledge.

At this stage, therefore, Putnam sees no conflict between a realist outlook which grounds mathematical truths in a process of rigorously formalised abstraction from certain objects, features, or properties of the physical world and an empiricist approach that considers such truths to be always, in principle, subject to revision should the evidence turn out to require it. Indeed, this second requirement follows directly from the first since if truth (or objectivity) in mathematics is dependent, at whatever 'abstract' remove, on those real-world features and properties, then of course it cannot claim any ideal or absolute exemption from revisability under pressures of empirical counter-evidence. Such is at any rate Putnam's proposal for avoiding mathematical Platonism – which he thinks a non-viable option – while maintaining the idea of mathematical truth as something more than mere convention, operational convenience, or habituated rule-following practice. Hence his claim, in the above-cited passage, that the mathematician 'is studying something objective, even if he is not studying an unconditional "reality" of non-material things'. Yet one can see already, in this same essay, how Putnam's idea of what counts as 'realism' or 'objectivism' with regard to mathematical truth is apt to lean over into something more like a conventionalist, constructivist, or even a Dummett-type anti-realist approach. 'In my view', he writes,

> there are *two* supports for realism in philosophy of mathematics: *mathematical experience* and *physical experience*. The construction of a highly articulated body of mathematical knowledge with a long tradition of successful problem solving is a truly remarkable *social* achievement … . If there is no interpretation under which most of mathematics is *true*, if we are really just writing down strings of symbols at random, or even by trial and error, what are the chances that our theory would be consistent, let alone mathematically fertile? (Putnam 1975[1]: 73)

On the face of it this is yet another strong argument for inference to the best (most rational) explanation, one that would count it nothing short of miraculous that mathematics should have proved so 'fertile' in its own and other, e.g., applied scientific fields except on a realist interpretation of statements about numbers, vectors, tensors, state-functions, and so forth. Yet to make this primarily a matter of *social* achievement (Putnam's emphasis), as evinced by its 'long history of problem solving', is already to suggest that the kinds of 'objectivity' and 'truth' in question might be subject to a different construal, one that inclined more in the direction of a practice-based (Wittgensteinian) or a verificationist (Dummett-type) appeal to the methods or criteria currently accepted within some given community of knowledge (Wittgenstein 1953, 1978; Dummett 1978). In which case Putnam's realist convictions would carry no force against these and other versions of the argument for replacing talk of mathematical 'truth' with talk of 'warranted assertability' or truth according to the standards and conventions of present-day best practice.

Indeed, Putnam acknowledges this point – or something very like it – when he goes on to counsel caution in deriving any strong (philosophically substantive) case for realism from the sorts of consideration that he has brought forward so far. Thus:

> [i]f this argument has force, and I believe it does, it is not quite an argument for mathematical realism. The argument says that the consistency and fertility of classical mathematics is evidence that it – or most of it – *is true under some inter-pretation*. But the interpretation might not be a *realist* interpretation. Thus [the intuitionist] might say, 'indeed, most of classical mathematics is true under some interpretation; it is true under an intuitionist *re*interpretation!' Thus our argument has to stand on two legs: the other leg is *physical experience*. The interpre-tation under which mathematics is true has to square with the application of mathematics *outside* of mathematics. (Putnam 1975[1]: 73–4)

Where the problems arise – at any rate the problems for Putnam's realist position – is with the appeal to physical 'experience' as means of assessing the fertility of mathematics when applied to other mathematically based sciences whose 'success' would otherwise have to be accounted a fluke or a downright miracle. No doubt this follows from Putnam's basically empiricist approach, that is to say, his basing the argument for mathematical realism on a strictly non-Platonist conception which eschews all talk about 'the "reality" of non-material things', and which accepts – in consequence – the empirically discoverable (and revisable) character of mathematical truths. Such, after all, is the chief lesson that Putnam derives from the cases of non-Euclidean geometry, Einsteinian relativity-theory, and quantum mechanics on the orthodox (Copenhagen) construal. (See the various essays on these and related topics collected in Putnam 1975[1].) However, it remains open to doubt whether a philosophy of mathematics that is 'realist' in this sense – i.e., which makes mathematical 'truths' revisable in response to empirical counter-evidence – can none the less claim to be realist in the sense of explaining how and why such truths differ from the general run of beliefs-held-true on the strength of our present-best (empirically warranted) knowledge.

Of course Putnam is well aware of this problem, as can be seen from his constant changes of mind (or shifts of emphasis) on the question as to whether there is a genuine difference or whether such an explanation can be had through recourse to the 'quasi-empirical' nature of mathematical discoveries and proof-procedures. What he hopes to establish is the pointlessness of raising this issue since the case for mathematical realism requires no more than a commitment to quantification over those various entities – numbers, sets, vectors, state-functions, etc. – which in turn play a crucial (indispensable) role in the current-best theories of physical science. But in that case there is no reason, Quinean 'pragmatic inclination' apart, to draw any definite line between the sorts of revision that are always possible with regard to empirical truth-claims and the sorts of revision that might be entertained with regard to mathematics or logic.

III

Putnam never quite embraces this doctrine since he sees very clearly what problems it creates for the widespread belief – shared by most physicists as well as mathematicians – that there *is* such a difference and that the truths of mathematics (like those of logic) *do* have a special status, whatever the difficulty of saying just what the difference is. This tension emerges once again toward the end of his essay 'What Is Mathematical Truth?' (in a section entitled 'Physics and the Future of Mathematics') where Putnam is typically unwilling to resolve the issue in either direction. Thus: 'I have not argued that mathematics is, in the full sense, an *empirical* science, although I have argued that it relies on empirical as well as quasi-empirical inference' (1975[1]: 77). Nevertheless, he continues,

> my expectation is that as physical science develops, the impact on mathematical axioms is going to be greater rather than less, and that we will have to face the fact that 'empirical' versus 'mathematical' is only a relative distinction; in a looser and more indirect way than the ordinary 'empirical' statement, much of mathematics too is 'empirical'. (*ibid.*)

What is most striking here is the 'looseness' and 'indirectness' of Putnam's own language, suggesting as it does a strong belief that this issue *should* be resolvable in terms of a 'quasi-empirical' approach, but also the nagging sense that there is something about mathematical truth – some objective or verification-transcendent property – that cannot be captured in any such terms. One is reminded of the passage from his essay 'There Is At Least One *A Priori* Truth' where Putnam remarks how often philosophers are torn between opposing arguments but how seldom they own up to such doubts in print. What usually happens, to repeat, is that 'we let ourselves be torn in private until we finally "plonk" for one alternative or the other; then the published paper only shows what we plonked for, and not the being torn' (Putnam 1983: 111–12). It seems to me that Putnam's plonking for (quasi)-empirical discovery-procedures and revisability in the case of mathematics is another instance of his taking a stance which conflicts not only with a large body of received philosophical thought but also with certain residual doubts in his own mind. Hence those repeated quote-marks around the word 'empirical' in the above-cited passage, along with the prefix 'quasi-' which likewise has a qualifying role to play, here as in other recent attempts to take up a middle-ground position on various aspects of the realism/anti-realism debate (Blackburn 1993). For the issue with regard to mathematical truth is like the issue with regard to *a priori* constraints in logic, where Putnam also 'plonks' for a theory of empirical revisability while none the less keeping an open mind as to just how far this process might go or just what limits might be placed on the scope for large-scale revisionism.

This is no great problem for postmodernists, cultural relativists, or 'strong' sociologists of knowledge whose grasp of mathematics and philosophy of logic – not to mention the history of science – is sufficiently vague to cause them no qualms when advancing such immodest proposals. (On this topic see Norris 1997.) But it is altogether different for a thinker like Putnam who is acutely aware of the problems that arise in all these areas if one simply rejects any thought of distinguishing between the various orders of analytic, *a priori*, and contingent (i.e., empirically warranted and hence empirically revisable) truth. There are many passages in Putnam's work which manifest a similar unresolved tension or reluctance to 'plonk' for either horn of this dilemma while inclining toward the (quasi-)empiricist 'solution' as that which possesses the greater degree of scientific-historical warrant. Thus his essay 'The Logic of Quantum Mechanics' makes the case for revising logic – more specifically, the principles of bivalence or excluded middle – if this enables us to 'keep the physics simple' and avoid forcing the issue with regard to such quantum-physical phenomena as wave-particle dualism (Putnam 1975[1]: 174–97). It begins, once again, 'by considering a case in which "necessary" truths (or rather "truths") turned out to be falsehoods: the case of Euclidean geometry' (*ibid.*: 174). This in turn raises the wider question: 'could some of the "necessary" truths of logic ever turn out to be false *for empirical reasons*?' (*ibid.*). As we have seen, Putnam's answer is a definite 'yes', borne out (so he believes) not only by the standing dilemmas of quantum mechanics but also by the evidence of previous shifts in what counted as instances of logical necessity or *a priori* truth. Thus:

> what is the nature of the world if the proposed interpretation of quantum mechanics is the correct one? The answer is both radical and simple. *Logic is as empirical as geometry.* It makes as much sense to speak of 'physical logic' as of 'physical geometry'. We live in a world with a non-classical logic. Certain statements – just the ones we encounter in daily life – *do* obey classical logic, but this is so because the corresponding subspaces of [Hilbert space] form a very special lattice under the inclusion relation: a so-called 'Boolean lattice'. Quantum mechanics itself explains the *approximate* validity of *classical* logic 'in the large', just as non-Euclidean geometry explains the *approximate* validity of *Euclidean* geometry 'in the small'. (Putnam 1975[1]: 184)

This Putnam takes to follow *necessarily* if it is accepted (1) that quantum mechanics in its basic ('uninterpreted' form) is a theory confirmed beyond reasonable doubt by its predictive-observational results; (2) that those results give rise to 'classically' unthinkable dilemmas or aporias; (3) that alternative (e.g., 'hidden-variable') theories can be safely ruled out as introducing 'an unknown physical force (the "quantum potential") obeying strange laws [and] introduced to account for the disturbance by measurement' (1975[1]: 140); and (4) that in this case a change of logic is the only recourse if one wishes to preserve an empirically adequate interpretation consistent with the full range of evidence. Nor is it a great price to pay, he thinks, if one considers that 'the only laws of logic that are given up are distributive laws ... and [that] every single anomaly vanishes once we give these up' (*ibid.*). All that is required is the simple recognition that we live in a non-Boolean world on the microphysical scale just as we live in a non-Euclidean world on the astrophysical scale at which the equations of General Relativity come into play.

Still, as I have said, there is a problem here when Putnam tries to square his logical-revisionist proposals with his case that such revision is justified solely by its pay-off in allowing a realist construal of the quantum-physical data. (See also Gibbins 1987; Haack 1974; Mittelstaedt 1994; Norris 2000.) After all, Putnam's chief objection to nominalism is that it fails to come up with any adequate account of why mathematics and logic *work so well* when applied to the physical world. Thus the burden of proof falls squarely on the nominalist to explain why this should be the case if numbers, sets, classes, functions and so forth are merely convenient posits adopted for the sake of empirical adequacy. Hence Putnam's firmly held view that '[t]here is no reason in stating logical principles to be more puristic, or more compulsive about avoiding reference to "nonphysical entities", than in scientific discourse generally' (1971: 14). For if reference to numbers, sets, classes, etc., is a well-established practice which has proved its worth in our dealings with various features of the 'classical' (i.e., macrophysical) world then the nominalist had better produce some strong arguments for drawing a line at the point of transition to such quantum-related functions as state-vectors, Hamiltonians, or lattices in Hilbert space. However, this makes it all the more difficult to see why Putnam should himself draw a similar line between the realm of macrophysical objects and events where the law of bivalence holds and the quantum realm where realism requires that we abandon that putative 'law' in order to save empirical appearances. 'All logicians agree', he writes, 'that, if there is such a thing as "the earth", [then] "The earth is round or the earth is not round", even if they disagree about the statement of the relevant principle in these cases too' (1975[1]: 325). So bivalence holds as a matter of empirical as well as of logical necessity in respect of objects in the macrophysical domain. But it is far from clear why this requirement should be lifted – or this 'law' considered empirically disproven – when it comes to issues in the interpretation of quantum mechanics. For we have it on Putnam's own submission that there is no good reason – nominalist prejudice apart – for adopting a different (non-realist) construal of such quantum-related 'entities' as state-vectors, Hamiltonians, Hilbert space, and so forth (Putnam 1971: 14). In which case, equally, there is no good reason for supposing that bivalence fails (or at any rate cannot be presumed to apply) in the quantum-physical domain.

Hence – I have suggested – one major problem with Putnam's attempt to salvage a workable realist conception of mathematical truth despite all the arguments brought against it by constructivists, intuitionists, conventionalists, and those who adopt a thoroughgoing naturalistic approach. On this latter view the

Platonist idea that such truths are discovered, not invented – that they belong to a realm of absolute ideal objectivity – should rather be seen as a belief brought about by their deep entwinement with the whole existing range of accepted scientific practices and methods. (See for instance Maddy 1990.) Putnam is unhappy with this naturalistic approach, whether applied to mathematics or logic, since it seems to make light of some powerful and widely shared convictions with regard to the difference in status between *a priori* truths (or those self-evident to reason) and empirical truth-claims that might yet be subject to revision. All the same, as we have seen, he goes a long way toward abandoning that distinction and adopts something very like Quine's outlook with respect to the revisability of logic under pressure from empirical counter-evidence. Thus the 'realism' that Putnam sets out to defend in the case of mathematical truths is one that has to do with their 'contextual apriority', or their figuring as strictly indispensable posits in our various scientific dealings with the physical world. This argument is put forward most explicitly in his book *Philosophy of Logic* where it concerns the necessity for physical science of quantifying over sets and assuming the 'existence' of those sets as something more than just a well-tried product of convenience. 'At present', he writes, 'reference to "classes", or something equally "nonphysical", is indispensable to the science of logic. The notion of logical "validity", on which the whole science rests, cannot be satisfactorily explained in purely nominalistic terms, at least today' (Putnam 1971: 23). However, this leaves it open for the Quinean to argue that Putnam's 'realism' amounts to no more than a *faute-de-mieux* holding strategy, or a covert acceptance that those various 'indispensable' items – numbers, sets, classes, state-vectors, etc. – have the status of so many convenient 'posits' adopted in order to expedite our dealings with the range of incoming sensory stimuli (Quine 1961).

Thus Putnam's is a basically empiricist approach to these issues, an approach that finds support in the twofold appeal to 'mathematical experience' and 'physical experience', the one having led to 'the construction of a highly articulated body of mathematical knowledge', and the other to 'a long tradition of successful problem-solving' (Putnam 1975[1]: 73). Hence his argument that there is no reason in principle why mathematicians should not use empirical – or at any rate 'quasi-empirical' – methods in finding out new constructions, hypotheses, proof-procedures, and so forth. After all, they would still be 'studying something objective', even if the kind of objectivity in question was not (as the hardline Platonist would have it) 'an unconditional reality of non-material things' (*ibid.*: 60). Rather, this would simply be a matter of acknowledging 'that the physicist who states a law of nature is abstracting a real feature of a real material world' (*ibid.*). And this realist claim would in no way be compromised by the fact that the physicist 'has to speak of numbers, vectors, tensors, state-functions, or whatever to make the abstraction'. On the contrary: it would gain just the kind of enhanced realism that comes of grounding these 'abstractions' in our various scientific practices, and of showing how those practices cannot do without the employment of mathematical methods and techniques. So what Putnam seeks to do is explain how we can give up the notion of mathematics as a paradigm case of *a priori* knowledge and accept that it 'resembles empirical knowledge', indeed, that 'the criterion of truth in mathematics just as much as in physics is success of our ideas in practice, and [hence] that mathematical knowledge is corrigible and not absolute' (*ibid.*: 61). Moreover, we can accomplish this seemingly drastic revision to received ideas of mathematical and logical truth without in the process giving up all claims to objectivity or realism in either domain. For those claims are much better served, Putnam thinks, by a sensibly scaled-down empiricist approach that grants them validity just in so far as mathematics and logic can convincingly be shown (like the methods of physical science) to have aided 'the success of our ideas in practice'. The trouble with alternative – e.g., Platonist or Fregean – accounts is that they purchase the absolute ideal objectivity of mathematics only at the cost of making it a mystery – a strictly insoluble problem – how we could ever gain knowledge of such truths by any means at our epistemic disposal (Frege 1953).

This is why Putnam is forced to the conclusion, along with others like Paul Benacerraf, that quite simply 'nothing works' in philosophy of mathematics, at least if the condition for a workable theory is that it should reconcile truth with knowledge (Benacerraf 1983; Putnam 1994[2]: 499–512). That is to say, no theory can possibly explain *both* how the truths of mathematics can be thought of as objective or verification-transcendent, *and* how we can none the less come to know them through various humanly achievable methods and proof-procedures. Putnam elects to resolve this dilemma by rejecting its Platonist–Fregean horn and opting for a qualified empiricist approach. On this view the 'entities' concerned – e.g., those of Peano arithmetic or axiomatised set-theory – do have a certain privileged status but only to the extent that they play a central role in our established mathematical practices, as well as in the methods and procedures of physical science. Of course there are well-known problems in the conceptual foundations of set-theory which make it a prime example, for Putnam, of the need to keep an open mind on the issue of what (if anything) should count as an instance of genuine (as opposed to 'contextual') apriority. However, it is clear that he means this argument to extend to *all and any* of those various candidate items which might lose their claim to *a priori* status should the empirical evidence so require. Thus they are always conceivably open to revision even if – as in the case of Euclidean geometry up until the early nineteenth century – they are *at present* so firmly and widely endorsed as to seem secure beyond rational doubt. In which case there can be no answer – certainly no answer on logically compelling or mathematically decisive grounds – to the Quinean claim that revisability reaches all the way from the empirical 'edges' to the logical 'core' of our existing web of beliefs (Quine 1961). What this distinction comes down to is merely the fact that the latter are more deeply entrenched and better protected against change under pressure from empirical counter-evidence. As I have said, Putnam has doubts concerning this wholesale empiricist approach, not least because it is so hard to reconcile with Quine's avowedly Platonist outlook in philosophy of mathematics, i.e., his acceptance of numbers and sets as existing (and deciding the truth-value of our various mathematical statements) quite apart from our present-best methods of verification (Quine 1981; Putnam 1983: 87–97, 98–114, 127–38). Thus, for Quine, since present-day physical science cannot do without quantifying over numbers – construed as classes of classes – then philosophy of mathematics had better tag along and admit numbers to its ontological scheme, that is to say, as values of the bound variables that play an indispensable role in our current-best scientific theories. Putnam is frankly perplexed by this and other aspects of Quine's address to the topic. All the same he sees no viable (non-Platonist) alternative to concurring with Quine on the revisability issue and thereby explicitly endorsing the case for empirical – or at any rate 'quasi-empirical' – methods of discovery and proof in mathematics.

From which, of course, it follows that those methods must be thought of as primarily inductive in character, rather than as axiomatic-deductive in the manner required by more traditional (*a priori*) conceptions of mathematical truth. 'By "quasi-empirical" methods', Putnam writes, 'I mean methods that are analogous to the methods of the physical sciences except that the singular statements which are "generalised by induction", used to test "theories", etc., are themselves the product of proof or calculation rather than being "observation reports" in the usual sense.' (Putnam 1975[1]: 62) In that case, clearly, those methods as applied to mathematics must inherit all the problems that have often been raised – not least by Putnam himself – with respect to the status of inductive reasoning in the empirical sciences. (See especially Putnam 1978, 1981.) No doubt he is obliged to adopt this stance in keeping with his generalised scepticism concerning *a priori* truth-claims and his belief that their character of seeming apriority comes of their entrenchment in our various empirically warranted (hence inductive) practices. Nevertheless, it is a claim that creates large problems for any approach that would seek to do justice to our standing intuitions in this regard. For if the truths of mathematics were indeed empirically revisable, or on a par with the kinds of result thrown up by empirical investigation, then there would seem little hope of explaining why they have yielded such a range of otherwise unattainable insights, discoveries and advances.

Putnam might appear to acknowledge this point when he speaks of 'mathematical experience' as the best warrant for realism, or when he rests his case on the evidence of 'a highly articulated body of mathematical knowledge with a long tradition of successful problem solving' (1975[1]: 73). However, this amounts to a pragmatist case for equating truth with the measure of achieved success, rather than a properly realist argument on which the 'success' of mathematical procedures is explained by their allowing us to get things right – objectively right – with regard to a realm of practice-transcendent mathematical truths. That these are two very different kinds of justificatory argument is a point brought home when Putnam proceeds – in the same sentence – to describe that record of problem-solving as 'a truly remarkable *social* achievement' (*ibid.*). For this is either a trivial claim to the effect that mathematics (like every other branch of enquiry) is a collaborative enterprise which involves certain shared standards of truth, method, procedural warrant, etc., or a much stronger claim to the effect that those standards are *ultimately* social in character, i.e., that they cannot be justified beyond the appeal to communally sanctioned practices or ways of carrying on.

Putnam never goes so far as to suggest – with the 'strong' sociologists of knowledge – that an approach of this sort could fully account for such deep-laid differences of view as that between (say) an empiricist like Mill and a Platonist like Frege on the status of mathematical truths. (See especially Bloor 1976; also Barnes 1985.) Indeed, as we have seen, he devotes a great deal of complex and sophisticated argument to the task of explaining just why mathematics has seemed to constitute a special kind of knowledge, one that eludes any wholesale conventionalist or social-constructivist account even though its truths should be counted *a priori* in a 'relative' rather than an 'absolute' sense. Still, Putnam is sufficiently impressed by various arguments against mathematical realism – among them the paradoxes of set-theory and the Wittgenstein-derived problem about 'following a rule' – for his statements to be often distinctly ambivalent in this regard. (See for instance Putnam 1993: 1–25, 115–26.) After all, it is just the point of those well-known passages in Wittgenstein, taken up and pressed further in a sceptical direction by exegetes like Kripke, that what counts as an instance of 'correct' rule-following cannot be decided by any criterion other than its meeting certain communal norms of rule-governed practice (Wittgenstein 1953: Part One, Sections 198–241; Kripke 1982). In which case it is pointless to seek some further justificatory ground, one that would somehow (impossibly) explain how the rule in question specified the rules for its own correct application.

The issue is raised most explicitly in *Philosophical Investigations*, Section 217, where Wittgenstein asks: 'How am I able to obey a rule?', and goes on to remark: 'if this is not a question about causes, then it is about the justification for my following the rule in the way that I do'. But then there is the further question – put into the mouth of Wittgenstein's imaginary interlocutor – as to what happens when 'my spade is turned', or when the justifying arguments come to an end. At this point, Wittgenstein responds, 'I am inclined to say: "This is simply what I do"'. Or again (Section 219): 'When I obey a rule, I do not choose. I follow the rule *blindly*'. This has struck many commentators – Thomas Nagel among them – as on the face of it such an utterly inadequate response that we must, in all charity, interpret Wittgenstein as having misspoken himself here and as surely leaving room for some other, more objectivist or truth-preserving construal (Nagel 1997). After all, if we asked someone to continue the series '3, 6, 9, 12 ....', and they went on '19, 27, 63, 14', then we would be justified in thinking that they simply hadn't grasped the relevant (correct) arithmetical rule, rather than concluding that their rule was one which just happened not to conform with the received practice of our own mathematical community. Or again, take Nagel's example of the set-theoretical concept of infinity according to which any finite arithmetical procedure (such as counting or addition) necessarily implies its valid application to an infinite range of further such cases. Thus:

> we know that $(x)(y)(\exists z)(x + y = z)$, but this is a judgement of reason about an infinite domain that at the same time our procedures of reasoning cannot fill out

in detail – though it is a further fact of reason that if iterated often enough, those procedures could reach any true proposition of the form 'a + b = c' …. Even where there is no decision procedure, or we don't have one, we may nevertheless be constrained to think that there is a right answer, and methods of trying to get it which are not guaranteed to succeed. (Nagel 1997: 70)

Putnam would no doubt agree with Nagel that any workable philosophy of mathematics must find room for standards of correctness – for judgements of objective truth and falsehood – which cannot be *entirely* practice-dependent in the sense of allowing *any* practice to set its own criteria for what counts as properly 'following a rule'. Yet there are aspects of his own thinking (not least the strong Wittgensteinian influence) which prevent Putnam from agreeing altogether that it *makes no sense* to conceive of mathematics in such practice-relative terms. After all, 'like empirical verification, quasi-empirical verification is relative and not absolute: what has been "verified" at a given time may later turn out to be false' (Putnam 1975[1]: 62). But if one puts this together with Putnam's doubts about the status and validity of inductive reasoning then it is hard to see what grounds he could have for rejecting the face-value (sceptical) version of Wittgenstein's rule-following argument. All the more so if the only reason that could count against a wholesale switch of mathematical procedures like that envisaged above is the kind of 'sociological' reason that presumably pertains to our existing, communally warranted 'practices' or forms of life.

IV

There might seem to be a striking parallel between Putnam's earlier 'Twin Earth' thought-experiments (1975[2]) and his use here of a kindred counterfactual hypothesis, namely that of the Martian mathematicians who have achieved a high measure of success by deploying 'quasi-empirical' methods that would strike their Earthian counterparts as simply not up to the mark (1975[1]: 61–4). In such a case, he asks, could we have any grounds for counting those methods 'irrational'? However, the main purpose of that earlier venture into possible-worlds logic was to distinguish between the various orders of contingent, *a priori*, and *a posteriori* necessary truth, this latter put forward as its most original or philosophically substantive claim. (See especially Putnam 1975[2]: 139–52, 215–71.) In short, it provided a means of explaining how reference could be fixed across various 'worlds' in terms of those essential (intrinsic) properties which enable us to pick out objects – prototypically natural kinds – despite any periodic shifts in the range of descriptive criteria applied to them. Thus the theory was intended not only to address certain problems with the standard (Frege–Russell) descriptivist account but also – less directly – as a means of resolving other philosophical quandaries, among them the Humean problem of induction (Hume 1955). That problem resulted from a failure to grasp how inductive reasoning could be grounded in something more than observed regularities or constant conjunction, that is to say, something more than the associative linkage of ideas brought about by repeated sequences of sensory stimuli. Rather such reasoning involved an appeal to those various real-world objects, properties, microstructural features, causal powers, dispositional attributes, and so forth, which sufficed to explain just *why* the regularities in question had been found to occur and could therefore be expected – with rational warrant – to occur on future occasions. (See also Harré and Madden 1975; Salmon 1967, 1984; Tooley 1988.) Thus the problem of induction arose only on a narrowly empiricist view of what counted as adequate evidence, or again, only on a narrowly deductivist view of what counted as adequate (rational) grounds for belief (Grünbaum and Salmon (eds) 1988; Salmon 1989).

My point in this brief return visit to Putnam's earlier work is that his thought-experiment with the Martian mathematicians works to very different effect. For the upshot of supposing these superior intellects to have used empirical (or 'quasi-empirical') methods in mathematics – and done so, moreover, with great success – is to create large problems for epistemology and philosophy of science. Thus, firstly, it becomes hard to explain why our own (Earthian) physical sciences should so often have achieved some signal advance by adopting a mathematics-based approach *despite and against* the empirical evidence, as with a whole range of such discoveries from Galileo to Einstein and beyond. Secondly, it fails to yield any reason why induction should be thought to possess its own proper standards of well-tried evidential warrant, standards that can only seem inadequate – and thus give rise to Humean scepticism – if measured by strictly deductive criteria. The most convincing defence of induction against those sceptical doubts is one that involves an appeal to counterfactual-supporting modes of causal explanation, i.e., claims to the effect that had x not occurred then neither would y, or again – in more elaborate versions of the case – that had a range of antecedent (jointly necessary and sufficient) conditions not obtained then events would not have turned out in the way that they did. (See Mackie 1974; Salmon 1984; Sosa (ed.) 1975.) Such arguments have a wide scope of application, from the physical sciences to history, economics, sociology and psychology. What they all have in common is the use of certain causal-explanatory hypotheses whose scope of application in any given case can then be assessed in counterfactual-supporting or subjunctive-conditional terms.

Indeed this is just the kind of reasoning that Putnam deployed in those earlier thought-experiments in order to demonstrate – as a matter of *a posteriori* necessary truth – that Twin-Earth 'water', 'gold', 'aluminium', 'molybdenum', 'tigers', and so forth, are not the same items that are properly picked out by qualified (expert or reliably informed) members of the Earthian linguistic community. Thus, for instance, if 'tigers' are discovered on Mars which then turn out – on closer inspection – to have a silicon-based rather than a carbon-based chemistry then we *might* want to carry on referring to them loosely as 'tigers' but we *wouldn't* in that case be talking about the same kind of creature that is properly so called in the Earthian context (Putnam 1975[2]: 215–71). That is to say, what fixes the reference for tiger-talk is (1) the fact of their having been originally so named; (2) the causal 'chain of transmission' through which that name has been passed down despite any interim changes of descriptive criteria; (3) our developed (e.g., genetic or molecular-biological) knowledge of the relevant species-membership conditions; and (4) the 'linguistic division of labour' which makes it possible for non-expert types to talk about tigers with a fair degree of confidence just so long as there are experts around who can always be consulted if need be. 'Are Martian "tigers" tigers? It depends on the context' (*ibid.*: 239). But if the context is that of sufficiently well-informed Earthian scientific knowledge and linguistic practice then clearly the answer must be no, Martian 'tigers' are *not* in fact tigers.

However, as I have said, it is a different matter when Putnam deploys his hypothesis concerning the Martian mathematicians who use quasi-empirical methods to obtain results that are far in advance of our Earthian achievements. For there is a problem here about *what could possibly qualify* as an instance of counterfactual-supporting evidential warrant, or a case in which the truth of a given mathematical proposition could be either confirmed or disconfirmed by appeal to some alternative (logically conceivable) 'world' where necessary truths still held firm but where sundry contingent matters-of-fact were subject to thought-experimental variation. Jerrold Katz makes the point – with acknowledgement to David Lewis – when he remarks that 'the necessity of a mathematical proposition exempts it from the requirement on empirical propositions to show that they counterfactually depend on the facts to which they correspond' (Katz 1998: 37; Lewis 1986). In other words, mathematics neither depends upon nor stands open to correction by any results turned up in the course of empirical enquiry. And the argument also works in reverse since there is no way that any factual or contingent state of affairs with respect to this or some other possible world can be affected by truths that necessarily obtain across all such worlds. As Lewis puts it, 'nothing can depend counterfactually on non-contingent matters. For instance, nothing can depend counterfactually on what mathematical objects there are …. Nothing sensible can be said about how our opinions would be different if there were no number seventeen' (Lewis 1986: 111).

Of course it might be claimed that such arguments take for granted exactly what Putnam is out to deny, i.e., the existence of mathematical truths that inhabit a realm of absolute ideal objectivity and which thus by very definition stand beyond reach of empirical claims or counter-claims. Still there is the question whether Putnam's proposal can possibly do justice to the range and extent of achieved mathematical knowledge, much of it going far beyond the limits of empirical (or even 'quasi-empirical') accountability. More than that: there is the problem as to how we should explain the extraordinary yield of mathematics in the physical sciences, or the fact that it has so often led to advances which outrun (or on occasion appear to contradict) the findings of empirical enquiry. And lastly there is the question why we should accept the dilemma that Putnam considers to exist between *either* endorsing a realist (= Platonist) conception which places mathematical truths beyond our furthest epistemic reach *or* endorsing a quasi-empirical (more-or-less naturalised) approach. For this dilemma takes rise from a further assumption, namely the idea that mathematical truth on any kind of realist construal *must* be epistemically inaccessible since we can only have know-ledge of objects that are those (or relevantly like those) of perceptual or sensory acquaintance. Yet of course it is just that empiricist way of setting up the debate which the realist seeks to challenge by asserting that there do exist forms of *a priori* knowledge – mathematics and logic preeminent among them – which don't involve the hopeless appeal to any such notion of perceptual contact with abstract objects or entities.

Thus we need not be driven to conclude, like Putnam, that in a certain (i.e., realist) sense 'nothing works in philosophy of mathematics' since objective truths are by definition unknowable, or beyond the compass of human discovery, while know-ledge necessarily falls short of objective (verification-transcendent) truth (Putnam 1994[2]: 499–512). Rather we should take it that we *can* have epistemic access to such truths though *not* through any mode of cognition analogous to that of sensory-perceptual acquaintance. For this is just another dogma of empiricism, one that continues to exert its influence even on those – Putnam among them – who would reject any hardline empiricist approach to issues of meaning, knowl-edge, and truth. Jerrold Katz puts the case with admirable clarity in a passage that is worth quoting at length. Thus:

> [t]he entire idea that our knowledge of abstract objects might be based on perceptual contact is misguided, since, even if we had contact with abstract objects, the information we could obtain from such contact wouldn't help us in trying to justify our beliefs about them. The epistemological function of percep-tual contact is to provide information about which possibilities are actualities. Perceptual contact thus has a point in the case of empirical propositions. Because natural objects can be otherwise than they actually are (*non obstante* their essen-tial properties), contact is necessary in order to discover how they actually are .... Not so with abstract objects. They could not be otherwise than they are .... Hence there is no question of which mathematical possibilities are actual possi-bilities. In virtue of being a perfect number, six must be a perfect number; in virtue of being the only even prime, two must be the only even prime. Since the epistemic role of contact is to provide us with the information needed to select among the different ways something might be, and since perceptual contact cannot provide information about how something must be, contact has no point in relation to abstract objects. It cannot ground beliefs about them. (Katz 1998: 36–7)

Again it may be said that this begs the question against Putnam since it assumes the truth of mathematical realism – i.e., of realism with respect to abstract 'enti-ties' such as numbers – and hence the untruth (or the unworkability) of any approach that would deny their objective existence and treat them as dependent on quasi-empirical methods and procedures. But the realist is then entitled to ask whether Putnam's proposed account can make sense of instances like those offered above, or indeed of other, more challenging cases where the truth-value of arith-metical statements exceeds our present or perhaps best-possible powers of verifi-cation. Goldbach's famous unproven conjecture – that every even number is the sum of two primes – would be one such example, as would the statement that the infinite (or indefinite) decimal expansion of *pi* contains a sequence of one hundred consecutive sevens. For there is simply no way that these could count as truth-apt or truth-evaluable statements on the theory that quasi-empirical methods are the only source of arithmetical knowledge.

What motivates the realist argument here is the conviction that in both cases there is a truth of the matter – an objective or verification-transcendent truth – which *would* settle the issue had we but the time, resources, computational power, or perhaps the requisite conceptual grasp to arrive at a definite answer. In Dummett's words, '[i]t is an essential feature of any theory of meaning that will yield a semantics validating classical logic that each sentence is conceived as possessing a determinate truth-value, independently of whether or not we know it or have at our disposal the means to discover it' (Dummett 1977: 371). What motivates the anti-realist argument, conversely, is the belief that it makes no sense to claim that such statements *must* be either true or false quite aside from our present-best methods or procedures for establishing their truth or falsehood. Thus (Dummett again):

> since ex hypothesi, from the supposition that the condition for the truth of a mathematical statement, as platonistically understood, obtains, it cannot in general be inferred that it is one that a human being need be supposed to be even capable of recognizing as obtaining, we cannot give substance to our conception of our having an implicit knowledge of what that condition is, since nothing that we do can amounts to a manifestation of such knowledge. (*ibid.*: 375)

Putnam has serious doubts concerning the consequence of this doctrine not only for disputed mathematical claims – where it seems to preclude any grasp of what would count as an adequate proof-procedure – but also in other fields where realism requires that there must be truths independent of our present-best means of verification. (See especially Putnam 1994[1].) After all, one decisive argument to this effect is that we now possess certain items of knowledge that were once beyond reach of adequate proof but which have since been borne out through more refined mathematical procedures or enhanced computational power. Thus, for instance, it has been shown that the integer produced by 317 successive iterations of the digit 1 is a prime number. Had someone (improbably) chanced to frame this conjecture before the relevant proof was devised then of course neither they nor anyone else could have been in a position to judge of its determinate truth or falsehood. On the other hand, they *would* have been fully justified – so the realist claims – to declare that it must be *either* true *or* false as a matter of objective mathematical fact quite aside from the lack of any present means for deciding the issue. And just as the question was resolved, in this particular case, when a proof-procedure turned up so likewise we can say of any well-formed but currently unproven conjecture that it might yet be proved by some future advance in our methods of verification but that its truth-value holds irrespective of the limits on our present-best knowledge.

The case for anti-realism often relies on a sceptical meta-induction which argues from the falsity of *some* past beliefs – among them, as Putnam points out, '*a priori*' truths like those of Euclidean geometry – to the verdict that *any or all* of our current beliefs might at length be shown up as empirically false or in need of revision under pressure from conflicting evidence. However one may then ask on what grounds the sceptic can claim with such confidence that those erstwhile 'truths' have failed to hold good or have turned out subject to revision in light of more advanced scientific knowledge. For at this stage the sceptic is obliged to respond that we now have good reason to count them false – or valid only in certain restricted domains – even though their 'truth' once appeared self-evident beyond any prospect of falsification. Thus the sceptical meta-induction can be turned around to support just the opposite (realist) conclusion, i.e., that the very possibility of arguing along such fallibilist lines presupposes the existence of objective or verification-transcendent truths. There is no making sense of the sceptic's case except on the assumption that we *do* possess standards of bivalent truth and falsehood which require – as a matter of logical necessity – that beliefs can be falsified in various ways and hence that truth cannot be coterminous with the scope and limits of our present-best knowledge or means of verification.

This case can be put in very general terms that extend from mathematics and formal logic to the whole range of disciplines, fields, or subject-areas where there exist statements of the 'disputed class' (neither true-nor-false so far as we know) as defined by an anti-realist like Dummett. Thus, according to Scott Soames, a proposition can be true even if it has never been expressed by an actual utterance.

> It is also not absurd to suppose that it can be true even if there is no sentence that expresses it. For example, for each of the nondenumerably many real numbers, there is a proposition that it is greater than or equal to zero. If each sentence is a finite string of words drawn from a finite vocabulary, then the number of propositions outstrips the denumerable infinity of sentences available to express them – that is, there are truths with no linguistic expression. Moreover, if languages are man-made constructions, then propositions that are expressed by sentences could have been true even if no sentences had expressed them. For example, the proposition that the sun is a star could have been true even if no one and hence no sentence had existed to express it. (Soames 1999: 19)

At this point the anti-realist may respond in various ways depending on the strength or scope of their commitment to the case against verification-transcendent truths. Thus they might argue (1) that the above line of argument is altogether wrong (or strictly unintelligible) since we cannot conceive how such truths might exist if we lacked any means of expressing them; (2) that there might be such truths for all we can know but that the issue is undecidable by very definition and hence of no genuine (epistemological) import; or (3), that anti-realism entails the non-existence of bivalent truth-values only as concerns our *present* state of knowledge with respect to items of the disputed class, and is thus uncommitted – necessarily and properly so – as concerns any future change in their status brought about by newly found proof-procedures or methods of verification. All three positions have been plausibly attributed to Dummett on the evidence of various passages in his work. At any rate it is clear that interpretation (1) puts the case in 'strong' anti-realist terms and flatly rejects Soames' claim that 'a proposition can be true even if it has never been expressed by an actual utterance'. For of course it follows from this interpretation that we cannot make sense of such realist talk about true (objectively valid) 'propositions' which exceed our means of articulate statement, any more than we can make sense of the realist position with regard to indeterminate (non-truth-evaluable) statements. Thus anti-realism of this sort cannot be valid if Soames' argument goes through and if it can indeed be shown – on the basis of a set-theoretical proof as described above – that there *must* exist a nondenumerable range of valid propositions with respect to the real numbers which necessarily exceeds 'the nondenumerable infinity of sentences available to express them'. As concerns (2), the realist will respond that this argument simply misses the point since what is at issue here is the objective truth or falsehood of statements in the disputed class and *not* the epistemological question of our present-best knowledge in that regard. When it comes to (3), the realist will most likely remark that this concession leans far enough in her own direction as to let the argument pretty much go by default. That is to say, if it requires that truth-values not be assigned *only in so far and for so long* as we lack any adequate proof-procedure, then again this is clearly an epistemological requirement which has no bearing on the existence or non-existence of objective (verification-transcendent) truths.

V

I should not wish to claim (absurdly) that this settles the question with regard to mathematical truth or even that it answers those particular problems that have so preoccupied Putnam's thinking over the past four decades. What it does bring out, I suggest, is the extent to which those problems have been forced upon him by the prevailing sceptical or anti-realist tenor of much recent work in this area. Also – more constructively – it points to the resourcefulness of Putnam's own work on the philosophy of mathematics and logic. For despite his receptiveness to certain aspects of the anti-realist case there is always a strong countervailing sense of the need to explain why mathematics should so often have opened the way to such a range of otherwise unattainable scientific advances. Indeed, it is precisely Putnam's grasp of its extraordinary fruitfulness in this regard that has led him to reject any Platonist approach that would locate mathematical truth in a realm of absolute ideal objectivity where it could have no bearing – no epistemic purchase – on the methods and procedures of real-world empirical enquiry. Yet of course it is just this 'realist' emphasis that also gives rise to Putnam's doubts with respect to the *a priori* status of mathematical truths and their unrevisability despite any show of empirical disconfirmation.

The resultant tensions are nowhere more apparent than in the first paragraph of his essay 'What Is Mathematical Truth?'. Thus:

> [i]n this paper I argue that mathematics should be interpreted realistically – that
> is, that mathematics makes assertions that are objectively true or false, inde-

pendently of the human mind, and that *something* answers to such mathematical notions as 'set' and 'function'. This is not to say that reality is somehow bifurcated – that there is one reality of material things and then, over and above it, a
second reality of mathematical 'things'. A set of objects, for example, depends for
its existence on those objects: if they are destroyed, then there is no longer such
a set .... Not only are the 'objects' of pure mathematics conditional upon material objects; they are, in a sense, merely abstract possibilities. Studying how
mathematical objects behave might better be described as studying what structures are abstractly possible and what structures are not abstractly possible.
(Putnam 1975[1]: 60)

This passage is remarkable for various reasons, among them its allowing the
antinomies of mathematical realism to emerge (so to speak) at full blast, while
none the less holding out for some solution – some alternative realist construal –
that would satisfy *both* the objectivist claim *and* the case for mathematics as a
branch of science subject to the usual procedures of empirical verification or falsification. On the one hand there is the radical-empiricist thesis (harking back to a
thinker like Mill) that mathematical sets have no 'existence' apart from the various
material objects of which they are comprised and in the absence of which they
would lack any content, reference, or valid application (Mill 1973–4). To this
extent they are 'merely abstract' functions which serve chiefly to expedite our dealings with empirical experience and which cannot be thought of as laying claim to
any order of objective (verification-transcendent) truth. Yet the emphasis seems to
shift quite markedly when Putnam describes mathematics as studying 'what structures are [and are not] abstractly possible', with the term 'abstract' seeming to
invite a more realist, objectivist, or even Platonist construal. Of course there is a
certain ambiguity about the phrase 'how mathematical objects behave', applying
as it might *either* to the kinds of relatively 'abstract' possibility that are recognised
through empirical investigation of the way that material objects combine into sets,
or to the ways in which our thinking discovers certain *a priori* rules and constraints
upon its powers of mathematical reasoning. The former (empiricist) reading
appears to gain credence from Putnam's firm anti-Platonist rejection of the notion
that 'reality is somehow bifurcated', or that there exists 'one reality of material
things' and then, 'over and above it, a second reality of "mathematical things"'. Yet
it is hard to make sense of this reading – or indeed of his empiricist premise that
the existence of sets depends on the existence of those physical objects that
compose them – if one gives full weight to Putnam's talk of 'abstract possibility'
and its clear implication that mathematical thought possesses at any rate a certain
degree of conceptual and epistemic autonomy.

This takes us back to the opening sentence and its twofold claim, first, that
'mathematics makes assertions that are objectively true or false, independently of
the human mind', and second, that '*something* answers to such mathematical
notions as "set" or "function"' (1975[1]: 60). If I seem to be placing an undue
weight of exegetical pressure on this and other passages from Putnam's essay then
my justification is that they capture certain tensions that go to the heart of his
thinking on these topics. Thus the idea of 'objective' mathematical truths that

exist 'independently of the human mind' would appear to rule out any empiricist construal according to which such truths are discovered (and must always be subject to later revision or abandonment) through further investigation of the way things stand with respect to physical reality. This would likewise be a plausible (realist) construal of his statement that '*something* answers to such mathematical notions as "set" and "function"', at least if one takes the 'something' in question to exist in a distinct ontological realm where mathematical truths can be arrived at through methods that are not (or not chiefly) those of the empirical sciences. Moreover, such a reading would make better sense of Putnam's claim for the 'objectivity' (or mind-independence) of those same mathematical truths, given that empirical discovery-procedures are the paradigm case of investigative methods that crucially depend on the scope and capacities of human cognitive grasp. Yet, again, this reading clearly meets resistance from his view of the one-way dependence relation that makes 'the "objects" of pure mathematics' strictly 'conditional upon material objects' (1975[1]: 60).

So there are various unresolved tensions in Putnam's essay which somewhat belie his confident opening statement that 'mathematics should be interpreted realistically', or as making assertions 'that are objectively true or false'. In my view those tensions have resulted very largely from his no longer applying the kinds of pertinent distinction – i.e., between *a priori*, analytic, contingent (empirical), and *a posteriori* necessary truths – which played such a crucial clarifying role in Putnam's earlier work (Putnam 1975[2]; also Kripke 1980; Schwartz (ed.) 1977; Wiggins 1980). One consequence of this is his pyrrhic conclusion that 'nothing works' in philosophy of mathematics, at least if the requirement for a workable theory is that it should somehow reconcile the opposed claims of objective (recognition-transcendent) truth and epistemic (recognition-dependent) knowledge. It seems to me that Putnam is overly impressed by the case for recognition-dependence and insufficiently responsive to realist arguments for truth – in mathematics and elsewhere – as independent of our present-best or even best-attainable state of knowledge concerning it. Nevertheless he has raised these issues with a sharpness of insight and tenacity of purpose which cannot be ignored by philosophers of either persuasion.

References

Barnes, Barry (1985). *About Science*. Oxford: Blackwell.
Benacerraf, Paul (1983). 'What Numbers Could Not Be'. In Benacerraf and Putnam (eds). 272–94.
Benacerraf, Paul and Hilary Putnam (eds) (1983). *The Philosophy of Mathematics: selected essays*, 2nd edn. Cambridge: Cambridge University Press.
Blackburn, Simon (1993). *Essays in Quasi-Realism*. Oxford: Oxford University Press.
Bloor, David (1976). *Knowledge and Social Imagery*. London: Routledge & Kegan Paul.
Boyd, Richard N. (1984). 'The Current Status of Scientific Realism'. In Leplin (ed.). 41–82.
Clark, Peter and Bob Hale (eds) (1993). *Reading Putnam*. Oxford: Blackwell.
Dummett, Michael (1977). *Elements of Intuitionism*. Oxford: Oxford University Press.
—— (1978). *Truth and Other Enigmas*. London: Duckworth.

—— (1991). *The Logical Basis of Metaphysics*. London: Duckworth.

Frege, Gottlob (1953). *The Foundations of Arithmetic*, trans. J.L. Austin. Oxford: Blackwell.

Gibbins, Peter (1987). *Particles and Paradoxes: the limits of quantum logic*. Cambridge: Cambridge University Press.

Grünbaum, Adolf and Wesley C. Salmon (eds) (1988). *The Limitations of Deductivism*. Berkeley & Los Angeles: University of California Press.

Haack, Susan (1974). *Deviant Logic: some philosophical issues*. Cambridge: Cambridge University Press.

Harman, Gilbert (1965). 'Inference to the Best Explanation', *Philosophical Review*, LXXIV. 88–95.

Harré, Rom and E.H. Madden (1975). *Causal Powers*. Oxford: Blackwell.

Hume, David (1955). *An Enquiry Concerning Human Understanding*. Indianapolis: Bobbs-Merrill.

Kant, Immanuel (1964). *Critique of Pure Reason*, trans. N. Kemp Smith. London: Macmillan.

Katz, Jerrold J. (1998). *Realistic Rationalism*. Cambridge, MA: MIT Press.

Kripke (1980). *Naming and Necessity*. Oxford: Blackwell.

—— (1982). *Wittgenstein on Rules and Private Language: an elementary exposition*. Oxford: Blackwell.

Leplin, Jarrett (ed.) (1984). *Scientific Realism*. Berkeley & Los Angeles: University of California Press.

Lewis, David (1986). *On the Plurality of Worlds*. Oxford: Blackwell.

Lipton, Peter (1993). *Inference to the Best Explanation*. London: Routledge.

Mackie, J.L. (1974). *The Cement of the Universe*. Oxford: Clarendon Press.

Maddy, Penelope (1990). *Realism in Mathematics*. Oxford: Oxford University Press.

Mill, J.S. (1973–74). *A System of Logic Radiocinative and Inductive: being a connected view of the principles of evidence and the methods of scientific investigation*, ed. J.M. Robson. London: Routledge & Kegan Paul.

Mittelstaedt, Peter (1994). *Quantum Logic*. Princeton, NJ: Princeton University Press.

Nagel, Thomas (1997). *The Last Word*. Oxford: Oxford University Press.

Norris, Christopher (1997). *Against Relativism: philosophy of science, deconstruction and critical theory*. Oxford: Blackwell.

—— (2000). *Quantum Theory and the Flight from Realism: philosophical responses to quantum mechanics*. London: Routledge.

Putnam, Hilary (1971). *Philosophy of Logic*. New York: Harper & Row.

—— (1975[1]). *Mathematics, Matter and Method* (*Philosophical Papers*, Vol. 1). Cambridge: Cambridge University Press.

—— (1975[2]). *Mind, Language and Reality* (*Philosophical Papers*, Vol. 2). Cambridge: Cambridge University Press.

—— (1978). *Meaning and the Moral Sciences*. London: Routledge & Kegan Paul.

—— (1981). *Reason, Truth and History*. Cambridge: Cambridge University Press.

—— (1983). *Realism and Reason* (*Philosophical Papers*, Vol. 3). Cambridge: Cambridge University Press.

—— (1987). *The Many Faces of Realism*. La Salle, IL: Open Court.

—— (1994[1]). 'Sense, Nonsense, and the Senses: an inquiry into the powers of the human mind', *Journal of Philosophy*, XCI: 9. 445–517.

—— (1994[2]). *Words and Life*, ed. James Conant. Cambridge, MA: Harvard University Press.

—— (1995). *Pragmatism: an open question*. Oxford: Blackwell.

Quine, W.V.O. (1961). 'Two Dogmas of Empiricism'. In *From a Logical Point of View*, 2nd edn. Cambridge, MA: Harvard University Press. 20–46.

—— (1981). *Theories and Things*. Cambridge, MA: Harvard University Press.

Salmon, Wesley C. (1967). *The Foundations of Scientific Inference*. Pittsburgh, PA: Pittsburgh University Press.

—— (1984). *Scientific Explanation and the Causal Structure of the World*. Princeton, NJ: Princeton University Press.

—— (1989). *Four Decades of Scientific Explanation*. Minneapolis: University of Minnesota Press.

Schwartz, Stephen (ed.) (1977). *Naming, Necessity, and Natural Kinds.* Ithaca, NY: Cornell University Press.

Soames, Scott (1999). *Understanding Truth.* Oxford: Oxford University Press.

Sosa, Ernest (ed.) (1975). *Causation and Conditionals.* Oxford: Oxford University Press.

Tooley, M. (1988). *Causation: a realist approach.* Oxford: Blackwell.

van Heijenoort (ed.) (1967). *From Frege to Gödel.* Cambridge, MA: Harvard University Press.

Wiggins, David (1980). *Sameness and Substance.* Oxford: Blackwell.

Wittgenstein, Ludwig (1953). *Philosophical Investigations*, trans. G.E.M. Anscombe. Oxford: Blackwell.

—— (1978). *Remarks on the Foundations of Mathematics*, trans. G.E.M. Anscombe, 3rd edn. Oxford: Blackwell.

Zermelo, E. (1967). 'A New Proof of the Possibility of a Well Ordering'. In van Heijenoort (ed.), 183–98.

9

Putnam, Peano and the *malin génie*: could we possibly be wrong about elementary number-theory?

I

As we have seen, in his later (post-1975) writings Hilary Putnam brings up a whole range of arguments from philosophy of logic and mathematics – among them arguments having to do with the conceptual foundations of set-theory – which he takes to count strongly against any realist or objectivist approach. (See, for instance, Putnam 1978, 1981, 1983, 1987, 1994, 1995.) Thus, for instance, there is Gödel's undecidability-theorem to the effect that any system sufficiently complex to generate the theorems of elementary arithmetic will contain at least one axiom incapable of proof within the system itself (Gödel 1962). Also there is the Löwenheim–Skolem proof that no formal or fully axiomatised system can adequately capture our intuitive and – in mathematical terms – our operationally well-tried notion of a set. This latter result Putnam thinks 'a serious problem for any philosopher or philosophically minded logician who wishes to view set theory as the description of a determinate independently existing reality' (1983: 4). What is more, it raises difficulties which can be seen to push Putnam a long way – perhaps (on occasion) somewhat further than he wishes to go – toward a radically contextualist or framework-relativist theory of truth, meaning and logical necessity. Thus: 'what can our "understanding" come to, at least for a naturalistically minded philosopher, which is more than *the way we use our language*? And the Skolem argument can be extended ... to show that the *total use of the language* (operational plus theoretical constraints) does not "fix" a unique "intended interpretation" any more than the axiomatic set theory by itself does' (*ibid.*).

Since late Putnam is himself strongly drawn toward a naturalistic position this creates large problems for his own approach, problems that would seem to have been further reinforced by his encounter with kindred sceptical *topoi* such as Wittgenstein's puzzle about rule-following and Goodman's 'new riddle' of induction. (Wittgenstein 1953: Part One, Sections 198–241; Goodman 1978; Putnam 1983: 115–26 and 155–69). Or perhaps – as Jerrold Katz suggests – this reinforcement has worked the other way around so that 'Wittgenstein's rule-following argument is the engine that drives Putnam's Skolemite argument' (Katz 1998: 114). Hence his distinctly under-motivated jump from the discovery of certain conceptual problems in set-theory to the full-fledged Wittgensteinian claim that, on the given construal, understanding can amount to nothing more than 'the way we use our language'. For this conclusion will appear to force itself upon us *only if* we assume that any realist philosophy of mathematics is a non-starter since it involves the idea of our somehow having epistemic contact with abstract entities such as numbers or sets. That idea strikes Putnam – along with most present-day mathematicians and philosophers, self-avowed realists and even some 'Platonists' among them – as beyond all hope of intelligible statement in non-contradictory terms. (See Benacerraf and Putnam (eds) 1983 for a broadly representative range of views.) Still, there would seem little merit in Putnam's proposed alternative approach if this means adopting a 'moderate' naturalist position which then becomes subject to Skolemite doubts and ends up by endorsing a broadly contextualist approach wherein truth is conceived as relative to language or to various possible ways of construing our talk about those same notional entities.

Katz cites a passage from Putnam's essay 'Models and Reality' where this dilemma finds expression in particularly sharp and poignant form. The Platonist has no problem with Skolem's theorem, according to Putnam, since

> he will take this as evidence that the mind has mysterious faculties of 'grasping concepts' (or 'perceiving mathematical objects') which the naturalistically minded philosopher will never succeed in giving an account of .... The extreme positions – Platonism and verificationism – seem to receive comfort from the Löwenheim–Skolem Paradox; it is only the 'moderate' position (which tries to avoid mysterious 'perceptions' of 'mathematical objects' while retaining a classical notion of truth) which is in deep trouble. (Putnam 1983: 4)

However, this will look much more like a forced or artificial dilemma if one accepts that realists need not subscribe to that self-refuting version of Platonism which supposes the mind to have epistemic contact with abstract (and hence epistemically inaccessible) objects like numbers, sets, or propositions concerning them. Rather, their argument should take the form of a case for the mind-independent existence of just such abstract objects but one that avoids any incoherent talk of our somehow knowing them by means analogous to those of perceptual contact. It is a 'Platonism' of this alternative kind that is implicit in Gödel's undecidability-theorem and in any result of mathematical reasoning – like the Löwenheim–Skolem Paradox – which claims *as a matter of objectively valid truth* to establish certain limits on the scope and reach of formal (axiomatic-deductive) methods for arriving at just such truths. Hence Gödel's cautionary statement that 'mathematical intuition need not be conceived of as a faculty giving an *immediate* knowledge of the objects concerned .... Rather, they, too, may represent an aspect of objective reality, but, as opposed to sensations, their presence in us may be due to another kind of relationship between ourselves and reality' (Gödel 1983: 484).

Anti-realists have typically given this claim short shrift, as when Dummett speaks of it as having 'the ring of superstition', or when Chihara declares that any such recourse to Gödelian objective intuition is 'like appealing to experiences vaguely described as "mystical experiences" to justify belief in the existence of God' (Dummett 1978: 202; Chihara 1982: 215). Still there is a strong case to be made – especially in view of Putnam's problems with steering a viable alternative course – that it is the only philosophy that 'works' for mathematics, or which can do full justice not only to the reach of our existing mathematical knowledge but also (crucially) to what we can surmise concerning the limits of that knowledge. For it is hard to see how that requirement could be met by an approach, like Wittgenstein's, that treats these issues solely in terms of rule-following behaviour, and which locates the standards of correctness for following a rule in the criteria laid down by communal practice or received usage. (See Wittgenstein 1956, 1976; also Kripke 1982, Wright 1980.) Such an argument may have considerable force against the mentalist conception according to which those standards can be fixed – or their validity checked – by reference to certain apodictic concepts or ideas that are taken to provide sufficient guarantee that we *must* be getting things right. For then of course there is the problem of infinite regress, that is to say, the necessity of searching one's mind for some rule that would apply for interpreting the rule that properly applies for interpreting the rule .... that decides what shall count as 'following the rule' in this or that particular case. Hence Wittgenstein's alternative appeal to a communal or practice-based conception of rule-following which avoids that predicament by simply rejecting any notion of privileged first-person epistemic access. Hence also Kripke's 'sceptical solution' which amounts to little more than a sharpened re-statement of the Wittgensteinian case for communal warrant as the sole criterion of correctness in such matters (Kripke 1982). However, this leaves it a mystery how mathematics – or any other branch of knowledge – could ever have achieved the kind of progress that results from breaking with received, commonsense, or customary habits of thought. Still less can it yield any plausible account of those major conceptual changes – like the advent of non-Euclidean geometry – which Putnam regards as posing a crucial challenge to any adequate philosophy or history of mathematics (Putnam 1975[1]: 60–78, 79–92, 174–7).

Putnam is both strongly drawn to this Wittgensteinian approach and keenly aware of the problems with it, not least the risk of its opening the way to a downright conventionalist or cultural-relativist position. So it is important to see just why such ideas have exerted a powerful hold on his thought despite these strong misgivings. Again Jerrold Katz offers some pertinent commentary on the way that Wittgenstein's thinking has appeared to offer the sole alternative to a mentalist conception of meaning and truth which manages to resolve all the above-mentioned difficulties. Thus:

> Wittgenstein's criticisms of Frege's (and Russell's) approaches to semantics were supposed to show that his own use-based approach to meaning and his interlocutor's mentalistic approach are the only ones left as serious contenders for our semantic allegiance. If those criticisms had succeeded, Wittgenstein's use-based approach would have emerged as the clear winner because his rule-following argument refutes the idea that 'what comes before the mind' provides the normative basis for fixing meaning in the use of language. But if those criticisms do not succeed in eliminating all other approaches to meaning, a refutation of the mentalistic approach does not settle the issue of what provides normative force. (Katz 1998: 114)

For Katz, the prime alternative contender is a realist theory of abstract objects which avoids the trap laid by various critics – whether naturalists, Wittgensteinians, or advocates of Dummett-style anti-realism – who make it out to involve our somehow having epistemic access to those objects through a mode of quasi-perceptual knowledge. This latter kind of Platonism is open to the standard range of anti-realist objections, involving as it does the impossible claim (which Gödel expressly disowns in the above-cited passage) that there exists a mysterious faculty of 'immediate' knowledge-by-acquaintance that puts us directly in touch with mathematical or other such abstract entities. Still there is no reason – anti-realist prejudice apart – to conclude that this amounts to a knockdown case against *any* argument which takes mathematical truths to be objective (verification-transcendent) yet amenable to proof or capable of discovery through advances in human understanding. Thus the thesis that 'nothing works' in philosophy of mathematics will seem to carry force only if it is assumed that the sole alternatives are a sensibly scaled-down empiricist conception of our cognitive capacities or a full-blown 'Platonist' metaphysics which fixes an untranscendable gulf between truth and knowledge (Benacerraf 1983; Putnam 1994: 499–512).

It seems to me that Putnam's retreat from a realist position can best be explained by his having very largely accepted the force of such sceptical arguments. Hence what he perceives as the ultimate dilemma between, on the one hand, a naturalistic approach that leaves no room for *a priori* truths of whatever kind and, on the other, a Wittgensteinian approach which counts them a product of linguistic convention or practice-based communal usage. The result has been not only a deepening scepticism with regard to the truth-claims of mathematics, logic and the formal sciences but also a gradual abandonment of his earlier outlook of causal realism as applied to issues in epistemology and philosophy of science (Putnam 1975[2]). Of course these are two very different kinds of 'realism', the one having to do with the objective existence of abstract entities such as numbers, sets and propositions, and the other with the existence of physical objects such as natural kinds along with their properties, causal powers, microstructural features, and so forth. Yet there is also a sense in which realism of either variety stands or falls with the acceptance or rejection of realism in the other domain. That is to say, the case for a realist construal of the progress of scientific knowledge depends on our accepting the extent to which advances in the realm of mathematics or formal theory can act as a spur to conjoint advances in the realm of 'applied' scientific research (Aronson, Harré and Way 1994; Boyd 1984; Rescher 1979; Smith 1981.)

II

Among the most significant texts in this regard is the essay 'Analyticity and Apriority', one of several where Putnam attempts to work through the consequences of Quine's radical-empiricist position (Putnam 1983: 115–38; Quine 1960, 1961, 1969). What concerns him chiefly is the issue as to whether *all* of mathematics can be thought of as 'revisable' in the same way as empirical propositions or those items of erstwhile 'synthetic *a priori*' knowledge – like Euclidean geometry –

which have since proved subject to revision. Thus Putnam remarks on the 'curious fact' that 'although *all* mathematical truths are "metaphysically necessary", i.e., true in all possible worlds, simply because nothing that violates a truth of mathematics *counts* as a *description* of a "possible world", *some* mathematical truths are "epistemically contingent"' (Putnam 1983: 124). What he means is that the only way to find out whether such truths actually hold is to implement a physical test-procedure. This might involve (say) constructing so many triangles by placing a number of rigid bars in a certain arrangement, or showing that a formal system contains an inconsistency or contradiction by programming a Turing machine to run until it halts at the crucial stage. Any knowledge thus gained – or any statement of it – would be *a posteriori* (and hence 'epistemically contingent') since arrived at on the basis of empirical results and not as a matter of *a priori* warrant or mathematically necessary truth.

No doubt we might still want to count this result among the class of such necessary truths despite the merely contingent fact that we had to apply an empirical method for want of any better (mathematically more elegant or compelling) alternative. Thus its truth *once known* would qualify for 'necessary' status since it could not but obtain in any 'possible world' where the same truth-conditions applied to all instances of valid mathematical proof. Nevertheless, Putnam says, 'my rational confidence in the mathematically necessary statement "it is possible to form *n* triangles with *m* rigid bars" is *no greater* than my confidence in the empirical statement' (Putnam 1983: 124). Moreover, any conflicting evidence that might turn up and shake my belief in the empirical statement would also – and to just that extent – shake my belief in the identical statement construed as a matter of necessary truth. In Putnam's words:

> [i]f I come to doubt the empirical statement, then, unless I have some *other* example that establishes the truth of the mathematical statement, I will come to doubt the mathematical statement too. Nor need there be any way in which I could 'in principle' *know* the truth of the mathematical statement without depending on some such empirical statement about mental or physical objects, diagrams, calculations, etc. (*ibid.*: 124–5)

According to Putnam the only reason why mathematical truths have so long been thought to possess a uniquely apodictic, self-evident or necessary character is the fact that we just *do* regard them as such, that is to say, our strong psychological disposition to place them beyond reach of empirical proof or counter-evidence. Thus we tend to assume 'that a fully rational ("ideally rational") being should be mathematically omniscient: should be able to "just know" all mathematical truths *without proof* (*ibid.*: 125). However this presumption can scarcely stand up if, as Putnam argues, there is no difference (in pragmatist terms: no difference that makes any difference) between the standards for empirical verification or falsification and the standards for acceptance or rejection as a matter of so-called 'necessary' truth. Quite simply, that distinction has to drop out, along with the idea of mathematics as possessing any kind of distinctive or privileged status save that conferred by our propensity to think in such ways.

But then, Putnam asks, could we possibly be justified in extending this doubt with regard to the unrevisability of mathematical truths to the point where it questioned such basic (presumptively self-evident) principles as those of Peano arithmetic, or the procedure for counting so as to yield a statement like '2 + 2 = 4'? Of course it may be said that these truths have a different – perhaps unrevisable – status since they are not the kind of thing that we could reasonably doubt, or for which we could require a more adequate proof-procedure (i.e., beyond that supplied by Peano arithmetic) before accepting them as valid for all arithmetically legitimate purposes. Thus '[w]e do not need a *proof* for this statement (barring epistemological catastrophe, e.g. coming to doubt *all* our past *counting*: but it is not clear what becomes of the concept of rationality itself when there is an epistemological catastrophe)' (*ibid.*: 125). All the same Putnam is more than half-way willing to entertain the possibility of just such a catastrophic collapse in our basic standards of rational warrant, even setting aside the hyperbolic Cartesian idea that *all* our knowledge (elementary number-theory included) might be the product of hallucination or false-memory syndrome. For it is still conceivable, so Putnam thinks, that the 'necessity' of basic arithmetical truths is a fact about our own psychological make-up or our strong disposition to grant them that status, rather than possessing any kind of objective (and hence unrevisable) warrant.

Thus: '[i]f we consider that "2 + 2 = 4" can sometimes be part of an *explanation*, is the fact (if it is a fact) that a rational being could not believe the denial of "2 + 2 = 4" (barring epistemological catastrophe) an explanation of the *truth* of "2 + 2 = 4"? Or is it rather just a fact about *rationality*?' (*ibid.*: 125). However, this raises the obvious question as to what should qualify as 'rational' conduct in our various procedures of counting, addition, multiplication, and so forth, if not the capacity to *get things right* with respect to both the necessary truths of elementary arithmetic (as yielded by Peano number-theory) and the application of those same procedures to objects and events in the physical world. For there is something decidedly odd about an argument, like Putnam's, which takes it that the existence of empirical proofs for certain mathematical claims is enough to throw a large paradox into the case for mathematical realism. After all, might it not be the case – quite unproblematically – that the truth of '2 + 2 = 4' is a truth that follows by strict necessity from the principles of elementary number-theory and which can also be known to apply (at any rate 'barring epistemological catastrophe') in our everyday or scientific reckoning with discrete particulars? Indeed, as Putnam says, a catastrophe like *that* is one that would make such a mess of everything – right down to the ground-rules of rational thought – that it amounts to no more than an empty threat or a conjuring of doubt where no such doubt can be seriously entertained.

Nor is it clear why Putnam should think that the explanatory role sometimes played by a statement such as '2 + 2 = 4' makes the fact that it cannot be denied by any rational being 'just a fact about rationality', rather than a necessary truth about numbers and their logical entailment-relations. Here again Putnam takes it as self-evident that there *must* be a conflict – an either/or choice – between the realist conception of mathematical truth which places it ultimately beyond reach of empirical confirmation (or disconfirmation) and the idea of such truth as none the less sometimes attainable through methods akin to those of the physical sciences or everyday practical experience. Thus, on Putnam's account, the realist deludedly thinks that an omniscient ('ideally rational') being should somehow be able to know the entire range of objective mathematical truths 'without proof ... perhaps by surveying all the integers, all the real numbers, etc., in his head' (1983: 125). Of course this belief is open to various familiar criticisms, among them the Wittgensteinian case against 'mentalist' conceptions of meaning and truth, and also – not least – early Putnam's whole battery of thought-experimental arguments to the effect that 'meanings just ain't in the head' (Wittgenstein 1953; Putnam 1975[2]: 139–52, 215–71). Still there is a great difference between the force of such arguments as applied by early Putnam and their presumptive force as applied against realist conceptions of mathematical truth. In the former context their purpose was to demonstrate the reference-fixing character of certain real-world properties and attributes (especially in the case of natural-kind terms) and the need to think of them as existing quite apart from any past or present range of descriptive or identifying criteria. (See also Kripke 1980; Schwartz (ed.) 1977.) In the latter, conversely, their point is to deny that we could ever have justification or legitimate grounds for supposing some statement to possess an objective truth-value aside from our present-best methods of proof or verification. For '[t]his is just forgetting, once again, that we *understand* mathematical language *through* being able to recognise *proofs* (plus, of course, certain empirical applications, e.g., *counting*)' (Putnam 1983: 125).

Thus Putnam has by now (as of 1983) come around to accepting something very like Dummett's anti-realist position with regard to the highly restrictive conditions on truth-evaluable statements in mathematics and the physical sciences (Dummett 1977, 1978). That is, he thinks of such statements as true (or false) only in so far as we dispose of an adequate proof-procedure for finding out their truth or falsehood. Otherwise they belong to the 'disputed class' and are hence neither true nor false to the best of our present knowledge, which is also to say – if one accepts this anti-realist logic – neither true nor false *sans phrase*. (See also Dummett 1991; Tennant 1987; Wright 1987.) So there is no intelligible basis for the claim that such statements possess an objective truth-value which we may (now or later) be able to verify, but which hold quite apart from our present or future state of knowledge concerning them. After all, as Putnam plausibly remarks, '[i]t is not irrational to need a *proof* before one believes, for example, Fermat's last theorem – quite the contrary' (1983: 125). However this argument lends support to his strong revisability-thesis *only if* one accepts the anti-realist view that 'truth' should drop out in favour of 'warranted assertability' as the sole criterion by which to assess mathematical and other statements. Otherwise it will seem strictly irrelevant to the question whether well-formed but as yet unproven conjectures should properly be construed in bivalent terms, i.e., as possessing an objective truth-value despite our inability to specify that value by the best means at our disposal. The fact that belief (or rational assent) in such matters requires the knowledge of an adequate proof-procedure is no good reason to suppose, with the anti-realist, that any statement concerning them is neither-true-nor-false so long as the relevant procedure is unknown (Dummett 1977, 1978). Thus if indeed it is the case – as recently claimed – that Fermat's last theorem has at last been proved then anyone who asserted its truth at some previous time when the theorem was still in doubt would none the less have made an objectively valid (though epistemically unwarranted or rationally under-motivated) claim.

Of course the same applies to other unproven mathematical conjectures, like that which holds it to be either true or false – quite aside from the limits of our current computational power – that the decimal expansion of *pi* contains a sequence of one hundred consecutive sevens. Or again, there is the case of necessary presuppositions such as Church's thesis to the effect that 'recursiveness is effective computability', i.e., those that are taken for granted in any mathematical proof-procedure. In Katz's words, such axiomatic premises, 'although they [themselves] have no proof, still can be shown to be *a priori* mathematical knowledge on the basis of an *a priori* justification that shows them to be essential to the best systematisation of a body of *a priori* mathematical knowledge' (Katz 1998: 197). They are beyond rational doubt not just in the sense – as Putnam would have it – that they define what *counts* as 'rationality' for us but in the sense that they express what philosophers since Kant have found so intriguing about mathematics, that is, its character of necessary truth conjoined with its extraordinary fruitfulness or power to generate new discoveries (Kant 1964). No doubt there is a deep philosophical puzzle as to *why* this should be the case, or how it is – if not by recourse to some kind of Pythagorean number-mysticism – that we can reasonably hope to explain it. However, there would seem little hope of getting clearer on this topic from any approach that sidesteps the issue by denying either the necessary status of mathematical truths or their immensely productive role in the development of the physical sciences.

Putnam has perhaps thought longer and harder about these issues than any other living philosopher. Indeed, what makes him such a truly *exemplary* thinker is the way that he has registered the impact and force of various anti-realist arguments while holding the line against other, more facile varieties of sceptical-relativist doctrine. (See especially Putnam 1988 for a striking re-statement of his earlier position with regard to naming, necessity, and natural kinds, albeit one that he now deems compatible with a suitably adjusted version of the case for 'internal realism'.) Yet it is also very clear that his extreme, almost barometric sensitivity to the present-day intellectual climate has led Putnam to accept the force of certain arguments – like the Wittgensteinian 'paradox' about rule-following or Dummett's denial of objective truth-values to statements of the 'disputed class' – which appear to invite just such a sceptical conclusion. Thus, having raised the question as to whether the sheer *impossibility* of denying '2 + 2 = 4' is 'just a fact about rationality' (i.e., just a fact about our predisposition to regard such truths as secure beyond 'rational' doubt), he goes on to propose some further thought-experimental arguments for the ultimate revisability of even such 'rationally' indubitable items of knowledge. 'Putting this question aside', he writes, 'like the hot potato it is, let us briefly consider the status of such mathematical truths as "Peano arithmetic is consistent" and the principle of mathematical induction' (Putnam 1983: 125). Since these truths are about as basic to the whole mathematical enterprise as any that Putnam could possibly adduce it is not at all clear that he has dropped the hot potato or resisted the temptation to pick up another with equally scalding properties. Where the difference lies, as Putnam sees it, is in the fact that our granting *a priori* status or rational self-evidence to truths of this kind belongs to an order of (seeming) necessity which strikes us as simply not admitting of empirical confirmation or disconfirmation. After all,

> [t]hese are not like the singular or purely existential combinatorial statements lately considered ('This formal system is inconsistent', 'There exists a way of forming *m* triangles with *n* matches', 'This Turing machine halts in less than *N* steps'). Certainly our beliefs in the consistency of Peano arithmetic and in induction are not epistemically contingent in the way that my belief that one can form *m* triangles with *n* matches (imagine I have just convinced myself by finding the arrangement) is epistemically contingent. I believe that arithmetic is consistent because I believe the axioms are true, and I believe that from true premises one cannot derive a contradiction; I have also studied and taught the Gentzen consistency proof; and these are *a priori* reasons. (Putnam 1983: 125)

Yet he then goes on to argue that we *can* in fact conceive (or at rate 'imagine') some circumstance in which we might be driven to renounce those beliefs or to revise our conviction that they are strictly *a priori* and hence neither subject to empirical proof nor open to empirical disconfirmation. What would force such a drastic shift, so Putnam maintains, is precisely the discovery of a standing *contradiction* in principles whose claim to rational, apodictic, necessary or *a priori* warrant had rested on the hitherto unchallenged belief that they *could not possibly contain* any such self-contradictory or inconsistent elements. For the fact (as he takes it) that we *can* imagine such a circumstance arising, however remote or unlikely the prospect by our own 'rational' lights, is sufficient to show that revision cannot be ruled out even in the case of axiomatic 'truths' which are so deeply entwined with our range of accepted mathematical procedures as to leave the whole enterprise in ruins were they found wanting through some future discovery of the kind here envisaged.

Of course Putnam sees that this entire line of argument will strike the realist as just another bad (and self-refuting) case of the sceptical propensity to raise doubts where no such doubts can consistently, rationally or intelligibly be raised. Thus she will deny that the argument can get off the ground since it involves conceiving *as a matter of genuine possibility* what we know to be impossible even at the furthest stretch of counterfactual-conditional (as distinct from merely fictive or imaginary) thought-experiment. So when Putnam claims that 'there are still circumstances under which I would abandon my belief that Peano arithmetic is consistent', namely 'if I discovered a contradiction', the realist will respond that 'this remark is "cheating"', [since] 'you *could not* discover a contradiction' (Putnam 1983: 125–6). However, while he accepts the force of this appeal to our present-best rational convictions, Putnam none the less denies that it carries any weight against his case for the ultimate (in-principle) revisability of even such seemingly self-evident truths. No doubt, he concedes,

> it is mathematically impossible (and even "metaphysically" impossible, in the recently fashionable jargon) that there should be a contradiction in Peano arith-metic. But, as I remarked above, it is not *epistemically impossible.* We can conceive of finding a contradiction in Peano arithmetic, and we can make sense of the question 'What would you do if you came across a contradiction in Peano arithmetic?' ('Restrict the induction schema', would be my answer). (*ibid.*: 126)

Now of course it is true that we can 'make sense' of such hypotheses to the extent that they are grammatically and semantically well-formed, that they belong to the 'language-game' of mathematics (at least on a liberal construal), and that they are made up of terms which play a well-defined role in other contexts or statements and can therefore be viewed as compositionally meaningful. More than that, they clearly have truth-values in so far as we can grasp – in some sense of 'grasp' – what would count as the kind of discovery (in some sense of 'discovery') that inflicted this catastrophic damage on all our hitherto accepted canons of mathematical truth and rational warrant. Still the realist will want to come back and respond that this is just another kind of thought-experimental 'cheating' since it requires us to accept – as a matter of genuine (mathematically thinkable) possibility – what can only be envisaged in such vague and unspecified counterfactual terms. In short, it may be said that Putnam is here playing fast-and-loose with just those modal-logical distinctions that occupied so prominent a role in his own early thinking and which would surely have prevented him from treating the idea of 'metaphysical impossibility' as just another piece of 'recently fashionable jargon'.

III

This contrast emerges to striking effect if one recalls the various well-known thought-experiments by which early Putnam sought to strengthen the case for causal realism in terms of strictly *metaphysical* (as opposed to epistemic) necessity (Putnam 1975[2]; also Kripke 1980; Lewis 1973, 1986; Wiggins 1980). The change in his thinking can be seen very clearly in Putnam's revival of the 'brain-in-a-vat' hypothesis as a means of confuting the realist objection to his claim that even the axioms of Peano arithmetic might be abandoned (or revised) under certain conceivable circumstances (1983: 126). Suppose, he invites us, that I am indeed such a brain-in-a-vat and that 'superscientist' manipulates my sensory inputs so that I hallucinate a situation where Kripke discovers some contradiction in Peano arithmetic and his discovery is accepted as valid by the entire community of qualified logicians and mathematicians. Suppose further that the proof is checked to the utmost of existing computational powers and holds up under every such test. In that case, although I was unable to perform the relevant checks myself, still

I should be *rationally justified* – so Putnam contends – in believing that Peano arithmetic was inconsistent on the best evidence to hand. From which it follows that 'even "Peano arithmetic is consistent" is not a fully rationally unrevisable statement' (1983: 126). And if this can be shown by means of an apt (albeit rather *outré*) thought-experiment then quite simply there is no item of supposed *a priori* mathematical knowledge, necessary truth, or rationally warranted belief that can stand proof against sceptical doubt. Thus first-order induction must likewise go by the board since 'an inconsistency in Peano arithmetic would make it rational to suppose that unrestricted induction was contradictory' (*ibid.*). So long as we can *make sense* of the given hypothesis – construe it as belonging to the realm of conceivable (no matter how remote) possibility – then all our present ideas of rationality and truth might be subject to drastic revision should some decisive piece of counter-evidence at length turn up.

But then, one may ask: what could possibly constitute such evidence if indeed (*ex hypothesi*) we were in a situation where our every last standard of rational warrant – from the grounding principles of deductive logic to those of first-order mathematical induction – has been shown not to hold or at any rate to stand in need of 'rational' revision? For there could then be no *reason* whatsoever to accept any *evidence* whatsoever as entailing any *conclusion* whatsoever with regard to whatever *premises* or *beliefs* we happened to entertain. In other words the thought-experiment is 'conceivable' only as a matter of vaguely imagined possibility and can be shown to self-destruct or collapse into manifest absurdity when examined in a more critical light. These problems emerge most sharply when Putnam comments – speaking *qua* brain-in-a-vat – that 'perhaps I do not have time to check the proof myself', but that 'I would believe, and rationally so, … that Peano arithmetic is inconsistent on such evidence' (1983: 126). That is to say, it is not merely for lack of time or through not having access to the requisite computational resources that the envatted brain is *necessarily* incapable of running such a proof for itself. Rather, it is because – even setting aside all the usual objections to this sceptical hypothesis – the brain (or mind) in such a predicament would be wholly bereft of means for assessing the truth or falsehood of any statement that came its way. So the clause that Putnam here slips in as an apparent side-issue is one which effectively wrecks the idea that this thought-experiment could work as a case for the rationally motivated choice to give up those (hitherto-accepted) necessary truths.

Of course there are arguments – some of them deriving from early Putnam – for the claim that we *can* have rational warrant for accepting the validity of proof-procedures which we have not actually worked through or figured out (so to speak) on our own behalf. This was just his point in appealing to the so-called 'linguistic division of labour' as a means of explaining how non-experts could reliably talk about objects (e.g., natural kinds) whose precise microstructural details they didn't know, or despite their lack of an adequate referential grasp as measured by the best (scientifically warranted) means of verification (Putnam 1975[2]: 223–9; also 1988: 22–6). Thus in the case of mathematics the issue falls out between, on the one hand, those who insist that we *must* have understood the proof or be able to manifest a grasp of its logical necessity, and on the other hand those who would relax that stringent condition just so long as there are experts around to whom we can appeal if pressed for an answer. But this latter line of argument clearly doesn't work when applied to the brain-in-a-vat hypothesis or to Putnam's ingenious update on the Cartesian sceptical theme. For here there is no question of a saving appeal to shared understandings or communal resources which can always be called upon to rescue the *cogito* from its state of epistemic solitude. Any limits on my knowledge must then be conceived as *absolute and necessary* limits, imposed by my having no recourse – again *ex hypothesi* – to anything beyond the scope of my own self-reliant cogitative powers. And if the sceptic's challenge extends to even the most basic standards of truth, rationality and logical warrant then there would seem no hope – as Descartes believed – of defeating the *malin génie* and reestablishing at least some minimal grounds for our knowledge of mind-independent reality or truth.

Putnam remarks in passing that 'Descartes was clearly aware of this problem', although 'it has not been very much appreciated in the past', most likely because of our tendency to think 'that a fully rational ("ideally rational") being should be mathematically omniscient' (1983: 125). However, what distinguishes Putnam's version of the sceptical hypothesis from Descartes' original version is his thought that we might be 'rationally' motivated in renouncing or revising the very idea of rational self-evidence or necessary truth. To be sure, he allows that we don't *need* a proof for statements such as '2 + 2 =4', since to doubt them would entail coming to doubt all our past activities of counting or simple addition, and can thus be ruled out 'barring epistemological catastrophe'. Moreover, as he says, if catastrophe were to strike on this scale then 'it is not clear what becomes of the concept of rationality itself' (*ibid.*). Yet neither is it clear what becomes of that concept in the surely catastrophic circumstance of my being – of course unbeknownst to myself – a brain-in-a-vat cunningly supplied with sensory inputs which lead me to think that I inhabit a world where Kripke has proved the inconsistency of Peano arithmetic. For in that case such basic arithmetical statements as '2 + 2 = 4' must be thought of not only as standing in need of proof but as strictly unprovable by the best (most 'rational') procedure to hand. So the scenario envisaged is one of catastrophe in both senses, i.e., 'epistemic' in so far as it deprives me of evidential grounds for anything I might claim to know, and rationality-destructive in so far as it involves the idea that my ground-rules of rational inference might turn out to contain some hitherto concealed contradiction or logical inconsistency.

'This is messy', Putnam writes, but perhaps inevitably so since after all 'philosophy of mathematics is *hard*' (1983: 126). Still one may doubt that it is as hard (or downright impossible) as would be the case if the brain-in-a-vat hypothesis captured anything of relevance to our actual procedures of counting, addition, numerical inference, deductive reasoning, and so forth. What gives that hypothesis its character of seeming plausibility is Putnam's acceptance of the basic anti-realist premise that there *must* be something wrong (or self-refuting) about the idea of verification-transcendent truths, or truths that lie beyond our present-best – maybe our utmost – powers of definitive proof. For there is otherwise no accounting for his flatly paradoxical (even, one might think, nonsensical) statement that 'there are circumstances in which it would be rational to believe that Peano arithmetic was inconsistent *even though it was not*' (*ibid.*: 126). If one asks what sense the term 'rational' can bear in this context then it can only be something like: '"rational" for a thinker whose reasoning is based on faulty premises, unreliable evidence, ignorance of the relevant proof-procedure', or whatever. In other words it is an *epistemic* sense according to which rationality consists in constructing the best hypothesis that fits the available sensory or experiential data. Thus I might (Putnam thinks) be rationally warranted in rejecting the 'axiomatic' status of the principles of Peano arithmetic if they *really turned out* – at some future date – to contain an inconsistency or contradiction shown up by applying some new and more exigent proof-procedure. But, then again, I would be rationally justified also if the procedure in question was one devised by an imaginary Saul Kripke who figured (along with a peer-group of likewise imaginary expert thinkers) in the world that superscientist had managed to create by feeding me the appropriate sensory stimuli. In both cases the 'rational' response would be to suspend belief in the hitherto accepted ground-rules of rational thought and endorse what was given as a matter of empirical (albeit illusory) warrant.

Hence Putnam's curious claim – in the latter instance – that it would indeed be rational to doubt (or reject) the principles of Peano arithmetic *even if* those principles were fully valid and my belief to the contrary was brought about by my suffering some form of wholesale systematic delusion. Still one has to ask what distinguishes this wildly counterfactual (and, as I have argued, strictly inconceivable) hypothesis from the other thought-experimental scenario where I am *not* a brain-in-a-vat but where a contradiction nevertheless shows up and requires just the same willingness to doubt all the ground-rules of basic arithmetic. 'Perhaps', Putnam writes, '"2 + 2 = 4" is rationally unrevisable (or, at least, rationally unrevisable as long as "universal hallucination", "all my past memories are a delusion", and the like are not in the field)' (1983: 125). But it is far from clear how Putnam can draw the line at extravagant sceptical hypotheses of this sort given that he goes straight on to reject any argument which counts it merely a kind of 'cheating' to talk about discoveries that could not possibly be made, or contradictions (e.g., in Peano arithmetic) which could not possibly exist. Sure enough, he concedes, their existence is 'mathematically' and even 'metaphyically' impossible. All the same they are 'epistemically possible' in so far as we *might* be placed in a situation where the weight of expert evidence required that we accept them as a matter of established (mathematically proven) fact. For then the only *rational* response would be to adjust our conceptions accordingly and – at the limit – give up belief in all the 'necessary' truths, arithmetical axioms, or ground-rules of logical reasoning that had guided our thought until then.

However this limit-case scenario is surely just another sceptical extravagance on a par with the brain-in-a-vat hypothesis and other such far-fetched speculative ventures into the realm of imaginable (but not logically thinkable) alternative worlds. Putnam would of course rebut this line of counter-argument by insisting that we *can* quite readily envisage a world – and not just the virtual-reality 'world' inhabited by brain-in-a-vat – where the above situation obtained. Thus, to repeat: '[w]e can conceive of finding a contradiction in Peano arithmetic, and we can make sense of the question "What would you do if you came across a contradiction in Peano arithmetic"?' (1983: 126). But there is a crucial ambiguity here which I think goes to the heart of these issues about realism and anti-realism in philosophy of mathematics and which helps to explain why Putnam has been pulled so sharply in opposite directions. No doubt we can 'make sense' of that question in so far as we possess an adequate grasp of what the words mean, how they function grammatically, what we have understood them to mean in other (more familiar or less problematical) contexts, and so forth. This follows straightforwardly from the principle of compositionality, that is, the principle that the meaning of a sentence derives from the meaning of its various component parts, each of which in turn has a functional role defined by its use in just such sentences. But it is a very different matter to claim – as Putnam does here – that the question 'makes sense' in so far as we can actually *conceive* what it would mean for Peano arithmetic to turn out inconsistent or contradictory. For we should then be in just the kind of downright 'catastrophic' situation that required us (absurdly) to deny the truth of certain necessary truths, or to endorse the possibility of that which was both 'mathematically' and 'metaphysically' impossible.

Putnam ends up in this awkward predicament partly by pursuing his sceptical thought-experiment far beyond the limit of genuine intelligibility and partly through adopting an epistemic approach which very easily slides into a form of Dummett-style verificationism. Thus, if we are tempted by the notion of mathematical truth as that which would be known by an omniscient (or 'ideally rational') being – 'perhaps by surveying all the integers, all the real numbers, etc., in his head' – then we can best be weaned off that delusory idea by recalling 'that we *understand* mathematical language *through* being able to recognise *proofs* (plus, of course, certain empirical applications, e.g., *counting*)' (Putnam 1983: 125). But, again, this assumes that any results thus achieved will depend for their validity (or truth-value) on our possessing the relevant proof-procedure and also on our not in future discovering some alternative procedure or some item of empirical evidence that calls them into doubt. To this extent Putnam goes along with the anti-realist argument according to which it *cannot make sense* to posit the existence of objective (recognition-transcendent) mathematical truths that would hold necessarily whether or not we possessed any means of finding them out. For Dummett this follows from the twofold requirement (1) that any knowledge we can properly be thought to have must be knowledge that we are capable of *acquiring* through a grasp of the relevant meanings, methods, procedures, rule-governed practices, etc., and (2) that we must also be capable of *manifesting* such knowledge in accordance with those same essentially shared or communal standards (Dummett 1977, 1978). So there is just no way – on this verificationist account – that we could (without lapsing into self-contradictory nonsense) claim warrant for asserting the existence of truths that lay beyond our utmost epistemic reach or powers of ascertainment.

Still, the argument goes through *only if* one accepts what Dummett takes as sheerly self-evident, that is, the Wittgensteinian premise that truth-values extend just so far as the limits of our understanding, and furthermore that understanding (prototypically, the understanding of a language) entails our being able to acquire and manifest the right responses in the right situation. Thus, in Dummett's words:

> we may identify someone's knowledge of the condition for the sentence to be true as consisting in his readiness to accept it as true whenever the condition for its truth obtains and he is in a position to recognise it as obtaining, together with his practical knowledge of the procedure for arriving at such a position, as manifested by his carrying out that procedure whenever suitably prompted. (Dummett 1977: 374)

From which of course it follows that we could never be justified in asserting the existence of recognition-transcendent truths or in taking certain statements – those of the 'disputed class' – to possess an objective truth-value despite our lack of a proof-procedure or adequate evidential warrant. Other thinkers of a broadly anti-realist persuasion – Crispin Wright among them – have queried various details of Dummett's case, including the strength of the acquisition-argument, the precise scope of the manifestation-principle, and the extent to which this latter might be scaled down to admit some kind of (likewise scaled-down) realist response (Wright 1992). Dummett has himself made a number of significant moves in this direction. (See for instance Dummett 1991.) Yet the whole debate has been conducted in terms that effectively endorse his basic thesis, that is to say, which take it as self-evident that there cannot be any appeal to recognition-transcendent or unverifiable truths since nobody could possibly be in a position to manifest a knowledge of such truths through appropriate verbal or rule-governed practical behaviour when presented with sufficient (recognisable) evidence. After all, what could *count* as such evidence for one thus placed if it lay by definition beyond their furthest powers of cognitive or intellectual grasp?

No doubt this argument is strictly irrefutable on its own terms, as can be seen if we suppose somebody to say: 'I recognise *this* as evidence for the truth (or falsehood) of proposition X although the truth-value of X is recognition-transcendent', or again, 'I know X to be the case (or not) despite my lack of any evidential grounds or rational warrant for that claim'. However these assertions are nonsensical only to the extent that they specify some determinate assertoric content to X and hence fall into a patently absurd or self-contradictory posture. What the realist maintains is nothing so absurd or so readily reducible to nonsense under pressure from the anti-realist quarter. Rather, it is the case – simply put – that there are many things we just don't know and have no means of finding out,

whether through the limits of our present-best knowledge or owing to some ultimate restriction on our powers of perceptual, conceptual or intuitive grasp. Moreover, we can quite legitimately say that there *must* be some objective truth of the
matter for statements (such as Goldbach's conjecture or the claim that the decimal
expansion of *pi* contains one hundred consecutive sevens) for which as yet we
possess no means of verification. And again, there are truths – preeminently those
of mathematics and logic – whose necessity we are capable of grasping even
though, in some cases, they cannot be proved by any fully adequate (formal or
axiomatised) procedure at our disposal. Indeed, such procedures may themselves
on occasion turn out to be inconsistent or to involve some paradoxical limiting
case, as famously happened with Russell's and Frege's work on the logical foundations of arithmetic, and – more generally – with Hilbert's grand programme when
Gödel produced his undecidability-proofs (See Gödel 1962; also Detlefson (ed.)
1992; Kitcher 1983; Putnam 1975[1]; Shanker (ed.) 1987). But these were themselves the unexpected outcome of some complex chains of logico-mathematical
reasoning which alone made it possible to raise such issues about the scope and
power of any purely formal proof-procedure. What they clearly *don't* license is any
generalised claim that we might come to doubt even the most elementary truths
of arithmetic or principles of logic should these come into conflict with some
result thrown up in the course of enquiry.

Thus, in Penrose's words, Gödel showed 'that there could be no formal
system F, whatever, that is both consistent … and complete – so long as F is taken
to be powerful enough to contain a formulation of the statements of ordinary
arithmetic along with standard logic' (Penrose 1995: 90). However, this offers
no support for Putnam's 'strong' revisability thesis, that is to say, his thought-
experimental conjecture that the Peano axioms might prove inconsistent or
contradictory, thus throwing the whole of arithmetic into a state of unprece-
dented turmoil. For it is Putnam's belief that this could come about – improbably
but just conceivably – as the result of an *empirical* discovery (like finding that the
m rigid bars of equal length didn't after all make *n* triangles, or that the Turing
machine came to a halt before completing some logically 'self-evident' proof)
which would then require just such a massive revision to our sense of what counts
as a necessary truth of mathematics or logic. What Gödel's theorem tells us, on
the contrary, is that so far from being empirically revisable these truths are both
objective (i.e., verification-transcendent) and possessed of a rational-intuitive
force that may on occasion surpass the limits of any formal proof-procedure.
Thus: 'the insights that are available to human mathematicians – indeed, to
anyone who can think logically with understanding and imagination – lie beyond
anything that can be formalised as a set of rules' (Penrose 1995: 72). Whence
Gödel's realist conviction that mathematics, and arithmetic especially, has a
character of necessary truth which cannot be reduced *either* to the limits of purely
computational proof *or* to a matter of the arbitrary choice between various possible systems, all of them equally valid since none of them can be both complete
and consistent. On this latter view, as Penrose describes it, 'we can keep adjoining

new axioms, according to our whim, and obtain all kinds of alternative consistent systems within which we may choose to work' (Penrose 1995: 110). Thus the case with mathematics would be something like that with the physical sciences in Quine's holistic conception (Quine 1961). That is to say, there would always be scope for pragmatic adjustment – for reinterpreting data, redistributing predicates or truth-values, introducing alternative 'auxiliary hypotheses', and so forth – at any point in the system so as to preserve overall coherence while retaining some particular cherished or firmly held item of belief.

However, the price of this interpretative freedom is a failure to explain how genuine advances in knowledge (as distinct from negotiated trade-offs between evidence and theory) could ever come about, or why mathematicians or physicists should ever feel compelled to abandon a theory in the face of conflicting evidence. For it would always be more 'rational' to take the pragmatist line of least resist-ance and make whatever local adjustments were required in order to avoid such conflict. The only reason for revising one or another in our range of extant beliefs would be the basically conservative (coherence-preserving) desire to reinterpret anything – whether at the observational 'periphery' or at the logical 'centre' – which threatened to disrupt or to complicate the overall picture. Yet, as Putnam sees it, this revisionist approach is incapable of yielding any adequate account of why certain episodes of theory-change – like those which led (to take Quine's own examples) from Ptolemy to Kepler, or Newton to Einstein, or Aristotle to Darwin – are such as to compel rational assent from the standpoint of informed present-day scientific knowledge (Quine 1961; Putnam 1983: 87–97, 98–114, 127–38). That is, they cannot be rationally explained as instances of the wholesale Quinean switch between different 'ontological schemes' or the Kuhnian process of radical paradigm-shift where theories are 'underdetermined' by the evidence and the evidence always 'theory-laden' to the point where it makes no sense to propose an evaluative ranking of different ('incommensurable') paradigms (Kuhn 1970; also Harding (ed.) 1976). 'My own guess', Putnam writes,

> is that the truths of logic we are speaking of are *so* basic that the notion of expla-nation *collapses* when we try to 'explain' why they are true. I do not mean that there is something 'unexplainable' here; there is simply no room for an explana-tion of what is presupposed by every explanatory activity, and that goes for philosophical as well as scientific explanations, including explanations that purport to be therapy. (1983: 138)

So to this extent at least – when confronted with the case for revisability in its across-the-board Quinean–Kuhnian form – Putnam acknowledges the need to distinguish between revision-proof standards of rational warrant and truth-claims whose status is a matter of our present-best empirical evidence. And he is likewise wary of 'therapeutic' arguments in the late-Wittgensteinian mode which purport to relieve us of such pointless 'metaphysical' anxieties by showing how they simply don't arise once we see that truth is nothing more than communal warrant within this or that language-game or acculturated 'form of life' (1983: 115–26).

Yet here again Putnam is frankly embarrassed to find himself propounding a theory that appears to affirm the existence of *a priori* (unrevisable) truths in mathematics and logic. What he considers problematical about Quine's approach is its departure from 'moderate conventionalism in the direction of *empiricism*' (Putnam 1983: 127). Thus, on Quine's radically holistic account, '[t]ruths of mathematics are partly empirical and partly "conventional" like *all* truths; mathematics is as factual as physics, only better "protected"' (*ibid.*). In Putnam's view this veers too far toward a strong-revisionist approach that would flout some of our most basic beliefs with regard to the truth-value of mathematical statements and their immunity (or at any rate *relative* immunity) from empirical disconfirmation. Yet of course to enter this relativising clause is already to treat such truths as *in principle* subject to revision on empirical grounds, no matter how rarely or whatever the unlikelihood – in some cases the near-impossibility – that such evidence might turn up. Thus Putnam effectively concedes the crucial point to Quine even though he thinks Quine's position too extreme and hopes to find some alternative approach that would *both* do justice to our standing convictions in this respect *and* make allowance for the limit-case scenario where we might (just conceivably) find ourselves in that predicament. On the one hand Putnam is keen to insist that his difference with Quine should not be viewed as involving a commitment to the *a priori* status – and hence the *absolute* unrevisability – of truths such as those of classical logic. After all, he is on record elsewhere as arguing to precisely the opposite effect, i.e., that logic is indeed revisable and that certain empirical discoveries – notably in quantum mechanics – may very well force us to accept such revision as the best (most rational) option (Putnam 1975[1]: 130–59, 166–74, 174–98.). Yet he still thinks that Quine underestimates the problems with taking this argument on board, or – what amounts to much the same thing – overestimates the likelihood that this option might be forced upon us as a matter of rational necessity. In other words there must surely be some middle-ground position from which to adjudicate the issue and avoid being pushed to either extreme in the manner of full-fledged 'metaphysical' realists or full-fledged Quinean revisionists.

IV

However, it is by no means clear that Putnam manages to strike that stance or that any such position is available to him, given his own well-publicised (and here reiterated) views on the revisability of logic. 'What I think (I blush to confess) is that what *is a priori* is that *most* statements obey certain logical laws. This will very likely offend both Platonistically minded and constructively minded philosophers (and both Wittgensteinians and Quineans); nevertheless, I shall try to make it plausible' (Putnam 1983: 127). It is a moot point whether Putnam's blush has to do with the extreme modesty of his claim – indeed, its well-nigh trivial character – or with the fact that it seems markedly at odds with some of his strong-revisionist statements elsewhere. At any rate, he has good reason to suspect that it can satisfy neither the realist party (to whom it will seem the merest of face-saving devices) nor the Quinean proponent of across-the-board revisability (who will dismiss such shamefaced *a priori* talk as at best a kind of closet ontological relativism that dare not speak its name and at worst a covert slide back into old, presumptively discredited modes of thought). Still, it is Putnam's belief that the trick *can* be worked and that there *is* a viable course to be steered between these opposite extremes. Hence his idea of 'contextual apriority', or of truths that are so deeply entrenched in our whole existing range of theories, practices, canons of evidence, standards of deductive or inductive warrant, and so forth, that we are justified in treating them as *a priori* for want of any genuine alternative. (See Putnam, 'It Ain't Necessarily So', 1975[1]: 237–49.) Yet of course this is just what the realist will point to as evidence of Putnam's not having grasped – or not having left himself room to admit – that their *a priori* status is precisely a matter of their unrevisability in *any conceivable* context of enquiry and *despite* any apparent conflict with the findings of empirical investigation. For on the realist account it is an essential property of mathematical or logical statements that if valid then they hold good necessarily as a matter of objective (recognition-transcendent) truth and are hence in no way subject to empirical testing or possible disconfirmation.

Here again Putnam seems to blur the distinction – so firmly maintained in his early work – between logical necessity and epistemic warrant, or truths self-evident in virtue of their logical form and truths self-evident in virtue of our knowing some proof-procedure or method of empirical (or 'quasi-empirical') verification. For if one lets that distinction go – or reinterprets it in context-dependent terms – then the way is wide open to empiricist construals which find no room for logical necessity except as a function of epistemic warrant. The following passage shows very clearly how Putnam is pushed in this direction despite his wish to come up with some workable middle-ground alternative.

> Are there *a priori* truths? In other words, are there true statements which (1) it is rational to accept (at least if the right arguments occur to me), and (2) which it would never subsequently be rational to reject no matter how the world turns out (epistemically) to be? More simply, are there statements whose truth we would not be justified in denying in any *epistemically* possible world? Or is it rather the case that for *every* statement s there is an epistemically possible world in which it is fully rational to believe that not-s? (Putnam 1983: 127)

Clearly these are rhetorical questions in the sense that they invite a certain response and are meant to rule out certain other responses – like a straightforward 'yes' on the first three counts – which the reader might come up with. Thus, according to Putnam, there are *a priori* truths in so far as there are truths which it is 'rational to accept', or whose acceptance is rationally warranted 'at least if the right arguments occur to me'. Moreover, there are truths of a highly restricted (since trivially self-evident) class – such as 'not every statement is both true and false' – of which it can safely be asserted that we could not have rational warrant for rejecting them 'no matter how the world turns out (epistemically) to be'. But this is *not* to say that the realist is justified in supposing the claim to extend beyond that highly restricted sphere or to have any bearing on significant issues of rationality, knowledge or truth. For, as we have seen, Putnam takes it that such issues must involve the question as to whether there might not be some '*epistemically possible world*' in which we would be warranted ('rationally' justified) in denying the truth of a statement now regarded as a matter of logical necessity or rational self-evidence.

Thus the thrust of his argument – here as elsewhere – is at once to narrow down and to broaden the class of *a priori* truths to the point where they are either sheerly tautologous (products of logico-semantic definition) or construed in context-relative terms as holding under certain epistemic conditions, i.e., the state of our present-best knowledge or available methods of proof. There is a curious passage that occurs just before the series of rhetorical questions cited above and which brings out very clearly the character of Putnam's dilemma. Its purport is to show that there must be something wrong with the Wittgensteinian claim according to which (1) 'mathematical statements do not express objective truths', and (2) 'their truth and necessity (or appearance of necessity) arise from and are explained by *our* nature' (1983: 126). Yet surely, Putnam writes,

> [i]f *our* nature explains why we shall never come across a contradiction in Peano arithmetic then, in exactly the same sense and to the same degree, it explains why there is a Mountain Ash in my yard. Both facts are dependent on my conceptual lenses; but neither fact is an artifact of these lenses. I do not create the properties of individual proofs in Peano arithmetic any more than I create the berries on the Mountain Ash. (*ibid.*)

What is chiefly problematical about this passage is knowing just where – if anywhere – the transition occurs between Putnam's dissident commentary on Wittgenstein's philosophy of mathematics and his own view concerning the status of mathematical truths. Thus it differs from the passage cited one paragraph above in so far as we were there left in no doubt that Putnam's questions were rhetorical in tone and sought to preempt the reader's response, whatever the problems when it came to construing their precise philosophical import. In this case, however, it is more difficult to see what Putnam is driving at even as a matter of basic utterer's intent. The first sentence seems quite unambiguous, at least given the immediate context of argument. It holds that Wittgenstein simply *cannot* be right in adopting a naturalised (which is also to say a radically conventionalist) position that would locate the source of such truths in our various deeply acculturated practices, role-following procedures, accepted standards of mathematical proof, etc. (Wittgenstein 1953, 1956). For if this were the case then there would be no difference – philosophically speaking – between the appeal to 'our nature' as a bottom-line explanation for why we shall never find a contradiction in Peano arithmetic and an appeal to the sheer self-evidence of certain none-the-less contingent facts like the existence of a Mountain Ash (with berries) in Putnam's yard. Each would involve – so the sentence implies – a serious underestimation of the extent to which the truth-value of statements in either domain is fixed by the way things stand objectively quite aside from 'our nature' or the various deep-laid conventions and protocols that decide what counts as warranted assertability. Moreover, by suggesting that the two cases are pretty much on a par in this respect the conventionalist approach fails to explain why we should find the idea of discovering a contradiction in Peano arithmetic *unthinkable* in a very different sense from the idea that we might be brought to doubt the evidence of our senses, or the presence of berries on the Mountain Ash. For where the latter kinds of doubt are at least rationally conceivable – as shown by a long history of philosophic thought-experiments from Descartes to early Putnam – any doubts with respect to the axiomatic principles of logic or arithmetic are such as to impugn the very possibility of self-consistent reasoning and hence the force of whatever counter-argument the sceptic might think to deploy.

So it would seem that Putnam has here come around to the position of accepting that there must (*contra* Wittgenstein and Quine) be certain truths that are indeed *a priori* in a stronger sense than 'contextually *a priori*' or '*a priori* by the standards that define *for us* what shall count as an instance of strictly unrevisable or self-evident truth'. This reading appears to be borne out when Putnam goes on to remark that '[b]oth facts are dependent on my conceptual lenses', although 'neither fact is an artifact of those lenses'. And again, yet more emphatically: 'I do not create the properties of individual proofs in Peano arithmetic any more than I create the berries on the Mountain Ash' (1983: 126). All of which implies a strong commitment to the realist thesis which holds that truth-values are recognition- or verification-transcendent, i.e., that they possess an objective character and determine the validity of any well-formed statement concerning them, whatever the scope or limits of our present-best knowledge in that regard. Yet there is also a sense in which the running-together of these two examples – Peano arithmetic and the Mountain Ash – is such as to undermine any realist claim for the distinctive *kind* of objectivity that obtains in the case of arithmetical or logical statements. This ambivalence comes out most clearly when Putnam says that *both* are 'dependent on' but not an 'artifact of' my 'conceptual lenses', and that I don't 'create' the logical structure of proofs in Peano arithmetic any more than I 'create' the berries on the tree (1983; 126). For on a realist view – such as Putnam espoused in his earlier writings – this is to confuse two quite distinct orders of truth: on the one hand that of necessity across all logically possible worlds and on the other hand that of epistemic warrant as pertaining to our knowledge of contingent (though none the less mind-independent) objects and events.

This helps to explain why Putnam's objection to Wittgensteinian naturalism in philosophy of mathematics gets so oddly out-of-focus as his argument goes along. If it is hard to make out just where the above-cited passage shifts from criticising Wittgenstein to defending the claims of a qualified realist outlook this is mainly because his implicit reservations can be read as reopening the way to a (no doubt qualified) naturalistic approach. After all, it is a far from 'realist' conception of truth in mathematics or logic that would treat such truth as epistemically on a par with the kinds of truth that we can hope to capture in those always corrigible statements which apply to objects, processes and events in the empirical domain. This is why, as I have argued, Putnam finds himself beset by such a range of conflicting intuitions when he attempts to explain just what is wrong with the Quinean and Wittgensteinian approaches (i.e., that they relativise or naturalise truth to the point where that distinction drops out), while himself adopting a compromise stance – the idea of 'contextual apriority' – which differs from theirs only to the extent that he sees more problems with it. What has led him into this dilemma is Putnam's epistemic conception of truth as applied to logic and arithmetic, that is, his assumption that the revisability-issue can always be raised and (in principle) answered by asking some question of the kind: 'are there statements whose truth we would not be justified in denying in any *epistemically* possible world?'. And from here it is no great distance to the brain-in-a-vat type of thought-experiment where I am programmed to believe that I inhabit a world in which Kripke has discovered a contradiction or inconsistency in Peano arithmetic.

Thus (to repeat): '[t]he proof is checked by famous logicians and even by machine, and it holds up. Perhaps I do not have time to check the proof myself; but I would believe, and rationally so, I contend, that Peano arithmetic is inconsistent on such evidence' (Putnam 1983: 126). However, this belief would be 'rational' only in the sense: arrived at on the basis of *rational-seeming* inferential warrant from *false* (delusory) expert sources under *wholly unreliable* and *systematically misleading* epistemic conditions. Besides, as I argued above, this thought-experiment would carry real force – or lend real weight to the revisability thesis – only if 'I' (the envatted brain) could be conceived as having 'checked the proof myself' for logical consistency and hence as possessing rational grounds (not just delusory hearsay evidence) for believing Peano arithmetic to be inconsistent. Otherwise it goes to prove just the opposite thesis: that truths of this order *cannot* be reduced to a matter of epistemic warrant, whether in terms of some future (real-world) empirical discovery that would actually count as evidence against them, or when subject to a speculative thought-experiment that exploits the wilder limits of counterfactual imagining. This seems to me the most 'rational' construal to be placed on Putnam's statement that 'I do not create the properties of individual proofs in Peano arithmetic any more than I create the berries on the Mountain Ash' (1983: 126). However, it goes clean against a great deal of what Putnam has to say elsewhere about the revisability of arithmetical and logical truths, or 'contextual' apriority as the most that can be had except in cases – like 'not every statement is both true and false' – whose sheer self-evidence comes at the cost of their trivial or vacuous character. Or again, if the proofs of Peano arithmetic are *really* to be taken as epistemically equivalent to the fact of a Mountain Ash existing in Putnam's yard then the revisability thesis might yet be maintained – on Quinean radical-empiricist grounds – but only at the cost of giving up any claim to conserve some version (no matter how modest) of the apriority argument. And this is not an option that Putnam is willing to embrace, despite the strong pull that it has exerted on his thinking over the past three decades and more.

V

So it seems, once again, that Putnam is caught on the horns of a dilemma that results from his accepting the force of sceptical arguments or far-out counter-factual hypotheses which go well beyond the limits of genuine (rational) accept-ability. His objection to Quine's strong-revisionist approach gives a fair indication of Putnam's uncertainties in this regard. 'In Quine's view', he writes, 'the unrevis-ability of mathematical statements is greater in degree than that of, say, the three-dimensionality of space or the conservation of energy, but not absolute. Truths of mathematics are partly empirical and partly "conventional", like *all* truths; mathematics is as factual as physics, only better "protected"' (1983: 127). It is odd that he should cite the three-dimensionality of space as an instance of *relative* 'unrevisability', given that it is now (post-Einstein) regarded as belonging to that class of erstwhile self-evident or supposed *a priori* 'truths' – like those of Euclid-ean geometry – that have turned out false, or at any rate applicable only within a certain restricted spatio-temporal domain. So there is no sense in which Quine could rank it at some midway point on the revisability-scale, any more than could Putnam, who after all takes the *de facto* relativisation of Euclidean geometry as a prime exhibit in his case for extending the revisionist claim to other (e.g., arith-metical and logical) items of currently accepted *a priori* truth. (See especially Putnam 1975[1]: 49–50, 77–8, 88–91, 174–7, 240–3.) Then again, what are we to make of his classing the three-dimensionality of space with the law of conserva-tion of energy, one that has stood firm against empirical revision even in the context of quantum mechanics? (Armstrong 1983; Feynman 1992; Harré 1993). Thus the whole debate about quantum non-locality and kindred phenomena – from Einstein *versus* Bohr to the present – has been premised on the conservation of angular momentum in a system where widely separated particles are assumed to start out from a singlet-state with joint spin-value zero and thereafter *neces-sarily* to possess anti-correlated values (i.e., still equal to zero) no matter how distant from source (Maudlin 1993; Norris 2000; Redhead 1987). So it is, to say the least, very strange that Putnam should place this law on a footing with instances – like the three-dimensionality of space – which no longer lay claim to empirical scientific warrant let alone *a priori* status.

What I think best explains this curious feature of his argument is the deep uncertainty in Putnam's mind as to whether it is conceivable (logically possible) that the truths of so entrenched and axiomatic a system as Peano arithmetic might yet prove subject to revision like those of Euclidean geometry. For in that case – so the argument seems to imply – there is simply no holding the line at any point between empirical facts-of-observation which are always revisable under pressure of conflicting evidence and arithmetical or logical 'truths of reason' which we treat as unrevisable only in virtue of their deep entwinement with our entire existing fabric of beliefs. Of course this is just Quine's position and one that Putnam avowedly rejects on account of its manifest failure to explain why it should seem so *wrong* – philosophically perverse – to place the truths of arithmetic and logic on a par with the claims of empirical knowledge or observational warrant. Thus, 'whereas Wittgenstein departed from moderate conventionalism in the direction of radical conventionalism (which holds that the truth of the theorems as well as that of the axioms arises from us), Quine departed from moderate conventionalism in the direction of *empiricism*' (Putnam 1983: 127). And this – we should take it – is a comparable error in so far as it blocks all paths toward explaining why such truths should possess so powerful a claim (short of absolute *a priori* warrant) to stand fast against empirical revision. Yet Putnam is himself hard put to produce an alternative account of arithmetical and logical truths that would somehow conserve this distinctive property while treating them as none the less revisable under certain (albeit far-out counterfactual and to us highly bizarre) epistemic conditions.

Thus '[t]he view I wish to defend is not that classical logic or mathematics are *a priori*; I myself have argued elsewhere that logic is revisable, and that a form of modular logic ("quantum logic") should be adopted for the purpose of formalizing physical theory, and not classical logic' (Putnam 1983: 127; see also 1975[1]: 166–73 and 174–97). However, that suggestion is itself problematic in several respects, among them its failure to take due account of David Bohm's realist (and non-logical-revisionist) approach to quantum mechanics, its confessed lack of any adequate solution to the quantum measurement-problem, and – most importantly here – the issue as to what could ever *count* as a reason for revising some established theory or truth-claim if logic were itself revisable in the way that Putnam proposes (Bohm 1957; Bohm and Hiley 1993; Holland 1993). In the present context it seems to me that Putnam has left himself with no alternative except to adopt a standpoint of 'moderate' conventionalism and empiricism. This allows him to reject the more 'extreme' (Wittgensteinian and Quinean) positions while upholding the existence of at least one *a priori* truth, i.e., the surely indubitable statement that 'not every statement is both true and false'. Or again, as Putnam confessedly blushes to confess: '[w]hat I think … is that what is *a priori* is that *most* statements obey certain logical laws' (1983: 127). But if this leaves arithmetic and logic still open to revision right down to their basic principles – i.e., the axioms of Peano arithmetic or the laws of bivalence and excluded middle – then it is hard to see that Putnam has provided an alternative approach that succeeds in avoiding those extreme conclusions. And the dilemma must appear all the more acute if one considers his attribution to Quine (a self-avowed Platonist in philosophy of mathematics) of the idea that mathematical unrevisability is greater in degree – though not different in kind – from the 'relatively' unrevisable character of statements concerning the three-dimensionality of space or the classical conservation-laws. For whereas classical space-time physics is now considered false for all but a limited range of applications it is strictly unthinkable that the conservation laws should be subject to revision *in any degree* without undermining the entire edifice of modern physics from Galileo to relativity-theory and even quantum mechanics.

My own view is that early Putnam came closer to explaining how mathematics can possess both the character of objective (verification-transcendent) truth and also such a singular degree of explanatory, predictive, and problem-solving effectiveness when applied to the physical sciences. He did so by distinguishing clearly between the various orders of analytic, *a priori*, and *a posteriori* yet metaphysically necessary truth, and – on the other hand – matters of contingent fact or empirically revisable knowledge (1975[2]: 139–52, 196–214, 215–72). Along with this went an equally firm distinction between truth-claims whose warrant consisted in their being borne out by the best evidence or proof-procedures to hand and objective truth-values (in mathematics or the physical sciences) which in no way depended on any such appeal to evidential grounds or epistemic warrant. One measure of the change in Putnam's thinking is his deployment of those thought-experimental techniques which started out as a means of refuting the sceptic on epistemological issues and were then converted to a use more in line with the standard (Cartesian) method for inducing just such sceptical doubts. Take for instance the following passage from his essay 'Other Minds' (1975[2]: 342–61) where Putnam effectively explains what is wrong with the kind of counterfactual supposition that would later induce him to entertain doubts even with regard to such basic 'truths' as those of classical logic or Peano arithmetic. 'It is perfectly imaginable', he writes,

> that other people should be mere 'dummies' controlled remotely by some intelligence I know nothing of. But I do not grant that this hypothesis is 'in the field'. For a hypothesis to be in the field, it is not enough for it to represent a possibility that we can imagine; it must meet two further requirements. It must be elaborated, the details must be worked out to a certain degree, various questions which naturally occur to one must be answered, and, secondly, it must not be too *silly* to consider. (*ibid.*: 359–60)

Of course it may be said (and rightly) that such doubts are not so much 'silly' as products of a philosophic mindset whose distinctive character is to raise certain problems with our normal ways of talking, thinking, performing mathematical calculations, and so on. Nor would I wish to decry that function if the alternative is a Wittgensteinian 'therapeutic' appeal to our various received, conventional, or naturalised methods and procedures. However, there are limits to sceptical doubt which emerge most strikingly through Putnam's later excursions into the realm of hyperbolic thought-experiment. In the end what they show (as I have argued here) is the impossibility of rationally doubting the most basic principles of logic or the truths of elementary arithmetic. That Putnam very often brings this out while claiming to demonstrate just the opposite – i.e., their empirically revisable character – is itself a strong mark of his searching and keenly self-critical approach to these issues.

References

Armstrong, David (1983). *What Is a Law of Nature?* Cambridge: Cambridge University Press.

Aronson, J., R. Harré and E. Way (1994). *Realism Rescued: how scientific progress is possible.* London: Duckworth.

Benacerraf, Paul (1983). 'What Numbers Could Not Be'. In Benacerraf and Putnam (eds), 272–94.

Benacerraf, Paul and Hilary Putnam (eds) (1983). *The Philosophy of Mathematics: selected essays*, 2nd edn. Cambridge: Cambridge University Press.

Bohm, David (1957). *Causality and Chance in Modern Physics*. London: Routledge & Kegan Paul.

Bohm, David and Basil J. Hiley (1993). *The Undivided Universe: an ontological interpretation of quantum theory*. London: Routledge.

Boyd, Richard N. (1984). 'The Current Status of Scientific Realism'. In Leplin (ed.), 41–82.

Chihara, Charles S. (1982). 'A Gödelian Thesis Regarding Mathematical Objects: Do they exist? And can we see them?'. *The Philosophical Review*, XCI. 211–27.

Detlefson, Michael (ed.) (1992). *Proof and Knowledge in Mathematics*. London: Routledge.

Dummett, Michael (1977). *Elements of Intuitionism*. Oxford: Oxford University Press.

—— (1978). *Truth and Other Enigmas*. London: Duckworth.

—— (1991). *The Logical Basis of Metaphysics*. London: Duckworth.

Feynman, Richard P. (1992). *The Character of Physical Law*. Harmondsworth: Penguin.

Gödel, Kurt (1962). *On Formally Undecidable Propositions of* Principia Mathematica *and Related Systems*, trans. B. Meltzer. New York: Basic Books.

—— (1983). 'What is Cantor's Continuum Problem?'. In Benacerraf and Putnam (eds), 470–85.

Goodman, Nelson (1978). *Ways of Worldmaking*. Indianapolis: Bobbs-Merrill.

Harding, Sandra S. (ed.) (1976). *Can Theories Be Refuted? essays on the Duhem–Quine thesis*. Dordrecht D. Reidel.

Harré, Rom (1993). *Laws of Nature*. London: Duckworth.

Holland, Peter (1993). *The Quantum Theory of Motion: an account of the de Broglie–Bohm causal interpretation of quantum mechanics*. Cambridge: Cambridge University Press.

Kant, Immanuel (1964). *Critique of Pure Reason*, trans. N. Kemp Smith. London: Macmillan.

Katz, Jerrold J. (1998). *Realistic Rationalism*. Cambridge, MA: MIT Press.

Kitcher, Philip (1983). *The Nature of Mathematical Knowledge*. Oxford: Oxford University Press.

Kripke, Saul (1980). *Naming and Necessity*. Oxford: Blackwell.

—— (1982). *Wittgenstein on Rules and Private Language: an elementary exposition*. Oxford: Blackwell.

Kuhn, Thomas S. (1970). *The Structure of Scientific Revolutions*, 2nd edn. Chicago: University of Chicago Press.

Leplin, Jarrett (ed.) (1984). *Scientific Realism*. Berkeley & Los Angeles: University of California Press.

Lewis, David (1973). *Counterfactuals*. Oxford: Blackwell.

—— (1986). *On the Plurality of Worlds*. Oxford: Blackwell.

Maudlin, Tim (1993). *Quantum Non-Locality and Relativity: metaphysical intimations of modern science*. Oxford: Blackwell.

Norris, Christopher (2000). *Quantum Theory and the Flight from Realism: philosophical responses to quantum mechanics*. London: Routledge.

Penrose, Roger (1995). *Shadows of the Mind: a search for the missing science of consciousness*. London: Vintage.

Putnam, Hilary (1975[1]). *Mathematics, Matter and Method* (*Philosophical Papers*, Vol. 1). Cambridge: Cambridge University Press.

—— (1975[2]). *Mind, Language and Reality* (*Philosophical Papers*, Vol. 2). Cambridge: Cambridge University Press.

—— (1978). *Meaning and the Moral Sciences*. London: Routledge & Kegan Paul.

—— (1981). *Reason, Truth and History*. Cambridge: Cambridge University Press.

—— (1983). *Realism and Reason* (*Philosophical Papers*, Vol. 3). Cambridge: Cambridge University Press.

—— (1987). *The Many Faces of Realism*. La Salle, IL: Open Court.

—— (1988). *Representation and Reality*. Cambridge, MA: MIT Press.

—— (1994). *Words and Life*, ed. James Conant. Cambridge, MA: Harvard University Press.

—— (1995). *Pragmatism: an open question*. Oxford: Blackwell.

Quine, W.V.O. (1960). *Word and Object*. Cambridge, MA: Harvard University Press.

—— (1961). 'Two Dogmas of Empiricism'. In *From a Logical Point of View*, 2nd edn.

Cambridge, MA: Harvard University Press. 20–46.

—— (1969). *Ontological Relativity and Other Essays.* New York: Columbia University Press.

Redhead, Michael (1987). *Incompleteness, Nonlocality and Realism: a prolegomenon to the philosophy of quantum mechanics.* Oxford: Clarendon Press.

Rescher, Nicholas (1979). *Scientific Progress.* Oxford: Blackwell.

Schwartz, Stephen (ed.) (1977). *Naming, Necessity, and Natural Kinds.* Ithaca, NY: Cornell University Press.

Shanker, S.G. (ed.) (1987). *Gödel's Theorem in Focus.* London: Routledge.

Smith, Peter J. (1981). *Realism and the Progress of Science.* Cambridge: Cambridge University Press.

Tennant, Neil (1987). *Anti-Realism and Logic.* Oxford: Clarendon Press.

Wiggins, David (1980). *Sameness and Substance.* Oxford: Blackwell.

Wittgenstein, Ludwig (1953). *Philosophical Investigations*, trans. G.E.M Anscombe. Oxford: Blackwell.

—— (1956). *Remarks on the Foundations of Mathematics*, trans. G.E.M. Anscombe. Oxford: Blackwell.

—— (1976). *Lectures on the Philosophy of Mathematics*, ed. Cora Diamond. Chicago: University of Chicago Press.

Wright, Crispin (1980). *Wittgenstein on the Foundations of Mathematics.* Cambridge, MA: Harvard University Press.

—— (1987). *Realism, Meaning and Truth.* Oxford: Blackwell.

—— (1992). *Truth and Objectivity.* Cambridge, MA: Harvard University Press.

Afterword

This book has gone a long way around in addressing what I take to be some of the basic problems with Putnam's later (post-1975) thinking about issues in logic, philosophical semantics, epistemology, and philosophy of science. I have made no secret of my own belief that those issues are more adequately treated – in scientific as well as philosophical terms – through the causal-realist theory of reference and truth which Putnam worked out to a high degree of conceptual refinement in his writings of the previous decade. That is to say, he was then in a strong position to account for our knowledge of the growth of knowledge as a matter of rational inference to the best explanation as regards both the physical sciences and the singular effectiveness of mathematics and formal logic when applied to objects and events in the physical domain. His subsequent pilgrim's progress though the travails of sceptical doubt is one that I have charted in detail here, together with his ultimate failure – as I see it – to arrive at the Celestial City. This pilgrimage seems to have started out from Putnam's early tutelage with Carnap, who at first impressed him with the achievements of a thoroughly formalised or axiomatised approach to the canons of deductive logic. 'It inspired the hope' Putnam writes,

> that one might do the same for so-called 'inductive logic' – that the 'scientific method' might turn out to be an algorithm, and that these two algorithms – the algorithm of deductive logic (which, of course, turned out to be *incomplete* when extended to higher logic) and the algorithm-to-be-discovered for inductive logic – might exhaustively describe or 'rationally reconstruct' not just *scientific* rationality, but all rationality worthy of the name. (Putnam 1981: 125)

However, this hope soon faded when it ran up against a range of philosophically intractable problems, among them some 'powerful considerations' due to Nelson Goodman and – one may conjecture – kindred arguments of a Wittgensteinian, Quinean, and Dummett-type anti-realist provenance. Thus '[t]he story Carnap told me supports the idea that it was the success of formalization in the special case of deductive logic that played a crucial role' (*ibid.*: 125). For the result – so Putnam suggests – was to show up by contrast the failure to achieve any corresponding formalization for inductive logic, which then provoked doubt as to whether such a 'logic' really merited that name.

Hence Putnam's increasing readiness – despite residual misivings – to grant the force of sceptical arguments (such as those deployed by Goodman) which would relativise the status of inductive warrant to the point where it becomes no more than the product of some favoured or agreed-upon scheme of 'projection' for picking out objects and assigning predicates (Goodman 1955, 1978). To be sure, Putnam says,

> [s]ome important aspects of inductive logic can be formalized (although the adequacy of the formalisation is controversial), but there is always a need for judgements of 'reasonableness', whether these are built in via the choice of vocabulary (or, more precisely, the *division* of the vocabulary into 'projectible' predicates and 'non-projectible' predicates) or however. Today, virtually no one believes that there is a purely formal scientific method. (Putnam 1981: 125)

However, one might just as well argue that what this passage brings home is not so much the hopeless predicament of inductive reasoning as the fallacy – plainly evident in Hume and remarked upon by J.S. Mill, among others – of supposing that induction *could or should* measure up to the standards required of deductive logic (Hume 1955; Mill 1843). Thus if indeed there is no 'purely formal' scientific method (with 'formal' defined by strict deductivist standards) then this is scarcely surprising – and no cause for scepticism – given that the physical sciences cannot possibly get along on deductive reasoning alone. Putnam is right enough in drawing this negative conclusion despite the high hopes that were once entertained by logical empiricists like Carnap and Reichenbach for a scientific method securely based on the formalised deductive treatment of empirical observation-sentences (Carnap 1956, 1967; Reichenbach 1938, 1951; also Salmon (ed.) 1979). But there is no good reason for his drawing the further (sceptical) lesson that induction can only be a matter of our 'choice of vocabulary' or of which predicates we treat as 'projectible' according to some given schema, convention or descriptive framework. For of course this Goodmanian approach puts the emphasis squarely on the open-ended range of possible 'projections', rather than the various intrinsic *properties* that justify our picking out some such predicates as applying to certain objects – prototypically natural kinds – in virtue of their subatomic structures, molecular constitutions, chromosomal attributes, and so forth. Thus it leads straight to Goodman's 'new riddle' of induction, and thence – for all Putnam's misgivings at this point – to an outlook of wholesale epistemological and even ontological relativism (Goodman 1955; Putnam 1983: 155–69).

Moreover, as Putnam remarks, the logical-empiricist programme encountered problems not only when applied (with such unfortunate results) to the logic of induction but also on its own privileged terrain, i.e., when extended beyond first-order logic to higher levels where its application turned out to generate paradoxes or inconsistencies (Putnam 1981: 124–6; also 1975[1] and 1983: 1–25). I have already had a good deal to say about the impact of this and similar discoveries on Putnam's thinking about philosophy of logic, mathematics, and the physical sciences. His response has been marked by an alternating pattern where periods (or passages) of relative confidence with regard to the objectivity of truth and the existence of rational norms of enquiry have given way to the admission of far-reaching doubts under sceptical pressure and then – most often – to a compromise settlement in the form of a pragmatist or 'commonsense' line of approach. Such is at any rate Putnam's advice in the series of Dewey lectures which offered a review of the chief stages in his own philosophical development and a defence of this commonsense-realist position as the best that could reasonably be hoped for given all the problems and perplexities thrown up in the quest for some stronger alternative (Putnam 1994).

No doubt there is a sense – as anti-realists are fond of reminding us – in which objectivism about reality and truth will always give a handle for the sceptic to argue that we cannot gain epistemic access to any such noumenal or 'verification-transcendent' truths, and must therefore in all consistency adopt a thoroughgoing sceptical outlook. Hence the basic thought behind such arguments, as described by Michael Williams: that 'if the world is an objective world, statements about how things appear must be unconnected with statements about how they are; this lack of connection is what familiar thought experiments dramatically illustrate' (Williams 1996: 56). From which the anti-realist typically concludes – like Putnam when defending his own more qualified 'internal' realist viewpoint – that the only means of defeating scepticism is to to give up such talk of objective 'truth' and adapt our standards of warranted assertability to what we can reasonably claim to know concerning some particular object domain. Where Putnam differs from a full-scale doctrinal anti-realist such as Dummett is not so much on this point about the need to bring truth-talk more into line with our epistemic capacities but rather on the issue as to whether it is at risk of falling back into another (more logically refined) form of scepticism by denying the very existence of objective truth-values for statements of the so-called 'disputed class'. The issue is stated most sharply in a passage from Dummett's *The Logical Basis of Metaphysics* (1991) which is worth citing at length since it seems to contradict any notion of his having backed away from the more extreme implications of his own doctrine. Thus:

> [r]ealism about the past entails that there are numerous true propositions forever in principle unknowable. The effects of a past event may simply dissipate .... To the realist, this is just part of the human condition; the anti-realist feels unknowability in principle to be simply intolerable and prefers to view our evidence for and memory of the past as constitutive of it. For him, there cannot be a past fact no evidence of which exists to be discovered, because it is the existence of such evidence that would make it a fact, if it were one. (Dummett 1991: 7)

Putnam understandably balks at this since he is still enough of a realist to find it incomprehensible that the occurrence or non-occurrence of past events or the existence or non-existence of a solar system in some region of the expanding universe beyond our epistemic ken should in any way depend upon the scope and limits of *our* cognitive grasp. (See Putnam 1994.) Yet there is, as we have seen, a powerful undertow of sceptical thought in Putnam's later writing which nevertheless draws him against the grain toward just such a 'strong' verificationist position.

My own view – to repeat – is that Putnam was very much on the right track in his early writings and that these problems in the wake of logical empiricism are better addressed through a full-fledged realist approach that (in the words of

Wesley Salmon) 'puts the "cause" back in "because"' (Putnam 1975[2]; Salmon 1984). All the same no philosopher has done more than Putnam to give these issues a contemporary force, not least through the exceptional range and grasp of his knowledge of mathematics and the physical sciences. In the end there is no *philosophical* answer to philosophical scepticism, or none could possibly satisfy the sceptic so long as the debate continues to be played by established intra-philosophical rules. Thus, as Barry Stroud puts it, the sceptic can always come back with the argument that 'all possible experience is equally compatible with the existence and with the non-existence of the world' (cited in Williams 1996: 73). On the other hand – Stroud again – this sceptical outcome will seem unavoidable only so long as we accept a certain premise, namely that of 'the epistemic priority of sensuous experiences over independently existing objects' (*ibid.*: 43). If this condition is rephrased in Dummettian terms – as something like 'the evidential priority of linguistically acquirable and manifestable understanding over realist truth-values' – then it captures another prominent feature of present-day sceptical thought. Both doctrines have exerted a powerful influence on Putnam's work over the past three decades, along with other forms of anti-realist or constructivist thinking which still leave their mark – as I have argued here – on his latest attempt (in the Dewey lectures) to formulate a version of 'commonsense' realism that would prevent such doubts from arising in the first place.

'Our journey has brought us back to the familiar', he writes: 'truth is sometimes recognition-transcendent because what goes on in the world is sometimes beyond our power to recognize, even if it is not beyond our power to conceive' (Putnam 1994: 516). It seems to me that this commonsense conviction finds its best, most compelling argumentative support in the objectivist and causal-realist approach which Putnam worked out in those landmark essays of his early period. Nevertheless, his later writing is a fine example of the capacity to question strongly-held beliefs in the light of searching criticism and, most of all, the exceptional willingness – rare among prominent thinkers in any discipline – to offer up his various changes of mind as matter for open debate. I started out on this book with a great admiration for these qualities in Putnam's work and finish it now, after so many pages of detailed critical commentary, with that feeling amply confirmed.

References

Carnap, Rudolf (1956). *Meaning and Necessity*. Chicago: University of Chicago Press.
—— (1967). *The Logical Structure of the World and Pseudoproblems in Philosophy*, trans. R. George. Berkeley & Los Angeles: University of California Press.
Dummett, Michael (1991). *The Logical Basis of Metaphysics*. London: Duckworth.
Goodman, Nelson (1955). *Fact, Fiction and Forecast*. Cambridge, MA: Harvard University Press.
—— (1978). *Ways of Worldmaking*. Indianapolis: Bobbs-Merrill.
Hume, David (1955). *An Enquiry Concerning Human Understanding*. Indianapolis: Bobbs-Merrill.
Mill, J.S. (1973–74). *A System of Logic*, ed. J. M. Robson. London: Routledge & Kegan Paul.
Putnam, Hilary (1975[1]). *Mathematics, Matter and Method* (*Philosophical Papers*, Vol. 1).

Cambridge: Cambridge University Press.

—— (1975[2]). *Mind, Language and Reality* (*Philosophical Papers*, Vol. 2). Cambridge: Cambridge University Press.

—— (1981). *Reason, Truth and History.* Cambridge: Cambridge University Press.

—— (1983). *Realism and Reason* (*Philosophical Papers*, Vol. 3). Cambridge: Cambridge University Press.

—— (1994). 'Sense, Nonsense and the Senses: an inquiry into the powers of the human mind'. *Journal of Philosophy*, XCI: 9. 445–517.

Reichenbach, Hans (1938). *Experience and Prediction.* Chicago: University of Chicago Press.

—— (1951). *The Rise of Scientific Philosophy.* Berkeley & Los Angeles: University of California Press.

Salmon, Wesley C. (1984). *Scientific Explanation and the Causal Structure of the World.* Princeton, NJ: Princeton University Press.

Salmon, Wesley C. (ed.) (1979). *Hans Reichenbach: logical empiricist.* Dordrecht: D. Reidel.

Williams, Michael (1996). *Unnatural Doubts: epistemological realism and the basis of scepticism.* Princeton, NJ: Princeton University Press.

Index

Note: I have not included entries for 'Putnam, Hilary' since he is mentioned on almost every page of this book and referred to implicitly throughout. Readers will be able to find their way around by consulting other prominent entries (e.g., Carnap, Dummett, Goodman, James, Quine, Rorty, van Fraassen, and Wittgenstein) which track Putnam's evolving response to a range of shared or opposed philosophical arguments. For the same reason – not just laziness on my part – I have decided to omit an index of topics since this would cover much the same ground. Thus for 'logical empiricism' (Putnam and), see especially the various page-entries under Carnap, Reichenbach, and Tarski; for 'anti-realism' and 'constructive empiricism' (Putnam on) see those under Dummett and van Fraassen; likewise for Goodman-type constructivism and the 'new puzzle' of induction, Jamesian pragmatism, Quinean radical empiricism and ontological relativity, Rortian 'strong descriptivism', and Wittgenstein on language-games, cultural life-forms, rule-following, and so forth. Other main topics of discussion – such as Putnam's thinking about conceptual problems in quantum mechanics – can be followed up by reference to the index of names (in this case Bohm, Bohr, Einstein, Heisenberg, Schrödinger) along with the chapter endnotes. On balance this seemed the most sensible arrangement and I hope that it will serve the reader well.

Albert, D.Z. 44
Allison, H. 86, 118
Alston, W.P. 17, 72, 81, 110
Angel, R.B. 79
Aristotle 3, 10, 97, 105, 157, 181, 196, 199–200, 262
Armstrong, D.M. 115, 268
Aronson, J. 90, 121, 249
Austin, J.L. 8, 23, 104
Ayer, A.J. 79, 117
Ayers, M.R. 183

Baker, G.P. 74, 88
Barnes, B. 109, 234
Behler, E. 18
Beiser, F.C. 15, 18, 86, 118
Bell, J.S. 46, 58
Beltrametti, E. 192
Benacerraf, P. 141, 154, 232, 247, 249
Berkeley, G. 17, 23, 151
Blackburn, S. 116, 228
Bloor, David 61, 73, 109, 234
Boghossian, P.A. 74
Bohm, D. 5, 44–7, 49, 51, 53–5, 57–8, 62, 63, 66, 67, 138–40, 171, 179, 190, 269
Bohr, N. 13, 32–3, 42–5, 48, 53–4, 57, 66, 107, 163, 167–71, 178, 189–90, 193, 268
Boole, G. 194, 229–30
Borges, J.-L. 212
Boyd, R. 40, 131, 168, 176, 219, 249
Boyle, R. 188–9

Brandom, R.B. 15, 86
Brink, D.O. 99

Caesar, Julius 3, 131
Carnap, R. 15, 30, 117, 119, 128, 129, 135, 145–6, 148, 213, 273–4
Cavell, S. 71
Chihara, P. 277
Church, A. 253
Clark, P. 218
Clauser, J.F. 58
Coffa, J.A. 24
Copernicus, N. 136, 195
Cushing, J.T. 44, 46, 58, 66, 138, 171

Dalton, J. 13, 45, 91, 93, 100, 107, 110, 162, 188–9
Darwin, C. 159–60, 262
Davidson, D. 9–10, 16, 17, 23, 25–7, 104, 113, 143–4, 170
de Broglie, L. 44, 62, 66
Democritus 13, 21, 59, 107
Derrida, J. 6
Descartes, R. 9, 13, 23, 36, 40, 42, 77, 82, 135, 143, 201, 251, 257, 266, 270
Detlefson, M. 261
Devitt, M. 20, 72, 90, 115
Dewey, J. 8, 18, 73
Diamond, C. 60, 73–8, 83, 86, 87, 89, 116, 149
Duhem, P. 27, 122

Dummett, M. 3, 6–8, 15, 21–2, 24, 28–30, 37, 42, 49–50, 52, 54–5, 60, 63–5, 67, 72–5, 78–81, 85, 89, 94, 100, 106–12, 116–18, 124–6, 135, 140, 145, 147, 151–3, 156, 160, 200, 219, 225–7, 239–40, 247, 252–3, 259–60, 275, 276
Dupré, J. 105

Einstein, A. 5, 13, 44, 45, 54, 66, 79–80, 107, 123, 136, 170, 194, 219, 221, 227, 236, 262, 268
Euclid 5, 24, 33, 34, 35, 136, 155, 192, 193–5, 196, 199, 201, 204, 209, 222, 224, 227, 229–30, 232, 240, 248–50, 268
Ewing, A.C. 18

Fermat, P. de 252–3
Feyerabend, P. 48
Feynman, R.P. 268
Fichte, J.G. 15, 18, 86, 120
Field, H. 122–3, 184
Fine, A. 42
Fodor, J. 156
Folse, H. J. 57
Foucault, M. 95, 212
Frege, G. 10, 13, 16, 17, 35, 41, 49, 91, 163, 232, 234, 235, 248, 261
Fuller, S. 109

Gadamer, H.-G. 6
Galileo 16, 25–6, 85, 104, 144, 219, 221, 236, 269
Garden, R.W. 47, 192
Gardner, M. 34–7
Geertz, C. 109
Gentzen, G. 254
Gibbins, P. 47, 48, 138, 192, 230
Glendinning, S. 15, 18
Gödel, K. 155–8, 204, 246, 247, 249, 261–2
Goldbach, C. 29, 238–9, 261
Goodman, N. 1, 3–7, 21, 33, 37, 41, 67, 72, 85–6, 88, 94, 105, 128–30, 151–4, 160, 173–5, 178, 186, 204–9, 211–16, 246, 273–4
Grünbaum, A. 117, 236
Guyer, P. 86, 118

Haack, S. 47, 138, 140, 192, 230
Hacker, P.M.S. 74, 88
Hacking, I. 23, 43–4, 46–7, 50–3, 55–6, 58–9, 67, 108, 137, 171–2, 184
Hale, R. 218
Hanfling, O. 79
Harding, S. 122, 262
Harman, G. 215, 221, 226
Harré, R. 90, 121, 177, 236, 249, 268
Hegel, G.W.F. 15, 158, 181–2
Heidegger, M. 18, 117, 120
Heisenberg, W. 42, 43, 44, 53, 62, 66, 193
Hilbert, D. 221, 229, 230
Hiley, B.J. 44, 63, 138, 171, 190, 269
Hodgson, P.E. 46, 58

Holland, P. 44, 45, 58, 63, 138, 171, 190, 269
Hollis, M. 96
Holtzmann, S. 74, 88
Home, D. 193
Homer 16
Honner, J. 42, 57, 167, 193
Horwich, P. 10, 28–30, 78, 84, 106, 109, 112, 113
Hume, D. 17, 23, 27, 88, 92, 93, 117, 128, 173, 204, 215–16, 235–6, 274
Husserl, E. 15

James, W. 8, 18, 23, 73, 84, 124, 145, 173, 218
Jammer, M. 193
Johnson, L. E. 113

Kant, I. 6, 9, 14–19, 23, 26–7, 36, 37, 85, 86, 89, 92–4, 117–20, 135–7, 143, 151–2, 155, 175, 193–4, 222, 224
Katz, J. 142, 237–8, 246–9, 253
Kepler, J. 262
Kim, J. 144
Kirkham, R. L. 113
Kitcher, P. 261
Kornblith, H. 215
Kripke, S. 10, 11–12, 33, 36, 41, 74, 88, 91, 123, 162, 163, 174–5, 179, 182–5, 201–4, 206, 208, 212, 214–16, 234, 243, 248, 252, 255, 257, 258
Kuhn, T.S. 14, 41, 80, 85, 86, 91, 96, 122, 123, 162, 170, 184, 186, 188, 262

Laudan, L. 90, 105, 121
Leich, C. 74, 88
Leplin, J. 72, 115, 177
Lewis, D. 31–2, 237, 255
Lipton, P. 90, 215, 221, 226
Locke, J. 17, 23, 105, 183, 204, 210, 213, 214
Loux, M. 214
Lovibond, S. 99
Löwenheim, L. 27, 32, 141, 204, 246, 247
Lucas, J.R. 46, 58
Lukes, S. 96
Luntley, M. 15

Mach, E. 43, 52, 94, 107
Mackie, J.L. 176–7, 236
Madden, E.H. 177, 236
Maddy, P. 141, 231
Malcolm, N. 60, 76
Margolis, J. 85
Maudlin, T. 46, 58, 268
Maxwell, J.C. 181
McCormick, P.J. 21, 85, 151
McCulloch, G. 12, 41, 93, 110, 124, 209
McDowell, J. 9, 15–18, 19, 21, 23, 26–7, 86, 94, 118–20
McMullin, E. 46, 57, 131
Mendel, G. 159
Mill, J.S. 128, 176, 204, 234, 242, 274

Misak, C.J. 43, 52, 79, 107
Mittelstaedt, P. 47, 138, 192, 230
Monod, J. 159
Moore, G.E. 100, 126–7
Musgrave, A. 35

Nagel, E. 129
Nagel, T. 15, 19, 23, 234–7
Newton, I. 24, 61, 81, 123, 136, 188, 209, 219–21, 222, 262
Newton-Smith, W. 170
Nietzsche, F. 18, 19, 120
Norris, C. 15, 48, 60, 63, 86, 105, 118, 140, 152, 229, 268
Nye, M.J. 45, 107

O'Connor, D.J. 113

Papineau, D. 170
Peano, G. 5, 35–7, 225, 232, 251, 254–9, 261, 265–7, 268, 269
Peirce, C.S. 63, 124, 214
Penrose, R. 155–6, 158, 261–2
Perrin, J. 45, 107
Phillips, D.L. 61, 73
Plato (and Platonism) 10, 37, 131, 136, 141, 154–8, 219, 222, 224, 226, 227, 231–4, 237, 241, 242, 247, 249, 263, 269
Podolsky, B. 44, 54, 66
Popper, K. 45, 48
Psillos, S. 121
Ptolemy 136, 195, 262
Putnam, R.A. 130
Pythagoras 253

Quine, W.V.O. 1, 2, 6, 7, 9–10, 13, 15–17, 25–7, 34, 37, 41, 42, 47–8, 85, 92, 96, 105, 122, 123, 128, 129, 138–44, 148, 170, 186, 195–202, 204, 223–4, 228, 231, 232–3, 249, 262–4, 266–9, 273

Rae, A.I.M. 42, 138, 179
Ramsey, F.P. 28
Redhead, M. 46, 58, 268
Reichenbach, H. 15, 47, 48, 128, 129, 274
Rescher, N. 24, 90, 115, 121, 131, 249
Rorty, R. 9–10, 13–14, 16, 17–19, 21, 25–6, 80, 84, 85, 99, 104, 105, 109, 115, 130–32, 144, 153, 186
Rosen, N. 44, 54, 66
Russell, B. 10, 13, 35, 41, 91, 163, 235, 248, 261
Rutherford, E. 13, 107, 170

Salmon, W.C. 90, 117, 128, 130, 177, 215, 221, 236, 274, 275–6
Schelling, F.W.J. 15, 18, 120
Schopenhauer, A. 120
Schrödinger, E. 44, 45, 54, 56, 57, 66, 138, 173, 180–1
Schwartz, S. 41, 91, 123, 162, 174, 207, 214
Sellars, W. 9–10
Shanker, S.G. 261
Shimony, A. 58
Skolem, T. 27, 32, 141, 204, 246, 247
Smith, P. 121, 249
Soames, S. 151, 240–1
Sosa, E. 236
Squires, E. 138, 193
Stern, D.G. 87
Strawson, P.F. 51, 86

Tarski, A. 79–80, 84, 86, 113, 114, 213
Teller, P. 51
Tennant, N. 15, 252
Thatcher, M. 3
Thomson, J.J. (Lord Kelvin) 13, 170
Tooley, M. 115, 177, 236
Turing, A. 250, 254, 261

van Fraassen, B. 21, 49, 52, 79, 105, 107–8, 117, 121, 192
Vision, G. 15
von Neumann, J. 47

Way, E. 90, 121
Weinberg, S. 211
Wheeler, J. 54, 56, 138, 152, 173, 179, 193
Whorf, B.L. 170
Wiggins, D. 174, 202, 214, 243, 255
Wigner, E. 34–5, 138
Williams, M. 17, 27, 71, 93, 106, 117, 127, 275, 276
Winch, P. 148–50
Wittgenstein, L. 1, 2, 4–10, 12–13, 33, 37, 41, 49, 50–1, 55, 58, 60–1, 67, 71–101 *passim*, 104, 108, 111, 116, 127, 132, 135, 144–51, 153, 156, 158–60, 186–8, 198, 211, 215, 216, 218, 227, 234–5, 246, 248–9, 252, 253, 260, 262, 263, 265–7, 269, 270, 273
Wright, C. 15, 65–6, 89, 116, 117, 248, 252, 260

Yeats, W.B. 7

Zermelo, E. 225–6
Zurek, W.H. 54, 56, 138, 173, 179, 193